www.workgroup.com

Workflow Mana

Modeling Concepts, Architecture and Implementation

Workflow Management

Modeling Concepts, Architecture and Implementation

Stefan Jablonski

Professor
Computer Science Department
University of Erlangen-Nuernberg

Christoph Bussler

Researcher
Computer Science Department
University of Erlangen-Nuernberg

INTERNATIONAL THOMSON COMPUTER PRESS

I (T) P An International Thomson Publishing Company

London • Bonn • Boston MA • Johannesburg • Madrid • Melbourne • Mexico City • New York • Paris
Singapore • Tokyo • Toronto • Albany, NY • Belmont, CA • Cincinnati, OH • Detroit, MI

Workflow Management
Modeling Concepts, Architecture and Implementation

I (T) P A division of International Thomson Publishing Inc.
The ITP logo is a trademark under licence.

For more information, contact:

International Thomson Computer Press
Berkshire House
168–173 High Holborn
London WC1V 7AA
UK

International Thomson Computer Press
20 Park Plaza
Suite 1001
Boston, MA 02116
USA

Imprints of International Thomson Publishing

International Thomson Publishing GmbH
Königswinterer Straße 418
53227 Bonn
Germany

International Thomson Publishing Asia
60 Albert Street #15–01
Albert Complex
Singapore 189969

Thomas Nelson Australia
102 Dodds Street
South Melbourne, 3205
Victoria
Australia

International Thomson Publishing Japan
Hirakawacho Kyowa Building, 3F
2-2-1 Hirakawacho
Chiyoda-ku, 102 Tokyo
Japan

Nelson Canada
1120 Birchmount Road
Scarborough, Ontario
Canada M1K 5G4

International Thomson Editores
Campos Eliseos 385, Piso 7
Col. Polenco
11560 Mexico D.F. Mexico

International Thomson Publishing South Africa
PO Box 2459
Halfway House
1685 South Africa

International Thomson Publishing France
Tour Maine-Parnasse
33 avenue du Maine
75755 Paris Cedex 15
France

British Library Cataloguing-in-Publication Data
A catalogue record for this book is available from the British Library

Library of Congress Cataloging-in-Publication Data
A catalog record for this book is available from the Library of Congress

First printed 1996

ISBN 1-85032-222-8

Typeset by Hodgson Williams Associates, Tunbridge Wells and Cambridge
Printed in the UK by Clays Ltd, St Ives plc

Contents

A man's heart deviseth his way;
but the LORD directeth his steps

Proverbs 16:9

Dedicated to Renate, Lisa
and my parents
S.J.

For Barbara, Maik
and my parents
C.B.

Preface

Often we have heard critics say that workflow management is nothing new but has existed in enterprises long before the advent of workflow management technology. In the sense that workflows are regarded binding and integrating the critical factors of an enterprise, people, organization and processes, this observation is correct. Nevertheless, workflow management technology introduces a new quality into the task of gluing together people, organization and processes to form a value chain. As database management systems have taken data management functionality out of application programs and have made it generally available in form of database management systems, workflow management systems take workflow management functionality out of application programs. This generally available workflow management functionality facilitates the more systematic writing of application programs, concentrating on application-specific details. Thus, workflow management offers a systematic approach to turn islands of automation into an effective and efficient vehicle with valuable commercial impact.

Workflow management is about the history, the present and the future of workflow executions; future executions have to be planned, controlled, supervised and audited. In order to contribute to these issues, this book is a first comprehensive introduction to the fundamental concepts of workflow management issues from a technical point of view.

The product-independent discussion of workflow management issues in this book helps readers to make objective and unbiased decisions when assessing commercial workflow management tools. It provides a general introduction and discussion of the fundamental constituents of workflow management. In detail, it brings out the fundamentals of workflow modeling and implementation. Also, it thoroughly reveals open research issues in the field of workflow management.

The book covers a step-by-step development of workflow management concepts, from analysis through modeling to implementation. It discusses requirements associated with the development of workflow management systems, along with useful details on both theoretical foundations and practical tools. Examples and case studies throughout the book aid the readers' understanding of workflow related issues.

The book is not intended to be a cookbook approach which describes benefits to be achieved from implementing workflow applications. Neither does it dwell on how to initiate, implement and maintain workflow applications. Nor is a discussion on the pragmatics of costing, buying and scoping workflow management systems in the scope of the book.

The book is intended for professional engineers, technical consultants and software architects who need a technical reference on workflow management or support in assessing and selecting workflow management tools. It is also appropriate for academics and students in computer science (e.g. systems engineering, software engineering) and business science who needs a scientific introduction to workflow management technology.

The book is divided into four parts. Part 1 provides a general introduction of the topic "workflow management". First, it demonstrates how workflow management is embedded into related research and engineering disciplines. The classification of workflow management within information systems engineering is given next. A brief overview on the fundamental constituents of workflow management closes this introductory part of the book.

Parts 2 and 3 contain the central chapters of the book.Part 2 discusses issues of workflow modeling. Syntactical elements of a workflow model and its semantics are discussed. Implementation issues are investigated in Part 3. Starting with an implementation model, an implementation architecture and a concrete example implementation are presented. Parts 2 and 3 are completed by introducing a suite of tools fundamental for workflow modeling and implementation, respectively.

Part 4 summarizes the book and provides an outlook on open issues in the realm of workflow modeling and implementation.

At the beginning of each part , a detailed overview of the chapters in that part is provided.

The clear structure of the book means we can describe guided tours through the text for readers with different interests. We classify three reader groups according to their main interests:

- to obtain an introduction to workflow management (solid-line tour)
- to obtain technical information (engineering perspective) (dotted-line tour)
- to obtain technical information (research perspective) (broken-line tour)

The figure below shows adequate paths through the book for these reader groups.

A book such as this cannot be written without having strong interrelationships and interdependencies with business and life. This is the reason for the following acknowledgments.

A large number of individuals contributed to this effort. Instead of listing them individually with the risk of forgetting somebody, we want to keep the

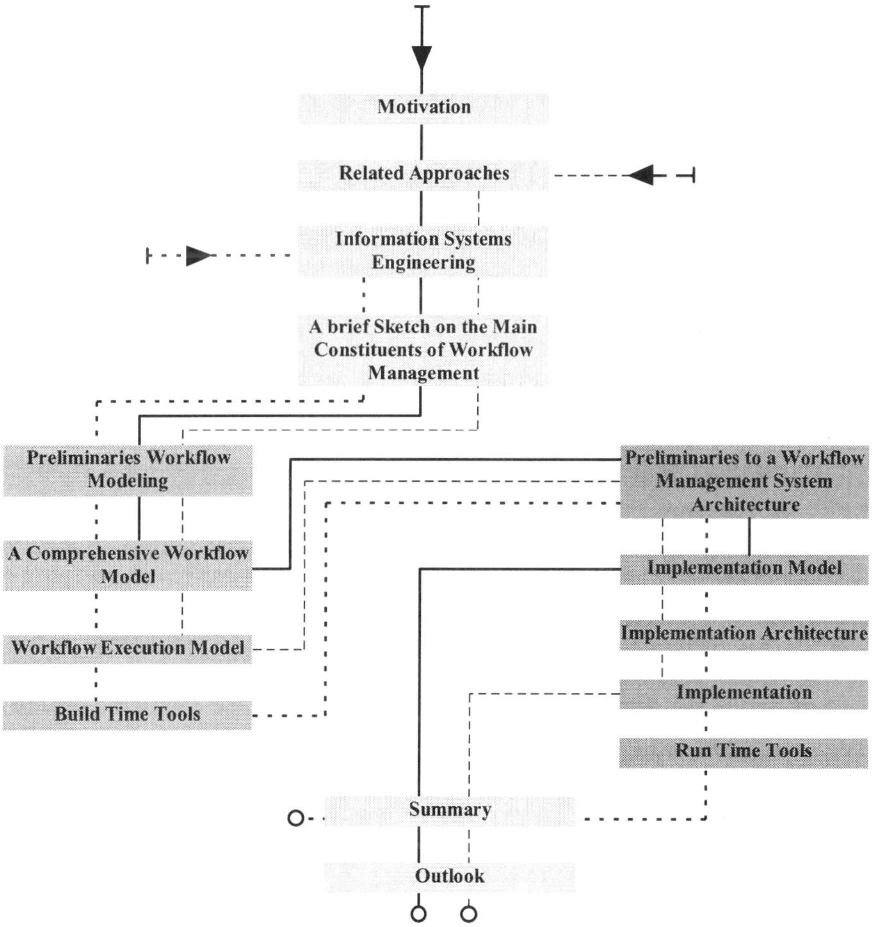

acknowledgments simple. However, this does not diminish the importance and significance of the persons who worked with us during the last few years.

Stefan Jablonski gratefully thanks Prof. Dr. Hartmut Wedekind who has been his teacher for the last ten years both in business and in life. Christoph Bussler thanks Prof. Dr. Hartmut Wedekind and Prof. Dr. Peter Kammerer (Technische Hochschule Darmstadt, Germany) for giving him the opportunity to pursue research on workflow management.

Both authors are grateful to Dieter Gawlick and their former colleagues at Digital Equipment's Activity Management Group in Mountain View / Palo Alto, CA. Finally, we thank our colleagues at the Computer Science Department (Database Management Systems) at the University of Erlangen-Nuremberg, Germany.

Last but not least, the authors would like to thank their families for their continuous encouragement, support, sacrifice and patience.

Part I: Introduction

1 Motivation

2 Related Work

3 Methodology

4 Main Constituents

This first part provides an initial understanding of the topic "workflow management". Before modeling and implementation details of workflow management are introduced in Part 2 and Part 3, the introductory part characterizes workflow management. Starting with motivation in Chapter 1, example workflow management systems either from academia or from professional vendors are presented in Chapter 2. Chapter 3 classifies workflow management into a comprehensive phase model of information systems engineering. Finally, Chapter 4 provides a brief sketch of the main constituents of workflow management. This last chapter predetermines the contents of the following parts which discuss the build time phase and the run time phase of workflow management systems.

After reading this first part, the reader should know about

- the historical development of workflow management technology,
- potential application areas of workflow management,
- purposes, challenges, pros and cons of workflow management,
- fundamental characteristics of workflow management,
- existing approaches to workflow management,
- the position of workflow management in a system engineering life cycle, and
- the main constituents of workflow management.

Readers who are merely interested in technical details about workflow modeling and execution should skip this first part. However, Part 1 conveys the authors' perspective on workflow management which is most relevant for the forthcoming discussion of workflow management systems.

Reader's Guide

The following table helps the reader to find out which sections are relevant to his needs.

Reader's Interest	*Sections to read*
history and origins of workflow management	Section 1.1
application areas of workflow management	Section 1.2
examples of workflow management	Section 1.3
basic definition of workflow management	Section 1.4
pros/cons of workflow management	Section 1.5
related work on workflow management	Chapter 2
role of workflow management in systems engineering	Chapter 3
components of workflow management	Chapter 4

1 Motivation

What is workflow management all about? To answer this question is the main purpose of this chapter. We start by analyzing the history of workflow management and investigate other areas in computer science and systems engineering that influenced and impacted the development of workflow management (Section 1.1).

In Section 1.2 workflow management will be related to computer supported cooperative work and groupware on the one hand; on the other hand, workflow management will be compared with cooperative information systems. Several case studies are presented in Section 1.3 to convey typical application scenarios of workflow management systems.

A characterization, a delimitation and a definition of workflow management are elaborated in Section 1.4. Section 1.5 reports about the pros and cons of deploying workflow management technology. Finally, Section 1.6 outlines the scope of this book.

Since our interpretation of workflow management will not be introduced until Section 1.4, some examples of definitions found in related literature are cited here at the beginning of the book. These definitions will convey a preliminary feeling of the concept "workflow management". We choose three definitions which originate from three different application areas: the first definition stems from the consulting area, the second one from the research domain and the third one from the industrial sector.

Hales and Lavery present a very comprehensive and adequate definition of workflow management (Hales and Lavery, 1991):

> Workflow management software is a proactive computer system which manages the flow of work among participants, according to a defined procedure consisting of a number of tasks. It co-ordinates user and system participants, together with the appropriate data resources, which may be accessible directly by the system or off-line, to achieve defined objectives by set deadlines. The co-ordination involves passing tasks from participant to participant in correct sequence, ensuring that all fulfil their required contributions, taking default actions when necessary.

In their definition, Hales and Lavery mention work organized as a set of ordered tasks, participants who have to execute the tasks, and data resources that are necessary to perform tasks. Additionally, a workflow management system is characterized by its major duties: passing tasks between the participants, controlling that participants fulfill their contributions and providing some kind of exception handling.

The above definition characterizes well the fundamental components of workflows. The forthcoming chapters of this book will show that this definition is very close to the concept of a workflow which we will follow.

Another definition of workflow management is given in Reinwald (1994):

> A workflow management system is an active system that manages the flow of business processes performed by multiple persons. It gets the right data to the right people with the right tools at the right time.

This definition sets business processes equal to workflows which we do not agree upon (cf. Chapter 3). Also, it restricts the execution of business processes to people. In accordance with the first definition given by Hales and Lavery we also like to include system participants into the list of agents that are eligible to execute a workflow. Three further components of workflows are mentioned in the second definition: data, tools and the right execution time (i.e. flow control). All three components are fundamental and will also be included in our conception of workflow management.

A third definition of workflow management stems from the industrial area, specifically from a industrial consortium called Workflow Management Coalition (WfMC, 1993) (cf. Chapter 2):

> A workflow management system is one which provides procedural automation of a business process by management of the sequence of work activities and the invocation of appropriate human and/or IT resources associated with the various activity steps.

This definition says that business processes are enacted by a workflow management system (cf. Chapter 3). Although the definition does not characterize activity steps in more detail, it stresses that activity steps are performed by human and/or IT resources. That means that the two fundamental parts of a workflow, the work that has to be performed and the actors that have to perform the work, are emphasized.

1.1 Historical Notes

This section gives an overview on the history of workflow management technology. Starting with some general remarks on fundamental prerequisites for workflow management (Section 1.1.1), origins and triggers for workflow management technology are discussed in Section 1.1.2. Finally, Section 1.1.3 introduces phases of workflow computing, i.e. generations of workflow management systems.

1.1.1 Prerequisites

Many analysts in the computer industry tout workflow management as the software technology of the 1990s. Since for a long time office workers have applied information technology to support their work, it is worthwhile to ask for the reasons why workflow management was not already the technology of the 1980s. What change between the 1980s and the 1990s made workflow management become so popular?

As early as the 1970s office work was already heavily impacted by computing technology. Database systems as the first major vehicle for an integrated office work infrastructure evolved rapidly and opened new dimensions for office activities. Computing power and intelligence available on the desktop has also grown dramatically. Nevertheless, the overall productivity of office workers has improved little due to lack of integration of the desktop products.

From our perspective, two fundamental trends have contributed to the broad advent of workflow management technology. The first trend is the enormous technological progress that characterized the last two decades. A second trend is set by a change in application system development: the global aim shifted from the automation of pieces of application systems towards the comprehensive development of integrated solutions.

We want to demonstrate the technological progress by three so-called "Laws" that describe the development of hardware in an illustrative way (Gray and Reuter, 1993).

- Moore's Law comments on the progress of electronic memories: starting from a rate of 1 Kb per chip in 1970, the capacity of a circuit memory chip has increased by a factor of four about every three years.

- Hoagland's Law states that the read and write density of magnetic disks and tapes has grown by a factor of ten every decade.
- Last but not least, Joy's Law predicts the mips rate of Sun Microsystems as $2^{year - 1984}$ for the years between 1984 and 2000. Although this formula is too optimistic, the major trend can be recognized and is impressive.

The predictions for memory and processor development can be completed by a forecast for bandwidth of communication networks. According to Gray and Reuter (1993), in the year 2000 local area networks will provide a bandwidth up to one gigabit per second and over a wide area will be able to transport 100 megabits per second.

The revolution in hardware technology allows to deploy computer software in a "revolutionary way". Workstations and specifically personal computers have become so cheap that each work-place can be equipped with computer hardware. Also, network technology has enabled the interconnection of these computers such that huge performant networks could be built up. The connectivity of hardware systems is a prerequisite for the connectivity of software systems: for the first time, integrated software environments could be established locally as well as globally.

Another consequence of effective and efficient hardware technology is the development of more sophisticated software technology. While at the beginning of the computing era computers were used as powerful calculators, now, sophisticated word processing, spreadsheet, and imaging applications can be supported on the desktop. Together with the hardware connectivity of computer networks, common database systems can be deployed which support the integrated application of all these software systems.

Not only technological progress has contributed to the development of workflow management technology, but also a new approach to define and develop application systems has to be reported. While in the past a task- or data-centric view was pursued – mainly predetermined by the existence of isolated (office) applications – modern approaches to application system development follow a (business) process- or work-centric view (Melling, 1994). This puts work into the center of interest. In contrast, a data-centric view merely emphasizes data integration, and a task-centric view aims at the effective and efficient implementation of single tasks and of execution dependencies defined between them. A process-centric approach takes up a broader standpoint and aims to integrate functions, data, programs, people (executing these functions), organizational structures, etc. Such an approach allows better to minimize (process) costs and to optimize an enterprise globally. The current trend in business process reengineering is exactly based on this observation (Hammer and Champy, 1993).

1.1.2 Origins

After having outlined the two fundamental prerequisites for workflow management we want to elaborate its origins. It is not possible to exactly determine one or more software technologies as origins of workflow management. However, there is a basic set of key developments in software technology which heavily influenced workflow management. We want to call these technologies the origins of workflow management. Without claiming to be complete, we classify seven software technologies as "conceptual ancestors" of workflow management, namely

- office automation,
- database management,
- e-mail,
- document management,
- software process management,
- business process modeling, and
- enterprise modeling and architecture.

Office Automation

Without any doubt, office automation must be considered as the main origin of workflow management (Ellis and Nutt, 1980). However, there is a fundamental distinction: task automation as one important discipline of office automation aims at the automation of individual office tasks, e.g. Lochovsky (1983), workflow management aims at controlling and driving the execution of (business) processes. Automation of control and not automation of tasks is at the center of interest. Thus, workflow management software assists human workers to execute processes. Workflow management has to be distinguished from "workflow automation" (Rusinkiewicz and Sheth, 1995). This related discipline aims at the automated execution of interdependent applications.

Despite the different interpretation of automation the close coherence between office automation and workflow management cannot be denied. Bracchi and Pernici (1984) lists some requirements for office information systems that seamlessly can be applied to workflow management systems. Some of the fundamental requirements are

- scheduling activities,
- function integration,
- personal assistance, and
- task management.

Chapter 2 presents some important examples of office management systems which can be regarded as early prototypes of workflow management systems that are tailored to deployment in office environments.

Database Management

In the research area of database management systems, workflow management was approached from a totally different angle. Conventional database management systems are passive, in the sense that they only manipulate data in response to explicit requests from users and applications. Besides, the only unit of work supported by conventional database management systems is a transaction. A transaction is an independent unit of computation.

Many applications are of long duration and involve multiple steps, executed by multiple clients. Activities, which implement those applications, access shared (persistent) data and therefore need to be synchronized among themselves. Another problem with long running activities is the higher probability of failures. When a long running activity fails shortly before it would have been completed, it is not acceptable to undo all the effects accomplished so far by the activity. Therefore, in order not to loose too much work after failures new failure handling strategies (e.g. forward recovery) have to be developed.

The above mentioned requirements of long running activities cannot be met by conventional database systems that only support conventional transactions. The discrepancy between available support from conventional database systems and requirements of long running activities led to the development of active database management systems (Dayal *et al.*, 1995). One of the first efforts in this research area was the HIPAC project (Dayal *et al.*, 1988).

The principal idea of active database systems is to enrich a (passive) database system by event–condition–action (ECA) rules (McCarthy and Dayal, 1989). The semantics of ECA rules is straightforward: when an event occurs the condition is evaluated; if the condition is evaluated to true, the associated action is executed. This trigger facility subsumes most of the functionality of an active database management system. Rules are considered as first-class database objects, i.e. they are managed and controlled by a database management system.

Each step of a multi-step activity is implemented as a transaction. But in contrast to the conventional approach where control flow between transactions is embedded into an application program, the control flow in the realm of active database systems is implemented by ECA rules which are themselves embedded into the database. Since data executed in transactions as well as ECA rules are first-class database objects, both access to shared data and synchronization among steps (i.e. transactions) can be controlled by the database system. This allows to implement multi-step activities, which can be regarded as simple workflows.

Another modern research direction in database management systems stems from the development of extended transaction models. It is called transactional workflow (Rusinkiewicz and Sheth, 1995). Following a similar purpose as with the introduction of ECA rules in active database management systems, in extended transaction models dependencies between transactions are taken to compose complex units of computation out of conventional transactions (Elmagarmid, 1992; Klein, 1991). Commit and abort dependencies are regarded as the most important forms of dependencies (Chrysanthis and Ramamritham, 1990).

As the term already implies, transactional workflows are tightly related to (extended) transactions. The approach starts out from specifying tasks which define work to be done. Although tasks are mostly set equal to transactions, in the realm of transactional workflow the interest does not lie in modeling internals of a task. Instead, only those aspects of a task are dealt with that are externally visible and relevant (e.g. the transition into a beginning, aborting or committing state). Therefore, a task is described by a set of execution states, a set of transitions between states, and a set of conditions enabling these transitions. The two main issues of transactional workflow execution is to handle failure atomicity and execution atomicity, i.e. only the behavioral and operational perspectives of workflows are tackled. This is the reason why we classify transactional workflow not as an approach to workflow management, but as a valuable approach to coordinate and synchronize application (i.e. task) execution in the context of workflow management.

E-Mail

Some characteristics of workflow management can already be found in e-mail systems. There is no need to explain the functionality of conventional electronic mail systems at this point. However, it is worth mentioning as exemplary an enhanced class of electronic mail systems which can be described as a simple predecessor of workflow management systems. Teamroute from Digital Equipment Cooperation is such a system (DEC, 1992). Electronic mail in an enhanced e-mail system like Teamroute does not merely consist of a header (an addressee, a title, etc.) and a body (the message) but also includes routing information. For example, all addressees who are to receive the electronic mail message are listed. This functionality with respect to routing is fundamental for workflow management as we will see later on in this book.

Document Management

The advent of computer technology in the office led to the replacement of paper documents with electronic documents. This caused the need for electronic document management systems (Khoshafian *et al.*, 1992). The first generation of document management systems can be called passive because it only reacts according to direct user requests. For instance, users can query for a certain document or they can request to lock a certain class of documents. Context-based retrieval and document management functions (e.g. lock, release, combine, destroy) are the major features of passive document management systems.

Active document management systems enhance passive document management systems by incorporating service functions which are based on time management. For instance, triggers can be incorporated that cause a document to be presented for review after a certain period of time. Oversimplified, this is a first step towards workflow management. Document-centric workflow management systems as discussed in Chapter 2 stem from active document management systems.

Software Process Management

Surprisingly, the research area of workflow management does not take very much into account the research conducted in software process management (Humphrey, 1989). Nevertheless, we think that in the area of software process management many of the design and execution issues of workflow management systems have already been discussed and investigated thoroughly. Software process management comprises three major phases:

- The model of a software process is developed.
- The software process model must be analyzed in order to detect errors and inconsistencies before the model is used to govern software process development.
- Software process models are executed, i.e. software is developed according to the rules and guidelines of the software process model.

A software process guides and assists people involved in the process of software development. For example, a software process coordinates the distributed development of large software packages such that the partial designs yield a consistent piece of software.

Naturally, the scope of software process management is limited to the development and execution of software process models. However, some selected approaches to software process management (e.g. Deiters and Gruhn, 1994) show concepts and techniques which are also essential for workflow management.

Business Process Modeling

There is a great deal of talk these days about redesigning business processes. Much of this recent interest in the subject can be traced back to Hammer (1990). Organizations today are going through something akin to a mid-life crisis, questioning and rethinking the ways in which they have been doing business. Fundamental questions are asked such as how their purpose and mission have changed during the last couple of years.

Over time, different departments have automated various processes within their functional areas using a variety of heterogeneous computer systems. For a period of time, this functional division worked well. However, on restructuring the organization, many companies find out that the way processes are defined and the technology in place is not optimal any more. For example, information sharing technologies like groupware and databases enable communication methods that have completely obliterated traditional sequential processing of work.

New information sharing technologies, network computer infrastructure and a broader view of application systems changed the way that application system development is pursued. Workflow management shares these concepts and attitudes and therefore allows to enact business process models adequately.

Business process modeling also takes in the broad standpoint we claim for workflow management. The accomplishment of work, not the execution of single tasks, is central. The broadness of business process modeling is nicely illustrated by Katz (1990):

> The term business modeling can be used to describe a number of different aspects of a business: financial, distribution, manufacturing lines, information and data requirements, flow of information and data across business processes, etc. ...

According to the above citation business processes span a wide range of aspects: economical, technological and computer-oriented aspects are directly mentioned.

Although matured approaches to business process modeling have come into existence rapidly, an enactment infrastructure is hard to find. Conventional enactment infrastructures mostly emphasize one or two specific aspects as already noticed in Section 1.1.1. Instead, an appropriated enactment infrastructure for business processes symmetrically supports multiple aspects of a business process. As we will see in Chapter 3, due to the broad scope of workflow management, this technology serves very well as an enactment infrastructure of business process modeling. To formulate it the other way around: the conceptual ideas of business process modeling, especially its broad, multi-aspect approach, triggered the development of workflow management software.

Enterprise Modeling and Architecture

Last but not least, enterprise modeling and architecture must be named as another trigger for workflow management (ICEIMT, 1992; Vernadat, 1996). In Section 1.1.1 we mentioned that one of the important prerequisites for workflow management is the process-centric view of work. For the discipline of enterprise modeling such a global, process-centric view is obligatory. Workflow management learnt from enterprise modeling to take all aspects of an application system into account and not just to concentrate on certain partial aspects.

Research work on enterprise architectures (Wortmann, 1994) demonstrates how enterprise models can be enacted. It defines a concrete path from modeling to execution that can be applied to the problem of mapping business processes to workflows. One of the interesting features of the enterprise architectures approaches proposed in Wortmann (1994) is how they modularize system components in order to define generic building blocks that can be composed into large systems. Workflow management can adopt this technique when multiple perspectives of an application system have to be composed into form a workflow.

1.1.3 Generations of Workflow Management Technology

Workflow management technology is still far from being mature. In contrast, we would rather say that workflow management technology is still in the beginning phase. Like any other technology, workflow management will evolve in phases (Abbott and Sarin, 1994): in the beginning phase, experiences with academic and commercial prototypes have to be gained. The outcome of this phase is a working knowledge of workflow management with respect to either modeling and execution issues. In the second phase, usually basic conceptual work is accomplished: based on the good and bad experiences of the first phase, conceptual models and architectures are developed. First design methodologies are also established in this phase. The proliferation of tools for workflow application development characterizes the third phase that emphasizes workflow infrastructure. Many technologies are finally embarking on the phase of standardization which aims at the development of norms and standards that makes the use of a technology possibly more effective and efficient.

Today, workflow management is on the road to phase two, i.e. first instances of conceptual work can be reported. However, the largest part of the workflow management market is flooded with "home-made" systems which all claim to contribute significantly to the overall conceptual developments. Nevertheless, we think that not more than a dozen workflow management systems deserve such an assessment. The unrestrained proliferation of the workflow management system market, which seems to make the topic "workflow management" unattractive for research people, stems from the software crises that many companies are currently suffering from. They regard workflow management as a panacea for most of their difficulties and therefore manipulate the workflow management market in an uncontrolled way. Nevertheless, it can be easily understood why companies wish to participate in the huge potential workflow manage-ment market, since it is quite lucrative.

This book intends to be a contribution to the conceptual phase in the development of workflow management technology, i.e. both conceptual work in the area of workflow modeling and execution are presented, and a design methodology for workflow management is introduced.

In McCarthy and Bluestein (1991) workflow management technology's development is classified into three stages: homegrown (1989–1992), rudimentary (1992–1995), and dynamic (1994–1999) workflow computing. Before this classification is compared with the classification scheme discussed above, each of the three stages will be characterized.

According to McCarthy and Bluestein (1991) the three stages of workflow management technology are differentiated by

- the ease of development,
- the sophistication of the underlying routing technology, and
- the adaptability of a workflow to changes in the structure of a firm.

The first point undoubtedly aims at tool support for workflow development. The second point assesses the capabilities of the execution system, mostly called the workflow engine, with respect to programmability, openness, and interoperability. The last point refers to the availability of a workflow model which can be adapted dynamically to changes in the business processes which are supported by workflows.

The generation of so-called homegrown workflow computing is identified by the lack of a distinguishable workflow model, such that all workflow related information like execution order and data flow have to be hard-coded into application programs. In turn, these application programs are written in a conventional programming language like C and do not use a specialized workflow description language. It needs no further discussion to see that such "workflow management systems" show little or no adaptability at all. From our perspective, we would not even call such approaches workflow management systems, since they are lacking in basic functionality.

The distinguishing feature between homegrown and rudimentary workflow management technology is the availability of an autonomous workflow engine for the second stage of workflow technology. This engine allows to execute workflow models which are defined independently from application programs. Although not stated directly in McCarthy and Bluestein (1991), we assume that also a rudimentary workflow model and basic workflow development tools are in place. Therefore, the development of workflows is alleviated. Also, changes to existing workflows should be easier to make. However, they will be restricted to a certain degree predetermined by the workflow model and the execution engine.

McCarthy and Bluestein do not state clearly what the distinction between rudimentary and dynamic workflow computing is, since techniques like client/server and object-oriented analysis can also be applied for rudimentary workflow computing. Our interpretation of these techniques is that in this third stage of workflow computing workflow management shows dynamics: the workflow model can be adjusted dynamically to new application requirements, the workflow management systems architecture can be adopted to new hard- and software infrastructures and it can be extended systematically with additional functionality.

In this book, we present either a workflow model and a workflow management system architecture which support dynamic workflow computing. Section 1.4 will show how we interpret "dynamics" in the context of workflow management. Part 2 of this book presents our approach to workflow modeling; Part 3 describes a dynamic execution infrastructure for workflows.

Finally, it is interesting to compare the two classification schemes introduced in this section (Figure 1.1). Experimental workflow technology reaches from the phase of homegrown approaches into the phase of rudimentary systems. Conceptual approaches start synchronously with the phase of rudimentary workflow management systems. This phase also is of importance during the phase of dynamic workflow management. Professional workflow management systems will be developed at the end of the phase of rudimentary approaches.

The evolution of workflow management technology is obvious. We stand at the beginning of a new technology. Therefore, the lack of matured systems is not surprising. However, we have to appreciate that some existing approaches are already very promising and point in the right direction.

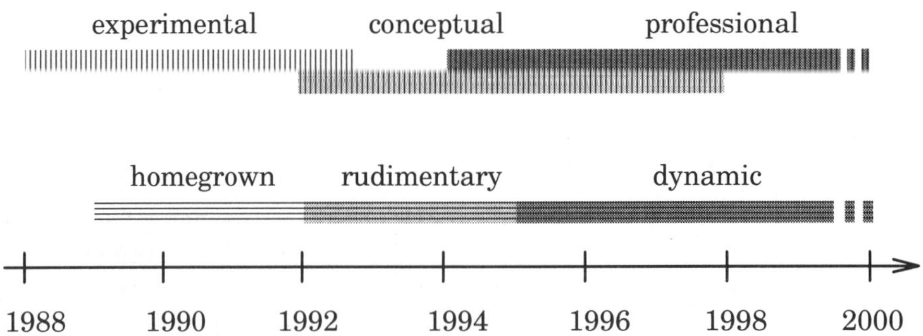

Figure 1.1: Phases of Workflow Management System Evolution

1.2 Area of Application

One way to find the application area of workflow management is to use an analytic approach. A well-known, encompassing application system range is selected first. Afterwards, the subrange of application systems that fit well to workflow management technology is selected. We will follow this methodology twice: first, the area of CSCW and/or groupware systems is analyzed; second, various classification schemes of application system types are investigated.

Computer supported cooperative work (CSCW) and groupware are regarded as one possible and suitable superordinated application area for workflow management (Bock, 1993). Section 1.2.1 will show which subrange of CSCW/ groupware systems are the home of workflow management.

In Section 1.2.2, a problem-oriented as well as a system-oriented classification scheme for application systems is investigated to find a suitable application area for workflow management technology.

1.2.1 Computer Supported Cooperative Work and Groupware

We do not want to embark on the almost philosophical discussion about the distinction and the similarities between the two notions "computer supported cooperative work" (CSCW) and "groupware". Nevertheless, some definitions are cited in the following which clarify the subtle difference between CSCW and groupware.

Wilson (1991) gives the following definition of CSCW:

> CSCW is a generic term which combines the understanding of the way people work in groups with the enabling technologies of computer networking, and associated hardware, software, services and techniques.

Ellis *et al.* (1991) characterizes CSCW as follows:

> Drawing on the expertise and collaboration of many specialists, including social scientists and computer scientists, CSCW looks at how groups work and seeks to discover how technology (especially computers) can help them work.

Both definitions put a conceptual aspect into the foreground. Although computer support is considered as being essential for CSCW, both citations emphasize more that computer technology has to be deployed for CSCW rather than point out how this technology should be conceived.

In contrast, definitions of groupware always put the software aspect into the center of interest. For instance, Johansen (1988) defines groupware as a term for specialized computer aids:

> Groupware is a generic term for specialised computer aids that are designed for the use of collaborative work groups. Typically, these groups are small project-oriented teams that have important tasks and tight deadlines. Groupware can involve software, hardware, services and/or group process support.

In Ellis *et al.* (1991) groupware is called a specialized computer-based system:

> ... we define groupware as: computer-based systems that support groups of people engaged in a common task (or goal) and that provide an interface to a shared environment.

According to the definitions shown above and in full agreement with the interpretation in Borghoff and Schlichter (1995), we use the term "CSCW" whenever we want to talk about conceptual and theoretical issues, and we apply the term "groupware" when we want to refer to system issues. This interpretation is also supported in many other publications; Marca and Bock (1992) is a very illustrative one.

Analyzing the term "CSCW"

In classifying the diverse disciplines that are subsumed under the notion of CSCW, we will find the special group of application systems that can be adequately supported by workflow management technology. But before this classification can be presented, the notion "CSCW" must be analyzed.

A very interesting approach to analyze the term "CSCW" is reported in Borghoff and Schlichter (1995): two different interpretations of the term "CSCW" are generated by inspecting it letter by letter from the beginning to the end and from the end to the beginning, respectively. Here is the result of the forward analysis:

- *C*: a computer based technology is the object of discussion
- *S*: the technology has to support some application type
- *C*: the application type puts cooperation into the center of interest
- *W*: the computer supported cooperation will accomplish some work

Borghoff and Schlichter call the forward analysis the interpretation from the perspective of computer science: the computer as a powerful tool to solve a problem (of cooperative work) comes to the fore.

The backward analysis of the term "CSCW" emphasizes the work that has to be done:

- *W*: the work to be accomplished is to the fore
- *C*: the accomplishment of the work is based on the division of labor and the cooperation of the workers
- *S*: the success of the work depends on adequate support
- *C*: the computer is one aid that can support the cooperative work

In the backward analysis the computer is just one possible tool that can support the accomplishment of the work. This interpretation is probably made by people of business and organization science.

Without any doubt, computers and work are two very important aspects of CSCW. However, we feel that one more aspect is under-represented in the discussion, namely the organizational environment (or infrastructure) where the computer supported cooperation actually takes place. Thus, CSCW is about the interrelationships and interdependencies of the three topics work, (computer) technology and organization[1] (Figure 1.2). Consequently, these three topics will also stand at the center of interest for workflow management.

The glue between work, organization and technology is the so-called group process (Borghoff and Schlichter, 1995) (Figure 1.2). We will see that the group process is the conceptual basis for business processes and workflows that will be introduced later in this book. Until we have defined workflows precisely, we will adopt the following definition of group processes for workflows.

To convey a first impression of how a group process is defined, we cite the definition of a group process given in Borghoff and Schlichter (1995). There, a group process is constituted by a static and a dynamic aspect. The static aspect comprises the factors:

- goals and objectives of the group process
- organizational structures and instances, i.e. people who participate in the group process
- a group protocol that orchestrates the group process

The dynamic aspect of a group process is defined by the following elements:

- a computer infrastructure (hard- and software) and non-computer infrastructure (e.g. buildings, facilities)
- group documents that document the group process (e.g. minutes)
- group activities that are performed during the group process (e.g. "fill out form", "archive document")
- group sessions that bundle group activities and assign people that execute them; group sessions can be performed synchronously and asynchronously by the people selected to participate (e.g. "process travel claim", "book trip")
- a group state that reflects the current state of processing (e.g. "started", "canceling")

It is time to come back to the origin of the discussion of CSCW. We wanted to interrupt the discussion in order to find the group of application systems that might be served well by workflow management systems. The last few paragraphs showed that the group process is a central part of CSCW application systems.

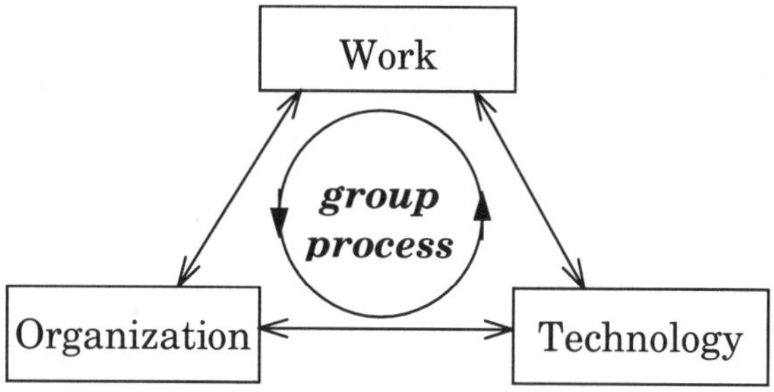

Figure 1.2: Three constituting Topics of CSCW (and Workflow Management)

We will see that a classification of CSCW systems can best be resolved by analyzing how group activities and group sessions are implemented. The next section will detail this observation.

Classification of CSCW

One of the classical classification schemes for groupware systems (and therefore also for CSCW applications) is reported in Johansen (1991) and Ellis *et al.* (1991). This scheme is called the time space matrix and classifies groupware/CSCW applications specifically with respect to time and place where the group activities and the group sessions, respectively, take place (Table 1.1).

The most popular example for face-to-face interaction is a conventional (non-computer supported) meeting: people are sitting together at the same time at the same place and performing a group activity.

Computer conference systems (Sarin and Greif, 1985) enable people distributed among various places to hold (synchronous) distributed meetings.

Multi-user editors like ForComment (Opper, 1988) allow asynchronous editing of a document which is a good example of asynchronous interaction (same place, different time).

Last but not least, asynchronous distributed interaction is a special form of groupware/CSCW applications. People are cooperating at different times sitting at different places. Workflow management systems support this type of cooperation well.

In Ellis *et al.* (1991) a functional classification scheme is also presented. Six different functional classes of groupware/CSCW systems are distinguished:

- message systems like e-mail systems for the asynchronous exchange of textual messages
- multi-user editors for the joint composition and editing of documents
- group decision support systems for the exploration of unstructured problems in a group setting

Table 1.1: Time Space Matrix of Groupware Applications

	Same time	*Different time*
Same place	face-to-face interaction	asynchronous interaction
Different place	synchronous distributed interaction	synchronous distributed interaction

- computer conferencing systems for the synchronous interaction of physically dispersed people through their workstations
- intelligent agents for the cooperation of human and non-human participants in electronic meetings
- coordination systems like Electronic Circulation Folders (Karbe *et al.*, 1990) for the "integration and harmonious adjustment of individual work efforts toward the accomplishment of a larger goal" (Singh, 1989)

Also in this functional classification of groupware/CSCW systems, workflow management can be categorized. Workflow management systems best fit into the class of coordination systems.

1.2.2 Cooperative Information Systems

This section introduces two classification schemes for application systems.

Problem-oriented Application Systems

The first system is problem-oriented; it is reported in Mertens (1985). Mertens classifies application systems according to the purpose and goals they are used for. He excludes special tools (e.g. compilers and editors) and single purpose application systems (e.g. CAD systems) from the classification scheme. Typical examples of application systems that are included into the classification schemes are manufacturing control systems or business administration systems. According to Mertens the following four types of application systems can be distinguished:

- *Administrative Systems*. The purpose of administrative systems is to support routine work that has to be performed very frequently and will almost never be changed. The main purpose of this application class is to rationalize mass data processing. Automatic control and data flow management are two characteristics of administrative systems.
- *Decision Support Systems*. Decision support systems help human users to make decisions. They process and analyze data in order to provide a

profound data basis for decision making. In many cases, operations research models are used.

- *Planning Systems.* Planning systems are problem solving systems. They are deployed when unstructured problems have to be solved. Expert systems and systems that are based on methods of artificial intelligence are typical representatives of planning systems.
- *Presentation Systems.* The main purpose of presentation systems is to prepare data is such a way that they can be easily comprehended by management staff. Typical examples of presentation systems are programs that support charts and diagrams.

The above classification demonstrates nicely that problem solving competence is the measurement that is used to classify the first three system types. The fourth system type, presentation systems, stands somewhat outside of the classification scheme and orthogonal to the first three types. It has to prepare, process and present information that is produced by the other system types.

Workflow management systems fit into the class of administrative systems, specifically, workflow management can be deployed to implement administrative systems. Their aim is not to provide sophisticated problem solving capacities but is to support routine work. Control and data flow management, having been introduced as main characteristics of administrative systems, represent two of the fundamental tasks for workflow management systems.

System-oriented Application Systems

A second classification scheme is reported in Brodie and Ceri (1992). Information systems are characterized as follows:

> ... a conventional information system is a computer-based system that represents aspects of the evolving state of an organization or of a topic area of interest to an organization. An information system consists of a collection of applications that implement required functions (representing state retrievals and changes) over a collection of shared, persistent information repositories (representing the pertinent aspects of the state).

Typically, multiple (mostly human) users are involved in simultaneous information processes by manipulating specific data through specific applica-tions. Well-known examples of information systems are airline reservation systems, employee administration systems, manufacturing control systems, accounting systems, etc.

The main characteristics of information systems are therefore

- application processes
- common data, and
- multiple (human) users.

It is not possible (and also not necessary) to exactly define information systems. The above discussion outlines sufficiently the main properties and behaviors of information systems. In particular, it is easy to realize that the following systems should not be considered as information systems (Brodie and Ceri, 1992): simulation systems, stand-alone and single user systems, knowledge-based systems, systems software (e.g. operating systems), editors, compilers.

It was common practice to develop information systems as application-specific but independent from each other. However, it was learned very quickly that information systems have to collaborate continuously. In order to accomplish work, group processes span multiple information systems and access their databases. The interaction of information systems is symmetric to the interaction of humans when working in an office, for instance. The required cooperation of information systems led to the notion of "cooperative information system". Formerly independent information systems now act in the role of component information systems under the control of a comprehensive cooperative information system. Nevertheless, the component information systems should maintain autonomy as far as possible.

Brodie and Ceri state that one of the main challenges of cooperative information systems is to provide communication protocols that allow efficient and transparent (with respect to systems software and hardware) cooperation in distributed and heterogeneous environments.

Summary

Comparing the system-oriented discussion with the problem-oriented discussion, it becomes very obvious that administrative systems can be implemented by cooperative information systems. This correspondence fits nicely to our interpretation that workflow management systems are a very typical and effective example of cooperative information systems.

The two classification schemes discussed in this section have given a first impression of the principal character and the principal goal of workflow management. Therefore, a vague picture of workflow management is already formed. Before this picture is concretized in Section 1.4, the subsequent section will report some selected case studies. The case studies will consolidate the first picture of the purpose and contents of workflow management.

1.3 Case Studies

In this section, four workflow[2] examples are presented stemming from different application areas. The first one is a software process example. The second example stems from the investment field. Example three covers the manufacturing area.

The last example describes a workflow from the office automation area.

The aim of this section is to check whether the example processes, which are regarded as typical workflows, fit into the two classification schemes introduced in Section 1.2.

We have selected examples from different application areas to show how similarly they can be treated with respect to workflow modeling and execution. It is not true that workflow management is well suited to office environments (e.g. within an insurance company) but does not comply with the requirements of engineering environments (e.g. the manufacturing environment). We had our first experience with workflow management in a manufacturing company (Jablonski and Ruf, 1990). Later, we found that the same concepts that we studied in that area could also be applied to office problems. The following examples will confirm this experience.

1.3.1 Software Process Example

In Section 1.1.2 we mentioned that software processes are very similar to workflows. This close relationship is the reason for demonstrating a software process example here.

The example software process reported in Kellner *et al.* (1991) is regarded as a standard software process modeling example. To use a standard benchmark problem facilitates comparisons of various modeling approaches in the software process field. We take it as a typical example of software process modeling. The principle goal of a software process is to control the development and maintenance of software.

Figure 1.3 depicts the principal structure of the standard software process. "Develop Change and Test Unit" is the name of the core problem. It is modeled by eight component tasks which are called

- Schedule and Assign Tasks,
- Modify Design,
- Review Design,
- Modify Code,
- Modify Test Plans,
- Modify Unit Test Package,
- Test Unit, and
- Monitor Progress.

In Figure 1.3 the full descriptions of the component tasks are not shown to afford better readability. Nevertheless, the example is sufficiently self-explanatory. Only the tasks themselves, responsible persons or groups who are dedicated to perform the tasks and data flow between tasks are revealed. Goals and objectives, data

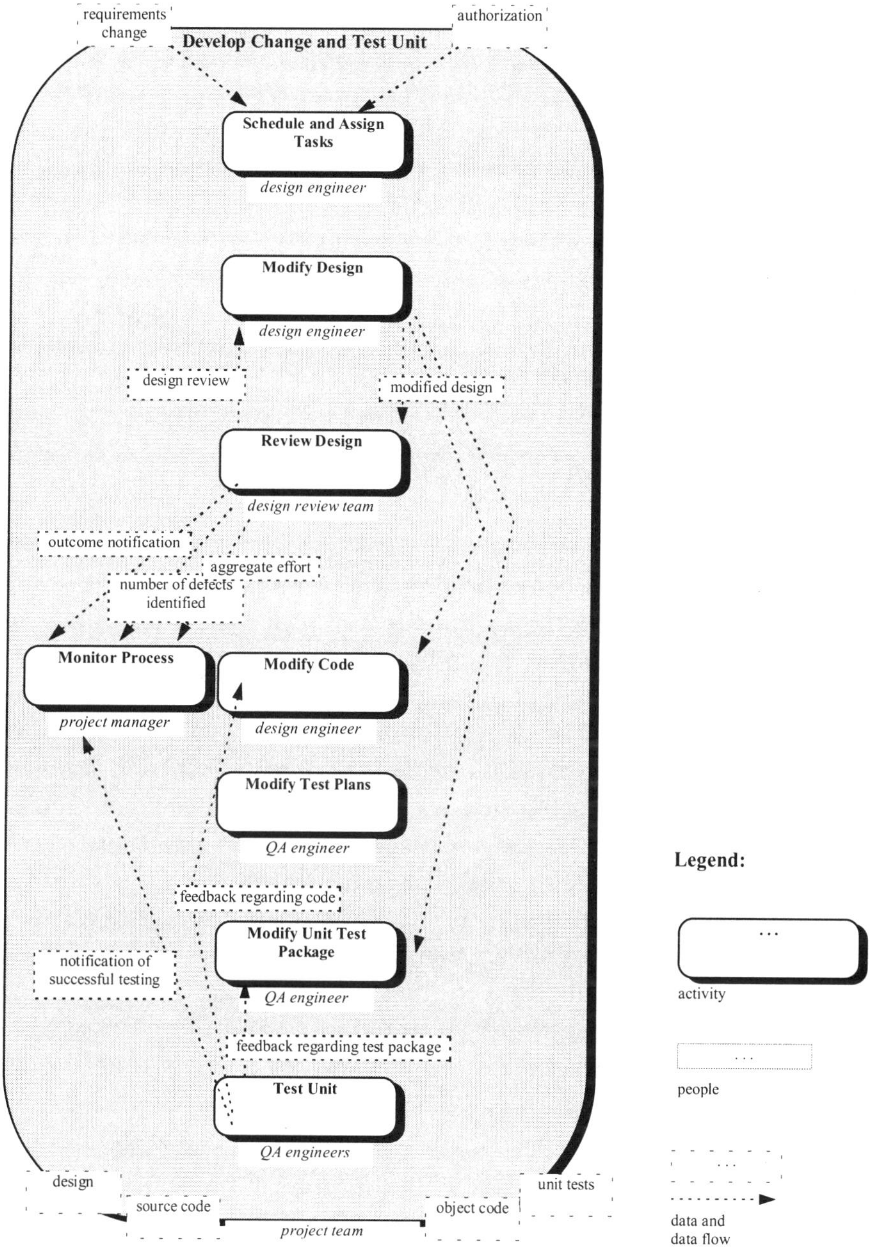

Figure 1.3: Software Process Example

consumption and production with respect to databases, the database schemes, the organizational structure and instances, the use of application programs (e.g. editors, compilers) and constraints restricting the execution of component tasks are neglected. They can be looked up in Kellner *et al.* (1991).

Even when Figure 1.3 omits essential parts of the component task descriptions and they are only mentioned briefly in the paragraph before, we can check that the example software process is defined like a group process (cf. Section 1.2.1). Goals and objectives, organizational structures and instances, computer infrastructure, group activities and group sessions are easy to find in the description of the software process. Therefore, we classify a software process as a special kind of group process. Moreover, a software process shows typical characteristics of an administrative process (cf. Section 1.2.2) that is performed on top of a cooperative information system.

1.3.2 Mortgage Request Handling in an Investment Company

The second example describes an administrative process, namely the mortgage handling request process in an investment company (Joosten *et al.*, 1994). The purpose of applying workflow technology in this example is to reduce paper traffic. During the processing of mortgage requests enormous streams of paper documents must be handled. Due to the inaccessibility of paper files and the lack of capacity to store the paper files people have to spend a significant amount of their time on non-productive activities which merely have to do with paper document handling. By introducing document management and workflow technology, the efficiency of mortgage processing is increased notably.

Figure 1.4 provides an overview of mortgage request processing. In order to preserve readability we omit to show data flow and electronic data containers (i.e. document and file containers) in the figure. Electronic documents and files are especially generated in the three initial tasks and in the task "Draw up Insurance Policy". All data are managed by electronic document management systems; they are available for all tasks that are executed in the global workflow. If employees of the investment companies need to access to one of the documents they can retrieve it from the corresponding document archive. In principle, the archives are accessible for all employees involved in mortgage request processing. Access rights control the integrity of document access.

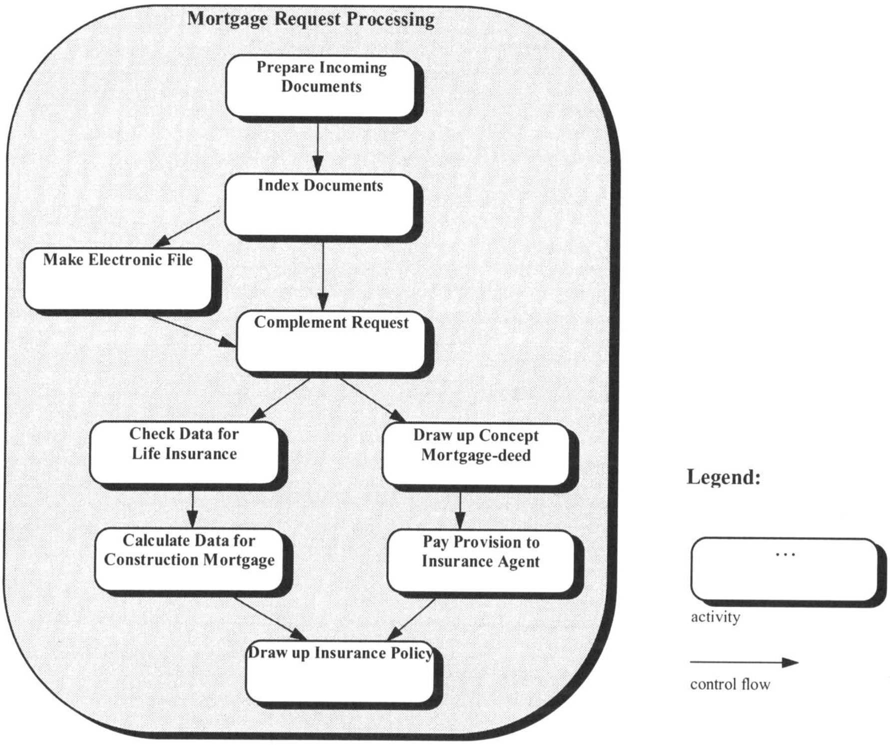

Figure 1.4: Mortgage Request Processing Example

1.3.3 Manufacturing Control

Our third example stems from the manufacturing area. We look at the first part of a manufacturing control process of one of the leading manufacturers of turbo chargers in Europe. In analogy to the two examples discussed above, only the fundamental parts of the process will be presented.

The manufacturing process analyzed in the following comprises the CAD (Computer Aided Design) and the CAPP (Computer Aided Process Planning) area. The major task of the design area is the generation of technical drawings for part manufacturing. The drawings are subsequently sent to the CAPP area, specifically to the two sub-areas "Bill of Material Generation" and "Process Planning". Here, bills of materials and process plans are defined. Next, the "Numeric Control" (NC) programming department is called to deliver NC programs for those operations of the process plans which refer to NC machines. At last, the NC programs are sent to the "Resource Management" department where the availability of reference NC machines, tools and fixtures is checked. Figure 1.5 shows the structure of the manufacturing process example.

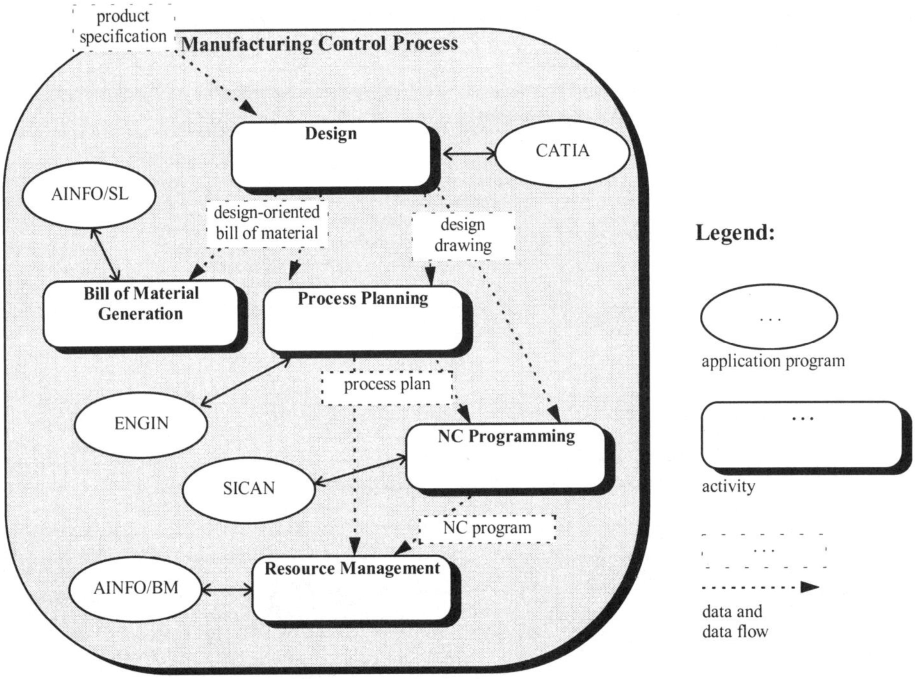

Figure 1.5: Manufacturing Process Example

In contrast to the software process example, no people are assigned to the process steps. Instead, each step is associated with an application program (CATIA, ENGIN, etc.). The semantics of this association is two-fold: first, the application programs are required to perform a particular step; second, people who are eligible to use a specific application program are indirectly responsible for executing a particular step.

Finally, we again want to check whether this workflow fits to the classification schemes that were developed in Section 1.2. Without going into details, the main characteristics of group process and administrative systems can be found in the manufacturing control process example. Therefore, we regard this as another proof of our classification schemes.

1.3.4 Lease Contract Management

The last example stems from office automation and describes the creation of a lease contract for real estate properties like flats, garages or business buildings. This workflow is deployed in a German company which leases properties professionally, see Dinkhoff *et al.* (1994).

We show a workflow and one of its subworkflows. The Create Lease workflow is a top-level workflow consisting of several subworkflows (see Figure 1.6). The first task, "Create Documents", is an automatic one. It is started after the workflow "Create Lease Contract" is initiated. Automatic means that no human user is involved in its execution. Basically, a batch job is initiated which calls the appropriate application programs. The result of this task consists of three documents, "Lesee", "Lessor" and "House Unity" each of which is sent to a separate subworkflow for further processing. One of the subworkflows, "Select Lessee", is discussed next. The others are omitted.

Figure 1.7 shows the subworkflow "Create Lessee". The first task ("Select Lessee") is a manual one. A decision is made if a person, the lessee, is already registered (i.e. is already leasing some property) or is not involved in any lease yet. In the first case the existent information about the lessee is selected and returned. In the latter case data about the new lessee is collected by another task ("Collect Lessee Dat") and inserted into a database by yet another subsequent task ("Insert Lessee Data"). Finally the newly inserted information is returned.

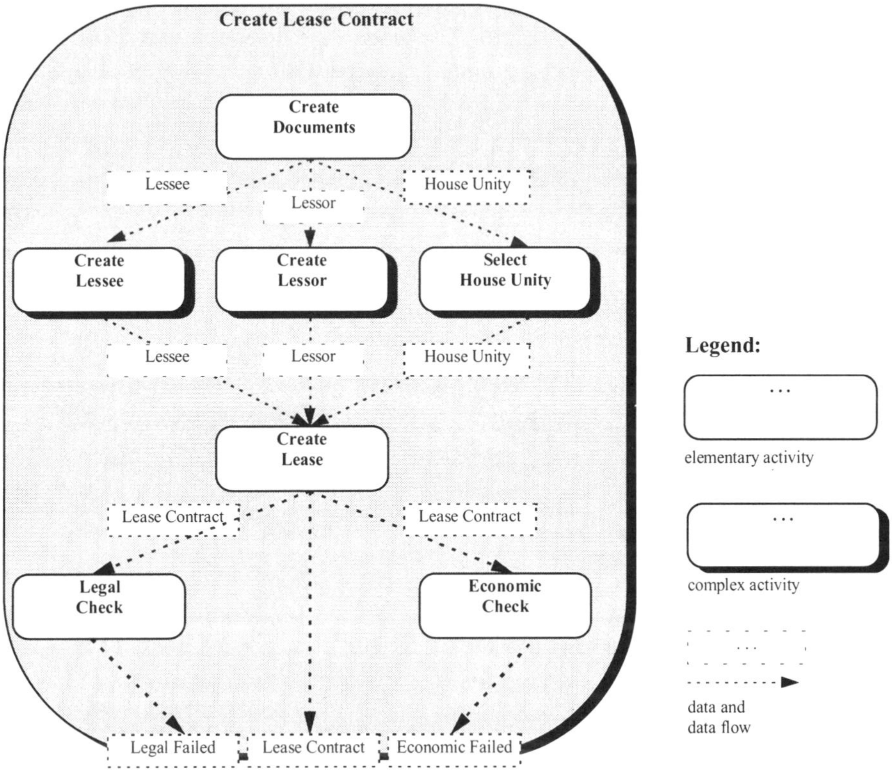

Figure 1.6: Creating a Lease Contract

As soon as this subworkflow ("Create Lessee") is finished as well as the other two ("Create Lessor" and "Select House Unity"), the task "Create Lease" can be started. This task is an automatic one and composes the three documents "Lessee", "Lessor" and "House Unity" into a "Lease Contract". After the composition of the "Lease Contract" a legal and an economic check is appended. The result of each check as well as the lease contract is the final result of the "Create Lease Contract" workflow. These results can be used for further processing.

Throughout the whole description the assignment of tasks to people as well as application programs to be used for task execution were intentionally left out. All the details can be found in Dinkhoff *et al.* (1994).

1.4 Formation of the Concept

After having been introduced to the historical development of workflow management, to a classification of workflow relevant application areas and to case studies, it is time to state more precisely what workflow management consists of.

Many definitions of workflow management can be found in the literature (e.g. Joosten *et al.*, 1994; McCarthy and Bluestein, 1991). Each of them is correct, however, none of them is complete. Because workflow management is a very comprehensive, extensive topic, this incompleteness is a logical consequence.

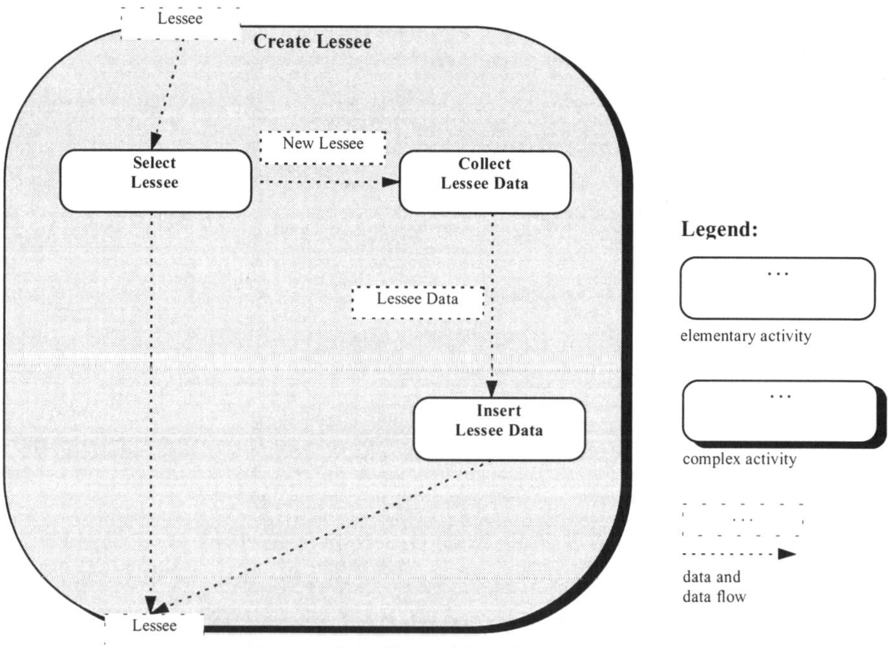

Figure 1.7: Create Lessee Subworkflow

Therefore, we characterize and delimit the scope of workflow management by defining workflow management indirectly through typical features, attributes, behaviors and application areas. Following this approach we hope to include most of the characteristics of workflow management.

Section 1.2 revealed that workflow management systems are used for

- distributed asynchronous interactions.

They are tightly related to

- coordination systems
- cooperative information systems, and
- administrative systems.

Taking these diverse classifications into consideration we characterize workflow management as follows:

- workflow management supports distributed asynchronous interactions
- workflow management integrates (individually developed and performed) work steps toward the accomplishment of a larger task
- workflow management supports routine work
- workflow management integrates applications (functions), technology (hard- and software), data and users into group processes; group processes aim at the accomplishment of work.

Analyzing the typical case studies of Section 1.3

- workflow management is general and generic

to support diverse application areas.

Besides these characteristics, another feature of workflow management must be mentioned which is most significant. Section 1.1.1 mentioned a new trend in application system development. Process-centric approaches are favored compared with task- or data-centric approaches. Since workflow management fosters this approach, one of its major challenges is to model all entities and relationships of an application system explicitly. A workflow, therefore, defines a comprehensive scheme which includes all aspects of an application system. This comprehensiveness and completeness opens up a most valuable opportunity for reengineering (Hammer and Champy, 1993). Such an accurate and complete scheme of an application system is the best basis to review and optimize processes in an enterprise.

Last but not least, it has to be mentioned that workflow management does not end with modeling. To execute workflows eventually is the final goal of workflow management.

1.5 Expectations and Fears

Whenever a new technology is developed and begins to proliferate, high expectations are associated with its introduction. Specifically the advent of workflow management technology raised expectations and received premature praise that was, first, not justified and, second, could not be sustained by most commercial products and research prototypes. In this section, expectations and fears about workflow management technology will be discussed.

Expectations

The contribution of workflow management to management and organizational effectiveness can best be assessed when group processes, the core of workflow management, are regarded from the perspective of the value chain concept (Porter, 1985). The value chain views an organization as a collection of activities that adds value to the product or the service of an organization (Koulopoulos, 1995). A value chain is a system of interrelated and interdependent (group) activities (i.e. they constitute a group session). The activities are linked together by either control or data connectors.

A very illustrative example of a value chain is a production process, where raw material is transformed to finished products. Another type of value chain can be found in service processes. A travel agency transforms customer specific data (date of vacation, favorite vacation resort, price limit, etc.) to a complete vacation trip booking.

Starting with the concept of a group process as a value chain and regarding a workflow as a special implementation of a group process, we now can present major positive business implications of workflow management (cf. Joosten *et al.* (1994)):

- *Increasing the quality of service.* Service provision is increased with regard to effectiveness and efficiency. Unnecessary delays are eliminated through automated routing and work division. This also leads to an increase of throughput.

  A higher quality service is provided since the failure rate is reduced due to validation checks that can easily be implemented for smaller parts of the production process.

  Service quality can also be improved by better ensuring on-going compliance with federal or state laws and enterprise (business) rules. Having implemented these regulations enables to execute processes according to their most appropriate versions.
- *Improving service to the clients.* There are two major services to be provided to a client. Information service is the first: many kinds of customer inquiries can be answered instantaneously since the service/production

process is implemented on top of huge databases that encompass all information relevant to the service/product and the clients.

Another valuable benefit of workflow management is flexibility with respect to the spectrum of service/product provision: alternative activities can effectively be composed to offer a new service/product.

- *Increasing productivity.* Due to the elimination of delays and higher throughput, the productivity of an enterprise can be increased.
- *Reducing costs.* The main cost reduction can be put down to the fact that workflow management increases throughput and therefore decreases the amount of time spent on a particular service/product.
- *Reducing vulnerability.* The introduction of workflow management technology requires thorough investigation of the group processes that have to be implemented. Increased knowledge about the group processes results from such a detailed study. This knowledge can be used to reschedule, defer or prioritize work to reduce its vulnerability.

Fears

Nevertheless, the introduction of a new technology often causes fears and reservations due to the unknown consequences of its deployment. Especially in this context, people are worried about workflow management being a straitjacket that controls and supervises human users who are degenerated to stupid agents that have to react to whatever the system prescribes. In detail, the fears and reservations break down into the following aspects (cf. Joosten *et al.* (1994)):

- *Too rigid control.* The workflow management system might control and direct its human users to an unacceptable degree. Users can only react to the system.
- *Too much inspection.* People fear the possibilities for management inspecting their work. In principle, all kinds of analysis are possible: what employee was spending what amount of time on what kind of task, of what quality was his/her work, etc.
- *Too little functionality.* Workflow management is not trusted to solve the major problems of an application area. This fear is caused by the overestimation of workflow management technology which often leads to the attitude that workflow management systems are a panacea for everything.[3] Since workflow management is not a panacea, the key issue is to balance the use of workflow management technology and not to blindly deploy workflow management systems to all kinds of problems.
- *Too much inflexibility.* The workflow as the implementation of the group process is too inflexible. It cannot be adjusted dynamically to new requirements posted by either the clients or the system environment.

It cannot be denied that workflow management imposes control on group processes and consequently also on people that are involved in performing them. However, this observation is common to most if not all computer technology that is introduced. If workflow management systems are used moderately they can offer helpful and valuable guidance throughout the execution of a group process.

1.6 Scope of the Book

This section tries to answer the three fundamental questions:

- Why was this book written at all?
- What is the perspective and the scope of this book?
- Who is the intended audience for this book?

The book market in the workflow management field is somewhat strange: every few months new comparison reports are published which summarize the main features of commercial workflow management products and compare them. Although in principle such reports would be beneficial, we are not in favor of them for the following reasons:

- The workflow management market is still very dynamic. This means that products change their main features drastically from version to version. Therefore, the validity of these reports is very limited.
- The comparisons are mostly very shallow. We have not found a publicly available technical report that compares workflow management systems sufficiently from a technical point of view. Scalability, customizability, extensibility, etc. are criteria that are fundamental for workflow management but they are not dealt with thoroughly in the reports.[4]

Therefore, comparison reports are neither sufficient nor adequate for consultants because they are out of date too fast; nor are they obligatory for technical people since from a technical viewpoint they are not profound enough.

Besides these comparison reports there are many papers on workflow management topics. Some of them are very interesting and present valuable ideas and concepts. The inherent problem with papers is that they merely deal with fragments of a problem and do not work on a topic broadly. They are more focused on introducing new technically sound concepts. Thus, it is very hard to get an overview on the current situation in workflow management by only studying the papers.

The only books on workflow management treat this topic from a business- and consulting-oriented perspective. This is justified due to the enormous popularity of workflow management that makes it one of the hot topics of business- and consulting-oriented people. Nevertheless, books on the technical aspects of workflow management are still missing. This is the niche into which our book fits. We want to discuss the workflow management topic for information technology professionals. However, we intend to do it in a way that business- and consulting-oriented people and also scientific-oriented people (e.g. students) can profit from. Our goal is to introduce a workflow model and a workflow management architecture which allows to classify and compare other workflow models and architectures. Thus, a clear conceptual preparation of the topics is fundamental.

We do not want to introduce another workflow model and architecture, but we want to introduce a classifying reference model and architecture which helps people to understand the principal concepts of workflow management. The idea behind developing a workflow reference model and architecture is that a large number of workflow problems have many characteristics in common. Thus, one comprehensive approach to workflow management might solve most of these problems. Very often, just the customization of some specific elements of workflow management suffices to provide an adequate solution. Therefore, the knowledge and experience put into such a comprehensive approach can be utilized when new workflow problems have to be solved.

This book can be characterized as a text book or a trade book which adapts the workflow management topic for a technology-oriented discussion.

Section 1.1 and Section 1.4 conveyed that workflow management follows a process-centric methodology and aims at the comprehensive treatment of an application scenario. The broadness of the approach makes it necessary that workflow management is not introduced separately and in isolation. However, we embed it into a global information systems engineering life cycle which shows the entire application path of this new technology. Specifically, we elaborate the relationship of workflow management to business process (re)engineering since both topics are – due to misinterpretation – set equal frequently.

The contents of this book are based on research in the workflow management area which we have conducted since 1987 as one of the authors worked on a project for "data and process (function) integration" at one of the largest manufacturing companies in Europe. Now, we know that "data and process (function) integration" is exactly what nowadays is called workflow management. Also, we gained much experience as (technical) consultants on real customer projects. There, we could prove the applicability of the concepts we had previously developed theoretically.

[1] Under the notion "organization" we subsume either the organizational structure of an enterprise (groups, departments, etc.) and the individuals working in/for an enterprise (employees, business partners, etc.).

[2] We should rather talk about group processes since we have not introduced workflows so far.

[3] It is a pity that many system vendors, consultant firms and even research institutes have disseminated this rumor.

[4] We heard of workflow management projects that failed (of course, these projects and their problems are never reported in public). This is mostly due to the unsufficient technical features of the workflow management products with respect to functionality, scalability, customizability, extensibility, etc. Thus it is fundamental to compare them against these technical measurements.

2 Related Approaches

During the first and second development phases (homegrown and rudimentary, see Section 1.1.3) many research prototypes as well as commercial products have been developed. To learn about the main features of workflow management systems, this chapter characterizes selected research prototypes and commercial products. The discussion gives insight into the functionality and behavior of the systems.

We structure the description of selected workflow management systems according to the following scheme:

- *Modeling Elements.* First, a discussion of the modeling elements available for the workflow modeler takes place. The elements of a workflow model (e.g. workflow, role, application, data) determine the expressiveness of a workflow management system.
- *Tools, Languages and APIs.* Workflow modelers as well as workflow management system users like clerks or managers have to interact with a system through user interfaces. Each of these two user groups uses a set of tools or languages for the specific tasks they have to fulfill. Sometimes it is necessary for an enterprise to build its own interfaces instead of using those supplied by a workflow management system. This might be important if a workflow management system has to fit into an already existing software infrastructure with a common look and feel. To support this, APIs (application programming interfaces) are made available in the form of function libraries by some workflow management systems.
- *System Architecture and Implementation.* Workflow types are instantiated during run time by workflow management systems (more specifically

by so-called workflow engines) in order to execute business processes. This section of the description focuses on execution or implementation related details of a workflow management system. Issues like distribution, scalability and reliability are discussed here as well as openness and interoperability.

- *Application Area Specifics.* In the ideal case, workflow management systems abstract from the semantics of a certain application area like office automation or shop floor processing (see Cleetus (1994)). However, in the early phases of workflow management system development not all systems followed this abstraction but were built for a specific application area. In this part of the description functionality for specific application semantics is reported.

We do not intend to enumerate all existing systems which are marketed as workflow management systems. This list is rather lengthy and contains more than 200 products. Hales and Lavery (1991) and White and Fischer (1994) provide an overview on various workflow management products. Instead, we restrict ourselves to those workflow management systems where sufficient and detailed documentation are available (e.g. research papers and user/programmer manuals).

Figure 2.1 positions the discussed systems onto a time axis. Section 2.1 and Section 2.2 discuss each system in more detail.

Besides commercial developments, the first steps in standardization of workflow management related issues have been accomplished. In 1993 a group of over 80 vendors formed an industrial standardization body named the Workflow Management Coalition (WfMC). A short overview of the aims and objectives of the WfMC is given in Section 2.4 as well as a summary of the first standardization activities.

At this point we want to make a note on the terminology we use to describe existing workflow management system prototypes and products. Throughout the descriptions we use the terminology found in the documentation of the respective systems. Another approach could have been to introduce a common terminology and translate the vendor specific terminology. We do not follow this second approach since we want to ensure that there are no translation errors from a specific to a common terminology. However, later on in this book (Section 5 and Section 6) we introduce a common terminology to describe workflow modeling elements independent from specific workflow management systems since we aim at presenting a general and comprehensive approach for workflow management.

The following sections are based on information available in autumn 1995. To the best of our knowledge we have summarized and classified the material in

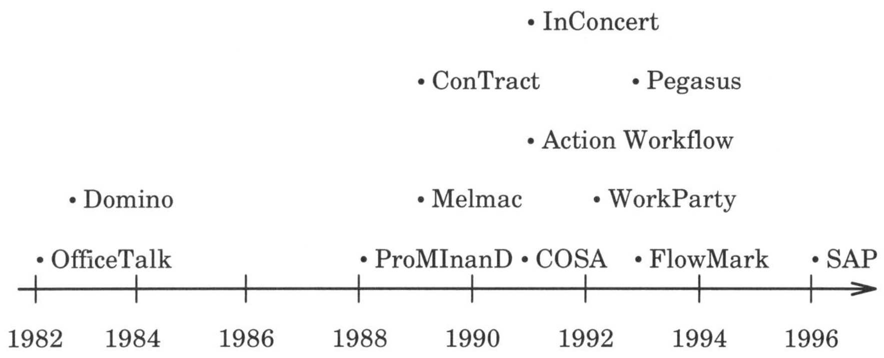

Figure 2.1: Time Axis of Workflow Management Systems

order to provide a homogenous overview on research prototypes and commercial products. Nevertheless, we are aware of the fact that at the time the book is finally published the contents of this chapter will be out of date. However, this chapter does not (and cannot) aim at completeness. Rather, it has to convey a first idea of workflow management technology on the one hand, and to introduce key players in the academic and commercial fields of workflow management on the other hand.

2.1 Research Prototypes and Efforts

The first research prototypes of workflow management systems were already built in the 1980s. Some of them are described in the following:

- ConTract (Section 2.1.1)
- Domino (Section 2.1.2)
- Melmac (Section 2.1.3)
- OfficeTalk (Section 2.1.4)
- Pegasus (Section 2.1.5)
- Transactional Workflows (Section 2.1.6)

The descriptions of these efforts are not complete since the information is derived from research papers. Research papers are focused in order to emphasize certain aspects of a prototypical development which is of interest to the research community.

2.1.1 ConTract (University of Stuttgart, Germany)

ConTract is a research effort at the University of Stuttgart in Germany. This effort focuses on the reliability and recoverability of long-living activities as well as on concurrency and resource conflict related issues in the context of database transactions. To provide a complete workflow model together with an execution system is not the goal of the ConTract approach. Therefore, we cannot structure the following description as indicated above since most parts of it could not be filled with information.

In contrast to conventional ACID (Atomicity, Consistency, Isolation, Durability) transactions which are intended to be short and touch only a few objects, complex long-living activities live significantly longer and touch probably a large set of objects. Furthermore, long-living activities have a complex internal control flow structure which has to be maintained by the system and has to be recoverable. Wächter and Reuter (1991) states that simple ACID transactions are not feasible to support the execution of long-living activities because of the divergence in requirements and characteristics.

Traditionally, applications call short transactions sequentially. The control flow between short transactions is managed by the application itself, not by an underlying service like a database system. After a failure of the application program (e.g. if a node crashes) the application has to know where to continue within the code it executes. The application itself has to find out which transaction is to be executed next. In contrast, data manipulated by the application is recovered automatically by an underlying database system. Because only the data manipulated by an application is recovered automatically but not the execution state of the application itself, the application has to reconstruct its state itself to continue execution after failure at the right place within the program.

The ConTract model aims at providing a base service for applications which recover their execution state automatically. This relieves applications from finding out by themselves where to continue after a failure. The basic idea is to build large applications out of short ACID transactions in order to provide an application independent system service. Such a large application is called a ConTract. A ConTract controls individual ACID transactions and is therefore a mechanism above ACID transactions. The ConTract model is therefore not merely a transaction model but a programming model.

Wächter and Reuter (1991) defined a ConTract as a consistent and fault tolerant execution of an arbitrary sequence of predefined actions (called steps) according to an explicit specified control flow description (called a script). A step is written in some traditional programming language accessing a database by performing queries. Steps are not hierarchically structured, i.e. a step cannot be a ConTract itself. Steps are programmed separately from ConTracts. No assumptions are made within a step about the calling environment. If it is used within a ConTract a step runs within the scope of a single ACID transaction. As soon as a step has been committed its effects are externalized even though the ConTract might not have been finished.

A ConTract is specified by a script. A script defines the steps to be used and the control flow between the steps using constructs like sequence, conditional branching, loop, parallel branching or loops spawning several steps. A script also defines context variables. These context variables are the local variables of a ConTract, store results from step executions and are used as input parameters for step invocations.

Steps can be combined into larger entities. It is possible to group several steps so that they are executed within one ACID transaction. This decision is made within the script using the steps. Dependencies between steps can be defined like

$$T1.abort \rightarrow begin.T2$$

The above dependency denotes that if a step T1 aborts, step T2 has to start. Dependencies enable to specify complex control structures between steps. For each step a compensation step (possibly an empty one) is specified. This compensation step performs database operations to semantically undo the externalized effects.

If a ConTract is interrupted (e.g. by a node crash or a user request) it is not rolled back. Instead, it waits for a resume command in order to continue. This is achieved by transferring it into an appropriate execution state from which resuming is possible. A ConTract recovers from a crash by starting at the nearest consistent state of computation. This is achieved by storing its context within a context database. This context is then used to determine the latest consistent state.

A ConTract can be canceled only by users, never by the system itself. Canceling a ConTract cannot be achieved by restoring before images, since the effects of steps within a ConTract are externalized while the ConTract is still active and not finished. Therefore a compensation strategy has to be in place to achieve a semantic undo. Within the script a compensation step is assigned to each step. To compensate a ConTract means to compensate each step which was executed within the ConTract by executing the related compensation step. The compensation of a ConTract might involve so many actions that a single compensation step is not sufficient. Instead, a whole ConTract might be assigned as a compensating ConTract to a step.

If a compensation fails, a note is sent to a responsible administrator. Compensation for faulty compensation steps is not supported due to the risk of steps endlessly compensating themselves.

Since ConTracts externalize effects of steps, ConTracts influence each other. This is no problem if no compensation happens at all. However, if some ConTract has to undo its effects it might be necessary to undo one or more other ConTracts which already made decisions on the externalized effects. Therefore, a run time system executing ConTract has to carefully log which step of a ConTract depends on the effects of which step of another ConTract to make compensation possible.

Cascading compensation however is not the ideal case, since it invalidates a lot of work already performed. Therefore ConTracts add invariants to steps. A ConTract modeler can add enter and exit invariants to steps. A step is executed only if the enter invariant holds. An exit invariant defines what the step expects the state of data to be (i.e. it specifies what is necessary so that its effects remain valid). Enter invariants define a state of data necessary for its execution. If the state is given, the step starts execution. If an exit invariant is necessary at the time another steps starts, the latter step has to check the exit invariants again in addition to its own invariants.

If an exit invariant fails two things could happen. First, the step could be rolled back (since it is an ACID transaction). Second, instead of rolling back the step a conflict resolution rule could be started. This conflict resolution rule could ask for some action to change the data in a way that the exit invariant holds. E.g. if the exit invariant says that the budget has to be higher than the cost of an airline ticket, but the budget is less, the conflict resolution rule could ask a manager to increase the budget.

The ConTract model is prototypically implemented by a system named APRICOT (*A Pr*ototypical *I*mplementation of a *Con*T*ract System) at the University of Stuttgart in Germany.

2.1.2 Domino (Gesellschaft für Mathematik und Datenverarbeitung, Bonn, Germany)

Domino is a research effort of the GMD in Germany which has been conducted since 1983. The following description is based on Kreifelts *et al.* (1993a, b), Kreifelts (1991), Kreifelts and Seuffert (1988) and Woetzel and Kreifelts (1993).

Modeling Elements

The model of Domino is very simple. The basic modeling elements are *procedure, role, action, form* and a *need* relationship as well as a *produce* relationship between an action and a form. There are several modeling elements to model an organization structure.

- *Form.* A form is a data structure which is worked on by a user. The fields of a form are not predefined and can be freely defined by a workflow modeler. Every field is accessible by a user at runtime.
- *Action.* An action defines a task a user has to perform. In order to carry out a task a user might use an application program. The data a user has available come with a form as input to the action. The data which are produced by a user are the result of an action.

- *Role.* Domino distinguishes two kind of roles: roles within a procedure attached to actions and roles within an organization. Roles within a procedure are placeholders for users. Attached to each role within a process is an expression of a role language which derives one or more users as soon as the action has to be performed. In Domino two roles are predefined: *initiator* and *office*. The initiator role of a procedure contains the user who started the procedure. The office role implements automated users. If an action is attached to this role the action gets executed automatically.
- *Organization.* Domino provides a set of modeling elements to model an organization. These are *organizational units*, *projects*, *jobs* and *people*. In addition to these objects multiple relationships are supported: *belongs to* (relates employee and organizational unit), *holds* (relates employee and job), *member of* (relates employee and project) and *supervisor of* (relates employee and organizational unit or another employee).

  Role language expressions are predicates over the modeled organization structure. If at run time a role attached to an action has to be resolved to employees the attached expression is evaluated against the organization structure.

  This evaluation might resolve into more than one employee so that a role might be assigned to several users. If several users play the same role they are able to execute the action in parallel.
- *Procedure.* A procedure is a net of related actions. An action is related to at least two forms, one containing its input data and one containing its output data. The form containing the output data of an action is the input data form of another action. This ensures that the network of actions within a procedure is not partitioned. Exceptions are the first and last form. They are related to the procedure itself.

  An action can have more than one form as input data. At run time the content of one is chosen as input parameters. The same applies to output forms. An action might be connected to several output forms. At run time one of them is chosen to receive the output values of the action.

  Modeling several input and output forms allows alternative execution paths within a procedure. This is important if at run time alternatives have to be followed depending on run time data values.

  Domino does not know the concept of control flow at all. There are no modeling constructs like sequence or loops or any other construct. The determination of the execution order of actions is solely based on the availability of data (forms). As soon as a form is available and related to an action this action is ready for execution.

The interplay of forms and actions can be easily mapped to Petri nets if forms are represented as places and actions as transitions. This is exactly what Domino is doing to represent procedures internally. In addition, the internal representation is used at run time to execute procedures.

After the work is done a user can choose to send the form to the next action (guided by the procedure), send the form back to the previous action (meaning to the user of the previous action) or delegate the procedure. This behavior resembles the paradigm of migrating folders or forms.

A specific property of the Domino system has to be mentioned here. The Domino system assigns actions to users according to the role and the result of the role language expression. If a user has finished the action the Domino system takes over and assigns the next actions if there are any. In addition to this execution paradigm it is possible for each user to send a message (possibly containing documents) to all procedure participants at any time. This way a simple form of free-style cooperation between users is incorporated.

Domino defines correctness of procedures. Structural and behavioral correctness is distinguished. The correctness rules for the structure of a procedure are:

- Every form is needed by a procedure or produced by an action.
- Every form is needed by an action or produced by a procedure.
- Procedures must not have partitions and must not have loops.

The correctness rules for the behavior of a procedure are:

- A procedure must not get stuck.
- A procedure must not have dead actions.
- A form is either needed by an action or produced by a procedure.
- A form must not be produced twice.
- At most one input and one output alternative to or from actions must be selected.

Tools, Languages and APIs

Domino provides a specification language for procedures as well as for organization structures and expressions. This language is called *CoPlanS* and is declarative in its nature. Even though the internal representation of procedures are Petri nets this is not visible at the language level at all. Domino provides a language compiler for compiling procedures into Petri nets.

Domino contains a user interface which is divided into two parts: a main window for getting an overview over procedures, and other windows. The main window indicates the status of each procedure from a user perspective (e.g. needs to be worked on, already finished, no action required, data has changed). Other windows are used to work on data of a single form, to track procedures, to start new procedures, to enter data or to select enclosures.

System Architecture and Implementation

Domino implements a client/server structure between its components. The management and supervision of procedures is done by a component called a *mediator*. This mediator has databases attached to store current states of running procedures as well as the organization structure. It also provides the compiler for the CoPlanS language which is used to compile and install office procedures. To perform the communication Domino uses e-mail to notify users about actions and to transport forms between the users and the mediator.

Application Area Specifics

Domino is designed to implement office procedures. It is deployed and tested in office settings.

2.1.3 Melmac (University of Dortmund, Germany)

The roots of *Melmac* are in software process management. Melmac is a software process management environment deployed to model and manage software processes. The following description is based on Deiters and Gruhn (1994), Deiters *et al.* (1993), and Gruhn and Jegelka (1992). Since software processes are specialized workflows in the area of software process management (cf. Section 5.1.3) we give an overview of Melmac here.

The software process model of Melmac is based on views. E.g. the specification of user activities happens within a different view than the specification of project management information. In order to derive a complete software process model all views are integrated into one representation. Therefore, modeling in Melmac means to model according to a divide and conquer paradigm. Furthermore, Melmac supports the delegation of partial models. So it is possible that multiple people model a software process.

Another interesting feature of Melmac is the possibility of dynamic change. It can be specified whether it is possible to change a software process at run time. This is supported by late binding and late modeling, meaning that it is possible to complete a model while it is enacted.

The modeling views supported by Melmac are:

- *Structural View*. Software processes in Melmac are based on Funsoft nets. Funsoft nets are high-level Petri nets adapted to the application domain of software process modeling. Funsoft nets are based on predicate/transition Petri nets.

The structural view provides three major modeling elements: *object types, activities* and *activity schedules.* Object types can be defined arbitrarily. They are used to type channels which store objects. Channels are the Funsoft net interpretation of places in traditional Petri nets. A channel can store several instances of the object type by which the channel is typed.

Activities (tasks) to be carried out are represented as agencies. An agency in Funsoft terminology corresponds to a transition in traditional Petri nets. However, agencies are enriched by more functionality. Either an agency has a service (tools) attached as specified by the service view (see below), or an agency is refined by another Funsoft net. In this case the agency is a *composite agency.*

An agency has an input firing behavior. The behavior is expressed in terms of the channels it reads from. The output firing behavior of an agency describes the channels an agency writes to. Here a decision can be involved in order to determine channels based on the result of decision function evaluation.

Activity schedules describe relations between agencies and channels by edges. Edges are defined between channels and agencies as well as between agencies and channels. Edges can be annotated to define special semantics: an edge annotation *CO* defines that an agency reads from a channel without removing an object; *IN* defines that an agency reads from a channel and removes the object from the channel; *OU* defines that an agency produces an object and writes it to a channel; *ST* defines a trigger to an agency from a channel to indicate that an object arrived; *FI* triggers a channel from an agency to indicate that the agency has finished performing an activity.

- *Service View.* The service view describes *tool services* provided to agencies. The service view provides a mechanism to envelope tools. An envelope consists of three parts: a startup, an action and a termination part. When an agency starts working the envelope assigned to it is executed. The startup part fetches documents from a project database into the workspace of the software developer on whose behalf the activity was started. The action part executes an application program with which the software developer performs his/her task. The termination part puts the results back into the project database.

In addition to tools the service view provides an *expertise service.* This service describes what has to happen in order to execute an activity. It suggests who should participate and how the activity is to be performed without controlling it. So a user might follow the suggestions but he does not have to.

- *Project Management View.* The project management view is concerned about the management of users as well as time and cost aspects of Funsoft nets. Activities are assigned to users for execution. This is done by building a role model. A role model assigns roles to activities as well as roles to users. If a role is assigned to an activity a user must be related to that role in order to get the activity assigned. A role assigned to a user therefore defines the activities he might be assigned. Furthermore, users can be directly assigned to objects (direct allocation). This expresses that only the assigned user can change the object. Besides the role model further specifications regarding the four-eye principle are possible. This allows to model that two activities have to be performed by the same user or by different ones.

  In addition to the management of users, milestones can be specified as well as start, end and duration time of activities. Furthermore, costs can be assigned to activities.
- *Profile View.* The profile view specifies qualifications and experiences required for activity execution. This enables different levels of guidance of users according to their experience in a certain area of expertise. In addition, based on this information, decisions on effective training for users are possible.

  Experience is expressed either as *novice, average* or *expert*. Qualification is expressed by qualification keys like *database, telecommunication* and so forth. Experience is assigned to users. Qualification keys can be assigned to users as well as to activities. A qualification key assigned to an activity expresses that a user to whom the activity is assigned has to have this qualification.
- *Change View.* The change view identifies points within a Funsoft model which might be subject to change during run time. These points are called *modification points.*

To produce a Funsoft net of a software process all these views are integrated. Basically all views of a software process model are mapped into one Funsoft net so that every model aspect is mapped to a common internal representation.

Melmac supports tools for modeling, analysis and enactment of Funsoft nets. Three forms of analysis are supported: validation, verification and process post-evaluation. Validation is based on simulating Funsoft nets. Simulation is done by token flows. A token is an abstract representation of an object within a Funsoft net. It completely abstracts from the object content. Simulation can take place in two forms: animated (before run time of a Funsoft net) and based on a process trace (after run time). Post process traces can be statistically evaluated, e.g. to find out how long agencies have been waiting for objects or where bottlenecks are.

Verification investigates a process model, not instances of process models. The goal of verification is to prove properties of process models. Melmac distinguishes between static properties like deadlocks (no firing possible any more), traps (a place remains marked if marked once) and dynamic properties. In addition to traditional Petri net properties Funsoft net specific properties are checked, such as useless or not processable object types. An object type is useless if no object occurs at run time or no object is produced. A not processable object type is one where objects are created but not read by an agency.

Enactment of Funsoft nets takes place to guide the users through a software process as well as to overview deadlines and to schedule activities according to priorities. Notification of users about activities to be executed is done by *agendas*. An agenda of a user is a graphical user interface displaying activities assigned to him. From there a user can choose an activity and start performing it. An activity which is scheduled to a user is called an *interaction activity*. In addition, Melmac supports automatic activities. An automatic activity is assigned to an application program. It starts the execution as soon as an automatic activity is assigned to it.

2.1.4 OfficeTalk (Xerox Palo Alto Research Center, Palo Alto, California)

OfficeTalk is a research effort conducted in the late 1970s and early 1980s at Xerox PARC (Palo Alto Research Center). The following description is based on Ellis (1983), Ellis and Bernal (1982), Ellis and Nutt (1980) and Ellis and Wainer (1993).

Ellis defines an office as a set of office procedures. An office procedure in OfficeTalk is specified by an ICN (information control net). ICNs provide the following modeling elements: *activity, procedure, task, repository, actor, role, goal* and relationships between them.

- *Activity.* An activity is a unit of work to be performed by an office worker. Sample activities are filling a time card, approving a time card or calculating employee pay based on a time card.

  Actions inside an activity are implemented by scripts. Opening files, retrieving information, invoking application programs, etc. are specified within a script language. As soon as a user starts working on an activity the script is executed for him.

  OfficeTalk distinguishes interactive from automatic activities. An interactive activity involves a user, an automatic activity is executed automatically as soon as it is ready for execution.

- *Repository*. A repository is a container of information represented as data. Sample containers are forms, files and folders.
- *Actor*. In OfficeTalk actors are the equivalent to users. Actors are related to roles by a *player* relationship. An actor might be related to more than one role at a time. Sample roles are employee, manager and clerk. Besides the player relationship a *reports to* relationship is available. This relationship expresses which actor reports to which other actor.
- *Role*. Roles are related to activities by a *performer* relationship. A role related to an activity expresses that an actor has to play this role in order to be eligible to work on the activity.

  At run time all role players are notified about an activity. The attempt of two or more users to start an activity might lead to access conflicts. However, only one agent is allowed to access an activity. All other agents are notified that they cannot start this particular activity any more.
- *Office Procedure*. An office procedure consists of a set of activities and a set of repositories. Activities are linked by a precedence structure which defines the order of execution. Available control flow constructs are *fork, join, choice* and *decision*. There are two kinds of joins: AND-join and OR-join. An AND-join requires all activities to be finished before execution can continue. An OR-join requires at least on activity to be finished before execution continues. A choice offers several paths to be followed. One of them has to be selected by a user. A decision selects one out of many possible paths based on some decision function.

  Office procedures can be nested to specify several levels of detail. An activity can be refined by an office procedure. This enables refinement of office work.

  An office procedure links to each activity a repository from which the activity fetches information or to which it stores results.

  In addition timing and probability information can be added to an office procedure. Timing information specifies duration of activities. A duration indicates how much time is available at most to execute an activity. A deadline defines at which point in time an activity has to be finished.

  Exception paths are supported by ICN nets. Skipping an activity is always possible and does not need to be modeled explicitly. Also returning to the previous user and returning to the initiator is automatically available.
- *Task*. A task is an individual transaction which may need to progress through many activities. E.g. processing a time card takes place by executing several activities: filling a card, approving a card and calculating an employee's pay. In this example processing the specific time

card is a task. In OfficeTalk several tasks can be processed concurrently. So if more than one employee starts processing his/her timecard several tasks are existent at the same time.

- *Goal*. ICNs allow to specify goals. Sample goals are customer satisfaction or increasing the number of orders. The applicability of a goal to an activity is specified by relating the goal to the activity. If an activity is related to a goal this goal has to be followed by the user executing the activity. An activity can be related to several goals at the same time. However, goals might conflict with each other causing problems in following them simultaneously.

When a user logs into the system at run time, operating system authorization is performed. OfficeTalk therefore knows which user is logged in and can derive roles and activities to be executed by the roles based on the authorization information. These activities are then made known to the user by a worklist. The notification is done by a scheduler which looks up a database for activities ready to be executed and subsequently notifies the appropriate users through worklists.

Besides worklists and a scheduler OfficeTalk has a simulation tool, an observer tool and an alerter tool. Simulation is done by running tokens through office procedures. A token represents a task without being concerned about task contents. Several tokens can run through an office procedure to simulate real tasks. Based on the behavior of the tokens work load, waiting times, queue lengths, etc. can be computed. These data can be further processed to derive throughput, turn-around times and to find bottlenecks.

An observer tool displays the actual tasks within an office procedure. It shows the current status of an office procedure. An alerter implements an event-action scheme. It is possible to specify actions to be taken if an event happens. An example scenario is: when on Friday afternoon no time card tasks have been submitted by an employee, notify the supervisor about this employee.

The OfficeTalk prototype is implemented in a three-component architecture. One part is a database system which stores the whole office information. This includes application independent entities like tasks, activities, etc. as well as application dependent data like files. A second part is a user interface. This runs on every workstation. The user interface displays the worklists and the application programs for filling in forms and so on. A dispatcher periodically scans the database and forwards new activities to the user interface. The third part is a modeling system. This is used to feed type information into OfficeTalk. A synthesis program takes the type information from the modeling part and updates tables within the database accordingly.

2.1.5 Pegasus (Hewlett-Packard Laboratories, Palo Alto, California)

Pegasus is a research effort of Hewlett-Packard Laboratories. Its goal is to provide an open and integrated information environment to support database and service interoperability for applications which access multiple data sources (Ahmed *et al.*, 1993; Shan, 1993). Sample applications are telephone service handling, computer integrated manufacturing processes, financial decision making, automated warehouses or travel reservations.

Pegasus uses an object-oriented model as framework for uniform interoperability. It is based on the OpenODB functional object model of Hewlett-Packard.

The architecture of Pegasus consists of four major layers (from "bottom" to "top"):

- *Individual Data Storage/Access Services.* This layer consists of the various "legacy" components. Examples are databases (relational, hierarchical, etc.), multimedia systems (with image, graphics, video, etc.) or legacy applications (like Lotus 1-2-3, Unix applications).
- *Basic Integrated Information Service.* This layer provides application neutral services like schema mapping and integration, distributed query processing, business operation flow management.
- *Domain Specific Information Service.* This layer deals with special needs for different application domains like information mining, query formulation for mobile computing devices, data caching.
- *End-user Applications.* This layer implements the applications which are needed by end-users to perform their tasks. These applications make use of the underlying layers to implement their functionality.

As mentioned already, the basic integrated information service layer contains an operation flow manager. It schedules and controls the flow of processes supporting complex work.

Noteworthy is that the operations flow manager is fully integrated into the Pegasus architecture. This ensures that all components the operation flow manager uses as well as all components that use the operation flow manager fit together seamlessly.

2.1.6 Transactional Workflows

There is a huge amount of literature available in the "transactional workflow" research area: Ansari *et al.* (1992), Attie *et al.* (1993), Breitbart *et al.* (1993), Georgakopoulos *et al.* (1995) and Krishnakumar and Sheth (1995). Instead of discussing them all, we want to elaborate the basic concepts of transactional workflows here. The following discussion is mainly based on Breitbart *et al.* (1993).

Dependencies between tasks of a workflow ensure correct control and data flow. Transaction management preserves data consistency by preventing execution of conflicting operations from multiple concurrently executing tasks. The goal of transactional workflow management is to provide an integrated infrastructure to ensure consistent data as well as correct control and data flow dependencies.

Large applications involve operations on multiple systems. Examples are travel reservation, service order processing and loan processing. The task coordination structure of an application is in almost all cases difficult to understand and to manage since related pieces of code are distributed throughout the application program code. Therefore a need to separate control and data flow from the rest of the application code is necessary. A workflow model which facilitates the separation is discussed in the following.

The workflow model is based on several kinds of dependencies. Specifying dependencies explicitly makes the computational structure declarative:

- *Control and data flow dependencies.* A task can pass through several task stages like *start, termination* and *execution*. The general form of control or data flow dependencies is: "Task *t* can enter state *s* only after task *u* has entered state *r*." These dependencies define data flow as well as control flow dependencies. Between tasks of a workflow multiple dependencies can exist depending on application semantics. Dependencies can be specified for example by precedence graphs, by predicate transition nets and by propositional logic.
- *Contingency dependencies.* Semantic success or failure is distinguished from the successful completion of a task indicated by task commitment (system success/failure). A negative decision on a loan request represents a semantic failure as far as a loan request is concerned. However, the task implementing the decision is successfully committed. Reactions to semantic failures are specified with contingency dependencies of the general form: "If task *t* fails semantically, then execute task *r* as a contingency task."
- *Task termination dependencies.* The general form of termination dependencies is: "If task *t* terminates in state *s* then task *r* must terminate in state *u*." Possible termination states are *committed with positive result* (semantic success), *committed with negative result* (semantic failure) and *aborted* (system internal reasons). Termination dependencies are called commit/abort dependencies if they refer to commit or abort only without

considering a semantic result. They are called success/failure dependencies if they refer to semantic success or failure.

A special kind of termination dependencies incorporates compensation (compensation dependencies): "If task *t* has committed and if some subsequent task *u* fails semantically or is aborted requiring the effects of task *t* to be undone, then execute task t^{-1} which must be guaranteed to commit in order to compensate *t*". t^{-1} is called a compensating task.

- *Critical task dependencies.* Critical tasks which affect the entire workflow are related by critical task dependencies. The general form of a critical task is: "If task *t* fails semantically or aborts then the entire workflow must fail, i.e. terminate in the semantic failure state".

The list of dependencies is not exhaustive. However, we do not extend this list further but want to give an idea about how to specify transactional workflows.

Breitbart *et al.* (1993) defines semantic transactions to ensure data consistency by executing an entire workflow as a single (semantic) transaction. A workflow submits a sequence of tasks for execution which are regarded as high level building blocks. In order to provide acceptable performance and simplify control of interleaving semantic properties of the tasks are exploited. Semantic transactions provide semantic serializability and semantic atomicity.

- *Semantic serializability.* Semantic serializability relies on the compatibility of tasks. Two tasks are compatible if their execution order is insignificant from the application point of view. A scheduler determines task inter-leaving based on task compatibility. The specification of which task is compatible to which other task is done by a human expert by means of a compatibility matrix. A schedule is semantically serializable if an equivalent serial execution exists with the same ordering of conflicting tasks.
- *Semantic atomicity.* Semantic transactions are aborted by invoking compensation tasks. Each task has one compensating task. It is assumed that input parameters are derived by well-defined rules. Within a schedule one task invocation is compensated by a second task invocation if the return values of all subsequent task invocations are the same as if neither had ever been executed.

A combination of workflow and transaction management is proposed by Breitbart *et al.* (1993) to combine the complementary aspects of dependencies and data consistency. An architecture composed out of three components is laid out comprising:

- *Semantic transaction manager.* This component handles the commit/abort dependencies in a system-oriented way and manages the interleaving between tasks of concurrent workflows.

- *Workflow dependency manager*. This component manages control flow, data flow and general termination dependencies.
- *Workflow manager*. This component manages all tasks of all workflows together with their states.

2.1.7 Further Research Work

There are many more research efforts being conducted than we can discuss here. So we devote this subsection to a list of efforts which are not further discussed in this book: ACTA (University of Massachusetts), ActMan (University of Erlangen), Carnot (MCC, Texas), CorMan (Fraunhofer Gesellschaft, Dortmund, Germany), Disdes (Fraunhofer Gesellschaft, IAO, Stuttgart, Germany), ESPRIT Project COMANDOS (Construction and Management of Distributed Office Systems) 834, 2071, Exotica (IBM Almaden Research Center, San Jose, California), Flex (Purdue University), PAPS (University of Bamberg), RFM/ECHO (Digital Equipment Corporation), Role/Interaction Nets (MCC, Austin, Texas), SCOOP (University of Pennsylvania).

2.2 Commercial Products

As indicated earlier a huge list of products exists in the area of workflow management. In the following some of them are described in detail:

- Action Workflow (Section 2.2.1)
- COSA (Section 2.2.2)
- FlowMark (Section 2.2.3)
- InConcert (Section 2.2.4)
- ProMInanD (Section 2.2.5)
- SAP Business Workflow (Section 2.2.6)
- WorkParty (Section 2.2.7)

2.2.1 Action Workflow (Action Technologies)

Action Workflow is the workflow management system of Action Technologies. The following description is based on Action Workflow (1992, 1993), and Medina-Mora *et al.* (1992, 1993).

Modeling Elements

The basic modeling element in Action Workflow is a *workflow loop*. A workflow loop defines work to be done. In general several workflow loops are used to build a complete workflow, here called a *business process*. Furthermore, *participants* and *applications* are part of the Action Workflow model.

- *Applications*. One of the goals of Action Workflow is to integrate application programs. Therefore an integration mechanism is developed which is based on STF (Standard Transaction Format). This format enables to specify workflow loops (see below). If an application submits a workflow loop specification to the workflow management system it initiates a workflow instance according to the submitted specification. After the workflow is finished the result is returned to the calling application.
- *Participants*. Participants within Action Workflow are characterized by roles and identities. Identities represent humans. Roles group humans by their organizational function like manager, director and engineer.
- *Workflow Loop*. A workflow loop consists of four parts and two participants as well as a cycle time and a condition of satisfaction. The four parts of a workflow loop are connected so that a closed loop emerges. The first part of a workflow loop is called *preparation*. It stands for a proposal of work to be performed. The preparation section originates at one participant who functions in the role of a *customer*. The second part of a workflow loop is a *negotiation*. It implements the agreement about work to be performed. It targets the second participant who plays the role of a *performer*. The third part of a workflow loop is called *performance*. Here work is actually accomplished. The fourth and final part of a workflow loop is named *acceptance*. In this phase, the customer evaluates the results.

  Acceptance is based on a condition of satisfaction which is attached to a workflow loop. This condition refers to the requirements which have to be fulfilled for successfully completing work. As soon as the performer delivers the result the latter is checked against the condition of satisfaction to determine success.

  Participants have application programs available to accomplish their tasks. They are notified about work to be done by the system.
- *Business Process*. Several workflow loops can be connected in order to build a more comprehensive workflow or business process. They can be connected sequentially such that one loop executes after another. Conditional branching is also possible; depending on the outcome of some condition a workflow is executed. Parallel workflow loop execution is also possible. Each workflow loop within a business process can be started several times. For instance, within a business process "hiring personnel" for each interview to be conducted a workflow loop can be started.

  Workflow loops can also be connected by replacing parts with another complete workflow loop. An example illustrates how this can be accomplished. In a hiring personnel workflow loop the negotiation phase is used to schedule interviews. Scheduling interviews is such a complex task that it can be implemented as a workflow loop. As soon as the scheduling interviews workflow loop has finished the performer of the hiring personnel business process can start the interview.

Two sorts of data are distinguished within a business process: data which are global to a business process and data which are local to a workflow loop. Global data can be accessed by all participants of a business process whereas local data can be accessed only by the customer and the performer of the respective workflow loop.

Tools, Languages and APIs

Action Workflow offers three tools. The Builder is used to model workflow loops (including cycle times and satisfaction conditions), business processes (including local and global data) as well as roles and identities. Everything can be specified graphically as well as in a script language. The basic modeling elements available on the graphic user interface are icons representing workflow loops and arcs to connect them. A combination of several loops connected by arcs forms a business process map.

The Analyst tool is used to run statistics on business processes. It can automatically compute, process and cumulate cycle times as well as process values based on workflow phases. Reporting facilities and what-if analysis functions are also supported.

The Manager tool executes workflow loops and business processes. It is used to instantiate new workflows, to query the status of workflows, to query and to sort pending work for a user, to set dates for work to begin and to remind users before or after deadlines. Events are scheduled to initiate automatic actions in workflows, to start new workflows, change their state and run applications. Furthermore, system configuration, start/stop of server processes and other system related functions are supported. Finally reporting facilities produce statistics on performance and workflow status.

Two sets of API exist: a client library and an application integration gateway. The client library provides functions to initiate workflows, to act within a workflow (execute a task), to bind process data, to query workflow status, to retrieve available activities and business processes and to fetch workflows in progress or pending actions. The library is used to build a user interface for the management of work since Action Workflow does not provide a default user interface.

The application integration gateway is used by applications and the Manager for communication. Communication is based on the STF exchange format. It constitutes a specification language used by applications to invoke workflow services. Instead of having a function for each service of the Manager a script is supplied by an application which specifies the services to be executed. Sample services create workflow loops, call external programs, send e-mail and trigger events.

System Architecture and Implementation

The Manager is the central component of the Action Technology workflow management system. It consists of several constituents:

- A *workflow processor* for processing business processes.
- An *agent processor* which manages the communication with agents.
- A *workflow language interpreter* which receives service requests and executes these services by calling other components.
- A *definition database* which contains the workflow and business process specifications.
- A *transaction database* which contains workflow/business process histories and states of running workflows.

The Manager can be deployed in two environments, with Lotus Notes or with SQL servers (Sybase/Microsoft). The basic functionality is the same in both environments: workflows and business processes are executed. However, additional functionality like security or transaction features is available depending on the environment (which we do not discuss further).

Special emphasis has to be put on STF processors. They translate between the native data format of an application and the STF format which is interpreted by the workflow language interpreter. Three types of STF processors exist:

- *Message-based.* Applications and the STF processor send each other messages containing service requests. Messages show the STF format.
- *Database-based.* Requests of services are stored by an application in a database from which the STF processor reads them. Results from the service executions are also stored within this shared database. Applications can query them from there.
- *Process-based.* Between an application and a STF processor an inter-process communication takes place in order to request services or receive results.

Application Area Specifics

The model is to specify workflows as conversations between humans. The four phases clearly indicate this. Therefore typical areas of deployment are human centered workflows. Since the modeling elements for the organizational embedding are not very expressive (only roles and identities), complex rules of responsibility cannot be modeled at all. This reduces the deployment to departmental settings where the expressiveness of roles is sufficient to model responsibility.

2.2.2 COSA (Software-Ley)

COSA ("*CO*mputerunterstützte *SA*chbearbeitung", computer-supported case-handling) is a workflow management system from the German software company Software-Ley. The following description is based on COSA (1994a, b, c).

Modeling Elements

COSA's workflow model can be partitioned into several aspects: *cases, workflows, activities, processes, data* and *organization*.

- *Processes.* Assigned tasks are carried out by users or are executed automatically by the workflow management system. A user can perform a task manually or by invoking application programs like editors or spreadsheet programs. In COSA it is possible to define several application programs to be called for the execution of a task. For each application program in a task, an operating system call is registered. A registered operating system call is called a *process* in COSA. Processes are executed at run time as soon as a task is accepted by a user.

  In COSA a so-called *storno process* can be related to each process (i.e. application invocation). It is invoked when a user wants to undo the effects of the primary process.
- *Data.* COSA allows to model two kinds of data: files and variables. Files are declared on an abstract level by providing a name and a type at definition time. Examples of file types are *ASCII* or *WordPerfect*. Files are referenced by name so that they can be passed around between different tasks of a COSA workflow. At run time a user associates a real file to an abstract file. So each time a workflow instance is to be started a different file can be referenced.

  Variables are also available in COSA. They can be read and set as needed.
- *Organization.* For the definition of an organization in COSA the following modeling constructs are available: *users, groups, group types, group membership, active substitutions, substitution plans* and *distributions*. A user is described by a user name, a password and further attributes. Also, the user's ability to change priorities of workflows, to forward assigned workflows, to access the history of a workflow and to access modeling tools

can be defined. COSA provides some built-in users. These "automatic" users are used for the automatic execution of workflows, i.e. without human intervention. If a workflow is assigned to such a user it is executed by that user automatically.

Groups are the basic building blocks of an organization hierarchy. A manager is responsible for a group and a group has several members. A group can also have other groups as members (subgroups). Groups are of a certain type enabling to group the users of an organization according to different criteria. E.g. one group type could be *functional* and another one *structural*. A group "clerks" of type "functional" would contain all users which are able to fulfill the function clerk. A group "sales" of type "structural" would contain all users of sales departments.

A user can substitute another user in case he/she is absent. A substitution plan specifies possible substitutions. For the duration of absence the tasks which can be carried out by a substituting user can be specified.

Finally, distribution plans can be specified. A distribution plan defines a set of users. Later on workflows can be assigned to distribution plans. This notifies all users which are part of the distribution plan.

- *Cases, Workflows and Activities.* In COSA a workflow consists of activities. A task for a user is specified by a *normal activity*. It is assigned to users according to a group language expression. COSA provides a group language which is used to select users from the specified organization structure. As soon as an activity is ready for execution the associated group language expression is evaluated. Notified users are able to accept an activity and start the defined processes.

  Besides normal activities *call activities* are part of the COSA workflow model. A call activity invokes other workflows which are called *subworkflows*.

  Additionally *start* and *end activities* are available to mark which activity is the first and which is the last within a workflow.

  An activity has a priority assigned as well as a flag which indicates that the priority can be changed. Furthermore, activities can be skipped. Another flag indicates that this is possible.

  For each activity a time limit for execution can be set. If the activity becomes overdue, a specified user is notified.

  The control flow between workflows is modeled with Petri nets. In addition to the usual Petri net semantics condition functions are available. Control flow between activities can be unconditional and conditional. In the latter case, condition functions determine whether a subsequent workflow is executed.

A *case* is an abstraction mechanism to group several workflows which belong together. An example is an order (case) which can be filled, mailed and paid. Filling, mailing and paying is implemented by three workflows. At the time a user starts a workflow the case the workflow belongs to must be indicated. This is important since data are attached to cases not to workflows. Thus, all workflows working in the context of one case can share the same data.

Variables which are valid for all workflows of a case are called *global variables*. They exist as long as the case exists. Variables within workflows are called *local variables*.

Users are notified of activities by memos. A memo is either used to notify a user about activities he has to carry out or it is used to merely inform a user about an ongoing activity. In the latter case, the informed user does not need to execute the workflow.

Tools, Languages and APIs

COSA provides several graphic tools:

- Case, workflow and activity definition tools which are also used to specify processes within activities.
- An organization definition tool.
- A form based administration tool with reporting facilities.
- A worklist which is used by users to view assigned activities and to start processes.
- A history access tool to view the history of a workflow.
- A statistics tool to get information about a set of workflows.

COSA provides a language for the specification of cases, workflows, processes, data and organization structures as well as a group language which is used to select users for activity assignment.

Also, a set of APIs is available. They contain all functions exported by the COSA server. So it is possible to build a worklist or other application programs accessing a COSA server directly. The functions can be used in a network transparent way. Access over the network is already contained within the function libraries so that an application program using the functions can deploy them as if the functions would be executed locally.

System Architecture and Implementation

The COSA system is built according to the client/server paradigm. A server builds the core of the COSA run time system. It manages running workflows and activities. The server stores run time information within a relational database system. This database also contains all type information about workflows, data and the organization structure. The tools are clients of the COSA server. COSA supports transparent access over a heterogeneous network.

As described earlier, processes are executed by users when they start assigned activities. A process can execute either on the client node where the memobox (worklist) resides or on the server node. This flexibility gives a workflow modeler the choice to invoke applications on the most appropriate node.

Load balancing and scalability is support by installing several servers. These servers cooperate to increase the overall throughput.

A distinct server is responsible for the management of the memoboxes. The memoboxes of the users can be moved to different memobox servers. So, the workload of the servers is reduced and the overall reliability is increased. If a server fails not all users are affected but only those assigned to that server.

COSA supports the distributed execution of workflows. This means that, for example, a workflow execution is distributed among several COSA systems. Each COSA system is set up in a different location, supporting different workflow types and organization structures.

An interesting feature of COSA is serverless computing. It is possible to install a memobox on a laptop. If a user wants to execute assigned tasks while he is disconnected from the network, he can download all necessary data from the server.

Application Area Specifics

COSA is almost free of specific application semantics. The only part of the model which is specialized towards an application area is organization structure modeling. The provided modeling elements are dedicated to model human organizations, not "organizations" of servers, machines and cells which might be useful in manufacturing environments.

For the support of workflows in which activities are executed automatically COSA provides predefined automatic users. There are seven different automatic users. They execute an activity when a specific event occurs:

- as soon as it is assigned,
- after a minute,
- after an hour,
- after a day,
- after a week,
- after a month, or
- after a year.

With respect to data handling COSA is restricted. The only data types which are supported are files and unstructured variables. Data flow of structured data between activities cannot be specified. So all data worked at in workflows have to be stored either in files or in unstructured variables.

2.2.3 FlowMark (IBM)

FlowMark is a workflow management system of IBM (International Business Machines). The following description is based on FlowMark (1994, 1995).

Modeling Elements

FlowMark's workflow model is partitioned into four modeling areas: *processes, programs, data structures* and *staff*.

- *Programs.* A program is a computer-based application like a text editor or a spreadsheet program. A program is used within a FlowMark process by a user to carry out an assigned task. Programs to be used within processes have to be registered within FlowMark. The registration of a program consists of a program name, its input and output parameters, protocol settings (like the location where the program is to be executed or the communication protocol), and platform specific settings (like OS/2 or AIX). This meta information is used by FlowMark at run time.
- *Data Structures.* A data structure in FlowMark is a list of variables. Some of them are predefined by FlowMark for internal use and cannot be deleted from the list, however, they can be accessed at run time. New data structures can be defined and variables can be added by a process modeler according to application area requirements. Data structures are used within processes to model the input and output parameters of a process. Input parameters are specified by a data structure which is called an *input data container*. Output parameters are specified by a data structure called an *output data container*. To transfer data from one process to another, variables of output data containers must be connected to variables of input data containers.
- *Staff.* Processes are assigned to users for execution. The assignment to users is based on several criteria one of which is the position of a user within an organization structure. Other criteria like the assignment based on history information are discussed later. FlowMark offers a basic set of modeling constructs to model the organization structure of an enterprise. These are *levels, people, roles, organizations* together with *people–role* and *people–organization* relationships.

  People correspond to employees who actually perform the work defined by a FlowMark process. A person is identified by a unique identifier, possesses a password and has further attributes like first and last names, phone number, etc. In addition, it is specified which persons may be substituted for another. Authorization can also be specified. Possible authorizations encompass the processes a person is able to perform, the people whose activities can be accessed and the people who have access to the person's activities. Furthermore, it can be specified whether a person is authorized to access management functions of FlowMark.

Role objects are used to specify organizational roles within an enterprise. A role has a name and has role members. Role members are persons who are assigned to this role.

Organization objects are used to define the structure of an organization. An organization object represents a group like marketing or research. Organizations can be hierarchically structured by decomposing it into suborganizations. An organization has a person assigned as manager and persons assigned as organization members.

Levels are introduced to distinguish people from each other based on some property like educational status. For example, levels like *novice*, *expert* and *guru* can be defined and assigned to people. At run time these levels are one possibility to select users for assignments.

- *Processes*. For the specification of processes several modeling constructs are provided: *process, program activity, process activity, block, bundle, control connector* and *data connector*. The basic modeling element is a process. A process defines all the activities that must be completed to accomplish the overall task. A process can have a duration assigned. If the process is not finished within the duration, the administrator of the process is notified.

  An activity within a process can either be a program activity or a process activity. A program activity is an activity which is to be executed by a user and has a program attached to it. This program is used to carry out the activity. A process activity is also an activity, however, it does not have to be completed by a single user. A process activity has a process attached to it. As soon as a process activity is ready to be executed, the attached process starts. This process is called a subprocess.

  The execution sequence between the activities of a process is defined by control connectors. A control connector relates two activities defining an execution order between them. In addition to control connectors *enter*, *exit* and *transition conditions* are supported for control flow specifications. An activity is finished only when its exit condition is true. Control passes to the next connected activity if a transition condition attached to the control connector evaluates to true. An activity starts only if its start condition evaluates to true. A start condition defines how many of the transition conditions of the incoming control connectors have to be true.

  Data connectors defined between activities specify the dataflow between the input and output containers of the connected activities.

A block groups activities within a process for better readability. In addition to this a block can be used to define loops within the control flow. As long as the exit condition of the block evaluates to false, the activities grouped by a block are executed again and again. A bundle is used to start a number of activities of the same type. The number of activities started is determined at run time and not at definition time.

Finally, for each activity an assignment rule has to be provided defining which people from the staff definition have to be notified about the activity. An assignment rule could be a role. This would cause all people assigned to that role to be notified about the activity. Assignment rules might also depend on historical information.

Basically programs, data structures and staff are defined independently of their use within processes. This approach supports their reuse and avoids multiple definitions of the same data type. Before a process can be specified, required programs for program activities have to be defined as well as data types required for data flow specifications. The same applies for staff definitions and processes. Only a formerly defined process can be reused within a process activity.

Tools, Languages and APIs

FlowMark groups its tools into two categories: build time tools and run time tools.

- *Build time tools.* Build time tools are used at process definition time. FlowMark provides several build time tools:
  - Tools to define staff like a people definition editor, a role definition editor, an organization definition editor and a level definition editor.
  - A graphical process editor to specify processes.
  - A program registration editor.
  - A data structure editor.
  - A process animation tool.
- *Run time tools.* Run time tools are used during process execution. FlowMark provides
  - a worklist which is used by users to view and execute their assigned tasks and
  - a bundle planning tool which is used to start several activities of the same type at run time.

FlowMark provides a set of APIs to control and access processes at run time. Processes can be started, terminated, paused and resumed. The APIs come with several language bindings.

System Architecture and Implementation

FlowMark is a database centered workflow management system. All data (build time data like process types and run time data like process instances) are stored within a (object-oriented) database. Even though a database is available, transactions are not available within processes.

FlowMark follows the client/server paradigm. Worklists are clients of FlowMark servers, which execute process instances. A server responds to client requests. It accesses the database to execute the services it offers to clients. It is possible to set up several FlowMark servers (which access the same database) so that clients can be distributed over several of them to avoid bottlenecks.

It is possible to operate on several databases at the same time. Each database defines an individual sphere, i.e. data is not shared between them. If a user logs on he/she can specify the database to be used. The possibility to run multiple databases can be used to set up one database for development and testing of processes, another one for operational processes and another one for education purposes.

Application Area Specifics

FlowMark is almost free from application area semantics. The only area where FlowMark is specific is staff definition. This part of the FlowMark model provides modeling constructs to model staff, i.e. employees and their interrelationships (like membership of organizations). However, there is no provision to model software services as agents nor machines or cells. The only way to execute a FlowMark process without human intervention is to declare program or process activities as *automatic*. In this case FlowMark starts the defined program or process automatically as soon as the start condition is true.

2.2.4 InConcert (XSoft)

InConcert is the workflow management system of XSoft. The following description is based on McCarthy and Sarin (1993) and Sarin *et al.* (1991).

Modeling Elements

InConcert provides a small set of modeling elements: *job, task, role, document, events* and *actions*.

- *Document*. A document is an abstract data object. It has a content, attributes and links to other documents. The content of a document is unstructured and contains information which is read by a user or worked on by an application program. However, structured information (e.g. data of forms) is stored solely in attributes. Documents are used within workflows (which are called jobs in InConcert). Every user who participates in a job can view and modify its documents. A user can follow the links of a document and can dynamically add further links.

If a user accesses a document it is automatically checked-out. If the user releases the document, it is checked-in. The automatic check-out/check-in mechanism ensures that users cannot simultaneously work on the same document. If a document is checked-in, a new version is created leaving the old one unchanged. New documents are created in checked-out state.

- *Task.* A task is a unit of work and represents the working context of a user. A task contains all information required by a user, i.e. one or more documents. In addition to data a task also refers to application programs which are used by users to work with the data.

  Documents are not attached to tasks physically but logically. So instead of providing an access path to a document a logical name is used to address a document. This means that in all jobs of the same type the documents are referred to by the same name even though different physical documents are attached.

  Applications work on the content of documents. In order to do so the content is copied into an operating system file which in turn is used by an application program. Results are also stored in files and copied back into the documents of a task.
- *Role.* A role is related to each task. A role represents a user, a group of users or an application program. Users represented by a role are eligible to carry out tasks assigned to that role. They are notified by work to-do lists about assigned tasks. A work to-do list contains all work in progress as well as future work. A work to-do list is the user interface to invoke operations on tasks, e.g. acquire a task, declare a task as complete, release a task or transfer a task to another user.

  If a role represents an application program a *routine task* is implemented. For each task type an automated agent exists. This automated agent passes the task to the application program. For instance, converting a document from one format to another can be implemented as a routine task where the format transformation is done by an application program.
- *Job.* A job is a multi-person collaborative activity which has a goal (e.g. process an insurance claim). A job consists of tasks which are related to each other by ordering dependencies. This ordering dependency defines possible execution orders of the tasks of a job. Documents are related not only to tasks but also to jobs. If a document is related to a job it is auto-

matically part of every task, i.e. it can be accessed by all involved users. The same applies to application programs. They also can be local or global to tasks.

Parallelism between tasks can be modeled. In order to enable parallel access of users to documents a fine granularity of documents is advised. Independent parts of one document can be accessed in parallel.

A special form of task is a subtask. A subtask represents a job instead of a unit of work. In this way, task decomposition can be implemented.

InConcert follows the paradigm of migrating tasks. Therefore it is possible that a document can be accessed by several tasks at the same time. Each task can work on a different (disjoint) part of the sme document.

InConcert enables dynamic changes at run time. Not only the contents of a document can be dynamically altered but also the task structure of a job. This supports dynamic adjustment of procedures depending on requirement changes at run time. Tasks can be executed as often as desired. Each time a task is executed again, a new copy of the task is created.

- *Events and Actions*. In InConcert events are related to operation executions (e.g. check-in, check-out, task status change, job create, job completion). An event description refers to the user executing the operation, the time of operation execution and the objects manipulated by the operation.

  Actions are triggered by events. An action can be the notification of a user via e-mail. Subscription lists can be implemented by this mechanism. A user subscribes to an event and asks for notification whenever the event happens (e.g. whenever a documents gets updated). Actions can also trigger operation executions. An example is to start a job as soon as an event happens.

The modeling of jobs results in templates of these jobs. A template contains all details which are necessary to run the job (including roles, documents, etc.). As soon as a request for job execution is issued the corresponding template is copied and an active job is created.

A characteristic feature of InConcert is that everything is modeled as an object. InConcert permits the extension of existing objects with further attributes. Documents can be extended (e.g. to add document format information) as well as links (e.g. to add information about the link destination).

Tools, Languages and APIs

InConcert supports a set of tools. There is an end-user interface called the work to-do list or task interface. This is used to access and perform tasks. A user can look at the work in progress, view eligible roles and groups, open a task, finish it and release it. InConcert provides a generic task interface which is applicable to all task types. In addition to this, task interfaces can be built which are adjusted to the specific needs of a task type.

InConcert offers a workflow editor. It makes all modeling elements necessary to model a complete job available to the job modeler.

A browser interface is also part of InConcert. It allows to look at job templates, active jobs, users, groups, etc.

Application programs are integrated by writing a piece of code which is bound to InConcert. There is no default mechanism which enables easy application integration like object request brokers.

Reporting is supported by standard database reporting tools of the underlying database. To do this, InConcert maintains an audit log which is a basis of report generation.

Through a set of APIs InConcert is accessible by application programs.

System Architecture and Implementation

The available literature does not detail the system architecture and implementation layers. A basic design decision is to use standard services like RPC, NFS (network file system) and databases.

InConcert is distributed over a heterogeneous network according to a client/server architecture. Service invocation is achieved by calling functions locally. The remoteness of a server is hidden from the client by using RPC within the libraries.

Application Area Specifics

InConcert does not prescribe special semantics from a certain application area. The term document might be misleading here, but it represents data in general, not office documents.

2.2.5 ProMInanD (IABG)

ProMInanD is a workflow management system developed at the German company Industrieanlagen-Betriebsgesellschaft (IABG). ProMInanD (Extended Office *Pro*cess *M*igration with *In*teractive P*an*el *D*evice) is an outcome of an ESPRIT (European Strategic Program for Research and Development in Information Technologies) project of the same name.

The following description is based on Karbe and Ramsperger (1989, 1990, 1991), Karbe *et al.* (1990, 1991) and Vogel and Erfle (1992).

Modeling Elements

ProMInanD follows the paradigm of migrating office folders. The concept of *Electronic Circulation Folders* (ECF) is introduced. An ECF consists of two parts, one containing a header with type information about the ECF, a unique identifier, a migration specification, the current state and the folder's history. The second part contains a folder slip used for informal notes for future users, a work sub-folder containing application related documents, an appendix sub-folder with auxiliary and explanatory information and a recovery sub-folder which is used by a rollback mechanism. An ECF represents an *office task.*

- *Migration Specification.* A migration specification defines all paths a folder might take while migrating through an enterprise. At run time a particular path is taken depending on individual data. A migration specification might consist of several elements:
  - *Step.* A step is an elementary task to be performed by an office worker (user) or to be executed automatically. In the first case an office worker uses referenced application programs to perform the step, in the latter case ProMInanD executes the referenced application programs by itself. A step might refer to multiple (or no) application programs which are required to execute the step.

    A step can either alter the contents of an ECF, can access one of the ProMInanD databases or can call an external program which in turn changes ProMInanD external data.

    An external application is integrated by writing code in the underlying programming language which embeds the application invocation. This code is later interpreted in order to invoke the application. No standard invocation mechanism (like operating system calls, remote procedure calls or object request broker calls) is supported by default.
  - *Decision Function.* A decision function is used to determine which out of two disjoint branches within the control flow has to be taken. A decision function might refer to ECF internal data for evaluation.
  - *Subtask.* Migration specifications can be reused by other migration specifications. Reuse takes place through subtasks. A subtask is an element of a migration specification referring to another one. At run time the migration specification referred to by a subtask is executed as soon as the subtask is ready for execution.
  - *Dependent Office Task.* A special feature of ProMInanD is the execution of dependent office tasks. A dependent office task is an ECF which runs in parallel to a so-called father ECF from which is was started. Two kinds of dependent ECFs exist: coupled ECFs, which join their

father later on, and uncoupled ECFs, which process independently from their father.

- *Routing Interventions*. Another special feature of ProMInanD are the possibilities for users to intervene a path at run time resulting in a behavior which was not specified within the migration specification. Some of the interventions actually change the migration specification, others do not change the specification but change the path only. The following possibilities for routing interventions exist:
  - *Refer Back*. An office worker asks a previous office worker for additional information. As soon as the previous office worker has responded the folder comes back to the asking office worker.
  - *Fetch Back*. The folder is returned to the last office worker if the next one according to the migration specification had not started processing yet. This intervention is used when an office worker forgot to do something.
  - *Delegate*. Delegation involves another office worker who executes the actual step. This operation changes the migration specification inasmuch as it adds two further steps to it. One for the office worker to whom the ECF gets delegated and one for the office worker who delegates. This makes it possible for the delegating office worker to view the result before normal execution continues.
  - *Add Step*. This operation adds a new step to the migration specification.
  - *Shortcut*. Shortcut leaves out one or more steps.
  - *Shift Step*. Shifting a step results in a changed execution order of steps within a migration specification.
  - *Forward To*. The forwarding operation passes an ECF to a specific office worker for further execution. In contrast to delegation the ECF does not return to the forwarding office worker.
  - *Start Dependent ECF*. An office worker can start a dependent ECF which is the son of the ECF the office worker works at.

  Freestyle routing, i.e. migration of an ECF without a predefined migration specification is possible. As soon as an ECF is created the *add step* operation can be used to move the ECF around freely. This is how ProMInanD supports *ad hoc* workflow processing.

- *Backtracking*. Not only migration specifications or actual paths can be changed; already performed work can also be undone in ProMInanD. To enable this the following operations are provided:
  - *Not Me*. The *not me* operator declares missing responsibility for a step. The folder is sent back to the preceding office worker.

    - *Cancel.* Canceling is used to delete an ECF. This is only possible if the migration specification has not reached a state where cancellation is not possible any more. If it is possible compensation takes place (see below).
    - *Roll Back.* Roll back puts an ECF back in the last consistent state.
- *Compensation.* Three requirements in the area of compensating steps are tackled by ProMInanD: compensating ECF internal data, compen-sating system data of ProMInanD and compensating data of the world outside of ProMInanD. The first case is accomplished by passive compensation: data are set back to a previous version. The second case (active compensation) is accomplished by a compensation program. The third case is done by notification of involved office workers. They have to perform the compensation manually.
- *Organization Structure.* ProMInanD has a rich set of modeling elements to model an organization structure. Office workers roles can be modeled expressing functions like manager or clerk within an organization. Office workers are related to roles to express their capabilities. Also, positions can be modeled which form the basic hierarchy together with organizational groups. Positions define workplaces which are occupied by office workers. Organizational groups cluster positions to larger entities. One position within a group is the manager position. Between organizational groups a subordination relationship exists. This expresses which group is subordinate to which other. A reporting relationship defines which office worker is subordinate to which other one. Substitutions can be expressed between office workers. They are either temporary (e.g. when an office worker is on vacation) or permanent.

  Assignment of steps to office workers is based on organizational functions, i.e. their office roles. An organizational function is evaluated at run time. All office workers able to perform the function are notified about the ECF. They can select an ECF to carry out the next task.
- *Programs.* Programs which are required to perform office tasks are integrated into ProMInanD by wrapping them with objects. For each program an object is defined which knows how to call the program. Using this technique every program can be included which has a language binding for the language ProMInanD is programmed with. At run time if an application has to be started the appropriate method for an object is called which in turn invokes the application.

Tools, Languages and APIs

There is a migration specification tool which displays the migration specification graphically. It is used also to change a migration specification. ProMInanD also offers a graphical editor for the definition and management of the organization structure. Office workers view assigned ECFs with their electronic desktop. It consists of an in-tray where incoming ECFs are displayed as well as an out-tray to send ECFs and a form box which contains all ECF types a user can start.

ProMInanD does not provide languages for the definition of migration specifications and of organization structure.

APIs are available to manage ECFs from user supplied applications.

System Architecture and Implementation

ProMInanD is based on a set of migration servers. Two kinds can be distinguished: local migration servers (LMS) and global migration servers (GMS). LMSs are installed at the workstation of each office worker to support local operations like executing step programs or providing functions on locally available ECFs. LMSs also derive the next step to be executed at the workstation. Each LMS has a database of its own to manage its data.

GMSs supervise the system-wide migration of ECFs. A GMS migrates an ECF from an LMS to the next LMS. In addition to this it evaluates the next office worker to whom a step has to be migrated. A GMS local database contains the organization definition, all migration specifications and step programs. ECF internal documents are also managed there. In addition to type information a GMS database stores run time information like the number of active workstations (where office workers are logged in), all logged in office workers, active roles as well as active ECFs and their location.

As indicated each LMS and each GMS has its own database for data required locally. Since ProMInanD uses a distributed database system it can partition its data instead of having a global database containing all the data.

Application Area Specifics

Since ProMInanD is based on the folder paradigm it is targeted at office environments. Besides the concept of folder forms, in-tray and out-tray as well as a human oriented organization structure indicate office work as target deployment of ProMInanD.

2.2.6 SAP Business Workflow (SAP)

SAP Business Workflow is a workflow management system from the German company SAP AG. SAP Business Workflow is part of version 3.0 of the R/3 system from SAP. Since the official release of SAP Business Workflow was in spring

1996, only preliminary documents were available which do not describe every detail (Fritz, 1994; SAP, 1995).

Modeling Elements

The following model elements constitute a SAP Business Workflow: *workflow, step (work item), task, object, application* and *organization.*

- *Object.* R/3 is a base systems which provides an enterprise with standard functionality for information processing. Sample functions are invoice processing, order processing, hiring processing, personnel administration, etc. R/3 as a base system provides an object model which supports object-oriented programming. This is done with a SAP internal language called ABAP/4. The functionality of R/3 can be altered by adding new objects and new methods. So basically whatever is to be done maps to a method invoked on an object.
- *Organization.* Since R/3 also supports personnel management, a module is available which implements objects to build an organization structure (R/3 module HR-ORG). This module models users, positions, workplaces, groups and their relationships to tasks and capabilities.
- *Task.* A task is described by several components. A task specifies a unit of work to be carried out by a user. One component is an object together with a method. This method is to be called when a user executes the task. Objects are either standard objects from the underlying R/3 system or user-defined ones which implement special requirements which are not already supported by R/3. Another component describes who has to carry out a task of this type (responsibility). This is done by referencing objects within an organization structure like users, positions, workplaces and groups. Another component is a reference to a role. A role can be used to detail further which user has to carry out the task. The reference to a role is used in addition to the references to an organization structure to determine eligible users for a task. A plain text is added which describes the contents of the task for explanatory purposes. Finally a set of events can be declared. Each of those events finishes a task execution.
- *Application.* External applications can be integrated into SAP Business Workflow through standard invocation methods like OLE and ODBC. The basic idea is to encapsulate external applications by objects.
- *Step (Work Item).* Steps are the basic building blocks of workflows. There are five different kinds of steps:
    - *Activity.* An activity is either a task (function), an external application, a transaction or a manual action. A transaction performs operations on data within transaction boundaries. A manual action is supported

since not all tasks a user has to do are supported by methods on objects or external applications.

- *User Decision.* Not all decisions can be made automatically by methods or programs. Therefore it is possible to model a decision which is based on a user's manual action.
- *Wait Step.* Parallel branches within a workflow are possible. Parallel branches have to be synchronized in order to be joined. Wait steps are available to model joining branches.
- *Subworkflow.* Parts of workflows can often be modeled in such a way that later reuse in different workflows is possible. A step can reference a workflow to reuse it. This is called a subworkflow.
- *Condition.* Depending on certain facts a workflow must branch and follow different paths. Two kinds of conditional branching constructs are available: *if then else* and *case* with the usual semantics.

A step references an actor role, which describes who is responsible for the execution of a step. This actor role is specified in terms of users, positions, workplaces or groups. It might take parameters in order to select appropriate users depending on run time values.

Steps are not necessarily assigned to just one person. Normally, a role can be played by several users. If a step is assigned to a role where several role players are available, this step appears on the desktop of all of them. As soon as one user decides to execute the step the step will be withdrawn from the desktops of all other users.

Steps can be executed automatically. If a task is to be performed which does not need a human user to execute it, it can be executed automatically. In this case the workflow management system takes care of the execution of the step.

- *Workflow.* Workflows in SAP Business Workflow are based on the concept of event-driven process chains. A process (workflow) step is triggered by an event. After a process step is finished it triggers another event which in turn might start another step. So between two steps of a workflow an event happens. Depending of how steps are linked, parallel as well as sequential execution of steps is possible.

The creation, synchronization and termination of workflows is controlled by events.

Data needed for workflow processing are obtained either from the underlying system or from so-called containers which hold workflow internal data. A container might also contain references to objects. Data flow between containers of several workflows is specified by source/sink definitions.

Since SAP Business Workflow is an integral part of R/3 the problem of integrating legacy applications is different from other approaches. SAP assumes that enterprises want to deploy workflow management in the context of R/3, i.e. they want to integrate R/3 functions through workflows. Since SAP Business Workflow is integrated into R/3 calling R/3 methods on objects is no problem at all. Therefore, as long as no external non-R/3 applications have to be called a legacy problem does not really exist. However, if an enterprise wants to deploy external applications, the problems known from other workflow management systems have to be faced (interfacing to invocation mechanisms, data transfer to and from external applications, data consistency between data of different applications).

In SAP Business Workflow data are not explicitly modeled. This is because the underlying system provides objects. In general, operations on data are encapsulated within objects. Therefore data are not explicitly visible at the workflow level. Documents are handled by an archiving system. They are scanned in and managed by a document management system. SAP R/3 makes sure that documents are available whenever they are needed. Here the same principle as discussed above applies: documents are encapsulated in objects.

SAP Business Workflow supports *ad hoc* workflow processing. In SAP terminology this means the creation and execution of a single work item.

Tools, Languages and APIs

SAP Business Workflow categorizes its tools into three categories:

- *Definition Tools.* Definition tools are available for the definition of workflows, tasks, objects, roles and the connection of events and their consumers and producers.
- *Run time Tools.* Run time tools are concerned with the execution of workflows (*Workflow Manager*), with the management of work items (*Workitem Manager*) and with the management of user interfaces (*Worklist Client*). A workitem manager assigns work items to users, supervises deadlines, does appropriate escalation and writes history information. A worklist client manages a user's interface (worklist) and selects, activates and forwards workitems according to user requests.
- *Reporting Tools.* Reporting tools of SAP Business Workflow support the retrieval of workflow related information, enable the analysis of workflows and provide statistics functions for evaluations.

In addition to the tools provided by the workflow management systems further tools of R/3 are available like the SAP Business Navigator. This tool provides a graphical representation of business processes, functions, communication, data,

data flow and organization. These areas belong to the R/3 system and therefore we will not embark on a detailed discussion here.

SAP Business Workflow supports APIs to access external systems. First, there are APIs which are concerned with event management. They allow to create workflow related events outside of the system and to report events to the outside. There are APIs to support the creation and management of workitems within SAP Business Workflow. The creation and management of workflows is also supported. It is possible to develop a worklist client by accessing the APIs directly. Finally, the access to attributes of objects as well as method invocation on objects is possible from the outside.

In addition to these APIs SAP Business Workflow intends to support the APIs developed by the Workflow Management Coalition (see Section 2.4).

System Architecture and Implementation

SAP Business Workflow is an integral part of R/3. It adds the functionality to process workflows. This execution environment has three major tasks to fulfill:

- *Work Management*, which is the assignment and supervision of steps.
- *Flow Management*, which is the evaluation of workflows to derive executable steps according to control flow definitions as well as the transport of data.
- *Worklist Management*, which manages the interaction of the execution environment with users.

Application Area Specifics

SAP Business Workflow is integrated into R/3 and not a stand-alone system. Enterprises which already deploy R/3 or plan to do it are therefore the target environment.

2.2.7 WorkParty (Siemens Nixdorf)

WorkParty is the workflow management product of Siemens Nixdorf Informationssysteme AG. The sources for our description are WorkParty (1994a, b).

Modeling Elements

The workflow model of WorkParty is based on the idea of a folder which migrates through an office. The main modeling elements are *tasks*, *workflows*, *variables* and *references* to folder external data. Modeling elements to model an organization structure are not part of the workflow model but available through a separate tool the *Organization Resource Management* (ORM, 1994a, b; Rupietta, 1994). WorkParty accesses ORM in order to derive the users responsible for a task.

However, in the following discussion we ignore the fact that two different software systems are involved and discuss this detail while discussing the overall architecture.

- *Tasks*. A task is an elementary step within a workflow. A task is performed by a user either with or without the use of an application program. In the first case an application program is referenced which is started as soon as the task is accepted by a user. An application program can take parameters as well as produce results.

  In case there is no application program referenced with a task, a description is delivered to the user. From this description the user has to derive what action to take. Results have then to be typed in.
- *Data*. WorkParty follows the folder paradigm. All data which are worked on by a workflow are carried along within a folder. Therefore no explicit data flow has to be specified since all data are present at all tasks of a workflow.

  A folder might contain up to three kinds of data: workflow variables, data values and references to folder external data. Workflow variables have to be typed with predefined types (string, integer, real and boolean). Other data are of type document or reference to documents. In most cases these are files within a file system.
- *Organization*. ORM supports the modeling elements *employee*, *function*, *position*, *authority* and *organizational unit*. An organization structure constructed in ORM is later accessed by WorkParty to evaluate users responsible for a task. In WorkParty users are called employees. Besides a first and last name, a phone number, an address and other attributes are stored.

  A position represents the workplace of an employee. It can be seen as a placeholder for an employee. A position has a set of tasks assigned for which an employee occupying this position is responsible. Therefore an employee has to be related to each position in order to get the assigned tasks of a position done. In ORM it is possible that an employee is related to several positions. However, one of those positions is the main one. Additionally, substitution relationships exist between employees and positions. If an employee is related to a position by this relationship he/she substitutes for the employee occupying this position in case of absence.

  Positions are grouped by organizational units. There are two types of organizational units: temporary ones and unlimited ones. Temporary organizational units define projects or task forces which are in almost every case of limited duration. Unlimited organizational units are units which form the basic organization structure. Examples are a sales or a manufacturing department. One position within an organizational unit can be defined as the manager position. This means that the organizational unit is led by the employee occupying this position. Organizational units can have other organizational units as members. In this way, a hierarchy of organizational units can be modeled.

An authority is a combination of authorizations and responsibilities. Authorizations are expressed by resource assignments and responsibilities by task assignments. An example of an authority is "John is authorized to sign payment orders up to $5000". Authorities can be related to employees. However, they also can be related to a position, a function or an organizational unit. Since at the end a user has to have an authority for executing tasks, assignments of authorities to non-employees like function or position have to be extended with inheritance rules. An inheritance rule defines how an authority assigned, e.g. to a position, is inherited. In this case an employee occupying the position inherits its authorities. If the position is substituted by another employee, the authorities are temporarily inherited by this employee also.

A function defines organizational functions like manager or sales clerk. A function groups positions which posses the same authorities or at least a common subset of authorities.

A special feature of ORM is that new attributes can be added to the schema of an object.

- *Workflows*. In WorkParty a workflow consists of tasks and/or subworkflows. Parameters of tasks are implemented as IN and OUT pins. Pins are formal parameters which are used to exchange actual values between a workflow and a task. Only values of variables can be passed through pins.

  A subworkflow is also itself a workflow. A workflow can be reused as subworkflow by referencing it. WorkParty provides a library where all workflows can be found which are available for use or reuse.

  Users performing tasks do not realize the existence of subworkflows since at run time they are executed as normal workflows.

  Tasks and subworkflows are ordered in an execution sequence by control flow constructs. These are *sequence*, *loop* (*while* loop and *repeat until* loop), *alternative* (with a default exit), *free choice*, *fork* and *parallel branching*. Sequence, loop and alternative as well as parallel branching have the usual semantics. Free choice means that all tasks or subworkflows which are connected by this control flow construct have to be executed, however the sequence of their execution is determined by users at run time and not prescribed at all. Fork means that control flow branches without joining again later on (this is in contrast to parallel branching).

A workflow belongs to a folder, i.e. it is part of a folder. Since folders contain documents only a workflow is viewed as a document. Subworkflows are also put into a folder, so that all necessary routing information is available. Priorities can be assigned to folders indicating the importance of work. Three levels are available: *low*, *normal* and *high*. In addition, the validity of a folder can be specified in terms of a date from which the folder can be used and a date until which the folder is available for use.

To find out which employee or employees are responsible for the tasks of a workflow an address expression is attached to each task. An address expression is used at run time to evaluate users. It consists of five fields, namely employee, function, position, authority and organizational unit. Each field can have a value or can have no value specified. The sample expression "<>, manager, <>, <>, <>" results in all employees associated to the function manager ("<>" means that there is no value assigned).

Besides performing employees there are other employees associated with a workflow: a workflow initiator and an employee responsible for a workflow. The workflow initiator is automatically derived. It is the employee who started the workflow. The person responsible for a workflow is derived also by an address expression. This employee can access the history of the workflow as well as perform other management functions. Furthermore, WorkParty distinguishes workflow administrators who make workflows available to performers. Workflow administrators cannot alter the workflow internals in contrast to the person responsible for the workflow.

WorkParty and ORM implement security functions. This means that objects like folders, workflows and employees can be protected by access rights.

Tools, Languages and APIs

WorkParty provides a set of tools to manage folders. First of all there is a folder management system which allows to store and retrieve folders in a structured way. It is based on a file system. To build folders a development environment is provided which supports workflow modeling. For viewing a workflow history a protocol (history) viewer is available. This viewer presents a workflow history in user readable form. In order to work on instantiated folders a run time environment is part of WorkParty. This run time environment displays all folders assigned to an employee. If a folder is within the run time environment of an employee he/she knows that some task has to be performed. The run time environment also provides a list of folders which can be started by that employee.

All these tools are graphical tools. In addition WorkParty provides a workflow definition language which can be compiled independently of the graphical development environment.

ORM as a separate software component provides its own tools. First of all there is a graphical tool for the definition of an organization structure. This includes the definition of all the above mentioned objects like employee and function. Furthermore, ORM provides an API to access its interfaces from other tools like WorkParty. In contrast to WorkParty there is no specification language within ORM to model an organization.

System Architecture and Implementation

The system architecture of WorkParty consists of several components. First of all WorkParty uses ORM as a separate component to manage the organizational part of workflow management. Another separate component is history management. Histories of workflows are stored in a separate database for security reasons.

WorkParty is fully integrated in an office desktop environment called ComfoDesk (White and Fischer, 1994). All components of WorkParty communicate according to the client/server paradigm. ORM as well as the history component exports APIs to support client access.

What are these

As an application integration mechanism WorkParty supports DDE and DLL.

On each user desktop (client) ComfoDesk runs with an embedded WorkParty client. A user desktop not only deals with displaying assigned workflows and executing applications but also with executing workflows. As soon as a task is finished the desktop client computes the next task to be carried out by a user. If the same user is eligible, the folder stays on the desktop. If not, the folder closes to be made available to other users.

Application Area Specifics

WorkParty's target environment is office procedure support. WorkParty is integrated into an office desktop environment following the idea of folders. Folders contain documents only (except variables of simple data types). ORM supports the modeling of human organizations.

2.2.8 Further Products

There are many commercial products available which serve as workflow management systems. There are too many to be listed here completely.

We tried to obtain substantial information about the best known products. However, the vendors were not able or willing to provide us with detailed information in all cases. Therefore we list some well-known products which we could not discuss here because of lack of information: Business Flow (COI, Consulting for Office and Information Management), FlowPath (Bull S.A.), Leu (LION), LinkWorks (Digital Equipment Corp.), Lotus Notes (Lotus Development Corp.), MultiDESK (Dialogika), OPEN/Workflow (WANG Laboratories Inc.), Plexus FloWare (Recognition International Inc.), PowerFlow, TeamFlow (ICL, International Computers Limited), ProcessIT (NCR Corp.), Regatta (Fujitsu Corp.), Staffware (Staffware), WorkFlo (FileNet), WorkMAN (Reach Software Corp.), WorkManager (Hewlett-Packard), X_Workflow (Olivetti).

2.3 WWW Resources

Whatever we write about academic prototypes and commercial products, in the fast moving area of workflow management this information will be out of date within a short time. Therefore, we maintain an index to various world wide web resources about workflow management at the University of Erlangen. This index will be updated whenever new information about workflow management systems is available. The index and the world wide web resources pointed at by the index provide the most accurate and actual information about workflow management systems. The index can be found at `http://www6.informatik.uni-erlangen.de/research/wf_references.html`.

2.4 Workflow Management Coalition (WfMC)

The Workflow Management Coalition (WfMC) was founded in 1993 as a non-profit international organization by several vendors developing or already selling workflow management systems. The group is now established and has stated its missions and objectives. Several working groups discuss and propose interfaces between the components of a workflow management system as well as between a workflow management system and its clients. In addition to this the WfMC (which can be seen as an industrial standards body) has defined the meaning of a product being compliant to its interface specifications.

In the following we give a short overview of the work the WfMC is conducting (WfMC, 1995a–d) and relate the scope of its efforts to the scope of this book.

Mission and Objectives

The WfMC states its mission as:

- Increase the value of customers investment with workflow technology.
- Decrease the risk of using workflow products.
- Expand the workflow market through increasing awareness of workflow.

The objectives of the WfMC are:

- Create specifications for a vendor consistent WFM Application Programming Interface which will provide a common method of access to WFM functions across heterogeneous products.
- Allow a WFM exploiter to potentially define and manage business processes with wider scope than might otherwise be possible.
- Preserve the investment in resources that a WFM user might have incurred with one WFM product while allowing another WFM product to be used in a different area.
- Create a model interchange format which will allow heterogeneous WFM models to be understood by multiple products.
- Create a specification which will allow WFM tools to be invoked in heterogeneous environments. This will improve the integration of workflow products with other I/T services such as mail, spreadsheets, word processors, processors, etc.
- Submit the results of the Coalition work (at the appropriate point in time) to appropriate standardization bodies as the basis for recognized international standards in the Workflow Management area.
- Encourage cooperative interoperability testing of WFM products using Coalition Specifications.

Member Structure

The WfMC has four types of members: regular members, guest members, personal members and members which declared their intention to join. To date there are about 80 regular members and 40 guest members registered. The main difference between the members is the right to vote in Coalition committees. Regular members are entitled to vote with one vote per member whereas guest members have no right to vote.

The Coalition is divided into two major committees, the Technical Committee and the Steering Committee. Basically the Steering Committee will set the Coalition policy whereas the Technical Committee is responsible for the drafting and interpretation of specifications. It provides recommendations to the Steering Committee on technical matters. Within each committee there are several small working groups which work on different areas like workflow terminology and interoperability standards. The committees as well as the working groups meet regularly.

Deliverables

The WfMC plans to deliver its work in the form of a series of documents which define or describe several areas of workflow management (WfMC, 1995e):

- *Reference Model.* Specification of a framework for workflow systems as well as identification of their characteristics, functions and interfaces (see Figure 2.2).
- *Glossary.* Development of standard terminology for workflow.
- *Process Definition Tools Interface (1).* Definition of a standard interface between the process definition tool and the workflow engine(s).
- *Workflow Client Application Interface (2).* Definition of standards for the workflow engines to maintain work items which the workflow client presents to the user.
- *Invoked Application Interface (3).* Definition of a standard interface to allow the workflow engine to invoke a variety of applications.
- *Workflow Interoperability Interface (4).* Definition of a variety of interoperability models and the standards applicable to each.
- *Administration and Monitoring Tools Interface (5).* Definition of monitoring and control functions.

Developed APIs are intended

- to allow workflow application to operate with different workflow management engines through standard interfaces
- to be supported by workflow management products today
- to provide consistent method to workflow management functions in cross-product workflow management engines

Compliance Rules

Compliance rules are set up by the WfMC members which define when a product is compliant to the interface specifications. Several levels of interoperability are defined. A level defines a set of interfaces and requirements. A workflow management system is compliant to a certain level if it implements the interfaces and fulfills the requirements defined by that level. The levels are

- *Level 1: Coexistence.* The ability for a number of workflow systems to reside on the same hardware and software base.
- *Level 2: Unique Gateways.* Developed to allow specific workflow systems to move work between themselves.
- *Level 2A: Common Gateway API.* An enhancement of Unique Gateways.
- *Level 3: Limited Common API.* A subset of workflow product functionality is reduced to an open API.
- *Level 4: Complete Workflow API.* All aspects of workflow systems behavior are embodied via an open API.
- *Level 5: Shared Definition Format.* Each workflow product can use the same process definitions at run time.

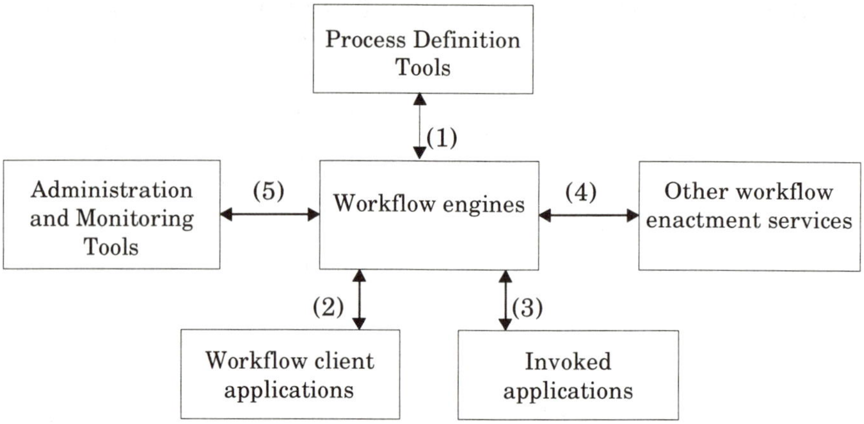

Figure 2.2: Interfaces identified by the WfMC

- *Level 6: Protocol Compatibility.* All APIs including transmission of definitions, work items and recovery is standard.
- *Level 7: Common Look and Feel.* Workflow product components appearance and method of operation are very similar.

In addition to the specified interface a product can implement further functions which are not within the specifications of the WfMC. To be compliant it is only necessary to have at least the specified interfaces. Having more does not harm compliance. The same is true for additional parameters of specified functions. Functions which are declared as optional by the WfMC do not have to be implemented by a product in order to be compliant. However, if a product implements some or all of the optional functions it has to be as specified.

A product which is compliant has to deliver a compliance document which describes the semantics of the implementation.

Scope of This Book vs. Scope of the WfMC

The WfMC focuses on the standardization of interfaces between modules of a workflow management system as well as between a workflow management system and its clients.

The interface specifications however are independent of a certain workflow model. The WfMC does not define the meaning of a workflow formally, i.e. neither C++ classes nor an Entity Relationship Model nor any other formal descriptions of a workflow type is provided. However, to interchange workflow descriptions a Workflow Process Definition Language (WPDL) is defined by the WfMC to serve as an interchange format.

In contrast to the work of the WfMC, this book has a broader scope. Not only interfaces of modules are discussed but also a complete architecture of a workflow management system (see Chapter 9). In addition to this a complete workflow model (Chapter 6) as well as the embedding of workflow management systems in the information processing infrastructure of an enterprise is provided (Chapter 5). Furthermore, the role of workflow management systems in the engineering lifecycle is discussed (Chapter 3).

3 Information Systems Engineering

When new methods or methodologies are introduced, it happens very often that the new method or methodology is considered as a global generic problem solver, i.e. as a panacea. The same phenomena could be observed at the introduction of workflow management technology. Without reflecting the meaning and purpose of workflow management and the interdependencies and interrelationships with adjacent topics, workflow management somehow "absorbed" the topics business process reengineering, enterprise modeling, process modeling, process execution, process analysis and process design, just to name a few.

This chapter classifies workflow management technology into the (traditional) framework of information systems engineering (Martin, 1990). Thus, we especially want to relate workflow management to the topics enterprise planning, business process modeling, system analysis, system design and information systems implementation. The goal of this chapter is to construct a methodology for information systems engineering in the realm of workflow management (Section 3.3).

In Section 3.1, a principal approach to information systems engineering is introduced. Section 3.2 discusses related methodologies which refine this principal approach. By integrating them into the principal approach, a workflow management oriented methodology for information systems engineering is constructed (Section 3.3).

3.1 Principal Approach

In this section a principal approach to information systems engineering will be introduced. However, before this can be done, we have to explain the meaning of the term "information systems engineering".

"Information systems engineering" is a combination of the two terms "systems engineering" and "information engineering" which mostly are used simultaneously and are interchangeable. They rather have to be distinguished from the area "software engineering" which aims at the construction of software of component systems on a project-oriented basis. Systems engineering and information engineering aim at the construction of software for a whole enterprise or a large sector of an enterprise. James Martin defines "information engineering" as

> the application of an interlocking set of techniques for the planning, analysis, design, construction and maintenance of information systems for a whole enterprise or across a major sector of the enterprise. (Martin, 1993, p. 241)

Information systems engineering facilitates the long-term evolution of information systems in an enterprise. Redesign and reengineering are therefore two constitutive aspects of information systems engineering. Thus, information systems engineering has to include phases of strategic planning as well as software implementation. In contrast, strategic planning is definitely not part of a software engineering process.

One of the most significant objectives of information systems engineering is to identify common objects[1] (data, processes, functions, etc.) across an enterprise. Redundant and unnecessary objects have to be removed and the maximum use of shared objects must be facilitated.

The principal approach to information systems engineering introduced in this section follows the concept presented in Martin (1990). This concept is very general and non-specific and therefore is very good as a starting point for the definition of information systems engineering for the area of workflow management. Figure 3.1 depicts the main components of the so-called information systems engineering cycle.

Two business-oriented phases, enterprise planning and business area analysis, can be distinguished from two system-oriented phases, system design and system implementation (cf. dotted brackets in Figure 3.1). The information systems engineering cycle starts with strategic planning of the enterprise at the top (enterprise planning). This phase is concerned with enterprise goals and critical success factors. Strategic business areas of an enterprise are defined and described on an overview level. Business strategies are established. These different information types lead into business area analysis.

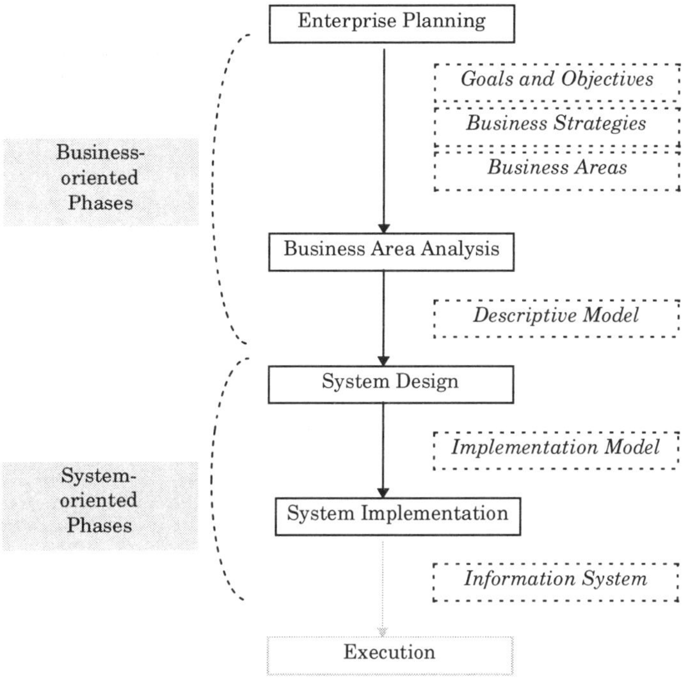

Figure 3.1: Phases of Information Systems Engineering

Business area analysis refines and revisits the results of enterprise planning. High-level object types are defined and requirements imposed by global goals, objectives and strategies are detailed. Business area analysis does not attempt to design systems; it merely attempts to understand and model the objects required to run the business areas. It is independent from current and future systems used to implement the business areas. Often, rethinking of objects is caused by business area analysis. Taking new or modified goals, objectives and strategies into account, the phase of business area analysis is the place where business process reengineering is performed.

The outcome of the second phase of information systems engineering is a descriptive model of a particular business area. Anticipating the discussion of Section 3.3, business processes are often the contents of such a descriptive model.

Next, the system-oriented phases of information systems engineering are entered. The main task of system design is to generate an implementation model. This model is derived from the descriptive model; it has to be precise. The implementation model describes object classes and object structures that can be directly implemented and finally will be executed. There are many different techniques that can be used for system design. Object Oriented Design (Booch, 1991), Responsible Driven Design (Wirfs-Brock *et al.*, 1990) and Object Modeling Technique (Rumbaugh *et al.*, 1991) are three well-known approaches.

In the phase of system implementation the objects generated during system design have to be implemented. For instance, an object "EMPLOYEE" is implemented as a table in a relational database management system, an object "ACCOUNTING" is implemented as a workflow and an object "PRINT" is implemented as a C procedure. The outcome of system implementation is an information system; for the special area of workflow management, this result is a Cooperative Information System (cf. Section 1).

Finally, applications will be performed by an information system generated during the phases of information systems engineering.

The two business-oriented phases are usually performed by experts of the various business units (domain experts). They know everything about how to conduct businesses but they are not very familiar with the information system infrastructure. The system-oriented phases are performed by information system professionals. They transform the requirements posted by the domain experts into technical implementations.

3.2 Refinements

The approach to information system engineering introduced in Section 3.1 is too shallow to facilitate the classification of workflow management. Therefore, two refining approaches are discussed in this section. They complete the principal approach of information systems engineering.

The first approach (Section 3.2.1) refines the phase of system design into method-independent and method-dependent layers. Section 3.2.2 introduces how system design and system implementation are treated in the context of software engineering.

3.2.1 Reconstruction of System Design

The dotted brackets in Figure 3.1 mark two work realms: the upper one is dedicated to domain experts, the lower one is dedicated to information technology experts. According to the figure, the final task of business experts is to define the descriptive model, while the initial task of the information technology experts is to construct an implementation model from the descriptive model. The transformation step from the descriptive model to the implementation model is one of the most critical steps of system development. Caused by misinterpretations – domain experts and information system professionals are "talking different languages" – a lot of inconsistencies might happen during this transformation. To bridge the gap between the two user groups, Ortner (1994, 1995) and Schienmann (1995) refine the system design phase: they split it up into a method-independent phase called "reconstruction" and a method-dependent phase named "system specification" (Figure 3.2). Before these two phases can be discussed, the meaning of "method" in this context has to be clarified.

A method directs to a certain type of implementation. Without aiming at completeness, the following list describes some example implementation strategies:

- *Object-oriented Implementation.* Following the paradigm of object-orientation, every piece of an application is an object. Therefore only objects and associated methods have to be developed.
- *Database-oriented Implementation.* A database-oriented implement-ation emphasizes the development of a conceptual database scheme. For example, relations, attributes and value domains have to be defined. The processing logic is somehow transparently hidden in application programs.

Consequently, also the deployment of workflow management systems defines another implementation strategy.

- *Workflow-oriented Implementation.* The workflow process is at the center of interest. Control flow, data flow, etc. have to be defined to integrate individual application programs into a workflow process.

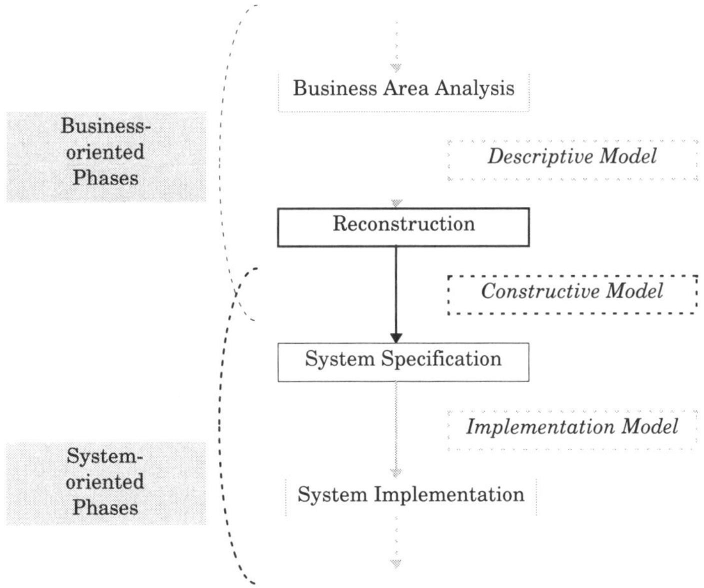

Figure 3.2: Refinement of the System Design Phase

The purpose of the phase "reconstruction" (cf. Figure 3.2) is to detail and complete the descriptive model such that an implementation could be derived easily. This task needs support by domain experts and by information technology experts. Domain knowledge is required since the descriptive model has to be extended in order to become complete. Information technology expertise is necessary since only the information technology expert recognizes the modeling elements that are still missing in order to reconstruct the descriptive model in such a way that an implementation model can be obtained.

The two constitutive components of a constructive model are a language, i.e. a grammar, to formulate correct sentences that describe the area of exploration, and a dictionary that defines terms and notions that can be used in these sentences. Thus, the constructive model is based on a material language approach (Ortner, 1995, 1994).

An example will illustrate the use of a constructive model. In the descriptive model, "documents" are referenced to describe an information resource. The description of this entity has to be refined in order to be able to implement it. A domain expert knows exactly what document bears what kind of information, and when a specific document has to be produced and consumed. In contrast, an information technology expert recognizes the most relevant parameters necessary to handle a document in an information technology infrastructure. For instance, the document management system that manages the document has to be specified. Location parameters and access rights have to be provided as well. Both domain-oriented and system-oriented information is described in the constructive model using an implementation-independent language. The entities of the constructive model are defined and their relationships are outlined. Although the content of an application system is determined thus, the way it is implemented is not determined yet due to the use of an implementation-independent language.

Only in the "system specification" phase do details about the selected implementation method come into the picture. For instance, workflow-specific or database-specific details appear. The outcome of system specification is an implementation model that precisely prescribes how an application system has to be implemented.

The advantage of separating out the method-independent phase of reconstruction is that a forum for communication between domain and information technology experts is established in the development methodology. The communication should avoid inconsistencies and failures due to misinterpretation. However, why does this phase have to be method-independent? If it were not method-independent, either the language of the descriptive model or a method-dependent language (e.g. a workflow language) would have to be used.

In practice, we experienced that a descriptive language usually does not allow to go into such a degree of detail that is necessary to describe an implementation model. On the other hand, use of a method-dependent language mostly expects too much technical knowledge from the domain experts and therefore real communication cannot be obtained. Also, the method-dependent language influences the constructive model too much and emphasizes specific features which are most relevant for the particular method-dependent language.

3.2.2 Software Engineering

In Section 3.1 the distinction between systems engineering and software engineering was discussed. In this section, software engineering will be incorporated into the information systems engineering cycle and therefore will be characterized as a special sub-discipline of information systems engineering.

Software engineering is a system-oriented discipline. According to Figure 3.2, software engineering deals with the phases reconstruction, system specification and system implementation. However, some approaches even omit the reconstruction phase.

In Denert (1991), a four-phase model of software engineering is proposed: system specification, system construction, module programming and system integration. However, there is a naming conflict: Denert's phase "system specification" corresponds with our phase "reconstruction" and Denert's phase "system construction" corresponds with our phase "system specification". Module programming and system integration both fit into our phase "system implementation".

A more detailed refinement of the phase "system implementation" is characteristic for software engineering. The implementation of a software system is split up into the programming of individual program modules, their testing, their integration into a comprehensive system and its testing. Figure 3.3 depicts this refinement of the system implementation phase. Towards a development methodology for information systems engineering, software engineering contributes to the system-oriented phases. Specifically, the construction of a comprehensive (information) system is dealt with by software engineering.

3.3 Information Systems Engineering for Workflow Management

Before we introduce information systems engineering tailored to workflow management we want to rephrase the purpose of this chapter. We stated that workflow management is neither a panacea that covers all phases of information systems

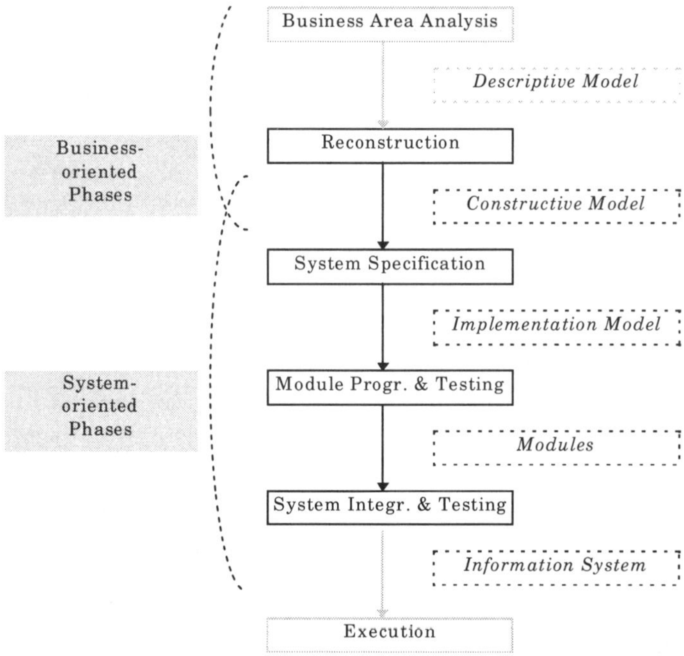

Figure 3.3: Incorporation of Software Engineering

engineering nor is it the only way to implement cooperative information systems. Workflow management is a well-defined part of an information systems engineering process. Therefore, in Section 3.3.1 a refined information systems engineering cycle is introduced. This phase model is used to classify workflow management, i.e. to select those phases of the information systems engineering cycle which can be implemented by workflow management technology (Section 3.3.2). A short overview on a development methodology for workflow management will finally be given.

3.3.1 Refined Information Systems Engineering Cycle

Figure 3.4 summarizes the figures from the preceding sections and shows a refined information systems engineering cycle. In practice, the cycle will usually not be processed completely. Depending on experience and local policies, some phases of this engineering cycle might be shortened or even omitted, some other phases might be expanded. Nevertheless, the information systems engineering cycle depicted in Figure 3.4 provides a working basis for the forthcoming discussion.

The Refined Information Systems Engineering Cycle allows to classify techniques and methods like system reengineering, system analysis and system design.

Reengineering an organization happens either in the phases Enterprise Planning or Business Area Analysis. The change of global strategic goals and the acquisition of new business areas are tasks typically performed during Enterprise Planning. Consequently, if a particular business area must be reengineered, Business Area Analysis is the place where this occurs.

A business area is characterized by a descriptive model. One way to specify a descriptive model is to use business processes. A business process abstractly defines how a particular business is conducted and relates it to business rules, strategies, policies, etc., i.e. to causalities that justify the constitution of a business process. Business process reengineering is the discipline that investigates whether

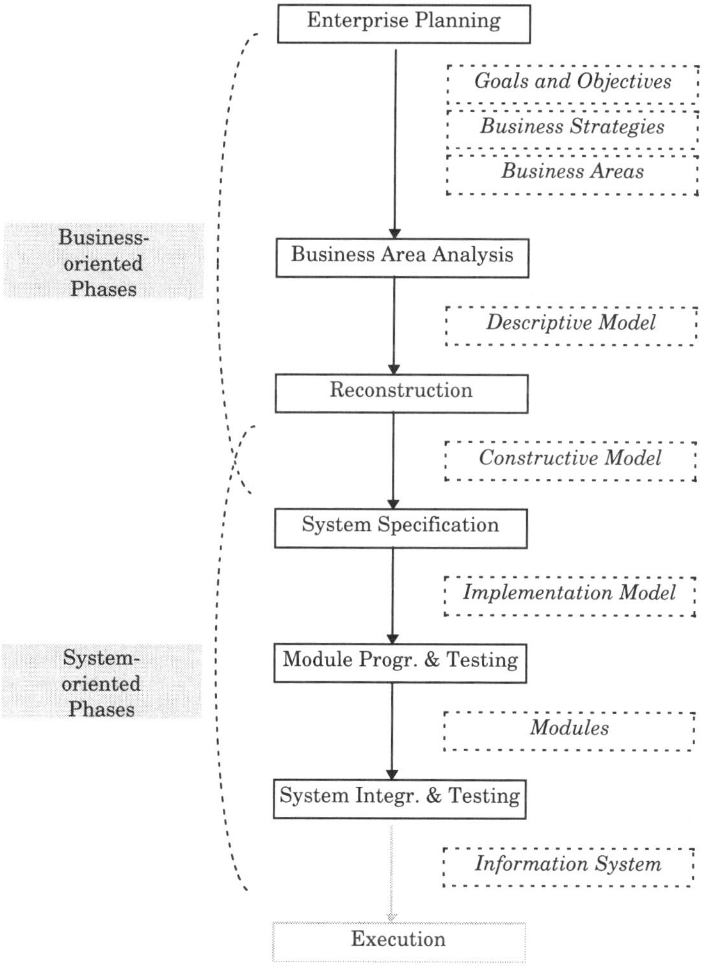

Figure 3.4: Refined Information Systems Engineering Cycle

the definition of a business process is still accurate and adequate and whether the causalities are still in place.

System analysis and system design (Fichman and Kemerer, 1992) are two closely related disciplines. The boundary between the two disciplines is fluid and imprecise. Just as fluid and imprecise is the application area of these techniques. For instance, Booch's method (Booch, 1991) is in principle applicable to Enterprise Planning, Business Area Analysis, Reconstruction and System Specification. This broad applicability is due to the fact that the method is so general that all kinds of application objects can be defined. This means that objects like "goal" and "purpose" as well as objects like "integer" and "float" can be defined. Thus, most phases of the information systems engineering cycle can be supported. However, this does not automatically mean that the method is superior to all others, especially to those that prescribe certain modeling elements and modeling steps. The flexibility of Booch's method can also lead to wrong design since the quality of a design is almost completely dependent on the knowledge and expertise of the modelers.

Other approaches are specialized to the requirements of particular phases. For instance, Responsible Driven Design (Wirfs-Brock *et al.*, 1990) is tailored to the requirements of the phases "System Specification" and "System Implementation" (Fichman and Kemerer, 1992).

3.3.2 Classification of Workflow Management

Last but not least, it is necessary to classify workflow management into the information systems engineering cycle. Since we regard workflow management as an implementation strategy (cf. Section 3.2.1) we first show the classification of implementation strategies into the information systems engineering cycle.

As stated in Section 3.2.1, the constructive model is independent of the implementation strategies. Therefore, implementation strategies cover the three lower steps of the information systems engineering cycle which are all characterized as system-oriented, i.e. implementation-oriented. Workflow management was defined as one possible implementation strategy. Hence, workflow management is only relevant for the phases System Specification, Module Programming & Testing and System Integration & Testing.

Figure 3.5 classifies implementation strategies into the information systems engineering cycle. An implementation strategy covers the system-oriented phases of information systems engineering. Thus, workflow management is characterized as a specific method to implement (cooperative) information systems. Consequently, it still requires methods for Enterprise Planning, Business Area Analysis and Reconstruction in order to define a complete information systems engineering cycle.

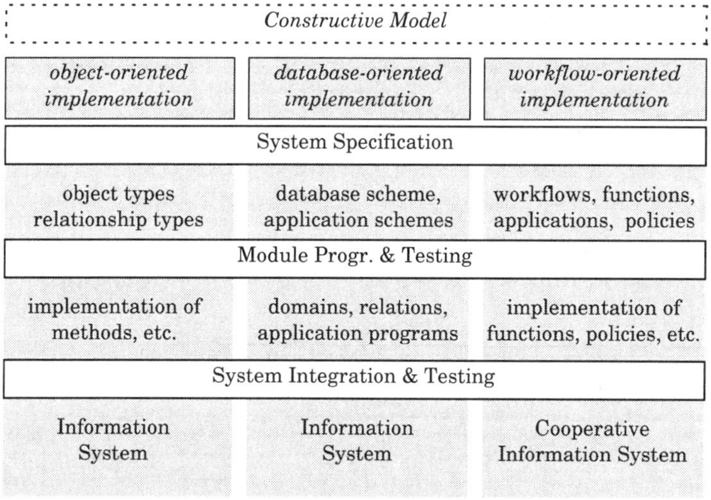

Figure 3.5: Classification of Implementation Strategies

Figure 3.5 is not complete in the sense that it shows all artifacts which are produced during the diverse development phases of the various implementation strategies. The figure only reveals some characteristic artifacts which are specified and implemented, respectively, during the phases. For instance, System Specification in the context of an object-oriented implementation strategy means to define object and relationship types. These types have to be implemented – for example with an object-oriented programming language – in the Module Programming & Testing phase. A database-oriented implementation strategy specifically requires the definition of a conceptual database scheme during System Specification. Its implementation, i.e. the specification of domains, attributes, relations, integrity constraints, etc. in a concrete database management system, is the main task of the Module Programming & Testing phase.

System Specification in the context of a workflow-oriented implementation strategy means to define schemes for workflows, functions (e.g. data conversion functions), applications, policies, etc. These artifacts will be implemented in the subsequent phase of Module Programming & Testing. For instance, data conversion functions and applications are implemented. The following chapters of this book will detail this workflow-oriented implementation strategy further; in particular, the artifacts generated during Systems Specification and Module Programming & Testing are elaborated.

A methodology for information systems engineering in the context of workflow management must take the process-centric view of workflow management into account. Therefore, the early phases of the development cycle must pursue this broad view and must put work and its manifold aspects into the center of interest (cf. Chapter 1). Enterprise Planning is scarcely impacted by a workflow-oriented implementation strategy. However, Business Area Analysis has to consider this implementation strategy. As remarked in Chapter 1, the descriptive model in the context of a workflow-oriented development methodology best consists of so-called business processes. Business processes are abstract descriptions of an application system. The main characteristic of a business process is its comprehensiveness, i.e. all aspects of an application system are included in the description. This is an ideal starting point for the derivation of workflows that also have to take up this broad, comprehensive standpoint. An example model for business processes which seems to be suitable for a workflow-oriented development strategy can be found in Hess *et al.* (1994). In this research paper, a business process meta model is proposed that includes entities like processes, business partners, tasks, applications, information technology, database, critical success factor, organizational unit, objective and reports. Most of these entities are also relevant for workflow management, as will be elaborated in the next chapters.

---

[1] For the time being, we use the term "object" in a very general manner according to the statement "everything is an object". This use does not imply any particular form of implementation (e.g. object-oriented programming).

4 A Brief Sketch of the Main Constituents of Workflow Management

The first three chapters of the book conveyed an overview on workflow management. This chapter divides the comprehensive task "workflow management" into two major subtasks and sketches both of them briefly. The subtasks will be elaborated in great detail in the following chapters.

Workflow management refers to several aspects which altogether compose a comprehensive job. A workflow management system consists of two parts (Leymann and Altenhuber, 1994): build time and run time. The build time part allows a modeler to define and maintain all the information necessary to eventually execute workflows. The workflows are finally performed by the run time part of the workflow management system.

Subsequently, we want to sketch briefly the main constituents of build time and run time. The constituents of each of the two parts are classified according to their main purpose and aim:

- *Conception.* Constituents that define the logical foundation of a whole part.

- *Enactment.* Constituents that define how the conceptual constituents are made available for use.
- *Handling.* Constituents that support the use of the enacted constituents.

Tasks, elements and requirements of the build time part will be discussed in Part 2 of this book. Part 3 will introduce the main aspects of the run time part of a workflow management system.

4.1 Build Time

The conceptual part, i.e. the logical foundation of the build time part, is the workflow model (cf. Figure 4.1). It contains all objects and relationships available to describe a particular workflow. The expressiveness of a workflow management system is decided by the content of this model. Thus, the workflow model is mainly influenced by requirements stemming from the application areas. For instance, if an application area needs to integrate multi media document management into workflows, the workflow model must incorporate corresponding means. Not only current application requirements but also future application requirements determine the workflow model. For instance, if the application area is highly dynamic and new model elements are required every once in a while, the workflow model must be easily extensible.

After the workflow model is principally settled, both the syntax and the semantics of the model elements have to be specified. This can best be done by providing a formal workflow language. A workflow language has to be specified in a formal grammar; it enacts the workflow model such that workflow modelers can use the workflow language to specify workflows. The constructs of the workflow language correspond with the elements of the workflow model.

Along with the workflow language the semantics of the model elements can be defined. Among other things, to define semantics by states, transitions and corresponding actions is a suitable approach.

The syntax of the workflow language is mainly determined by presentation requirements. A good language design supports the use of the workflow language fully.

It is worth mentioning that the workflow model and the workflow language, determine the expressiveness, the comprehensiveness and the functionality of a workflow management system. Only things that can can be expressed by the workflow language can eventually be executed.

In this chapter, we briefly want to mention the tools which are necessary to support build time. A workflow editor is necessary for the specification of workflows. The workflow language has to be compiled in order to check the integrity of the specified models. Simulator and animator tools are used to check the prag-

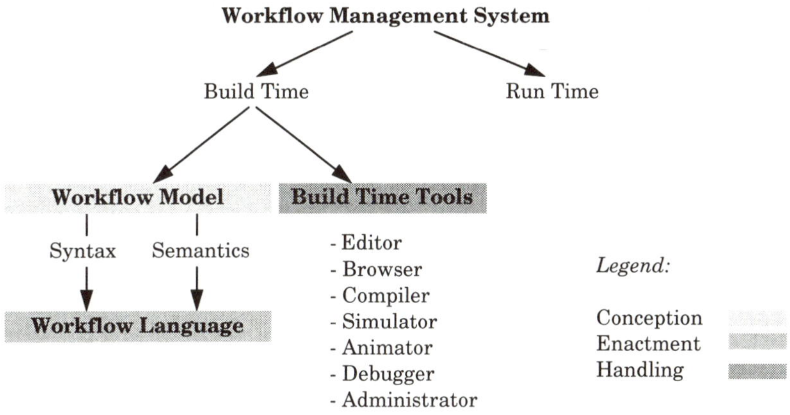

Figure 4.1: The Constituents of Workflow Management Systems – Build Time

matics of specified workflows. Last but not least, the workflow definitions have to be administered in a database, library or repository.

4.2 Run Time

The execution of workflows is the main task at run time. Therefore, an execution infrastructure has to be provided. We divide the execution infrastructure into three aspects:

- implementation model,
- implementation architecture, and
- implementation

The implementation model resolves into the functional components which form the conceptual basis for the run time part of a workflow management system (cf. Figure 4.2). For example, a module for application program integration is defined as abstract data type, i.e. its internal data structures and its interface are specified. The implementation model prescribes the components and the protocols between them, i.e. the application program interface (API) and formats and protocols (FAP) are defined.

Requirements referring to the architecture determine features like interoperability and portability. Also, implementation-related features (see below) are already predetermined by the functional architecture. For example, if a certain piece of functionality is not associated with a separate functional component, extensibility and replaceability of this piece of functionality are drastically reduced.

The implementation architecture is the second aspect of an execution infrastructure for workflows; the enactment of the functional components has to be performed. Three main tasks must be carried out:

- The functional components of the architecture have to be mapped to active elements of an operating system (e.g. processes, threads).
- Databases have to be designed for the data necessary to control and execute workflows.
- Communication mechanisms for component cooperation have to be selected.

The selection and configuration of the implementation infrastructure is driven by requirements like reliability, scalability, robustness and managability.

The implementation architecture must finally be instantiated with concrete systems that are available to implement a workflow management system. For example, when the implementation architecture says that a relational database management system is to be used, a concrete relational database management system is chosen (e.g. ORACLE, INFORMIX, SYBASE) to implement the workflow management system.

Last but not least, run time has to be supported by tools (handling). For instance, monitor tools are necessary to observe and control progress of workflow execution. Since we track the execution of workflows in a history database, analysis tools are used to assess effectiveness and efficiency of workflow execution. Administration and configuration tools are required to manage the execution infrastructure itself. The worklist manager provides worklists which are the user interface to the workflow management system.

The efficiency of a workflow management system is mainly determined by its implementation. However, if the functional design (architecture) is already poor, an implementation cannot become optimal.

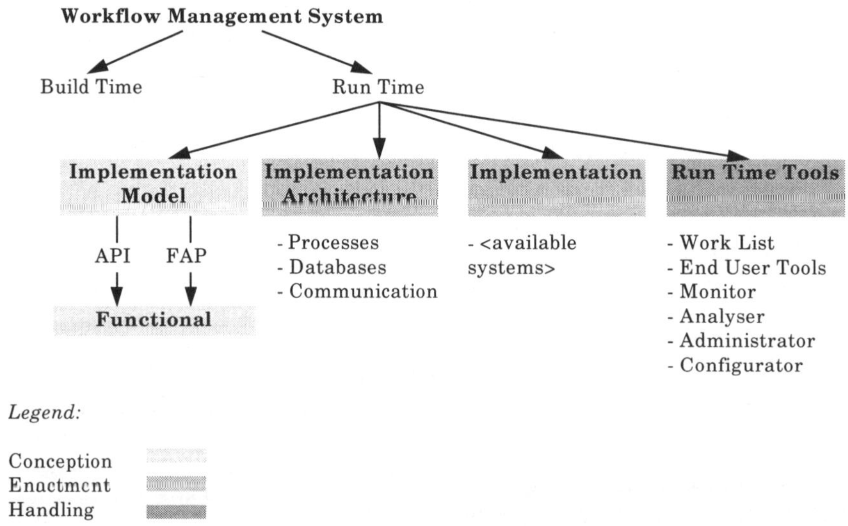

Figure 4.2: The Constituents of Workflow Management Systems – Run Time

Part 2: Build Time

According to Chapter 4, in Part 2 a workflow model, a workflow language and workflow tools will be introduced. Nevertheless, the main issue of this second part is to present a comprehensive workflow model. This general workflow model shows most of the relevant perspectives of any workflow model. The reader should know the reasons why we have structured this workflow model as described in Chapter 6; therefore, Chapter 5 describes design rationales that stand behind this workflow model. Reading this chapter is mandatory; if it were omitted, fundamental requirements towards the construction of a general workflow would not be understood. The operational semantics of the workflow model is discussed in Chapter 7. A brief overview on tools that support the build time part of a workflow management system is given in Chapter 8.

After having read this second part, the reader should know about

- design rationales of a comprehensive workflow model,
- major elements of a comprehensive workflow model,
- ways to extend and customize this workflow model, and
- tools that facilitate the definition and administration of workflows.

Since the workflow model determines the effectiveness of workflow management (cf. Chapter 4), this second part should be studied carefully. Whatever has to be executed in the context of a workflow must be expressible in the workflow model.

Reader's Guide

The following matrix guides readers with special interests.

Reader's Interest	*Chapters to read*
requirements for and classification of workflow models	Chapter 5
workflow model	Chapter 5 and Chapter 6
workflow modeling language	Appendix
workflow execution semantics	Chapter 7
build time tools	Chapter 8

5 Preliminaries to Workflow Modeling

This chapter outlines the rationales that stand behind the workflow model we are going to present in Chapter 6. The first three sections prepare the topic "workflow modeling". In Section 5.1, we look into related areas of workflow management technology in order to learn about meaningful and significant contents of a workflow model. Section 5.2 then summarizes requirements towards a workflow model. Modeling techniques which are suitable for the description of a workflow model are discussed in Section 5.3.

The last three sections prepare the presentation of our workflow model in Chapter 6. A classification scheme of workflow models is presented in Section 5.4 in order to discuss the design center of our workflow model. The workflow models introduced in Chapter 2 are also classified into this scheme. Section 5.5 provides a brief overview of our workflow model. Section 5.6 shows how the various elements of the workflow model are represented in Chapter 6.

5.1 Contents of a Workflow Model

What should be the contents of a comprehensive workflow model? To answer this question, we look into related research areas of workflow management. We expect to learn from these areas and to obtain substantial indications towards fundamental elements of a workflow model.

When looking into related research areas it is important to select only such areas which also pursue a process-centric view of work (cf. Section 1.1.1). The final goal of this section is to compile a set of relevant perspectives that could become parts of each comprehensive workflow model.

It is obvious that the manifold commercial and academic approaches of workflow management introduced in Chapter 2 are another source of information. However, we do not want to deal with them extensively in this section since they are already studied elsewhere (cf. Chapter 2).

Four research areas are analyzed in the following. We begin with the traditional area of business management (Section 5.1.1). After that, we study two research areas, namely enterprise modeling and architecture (Section 5.1.2) and software process modeling (Section 5.1.3), which we already mentioned as origins of workflow management systems in Section 1.1.2. We close this section with a brief sketch of coordination theory which theoretically outlines the scope of workflow management (Section 5.1.4). Section 5.1.5 abstracts the results of the former sections and compiles a comprehensive list of potential perspectives of a comprehensive workflow model.

5.1.1 Business Management

Traditionally, business management can be divided into structural organization and operational organization (Wöhe, 1984). Structural organization is concerned with interrelating basic organizational elements of an enterprise, like slots, positions and departments, in order to form the global organizational structure. The main task of operational organization is to organize the execution of work processes, i.e. to arrange work steps in order to form global work processes.[1] Structural organization regards an enterprise as an institution, operational organization deals with work performed in such an institution. Nevertheless, structural organization and operational organization are tightly coupled and neither can exist without the other.

The main result of structural organization is the definition of organizational elements (slots, positions, instances, departments, etc.) and the association of responsibilities. Thus, the organizational structure of an enterprise is determined. Based on the organizational structure the relationships between organizational elements are defined. For instance, a certain position is responsible for a whole department. An organizational structure also determines the formal flow of information and work objects (e.g. documents).

Structuring work processes (operational organization) is divided into four sub-tasks:

- definition of work content,
- definition of work execution time,
- definition of work execution place, and
- association of work to organizational elements.

The definition of work content refers to two independent issues: first, work objects have to be determined. For example, a travel claim form and a trip schedule are the work objects of the work process "travel claim reimbursement". Second, the tools available and usable to fill a travel claim form and to write a trip schedule are fixed.

The definition of work execution time is split up into three separated subjects: first, work steps constituting a work process have to be ordered. Second, the total/average/minimum/maximum execution time of a work step is specified and after that the accumulated execution time of a work process is calculated. Third, if it is necessary due to application-specific requirements absolute start and/or end times (so-called calendar time) for the execution of work processes and work steps must be fixed.

For each work process and work step, it has to be determined where it is executed. For example, a manufacturing step is scheduled for a specific manufacturing device which is located at a specific place on the shop floor. If information is processed on a computer network, the computers available for performing a particular step must be specified.

The tightest link between structural organization and operational organization is the association of work to organizational elements. For each work step and for each work process, one or more organizational elements must be selected which have to perform the work either together or exclusively.

The main objective of the above discussion is to analyze the discipline business management in order to find potential contents of a workflow model. The second column of Table 5.1 summarizes the previous discussion.[2]

5.1.2 Enterprise Modeling and Architecture

There are many methods in the area of enterprise modeling and architecture: CIM-OSA, Purdue Enterprise Reference Architecture, GRAI, IDEF, SADT, SSADM, TOVE, etc. Some of them are regarded as CIM-specific (CIM stands for "computer integrated manufacturing") although this distinction is not relevant for our purposes. It is more interesting that all these approaches follow a broad view of an enterprise and want to comprehensively model and execute the significant work processes of an enterprise.

It is far beyond the scope of this book to discuss the various approaches to enterprise modeling and architecture as mentioned above. Instead, we would like to summarize which elements are regarded as significant enough to be included into a broad enterprise model (cf. Table 5.1, third column). Therefore, CIM-OSA and TOVE will be analyzed with respect to the elements of their enterprise models.

CIM-OSA is an ESPRIT project being undertaken by the ESPRIT Consortium AMICE (Kosanke, 1992; Vernadat, 1992, 1996). CIM-OSA intends to use enterprise

Table 5.1: Potential Contents of a Workflow Model

Related area→ / *perspective ↓*	*Business Management*	*Enterprise Modeling and Architecture*	*Software Process Modeling*	*Coordination Theory*
Function	work steps	domain processes business processes enterprise activities functional operations events states	processes process elements process steps	activities
Operation	tools devices computers	resource capability inventory	artifacts	resources
Behaviour	ordering of	control flow in processes	control flow in processes	interdependencies between activities
Information	information flow work objects	information elements enterprise objects	artifacts	resources
Organization	organizational elements organizational structure responsibility association of work	organizational units organizational cells responsibilities authorities	agents roles	actors resources
Causality		causalities		goals
Integrity and failure recovery		integrity rules		
Quality	execution time start/end time	time cost quality		
History				
Security	permissions responsibilities			
Autonomy	places of execution			

models to monitor and control daily enterprise operations. For this purpose the development of CIM-OSA focuses on two major components:

- An executable enterprise model for the description of the total enterprise including all functions, information, resources and organizations. Static as well as dynamic aspects are covered.
- An integrating infrastructure containing information technology and machine technology services for the execution of a model under control of the daily enterprise events.

CIM-OSA considers four enterprise views: function view, information view, resource view and organization view. We simply want to list the diverse model elements which are associated with these four views of an enterprise:

- *Function View.* Event, domain process, business process, enterprise activity and functional operation.
  Modeling elements of the function view are used to model enterprise functionality and behavior, i.e. the flow of control. The activity-oriented elements of the function view are closely related to workflows.
- *Information View.* Information element, enterprise object, object view, object relationships and integrity rule.
  The modeling elements of the information view mainly describe the informational perspective of an enterprise. Examples of enterprise objects are documents, forms, files and orders.
- *Resource View.* Resource and capability.
  Resources are used in support of the execution of one or more activities. Examples of resources are tools, probes, carts, robots and operators.
- *Organization View.* Organization unit, organization cell, responsibility and authority.
  The elements of the organization view define the organizational structure of an enterprise.

Although a detailed discussion of the enterprise model is omitted here, the meaning of the modeling elements is understandable. We classify the elements of CIM-OSA's enterprise model into Table 5.1, column 3.

Another approach to enterprise modeling is called TOVE (Toronto Virtual Enterprise) (Fox and Gruninger, 1994). This research focuses on the creation of an enterprise design environment that allows for the exploration of different designs or models of an enterprise along various perspectives such as quality, costs and agility. In TOVE, these perspectives are called ontologies. An ontology is a formal description of entities and their properties. The ontologies defined in TOVE exhibit various dimensions of an enterprise model.

The following ontologies are considered in TOVE: activities and states, time, resources, quality, cost, inventory, orders, parts, organizational structures and causality.[3] We complete the third column of Table 5.1 (Enterprise Modeling and Architecture) with these ontologies. However, not all ontologies are added to the table, since some of them are just instances of objects already mentioned in the table (e.g. an order is a specific information element).

Together, the two presented approaches to enterprise modeling and architecture illuminate a broad spectrum of perspectives which should potentially be considered in a workflow model.

5.1.3 Software Process Modeling

Humphrey and Feiler (1992) define a software process as

> … a set of partially ordered steps intended to reach a goal.

According to their definition, the components of a process are called "process elements". Such process elements which are atomic, i.e. which do not have an externally visible substructure, are called "process steps". Curtis *et al.* (1992) complete the description of a process:

> Although there is no wide-spread consensus on the constructs that collectively form the essential basis of a process model, the following list includes many of those most frequently mentioned …

The list mentioned in the citation contains the concepts agent, role and artifact. Agents execute the components of a process. Process steps are enacted such that collectively the goals are accomplished for which the process was designed. Typically, process steps manipulate artifacts.

Curtis *et al.* name four most commonly represented perspectives of a process model:

- functional perspective
- behavioral perspective
- organizational perspective
- informational perspective

The modeling elements introduced in Section 5.1.1 and 5.1.2 can easily be mapped to these perspectives. All four perspectives are represented directly in Table 5.1.

5.1.4 Coordination Theory

While the former approaches can be categorized as practical cases, the following discussion is theory-oriented. Coordination theory provides an abstract view on coordination problems. Since workflow management can be considered as a specific coordination problem, coordination theory can provide a suitable background. The following discussion is based on Crowston (1991) and Malone and Crowston (1994).

Coordination is the act of working together. Work is acting in a goal-oriented way. Thus, there must be one or more actors performing some activities which are directed toward some ends. The activities are not independent from each other; the relationships between activities are called interdependencies. Therefore, the definition of coordination can be reformulated:

> Coordination is managing dependencies between activities. (Malone and Crowston, 1994)

A central concern in coordination theory is to understand the basic processes involved in coordination. Four components of coordination are identified:

- *Identifying goals.* Goals have to be selected that are worth being pursued.
- *Mapping goals to activities.* Goals are decomposed in order to identify activities. Activities have to be performed in order to accomplish associated goals.
- *Mapping activities to actors.* Tasks (i.e. executing activities) are assigned to actors. Actors are responsible for executing tasks accurately and adequately.
- *Managing interdependencies.* There are several causes for interdependencies. For instance, activities have to be executed in a specific time order. Sequencing and synchronization are two examples of timing interdependencies. Another kind of interdependence results from the use of the same resources: if an activity has to archive data on a tape and the tape device is allocated to another activity, the two activities are in conflict. Even an actor that has to perform multiple activities can be regarded as a special kind of resource. Data and applications are other examples of resources.

The theoretic reflections on coordination justify many of the perspectives depicted by Table 5.1. Coordination theory therefore rounds off the perspectives derived pragmatically from the approaches discussed previously.

5.1.5 Consolidation of Perspectives

In this section, the relevant subject areas of a comprehensive workflow model are consolidated. Here, consolidation means to introduce vocabulary that abstracts from the terminology of the previously discussed disciplines (e.g. business management, enterprise modeling). Using an independent naming scheme for perspectives, the specific concepts of the related disciplines can be classified more easily.

The perspectives elaborated in this section are potential candidates for perspectives of a comprehensive workflow model (Chapter 6) since these perspectives are considered to be relevant for related disciplines which also pursue a process-centric view on work. Table 5.1 summarizes the disciplines and introduces an abstract classification scheme for perspectives.

Although none of the four related research areas discussed in this section mentioned the history perspective directly, we added it to Table 5.1 since all research areas presume that something like an audit trail is available to check efficiency and effectiveness of work process executions.

5.2 Requirements

After having compiled a list of relevant subject areas for a workflow model, we collect requirements towards a workflow model in this section. The following discussion is divided into two parts: the first part is concerned with requirements stemming from the potential application areas of workflow management systems. The second part of the discussion pertains to the handling of the workflow model itself. In principle, splitting the debate into two parts is not necessary. However, by following the split we emphasize some typical features of the application areas of workflow management systems.

5.2.1 Application-oriented Requirements

The application-oriented set of requirements of a workflow model is found when typical uses of workflow management are investigated.

Many Different Forms of Workflows

When workflow management technology is applied in an enterprise, normally not just one application domain has to be served but potentially all that are significant for the enterprise. Examples of application domains are corporate management, finance, marketing and sales, administration, production management and shop floor management.

The workflows encountered in the different application domains of an enterprise show manifold characteristics. It is almost impossible to anticipate all features of workflows that have eventually to be designed for the different application domains. Thus, in order to cope with the upcoming requirements of new workflows, the workflow model must be

- extensible.

Dynamically Changing Business Requirements

Today, the competition between vendors is so high that fast response to changed market requirements is mandatory in order to stay in business. For instance, if a customer orders goods which are not part of the normal production program, a company will change its production program to serve the customer's order (if it is worth the effort from a business point of view). Workflows that implement production processes are long running; sometimes their execution takes several weeks or months. In case the production program has to be changed, these workflows have to be adapted. However, they cannot simply be terminated, modified and restarted, because this would cause great loss of effort and material; instead, they have to be

- dynamically customizable,
- adaptable, and
- must support the full life cycle of a model.

The last point includes the existence of a change process, a versioning concept and configuration management.

Continuously Growing Application Area

The deployment of a workflow management system is most beneficial if broad parts of an enterprise are using this technology. Therefore, new workflows will be defined continuously. In order not to duplicate effort, it is necessary that the elements of a workflow model are

- reusable.

For instance, workflows (cf. Chapter 6) are defined such that they can be used as subworkflows in arbitrary workflow definitions.

Distributed Heterogeneous Computing Infrastructure

Workflows span multiple parts of an organization that favor different hard- and software systems. Such computing infrastructures consist of heterogeneous, autonomous and distributed (HAD) legacy and new systems (Rusinkiewicz and Sheth, 1995). It is not economic and often not feasible to completely discard the already existing application systems. Instead, workflow models must be

- open

to be able to integrate existing and new application systems. Nutt (1992) characterizes an open system:

> An open system is one in which the components and their composition are specified in a non-proprietary environment, enabling competing organizations to use these standard components to build competitive

No Connetion with the next page

This definition of open systems emphasizes non-proprietary environments. Interoperability provides an application program access to others in a network which is the basic requirement of an open system (Umar, 1993). Sometimes the term "compatibility" is used alternatively to interoperability (Meyer, 1988).

In the context of workflow management, openness refers to the interoperability between application programs and a workflow management system. Specifically for a workflow model, openness requires constructs which allow to define API and FAP for external application programs to be integrated into workflow executions.

5.2.2 Model-oriented Requirements

Model-oriented requirements are valid globally; they are not specific for workflow models. Model-oriented requirements are also dealt with under the subject "software quality". Nevertheless, there is a variety of software: software products, software models, software implementation systems, etc. Therefore, not all aspects applicable to software in general are also significant for models. For instance, scalability is an appropriate quality of any form of software implementation, however, it is not relevant for a software model. The following discussion is customized to workflow models and integrates aspects presented in European Committee for Standardization (1994), Hindel (1993) and Meyer (1988).

We distinguish three different forms of representation of a workflow model which exhibit the three most significant perspectives of a workflow model:

- graphical representation,
- formal representation, and
- enactable representation.

The term "graphical" used in the first list element is somehow misleading. "Graphical" would be better replaced with "easy-to-use". However, graphical representations mostly bear this property. Another aspect of ease of use is the provision of abstraction mechanisms in order to facilitate stepwise refinement. Encapsulation, information hiding, classification, particularization and specialization are concepts which are of major interest in the context of abstraction. Abstraction mechanisms provide building blocks that make the specification of complex workflows easier. Thus, the graphical representation of a workflow model should support the following qualities:

- ease of use,
- readability, and
- abstraction.

A workflow model must also have a formal representation. This is necessary to prove the correctness and integrity of a workflow model itself and of the workflows modeled. A property of a workflow model that goes along with formality is preciseness. Having a formal workflow model in place, workflows are verifiable which is another quality of a workflow model. Altogether, the formal representation of a workflow model has to support the qualities

- correctness,
- integrity,
- preciseness,
- testability, and
- verifiability.

As shown in Section 4.1, a workflow language is the implementation of a workflow model, i.e. it represents its enactable representation. A language shows syntax and formal semantics; the latter can be provided by the formal representation of the workflow model. The graphical representation of the workflow model illustrates the constructs of the workflow language. Thus, the language is a melting pot where aspects of the graphical and the formal representations of a workflow model are unified. Therefore, the qualities associated with either the graphical and the formal representations also hold for a workflow language. We merely want to add the quality

- unambiguity

which equally holds for all three representations of a workflow model. Unambiguity means that there is only one unique representation of a certain artifact in a model and a language.

The qualities mentioned so far mostly refer to either model usage and model adaptation (cf. Section 5.2.1). Model revision posts another requirement on a workflow model, namely

- maintainability.

Several criteria which support maintainability have been mentioned already: unambiguity, ease of use and readability. If there is only one place where a specific artifact is to be specified, and this part of the workflow model is easy to comprehend, then it should not be a great effort to maintain the workflow model, i.e. to adapt it to new requirements.

The discussion of requirements for a workflow model must be concluded by mentioning the most important feature of a workflow model, that makes the enactment of all the requirements possible:

- modularity.

We agree with Hindel (1993), McCall *et al.* (1977) and Meyer (1988) that without modularity most of the required features of a workflow model cannot be enacted. Sometimes we use

- orthogonality

as a synonym for modularity. This mostly happens when we want to express that one of the key features of a modular (workflow) model is partial exchangeability and extensibility. Orthogonality refers to independently designed parts of a workflow type that can be composed to a complete workflow type description.

5.3 Representation Techniques

Workflow model representations (and languages) can be evaluated by the extent to which they provide constructs useful for representing and reasoning about the various aspects of a workflow (Curtis *et al.*, 1992). Curtis *et al.* identify various languages and approaches suitable for (software) process modeling. In principle, these approaches are potential candidates for the representation of a workflow model. The following list enumerates the approaches identified in Curtis *et al.* (1992):

- procedural programming languages (e.g. APPL/A)
- system analysis and design (e.g. STATEMATE, DFD, SADT)
- AI languages and approaches (e.g. GRAPPLE, MARVEL)
- events and triggers (e.g. STATEMATE)
- state transitions and Petri nets (e.g. RIN)
- control flow (e.g. MVP)
- functional languages (e.g. HFSP)
- formal languages (e.g. context-free grammar)
- data modeling (e.g. PMDB)
- object modeling (e.g. AP5)
- precedence networks (e.g. SPMS)
- quantitative modeling (e.g. system dynamics)

Curtis *et al.* assess the various approaches to software process modeling with respect to whether they cover the perspectives of software process models (cf. Section 5.1.3). They conclude that none of the approaches covers all perspectives adequately. This conclusion is one of the reasons why we have chosen another approach to workflow modeling which we simply call

- comprehensive object modeling

in order to distinguish it from the approach "object modeling" mentioned in the above list. Another reason to not to choose an approach that is identified in the in order to distinguish it from the approach "object modeling" mentioned in the above list. Another reason to not to choose an approach that is identified in the above list is the following: the approaches in the list already show severe deficiencies in representing the four perspectives of software processes. The comprehensive workflow model developed in this book is characterized by being broader than software process models (cf. Section 5.1.5) and, furthermore, by being extensible with new, still unknown perspectives. This leads to the conclusion that the above listed approaches cannot be suitable for workflow modeling.

Particularly for people stemming from the area of object-oriented programming there is nothing special about our approach of comprehensive object modeling. For people who are not very familiar with object-oriented programming we clarify the main concepts of our approach.

There is one fundamental concept which has to be followed strictly:

Every single artifact which is relevant for a workflow has to be modeled as an object.

Nevertheless, this rule has to be refined:

Every single type of artifact has to be modeled as an object type.

Instances of object types are obtained by instantiating object types. Each object type is characterized by its underlying data structure and operations that manipulate these data structures. An object type is constituted along the design rationales of abstract data types.

Some examples will shed some light into the comprehensiveness of the definition. To define document types and then to derive concrete document instances is quite obvious. However, the application of the above definition to control flow constructs is not so straightforward. For instance, an object type for the control flow construct "sequence" is defined. The meaning of this construct is apparent: if workflows w_1 and w_2 are connected by an instance of this control flow construct, workflow w_2 has to be started as soon as workflow w_1 has terminated. Among others, there is an operation "execute". This means to start workflow w_2 after workflow w_1 has finished. There might be data structures (attributes) for the object type "sequence". One attribute is called "limited evaluation time" with the following meaning: if the evaluation of the control flow construct, i.e. the search for the workflow to be executed subsequently, consumes more than the specified amount of time, the execution is regarded to have failed (cf. Chapter 6).

With the selection of the comprehensive object modeling approach the requirements discussed in Section 5.2 are met completely. We do not intend to dwell on this observation but refer to experiences in the realm of object-oriented modeling which support it.

5.4 Classification of Workflow Models

Before our comprehensive workflow model is presented a classification scheme for workflow models is introduced. This scheme shows that although workflow management puts the work process in the center of interest, there are various alternative approaches to this. A two-dimensional classification scheme is identified which allows to classify existing workflow models and, specifically, the workflow model which is introduced in Chapter 6.

Two major dimensions are distinguished: design center and deployment area. A design center identifies the primary focus of a workflow model. In principle, all perspectives of a workflow model can represent a design center. The other perspectives of the workflow model are arranged around the design center to complete the broad process-centric view of the workflow model. The second dimension, the deployment area, stems from the fact that many workflow management systems are developed for a special application area. Therefore, the corresponding workflow model contains model elements which are tailored to these specific deployment areas. In the following, various aspects of the two dimensions are discussed.

Design Center

Let us repeat the observation from Section 1.1.1. There, different approaches for the design of information systems were introduced. Data-centered approaches were distinguished from task-centered approaches; finally, the process- or work-centric view was presented as the ideal approach for workflow management.

Within the work-centric design center several streams can be identified. As we have seen in Section 5.1, a workflow model is constituted of many different perspectives. Principally, each perspective can establish a design center. Some common design centers in the realm of workflow management are listed below (Schwab, 1993):

- agent
- data (document)
- process (workflow)
- application
- history

In Table 5.2, the workflow management systems discussed in Chapter 2 are classified. The comprehensive workflow management system that is introduced in Chapter 6 (for the time being, we call it *MOBILE*) fosters workflows as its design center.

Table 5.2: Classification of Example Approaches

Deployment area → *Design center* ↓	*Specific*	*Partially*	*General*
Agent		Action Workflow	
Data (Document)	WorkParty, ProMInanD		
Process (Workflow)		FlowMark, SAP Business Workflow, Pegasus, Melmac, Domino, OfficeTalk, COSA, InConcert	ConTracts, *MOBILE*
Application			
History			

Deployment Area

The second dimension of the classification scheme is built by dependencies from deployment areas. Three degrees of dependencies are identified:

- *Specific*. Workflow models are fully dependent from an application area which consists of termini technici only. Almost no common concepts are incorporated into the workflow model.
- *Partially dependent*. The elements of the workflow model are a mixture of deployment area specific constructs and general constructs.
- *General*. The workflow model is exclusively composed of general modeling concepts. No specific deployment area is emphasized.

The dimension "deployment area" is represented by the columns in Table 5.2. *MOBILE* is classified as workflow management system that provides general modeling constructs.

Table 5.2 demonstrates that most workflow management systems favor the process-centric approach, which is not surprising. However, it is a surprise that most approaches offer a workflow model that is partially dependent from a specific deployment area, i.e. the vocabulary used in the workflow model and workflow language, stems from that deployment area.

Based on our experience in diverse deployment areas of workflow management, i.e. manufacturing (Jablonski and Ruf, 1990), office automation (Bussler and Jablonski, 1994) and enterprise modeling (Bussler, 1995b), we also believe that processes (workflows) are an ideal design center for workflow management. Additionally, our experience motivates to offer a workflow model that is independent from a specific deployment area. Our favorite workflow model which is represented in Chapter 6 is equally suited to be used for manufacturing scenarios, office automation problems and enterprise modeling tasks.

5.5 *MOBILE* – A Comprehensive Workflow Model

The comprehensive workflow model that will be introduced in Chapter 6 is based on research work, literature study and experiences from customer projects conducted since 1987. From this work, the workflow model *MOBILE*[4] evolved. As stated in Section 1.6, the workflow model and architecture introduced in this book is not another specialized approach which is the result of our personal research and professional work but the workflow model and architecture serve as a reference for the classification and assessment of other workflow models and architectures. Therefore concepts discussed in the following are general and not limited to the scope of our personal work.

5.5.1 Perspectives

In this section the main constituents of the *MOBILE* workflow model are introduced briefly in order to provide a preconception of Chapter 6. According to previous discussions in this chapter (cf. Section 5.1), these constituents are discussed as perspectives of the workflow model.

However, the succeeding examination is characterized by not being complete. Because of Section 5.2.1 this is not possible since the deployment area of workflow management is pervasive and new perspectives or extensions to existing perspectives will most probably be encountered. Nevertheless, due to the extensibility of the workflow model this incompleteness is harmless since the workflow model can be extended almost arbitrarily.

The comprehensive workflow model is split into two categories of perspectives,

- factual perspectives, and
- systemic perspectives.

Factual perspectives stem from the deployment areas of workflow management. They determine which artifacts can be included into a workflow specification, i.e. they determine the contents of a workflow model. Section 5.1 provides valuable hints for the factual perspectives of a workflow model. Factual perspectives exist independently from the enactment of a workflow description, i.e. whether there is a workflow management system in place which executes workflows automatically or workflows are completely processed manually is not relevant.

Systemic perspectives come into the picture because of a special form of enactment. Indeed, we pursue the enactment of workflow descriptions by workflow management systems. Therefore, systemic perspectives are derived from the execution of workflows by a specific workflow management system. Two examples shed some light onto this differentiation: an important factual perspective is formed by integrity and consistency which implies error treatment. On a factual level for instance, it is defined which part of a workflow has to be performed atomically. Such a part is probably called an atomic sphere of execution. On a systemic level, database transactions and persistent queues (cf. Gray and Reuter (1993)) might be used to guarantee atomicity. Alternatively, persistent objects are an implementation variant. Although the use of database transactions together (with persistent queues) and the use of persistent objects might be equivalent with respect to fulfilling the requirement "atomic sphere of execution", the language constructs needed to express these systemic features are rather different.

Another example of the differentiation of a factual and a systemic perspective is the history perspective of a workflow: on a factual level, the history perspective is important for providing features like auditing (e.g. in order to comply with tax laws) and revisions (e.g. in order to track the development of businesses). On a systemic level, the history perspective defines how formerly produced (historical) data can be reused in another context.

In this chapter, we want to concentrate on factual perspectives since they are the more general concepts in compliance with the global mission of this book. Nevertheless, systemic perspectives are partially considered in Part 3.

For each of the factual perspectives introduced next, a main question is presented which is answered by the introduction of the respective perspective. Additionally, basic model elements which represent the perspective and a brief description of the general meaning of the perspective are given.

According to Table 5.1 the following five perspectives are of fundamental importance for each comprehensive workflow model:

- *Function Perspective:* What has to be executed?
  Elementary workflows, composite workflows, subworkflows, superworkflows.
  The functional units of a work process to be executed are described. These functional units represent the core part of a workflow, i.e. they actually are the workflows.
- *Operation Perspective.* How is a workflow operation implemented?
  Workflow applications. We will see that workflows are merely functional units to structure a work process. The real work is accomplished by so-called workflow applications.

- *Behavior Perspective.* When is a workflow executed?
  Control flow constructs, control flow.
  According to Curtis *et al.* (1992) the behavior of a workflow is determined by the flow of control among its functional units.
- *Information Perspective.* What data are consumed and produced?
  Data, data flow.
  Workflows and workflow applications (and auxiliary functions) consume and produce data which altogether determine data flow.
- *Organization Perspective.* Who has to execute a workflow or a workflow application?
  Agents, people, roles, policies, organizational units.
  Each workflow (application) has to be performed by one or more members of an organization. Who is eligible to execute a workflow (application) is described by the organization perspective.

For most application areas, the above five perspectives are mandatory and sufficient. Most of the workflow approaches introduced in Chapter 2 are restricted to them. However, another group of six perspectives can be identified which is also very significant for a comprehensive workflow model and completes the specification of a workflow:

- *Causality Perspective.* Why is a workflow executed?
  Causalities, reasons, needs.
  The execution of a workflow mostly depends on requirements posted by the business. Only if such requirements still hold, the execution of a workflow is justified.
- *Integrity and Failure Recovery Perspective.* What constraints have to be fulfilled to execute a workflow properly?
  Consistency constraints, failure recovery.
  First, it has to be described what constraints have to be fulfilled to consider a workflow to have executed properly. Second, since failures are principally not avoidable, recovery measurements must be provided to get from an inconsistent, exceptional state back to a consistent state.
- *Quality Perspective.* Is the execution of a workflow efficient and effective?
  Execution time, execution costs.
  Execution time and cost are two potential criteria to assess the quality of workflow execution. Quality can be assessed before a workflow is executed, during execution and after it has been terminated.
- *History Perspective.* What workflow was executed when, what data were consumed and produced, who was executing it, etc.?
  Executed workflows, executing agents, evaluated control flow constructs.

The history perspective builds up an audit trail of workflow execution. All aspects of a workflow execution are logged.

- *Security Perspective.* Who is allowed to execute which workflow (application)?
  System user.
  While the organization perspective determines agents eligible to execute a workflow (application) in the context of an organization, the security perspective boils this aspect down to users on a computer system.
- *Autonomy Perspective.* Can or must a workflow (application) be executed autonomously?
  Mobility, distribution, execution threads.
  There are three aspects of autonomy: If a workflow (application) can be executed autonomously, it is possible to check it out onto a mobile computer and eventually check the results of execution back to the stationary (i.e. immobile) part of the workflow management system.
  Second, due to organizational requirements it might be demanded that parts of a workflow are performed independently (e.g. it is executed in an independent department).
  Subworkflows might be executed asynchronously. Thus, the execution of the superworkflow and the subworkflow(s) form independent, autonomous execution threads.

The list of perspectives of a comprehensive workflow model is still not exhaustive. As mentioned in Section 5.2 this list must be extended if the situation arises, that still unknown features must be covered. The modularity of a workflow model, i.e. the orthogonality of its perspectives, must allow this.

5.5.2 Design Principles

The *MOBILE* workflow model is based on the design principles which are discussed below.

Representation of Model Elements as Abstract Data Types

Model elements are represented as abstract data types (cf. Section 5.3); a model element is characterized by its data members which describe its structural part and a dynamic part which describes how to manipulate it. The structural part of a model element is constituted by its so-called components, the dynamic part of a model element comprises operations applicable to the model element.

Occurrences of model elements are attained by instantiating the abstract data type that represents the model element.

Constructive Approach (Differentiation between Definition and Use)

Elements of the workflow model are defined (constructed) autonomously and independently before they are used in the context of another model element. For instance, a workflow application is first defined independently from any use. Eventually, with the definition of an elementary workflow this workflow application is used, i.e. it is referenced.

Defining a model element means to specify a new element type. Using it in another context means to specify a variable of the corresponding element type.

There is one important effect when differentiating strictly between definition and use of a model element. Model elements are characterized by features. For example, for a workflow type a constraint is defined which restricts its start time. When a variable of the model element is used in the specification of another workflow, the workflow variable can be refined by additional constraints. When an instance of the workflow variable is created, the constraints defined for the workflow type and the constraints defined for the workflow variable are valid. Another way to interpret this situation is to assume that constraints attached to the workflow variable overwrite constraints that are attached to the workflow definition.

5.6 Representation of Model Perspectives

The perspectives of the comprehensive workflow model *MOBILE* will be elaborated in Chapter 6. Each perspective is discussed according to the following scheme:

- Description of the model elements associated with a perspective
  Each model element is regarded as an abstract data type. Therefore, its components and operations have to be investigated.
  - Informal introduction of major model elements
  - Formal definition of the components of a model element
  - Formal definition of the operations of a model element
- Language representation of the perspective
- Discussion of the implementation of the perspective by a related approach
- Discussion of further issues

For the formal description of model elements, specialized entity-relationship diagrams are used. In order to follow a constructive approach, only a restricted set of relationship types is used for the specification of interdependencies and interrelationships between the elements of the workflow model:

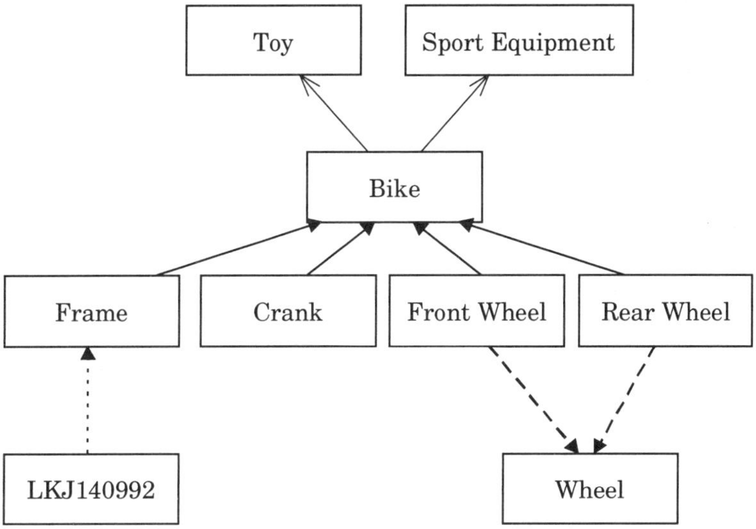

Figure 5.1: Bike Example

is_a (subordination)
is_part_of (whole/part relationship)
is_instance_of (subsumption)
is_used_as (role relationship)

"is_a" describes logical abstraction between model element types. "is_instance_of" also constitutes a logical abstraction, though it connects instances of model elements to the corresponding types. The relationship "is_part_of" denotes the components of a model element. A particular use of a model element is illustrated by the "is_used_as" relationship.

To demonstrate how the four relationships are applied a bike is reconstructed in Figure 5.1. We have chosen an example which is absolutely independent from workflow management in order to show the use of the relationships without confusing the user with workflow specific details which have not been introduced yet.

A bike consists of a frame, a crank, a front and a rear wheel ("is_part_of" relationship). Both front wheels and rear wheel are subtypes of wheel ("is_a" relationship). LKJ140992 is a concrete instance of a frame ("is_instance_of" relationship). Children see a bike as a toy, while sportsmen regard a bike as sports equipment ("is_used_as" relationship).

[1] Work processes might be implemented as workflows. However, this is not a must. Work processes can be implemented manually as well.

[2] The row titles of Table 5.1 use a classification scheme that complies well with the structure of the workflow model that is introduced in the next chapter. We determined this classification scheme by analyzing the related disciplines discussed in this section.

[3] It is not quite clear what ontologies are actually considered since different publications present different sets of ontologies.

[4] *MOBILE* does not directly refer to "mobile computing" but to the "ornamental structure with parts that move in currents of air" (Hornby, A.S.: Oxford Advanced Learner's Dictionary of Current English, Oxford University Press, 1974). Two main features characterize this work of art: it is balanced and all parts are mobile – two features that hopefully are also characteristics of our workflow model and architecture.

6 A Comprehensive Workflow Model

This chapter introduces a comprehensive workflow model which supports the key features discussed in Chapter 5: extensibility, reusability and openness. The presentation of workflow management systems in Chapter 2 reveals many different terms expressing more or less the same concepts and it introduces an even larger set of system features. The comprehensive model which is presented in the following can be used as a reference model to classify these concepts and features. Mapping concepts and features to one selected reference model makes it possible not only to understand the workflow management systems much better but also to compare them with each other more effectively.

The first five sections (Section 6.1 to Section 6.5) introduce the major five perspectives of a workflow model: workflows, data and data flow, control flow, workflow applications and organization. Section 6.6 discusses further perspectives which are of relevance in workflow modeling. However, they can be regarded as optional and only relevant for selected application areas. Therefore, they are discussed in less detail.

6.1 Workflow

While the concepts introduced in the following sections implement one dedicated perspective of a workflow model, the concept "workflow" solves two issues: On the one hand side a workflow defines the function perspective, i.e. *what* has to be done. On the other hand side a workflow constitutes a frame where the other perspectives like the behavioral or the organization perspective are embedded. The concept "workflow" is the design center of the overall workflow model (see Chapter 5). A workflow is the basic unit of execution and serves as the main interaction object to workflow management system users.

6.1.1 Model Elements

Basic Elements

The function perspective defines *what* has to be done. It is constituted of either elementary or composite workflows. An elementary workflow represents a basic task for a human user or an automated agent. A composite workflow consists of other workflows, so-called subworkflows. It represents a compound task which is composed of smaller tasks represented by subworkflows. Composite workflows coordinate their subworkflows. The encompassing workflow of a subworkflow is called superworkflow.

Workflow types are distinguished from workflow instances. At run time several instances can be derived from the same workflow type. An instance is called top-level workflow if it references subworkflow instances but is not referenced by any other workflow.

To ensure integrity and consistency constraints can be attached to workflow types. Enter constraints are checked at the time a workflow is instantiated to verify initial conditions. Exit constraints can be modeled to check integrity conditions before a workflow finishes. Finally, run time constraints can be modeled which are checked "continuously" during run time.

Workflows are assigned to users. Workflow operations are made available to users to process workflows. Besides application area independent workflow operations like start, pause and resume, application area dependent workflow operations like sign, reimburse, execute and commit should be modeled.

Components

Elementary and Composite Workflows

As discussed in Curtis *et al.* (1992), (software) processes can be decomposed further into (software) process elements. These refine the overall process. Process elements can be refined into further process elements until elementary process steps are reached. *Elementary* means that there is no further decomposition into other process elements.

Workflows also follow the idea of task decomposition. A workflow used for refinement is called a *subworkflow* whereas the refined workflow is called a *superworkflow*. The leafs of workflow refinement are *elementary workflows*. They are not further refined by workflows and are the smallest units of work to be performed. In contrast, *composite workflows* are refined. Superworkflows are

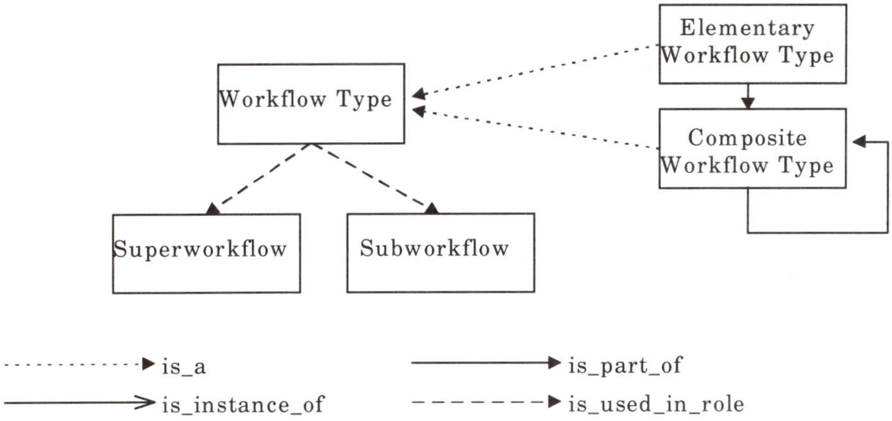

Figure 6.1: Elementary and Composite Workflow Types

always composite workflows. A composite workflow can be refined by elementary as well as composite workflows.

The following distinction is important for the design of a workflow model. A workflow is elementary or composite by definition. In contrast, a workflow is a subworkflow or a superworkflow by the way it is used. If a workflow references another one, it becomes a superworkflow from the viewpoint of the referenced one. The referenced workflow becomes a subworkflow from the viewpoint of the referencing one. In Figure 6.1 the terms defined above are related to each other.

Workflow types are distinguished from workflow instances. At runtime, workflow instances represent actual tasks to be carried out. A workflow instance is of a specific workflow type. Multiple instances might exist at the same time which belong to the same workflow type. A workflow type defines a scheme of a process whereas an instance instantiates the scheme.

Because of the distinction between workflow types and workflow instances the following model detail is emphasized here. A *top-level workflow instance* is a workflow instance which is not referenced by another workflow instance as a subworkflow instance. A workflow instance becomes a top-level workflow instance by use, not by definition. A top-level instance might be derived from an elementary or a composite workflow type. Therefore, no special workflow type for top-level instances (top-level workflow type) has to be introduced. If we introduced such a special workflow type it could not be referenced as a subworkflow. This violates the principle of reusability since reusing it as a subworkflow would be impossible. Therefore we carefully distinguish between the definition of workflows and their usage. Figure 6.2 relates terms in the realm of workflow types and instances.

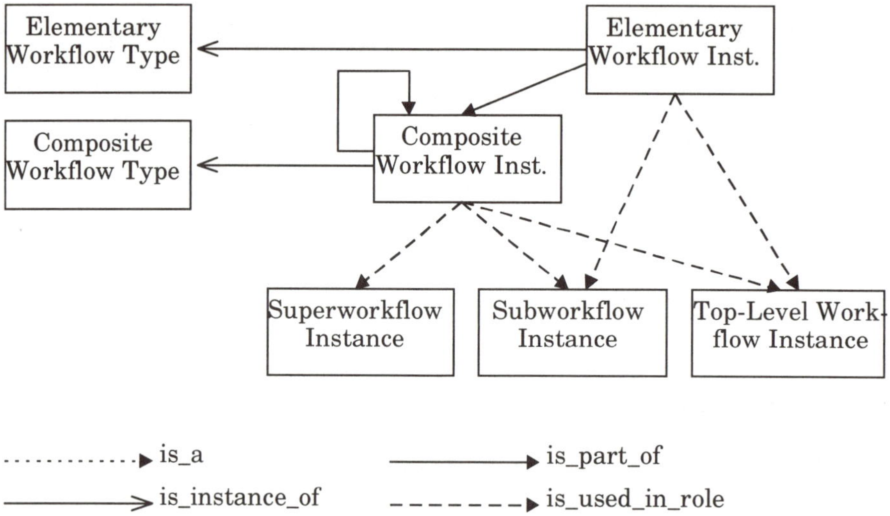

Figure 6.2: Elementary and Composite Workflow Instances

So far we can model the basic workflow type structure according to the concept of task decomposition. However, this is not sufficient to model the function perspective of workflows. The next section introduces constraints which are used to check consistency criteria before, after and during workflow execution.

Constraints

In general, a workflow cannot be executed arbitrarily. For instance, specific workflows may only be executed during normal working hours; a travel expense reimbursement workflow may only be started if the trip was previously approved. The trip approval check is executed exactly once when the reimbursement workflow starts. The working hour constraint has to be checked "continuously" during workflow execution in order to pause when normal working hours are over. Three kinds of constraints can be distinguished which are delimited by their execution time (see also Chapter 6.6.4):

- enter constraints,
- exit constraints, and
- run time constraints.

A workflow might be associated with several constraints. For instance, a workflow can have two enter constraints, no exit constraints and three run time constraints. If a workflow has several constraints of the same kind, they have to be connected by Boolean operators like *and*, *or* and *not* as well as by brackets.

Constraints are defined and evaluated on data values. For instance, the working hour constraint references a data structure "clock". The following data to be referenced can be distinguished (see Section 6.2):

- *Control data.* Control data are data available within a workflow.
- *Production data.* Production data are external to workflows. Only pointers to these data are available in a workflow.

For instance, if a trip approval constraint is checked, trip approval data have to be accessed; trip approval data are production data. Trip identifiers which are passed between workflows are typical control data.

As long as all constraints of a workflow are fulfilled processing continues normally. However, as soon as a constraint is violated a semantic error occurs (cf. Section 6.6.4). Semantic errors are application area specific. For example, if a trip was not approved, only the application expert can decide how the travel reimbursement workflow has to be continued. There are several solutions to repair semantic errors (Leymann and Altenhuber, 1994):

- terminate workflow execution
- wait for constraint fulfillment
- start of repairing workflow
- rollback semantically

A comprehensive discussion of semantic errors can be found in Section 6.6.4.

As far as enter and exit constraints are concerned, their time of execution is intuitively clear: an enter constraint of a workflow is evaluated as soon as the workflow is instantiated. An exit constraint is evaluated after a workflow has finished. In contrast, a run time constraint is evaluated "continuously". This means that it is evaluated between workflow instantiation and workflow termination. During processing it is evaluated "continuously". Since "continuously" cannot be implemented as the term indicates, certain points of workflow execution have to be marked determining when run time constraints are evaluated. It is possible to check a run time constraint before and after a subworkflow is executed. Alternatively, it is possible to check before and after a user action. Chapter 7 discusses this topic in more detail. Figure 6.3 shows the relationship between constraints and workflow types.

Workflow Body

Besides being part of the function perspective a workflow type builds a framework for all workflow perspectives. This framework is implemented by the *workflow body*.

Figure 6.4 gives an overview on the perspectives represented in a workflow body. The workflow body is constructed in a modular way. Each perspective is specified separately. The main benefits of this kind of approach are a more clear representation and the extensibility of the workflow body. Extensibility not only means to add a new perspective but it also allows to remove a perspective if it is not relevant for a specific application area.

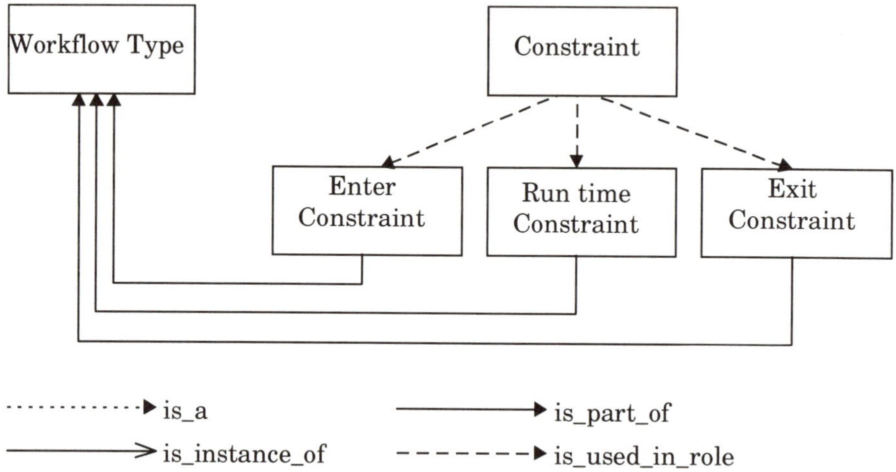

Figure 6.3: Constraints for Workflows

Function Perspective

The function perspective of a composite workflow is constituted by the set of its subworkflows. The function perspective of an elementary workflow is empty since an elementary workflow does not bear any subworkflows.

All constraints discussed so far are associated with a workflow type (Figure 6.5). However, the use of a workflow in the role of a subworkflow might impose further use-specific constraints. As an example, let us look at the working hour

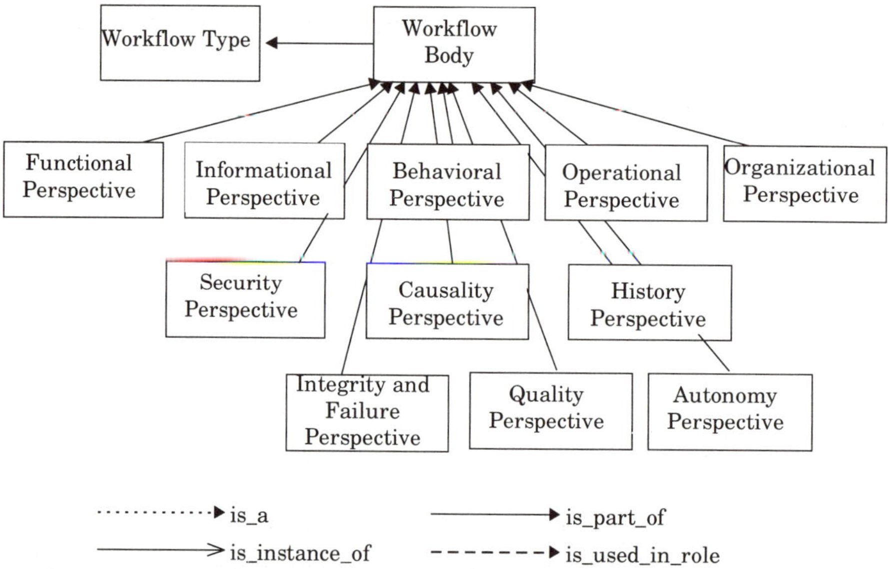

Figure 6.4: Workflow Body

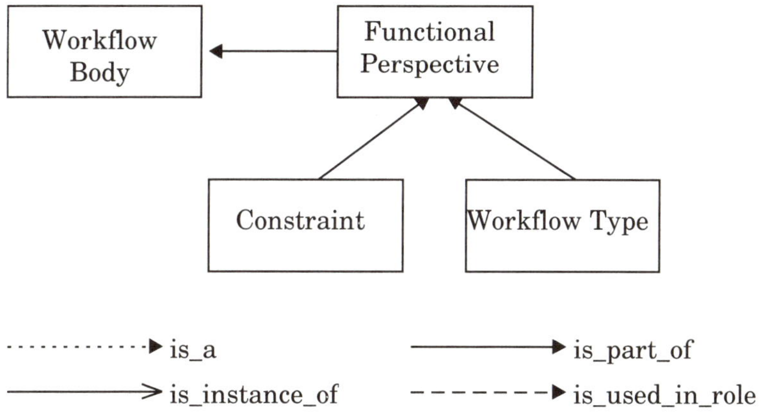

Figure 6.5: Function Perspective

constraint of a workflow type. This workflow type might be referenced as a subworkflow; a specific constraint says that the embedding superworkflow may only be executed on Mondays and Fridays. This constraint is also relevant for the workflow type introduced at the beginning of the example (see Section 6.6.4 for a general discussion of the use of constraints).

A default constraint execution strategy says that constraints introduced due to the use of a workflow as subworkflow override constraints defined for a workflow type. If no constraints are defined within a superworkflow all constraints of the subworkflow apply. This default strategy is not always appropriate. We omit the discussion of further strategies here and refer to Section 6.1.4 for a more flexible execution strategy.

Operations

A workflow is the basic unit of execution. It is therefore an active object. Operations are the means to access the functionality of a workflow. The example systems presented in Chapter 2 provide a standard set of operations (like *start, stop, resume, execute*) for each workflow type. These operations are available for all workflow types. This approach is neither adequate to model workflows realistically nor is it user friendly. To support this criticism, some examples are given which show the deficiencies of the above-mentioned approach.

Most approaches provide exactly one operation for an elementary workflow to perform; usually it is named *execute* or *start*. The following example shows that this is not adequate or sufficient. A user is asked to approve a meeting date. He would like to either approve the date or propose an alternative date. An ergonomic solution for this problem would be to support two operations, *approve* and *propose_alternative_date*.

In a second example a manager has to sign a travel expense reimbursement form. On request, he would like to inspect the approval form to look up details.

The operations *sign* and *show_approval* would support this scenario adequately.

As in object-oriented languages a distinction is made between operations for workflow types and instances. Operations for workflow types are among others *start* (creating a new instance), *deactivate* (making this type unavailable for future use), *activate* (releasing a workflow type for use) and *show* (displaying the workflow type specification). Representative operations on workflow instances are *stop, resume, delete, sign, disapprove* and *reject*.

An operation becomes a type or an instance operation by use, not by definition. The type operations as well as the instance operations of a workflow type are attached to the workflow type. If an instance of the workflow type exists, the instance operations are looked up at the respective workflow type. Figure 6.6 shows how operations are related to a workflow type.

Elementary workflows represent tasks to be fulfilled. Operations are used to perform required actions to fulfill the task. In contrast a composite workflow does not represent a task but organizes tasks. Composite workflows have operations, too. These are used to manage task organization. For instance, stopping a composite workflow execution might result in a state where no task can be executed further.

Operations are implemented by workflow applications (see Section 6.4). A workflow application augments application programs (e.g. a spreadsheet tool) with a workflow specific piece of code called a wrapper. This wrapper is necessary to implement the protocol between a workflow management system and an application program. Basically each workflow operation references one or more workflow applications. As soon as a user decides to execute a workflow operation the referenced workflow applications are executed. Details are discussed in Section 6.4.

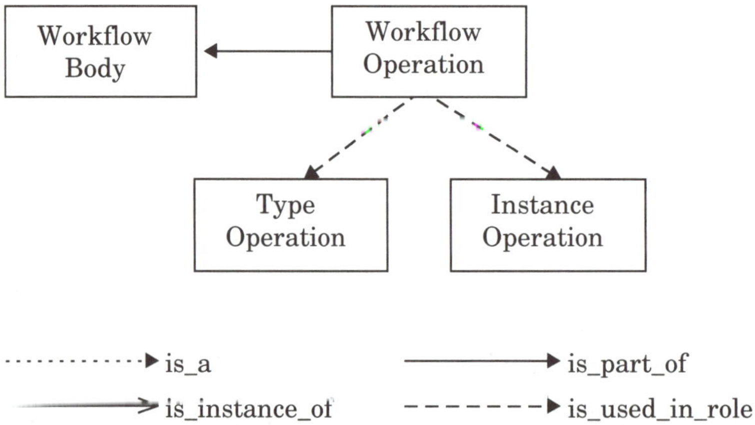

Figure 6.6: Workflow Operations

6.1.2 Example

Modeling a workflow type is a creative job investigating alternative designs. A modeler needs to have a way to write down a workflow type formally. In addition to documentary purposes a workflow type specification is also the basis for workflow execution.

In order to not overload this chapter we do not present the Backus Normal Form (BNF) of the workflow language here but separately in Appendix A. There, the BNF for the function perspective can be found.

Throughout this chapter we construct a workflow dealing with travel expense reimbursement. Here is the first part of a workflow scheme that specifies the example.

```
WORKFLOW_TYPE travel-expense-reimbursement (...)
  ENTER_CONSTRAINT     approved(...)
  RUNTIME_CONSTRAINT   during_hours(8:15, 17:45)
                       AND
                       during_days(Monday, Friday)
                       AND
                       within_weeks(2)
  EXIT_CONSTRAINT      sufficient_budget(...)
  END_CONSTRAINTS
  ...
END_WORKFLOW_TYPE
```

Parameters of the functions representing the constraints are not filled in since they are not defined yet. Later on we will see that *approved* will take a trip identifier and *sufficient_budget* the amount to be reimbursed as an actual parameter. Functions needed to implement constraints are specified separately (we omit their specification here).

Several subworkflows of the same type can be referenced within a superworkflow. For each of the subworkflows constraints can be specified separately. We extend the travel claim reimbursement example by six subworkflows, two of them being of the same type. We assume that each of the five types is already specified so that we can reference them here. Note that it cannot be inferred from the following specification whether a subworkflow is elementary or composite. To decide this the respective workflow type specification must be inspected.

```
WORKFLOW_TYPE travel-expense-reimbursement (...)
  ...
  SUBWORKFLOWS
```

```
    Fill: fill      RUNTIME_CONSTRAINT
                          within_days(2)
                    END_CONSTRAINTS
    Sign: sign_1    RUNTIME_CONSTRAINT
                          within_week(1)
                    EXIT_CONSTRAINT
                          signed() OR refused()
                    END_CONSTRAINTS,
          sign_2    RUNTIME_CONSTRAINT
                          within_week(1)
                    EXIT_CONSTRAINT
                          signed() OR refused()
                    END_CONSTRAINTS
    Reimburse: reimburse;
    Archive: archive;
    Information: inform
  END_SUBWORKFLOWS
  ...
END_WORKFLOW_TYPE
```

The task "fill" has to be done within two days whereas "sign_1" and "sign_2" have to be finished within one week. In addition, the workflow modeler wanted to make sure by assigning exit constraints to "sign_1" and "sign_2" that signing takes place or is explicitly refused.

Finally, the workflow operations of a workflow type have to be defined. Operations are either type operations denoted by "**T_**" or instance operations denoted by "**I_**". Parameters are to be specified also, their syntax is shown in Section 6.3. We extend the above example by three operations *start, pause* and *resume*:

```
WORKFLOW_TYPE travel-expense-reimbursement (...)
  ...
  OPERATIONS
        T_OPERATION start (...) ...END_OPERATION;
        I_OPERATION pause (...) ... END_OPERATION;
        I_OPERATION resume (...) ...END_OPERATION
  END_OPERATIONS
  ...
END_WORKFLOW_TYPE
```

The type operation "start" is specified to start a travel expense reimbursement workflow, i.e. to create a workflow instance. Two instance operations are defined, one to pause a workflow instance and one to resume it.

6.1.3 Example Implementation

As real example we briefly discuss how the function perspective is implemented in FlowMark (cf. Chapter 2). We relate FlowMark's modeling concepts to the concepts formerly introduced in this section. FlowMark distinguishes several building blocks:

- *Process.* A process corresponds to a composite workflow.
- *Program Activity.* A program activity is an elementary workflow which references one application program. Executing the program activity means executing the referenced application program. This is started by the fixed operation "execute". It is neither possible to have several application programs started nor to have several operations defined which start different application programs.
- *Process Activity.* A process activity corresponds to an elementary workflow which references another process. In this way it represents a subworkflow. At runtime executing a process activity means executing the referenced process.
- *Block.* A block groups activities of a process. A block has an input and an output container from which it gets data. A block is specified within a process and cannot be reused elsewhere. A block is introduced into FlowMark to model loops. It can be specified that a block can be executed several times.
- *Bundle.* A bundle contains a program or process activity. A bundle is used to initiate several instances of the activity it contains at runtime. The number of instances to be initiated is determined at runtime.

FlowMark supports exit conditions which can be viewed as exit constraints. There are neither enter nor run time constraints available in FlowMark.

Operations in FlowMark are fixed for all elementary and composite workflows. However, they are not specified explicitly as shown above but are implicitly available. The functionality to start a workflow or to execute the application program of a program activity is available at the user interface.

6.1.4 Further Issues

Some further issues have to be brought in the context of workflows as the implementation of the function perspective.

Subtyping

As in object-oriented languages subtyping might be a way to adjust workflow types to special application area requirements. Also, *abstract workflow types* such as abstract classes (classes which are never instantiated) (Goldberg and Robson,

1989) might be a way to structure class hierarchies of workflows. For instance, an "intergalactic" travel claim is designed to specify the necessary subworkflows *fill*, *sign* and *reimburse*. In some countries an additional step *check* is required whereas in other countries a step *archive* is needed. Inheritance might also be applied to the other perspectives introduced later on.

Object-oriented technology provides inheritance for object variables (class and instance variables) as well as for operations (class and instance operations). However, a workflow type contains much more than only variables and operations. In order to subclass a workflow, its superclass has to be named in the type specification. Furthermore, elements of the superclass might be overwritten. In order to overwrite an element of a superclass the element has to be referenced by name.

Constraint Execution Strategies

It is most flexible to let a workflow modeler decide upon the constraint execution strategy for each subworkflow individually. In some cases it is the only way to decide how constraints are combined. In an example scenario, a working hour constraint is attached to a workflow. From the use of the workflow as subworkflow another constraint is imposed, namely to execute it at night time. To provide a default strategy for constraint execution is not possible. The workflow modeler has to decide whether both or just one of the two constraints has to be applied finally.

Operation Availability and Execution Order

Operations have to be made available to users in order to be executed. Some operations might be attributed as "automatic", i.e. they are executed automatically without user intervention. Some operations are used by other operations as subroutines and therefore do not have to be made visible to users. It is necessary to specify which operations are visible to a user.

Besides the visibility issue the execution order of operations needs to be specified. For instance, if an elementary workflow has three operations available *accept*, *sign* and *done*, a workflow modeler might want to guide the user to first execute *accept*, then *sign* and finally *done*.

6.2 Data and Data Flow

One of the main tasks of workflow management is to provide the right data at the right time. Before introducing model elements to specify data flow some general remarks have to be given. Workflow management is neither document management nor office automation (cf. Chapter 1). Document management deals with the management of documents and related issues like document retrieval and storage. Office automation provides powerful tools to support office workers' work on these documents. However, workflow management systems might use document management systems to implement certain application systems, and workflow management systems might be deployed in an office environment configured as an office automation tool.

Documents will not be a modeling construct within the workflow model; instead, data are modeled in general. Documents are merely viewed as a special kind of data. During workflow execution new data will join the data flow whereas other data will leave it. Different data might take different migration routes. This more general model of data and data flow also allows to model document flow effectively since documents are regarded as a special kind of data. However, document flow does not take place on the production data level but on the control data level which will be clarified in the next paragraphs.

Workflow management systems are not general data management systems. To comprehend this differentiation, *control* and *production data* have to be distinguished. Control data are data which come into existence only because of workflow management; they are only relevant internally for a workflow management system. Typical control data are local variables of workflows or data (e.g. a pointer to a file) passed between subworkflows. As soon as a workflow is finished control data are discarded. In contrast, production data exist even without workflow management; they are external to a workflow management system and might be used by it. For instance, travel claim forms exist before workflow management is introduced. Handles which point to these forms are needed in a workflow management system to implement a travel claim reimbursement process. Production data which are relevant for a workflow management system are called *workflow relevant production data*. Nevertheless, workflow management systems do not manage these data. They are managed by some other system like a document management system or a database management system. Operations on these data are not provided by a workflow management system but are supported by other systems. The operations might be used in the realm of workflow management in order to access external data. Figure 6.7 illustrates these data categories.

6.2.1 Model Elements

Workflows as well as workflow operations have parameters. IN, OUT and INOUT parameters are distinguished. A parameter is either mandatory or optional. Workflows have local variables to store intermediate results. Local variables as well as parameters are typed. Basic data types are provided. However, it is possible

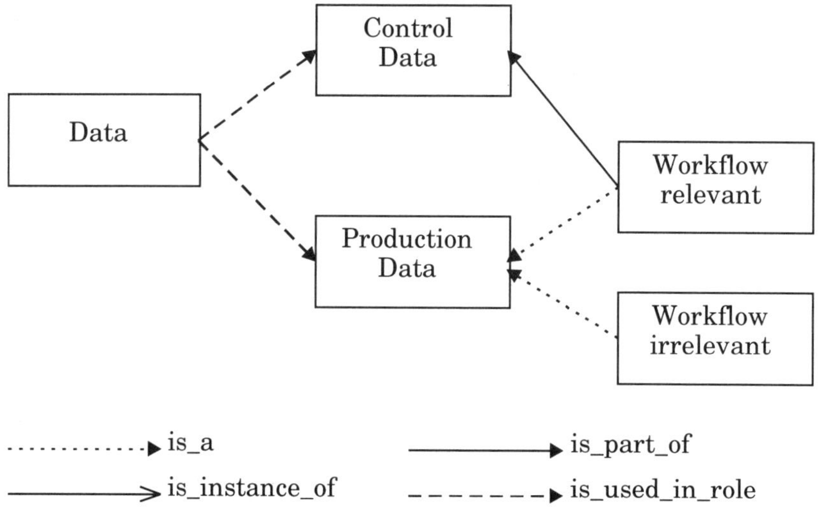

Figure 6.7: Categories of Data Used in Workflow Management Systems

to define further data types on demand. Last but not least, data flow has to be implemented. Data flow either between subworkflows or between subworkflows and workflow local variables. The above-mentioned concepts together make up the information perspective of a workflow.

Data Types

The distinction between data types and data instances has been proven useful. In general, data can be represented in several ways: as structures like in Pascal (Wirth, 1971), as objects like in Smalltalk (Goldberg and Robson, 1989) or simply as unstructured files of a file system (Tanenbaum, 1987).

For simplicity of representation and discussion we use a Pascal-like approach. A distinction is made between elementary data types like *integer, real, decimal, boolean, string*, etc. and composite types like *record* or *array*. Furthermore a distinction is made between the *value of data* and a *pointer to the value*. This distinction is important when data are passed through parameters since in one case a copy of the data is created and in the other case a pointer to a value is transferred. In addition, constraints can be attached to data types which implement consistency criteria. Data constraints are like run time constraints introduced in Section 6.1.1. A sample constraint might require that an integer value has to be greater than 1000. Finally, an initialization expression can be specified for data which defines the initial value of data right after it is created.

Data types consist of the specification of data as well as constraints and initialization definitions. Data types are reused in different contexts such as in another complex data type or within a workflow type. Because of reuse, constraints and initialization definitions might be overwritten by the using environment.

Parameters

Parameters are used to pass data between workflows and workflow operations (Figure 6.8). At definition time, formal parameters are specified. At runtime formal parameters are instantiated with actual parameters. There are three different kinds of parameters: IN, OUT and INOUT parameters. IN parameters are read-only, OUT parameters are write-only and INOUT parameters can be read and written arbitrarily. Parameters are scoped, i.e. they are only visible in the domain (i.e. workflow type or workflow operation) they are specified for.

By connecting parameters which are attributed by IN, OUT or INOUT, data flow is determined. Furthermore, parameters can be mandatory or optional. A mandatory IN or INOUT parameter of a workflow or workflow operation has to be filled before processing can be continued. A mandatory OUT or INOUT parameter has to be filled before processing can be finished. Optional parameters might be filled but this is not mandatory. If there is no value assigned the workflow or the workflow operation can still start processing.

The start of a subworkflow does not only depend on mandatory parameters but also on control flow specifications. It might happen that all mandatory parameters are filled but the subworkflow still cannot start because control flow has not reached it yet. Within this waiting period optional parameters might be filled.

It must be possible to find out if an optional parameter has a value assigned or not. This can be checked by a special function applied to a parameter which returns a boolean value. If the function returns true, the optional parameter is filled; it returns false otherwise. This way, a subworkflow can make internal computations dependent on the existence of optional parameters. The same applies to optional OUT parameters, symmetrically. There also a special function can be applied having the same semantics.

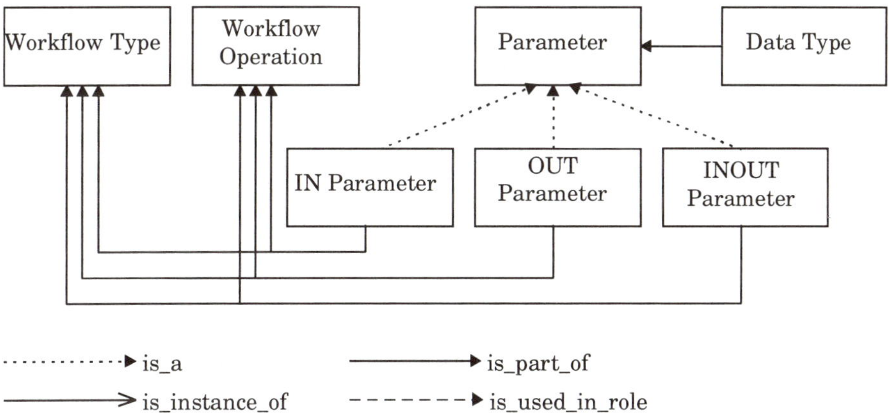

Figure 6.8: Parameters of Workflow Types and Workflow Operations

Basically a parameter might be a value parameter or a reference parameter. A value parameter contains a value of the data type. For instance, a parameter of type integer contains an integer value at runtime. In contrast, reference parameters contain pointers to values. For example, a parameter of type pointer to array contains a pointer directing to an array which is stored elsewhere.

When a superworkflow passes data to a subworkflow by the means of value parameters, the parameter value is a copy of the original data structure. This means that the subworkflow can change the value without affecting the original data structure. Reference parameters behave different. Since only pointers are shipped, manipulating the parameter also impacts the value of the parameter in the domain from which it is obtained.

Subworkflows of a workflow may run in parallel. When a pointer to a data structure is transferred to two subworkflows as an INOUT parameter each of the parallel subworkflows can change the structure independently, i.e. concurrency is possible. In order to make data access atomic, the writer of the data structure has to make sure that interference is avoided. In Tanenbaum (1987) this problem is discussed in the context of the producer/consumer problem. Synchronization of several writers to a data structure can be implemented by semaphores.

Workflow Local Variables

Since workflows are modeled as abstract data types they maintain *workflow local variables*. A workflow local variable is of a certain data type. Constraints and initializations can be specified for workflow local variables. It has to be specified how constraints defined for the data type of a workflow local variable relate to constraints defined for itself.

Workflow local variables are available within the workflow where they are specified. They are not automatically available in subworkflows. If a subworkflow needs access to the local variables of its superworkflow they have to be passed explicitly through parameters. This might involve more specification work, however, it improves reusability since no implicit scoping rules are applied.

In addition to *user defined* workflow local variables, *system defined* workflow variables are available, called *workflow context variables*. Workflow context variables contain information about a workflow. For instance, there might be a context variable "workflow type name" which contains the name of the workflow type; "workflow id" might contain the unique workflow instance identifier; and "start time" might store the time and date when the workflow started. All these variables are maintained by the workflow management system. They are managed automatically and cannot be manipulated within a workflow. Only read access is possible.

Data Flow

Data flow generally happens between parameters and workflow local variables. Data flow follows a producer/consumer (or source/sink) relationship. Sources and sinks might be both parameters as well as workflow local variables. On the one hand, data flow between a source and a sink can be direct. For instance, an OUT parameter of a subworkflow is directly connected to the IN parameter of another subworkflow. In this case the data flows directly and cannot be observed or accessed by any other subworkflow or workflow operation. On the other hand, data flow from a source to a sink can be implemented via a local variable. Other subworkflows or workflow operations can observe and access it.

In some situations the same meaning of data is represented by different data types. For instance, a Boolean value might be represented by two integers ("0" and "1") or by a data type Boolean. Since workflows are specified independently, a mismatch in data types might occur: one workflow expects a Boolean value to be represented by an integer whereas another workflow expects it to be represented by a Boolean data type. In order to resolve this problem a conversion between the integer representation and the Boolean representation is necessary. A *conversion function* converts the integer representation into the Boolean representation. Instead of flowing directly between the two subworkflows, data flow from the source subworkflow to the conversion function and from there to the sink subworkflow.

Mismatch in semantics is also possible. For instance, one subworkflow works with US Dollars whereas another workflow deals with Swiss Francs. In such a case, a conversion function is necessary to convert the money amount from one currency into the other. This involves some computation referring to an exchange rate. Since exchange rates are dynamic and change daily an external system has to be involved to get the actual exchange rate. This exchange rate is a workflow external piece of data, i.e. it is production data.

Production Data Access

As already discussed, production data are data stored and managed outside of a workflow management system. As the exchange rate example shows, access to production data may be necessary from within a workflow. Using conversion functions for production data access has some drawbacks. Conversion functions are executed in the realm of a workflow management system. If the data access operation requires interaction with a workflow user, the operation does not know how to contact him. The user resides in a workspace (cf. Chapter 9) which is not known to the conversion function. Error handling also has to be implemented by the conversion function. It is more appropriate to integrate access to external data into workflow operations (Section 6.1.1). There the issues of user interaction and error handling are tackled adequately (see Chapter 9). Application programs that access production data are integrated into workflow operations.

Figure 6.9 relates the elements of the information perspective: parameters, local variables and data flow.

6.2.2 Example

In the following the example introduced in Section 6.1.2 is extended by parameters, local variables and data flow.

```
WORKFLOW_TYPE travel-expense-reimbursemen
  (MANDATORY IN integer: trip_id)
  ENTER_CONSTRAINT approved(trip_id)
  RUNTIME_CONSTRAINT during_hours(8:15, 17:45)
  EXIT_CONSTRAINT sufficient_budget(amount)
  END_CONSTRAINTS
  ...
```

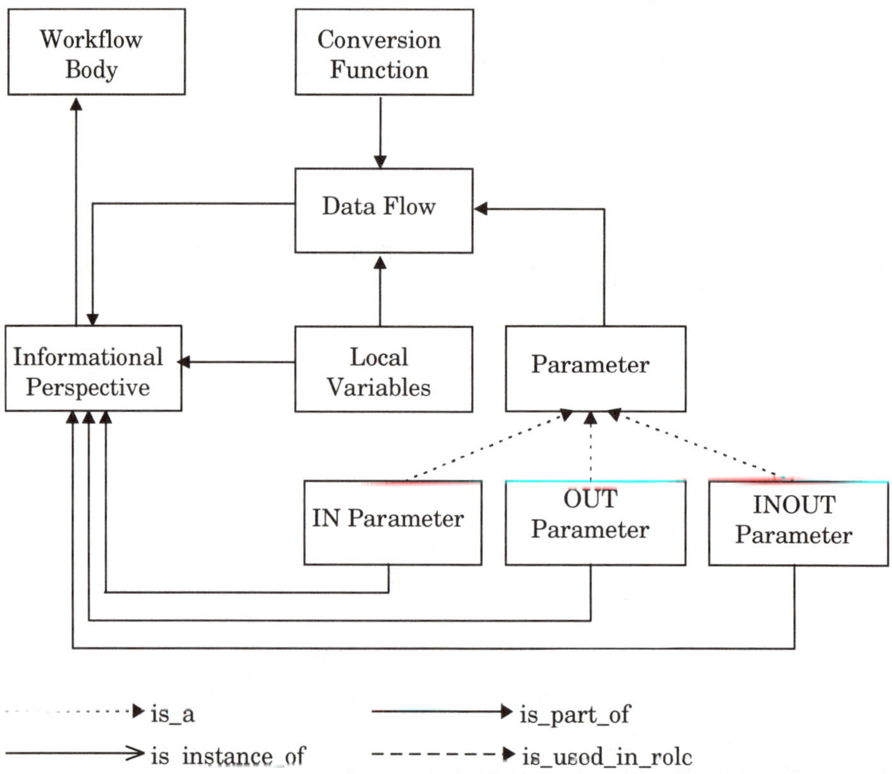

Figure 6.9: The Information Perspective of Workflows

```
WORKFLOW_DATA
  decimal: amount
    CONSTRAINTS amount > 0
    INITIALIZATION amount := -1;
  boolean: signed_1, signed_2
    INITIALIZATION signed_1 := false,
      signed_2 := false
END_WORKFLOW_DATA

DATA_FLOW
    travel-expense-reimbursement.trip_id
    → approved.trip_id;
    amount→ sign_1.amount;
    amount→ sign_2.amount;

    sign_1.result→ signed_1;
    sign_2.result→ signed_2;

    signed_1→ inform.signed_1;
    signed_2→ inform.signed_2;
    ...
    amount→ sufficient_budget.amount
  END_DATA_FLOW
  ...
END_WORKFLOW_TYPE
```

The interface specifications of the two workflow types "Sign" and "Information" are shown next:

```
WORKFLOW_TYPE Sign (IN decimal: amount;
                    OUT boolean: result)
  ...
END_WORKFLOW_TYPE

WORKFLOW_TYPE Information (
    IN POINTER TO boolean: signed_1, signed_2)
  ...
END_WORKFLOW_TYPE
```

As we will see in Section 6.3.2 the subworkflow "inform" can be executed any time. It is introduced to inform a caller about the status of the workflow, i.e. whether the form is already signed or not. The workflow type "Information" specifies a workflow operation "inform". Each time "inform" is called the actual status is queried. The local variables "signed_1" and "signed_2" are implemented as pointers such that they always point to the actual status. If they were implemented as data values they would not be updated if the status changed.

6.2.3 Example Implementation

Domino (Chapter 2) uses forms as data carriers. All data produced or received are put into forms which migrate between subworkflows. Between two subworkflows exactly one form flows. Nevertheless, a subworkflow may receive forms from several other subworkflows. However, only one form is chosen and consumed. Domino implements neither parameters nor local variables. Conversion functions are not implemented either.

FlowMark (Chapter 2) pursues a similar approach to that introduced in Section 6.2.1. A FlowMark workflow has an input data container and an output data container where the input or output parameters are stored. Data flow is direct only. Data elements of an output container are directly connected to data elements of an input container. FlowMark neither supports the distinction between mandatory and optional parameters nor the concept of INOUT parameters. Conversion functions and local variables are not supported.

6.2.4 Further Issues

Type Conversions

Production data are implemented in an own data type system which is in general different from the data type system of a workflow management system. In order to transfer production data to the local variables of a workflow special data *type conversion* has to take place. Data type conversions are implemented by functions. These functions are called before or after the production data are stored or read by an appropriate application program within a workflow operation.

Merging Results

Sometimes two parallel subworkflows produce data which have to be merged before they can be processed further. For instance, an average is to be computed out of several output data. Conversion functions can be used to implement this; all subworkflows contributing to the average deliver their result to one conversion function. As soon as all values have arrived the function computes the average and stores the result in a workflow variable.

6.3 Control Flow

A major issue of workflow management is to specify the execution order of workflows (also called *control flow*). Sometimes the execution order is not known exactly in advance; only partial orders are recognized. The example of a travel agency illustrates this observation. Hotels, flights and rental cars can be booked. However, the order of booking a hotel, a flight and a rental car differs from case to case. Sometimes only a hotel is booked, sometimes a rental car and a flight is booked. Nevertheless, the booking steps have to be finished before an invoice is printed.

From the discussion so far we can span the whole spectrum of execution order specification. At one end of the spectrum the control flow is completely specified. Every execution path which is possible is laid down in the workflow specification. At the other end of the spectrum no control flow is specified at all. No restrictions are made on the execution order of subworkflows. At runtime, the workflow users determine the sequence "on the fly". It is optimal to specify exactly those execution order dependencies which are fundamental, even if only partial ordering results.

An execution order specifies control flow dependencies between subworkflows of a workflow independent of data flow dependencies (as discussed above). At run time data flow and control flow specifications have both to be considered when the execution order of subworkflows is determined.

6.3.1 Model Elements

The behavior perspective of a workflow is specified by control flow constructs. A control flow construct determines a set of possible execution orders for workflows. Several control flow constructs can be composed into a control flow expression to specify complex behavior of workflows.

Control Flow Constructs

A standard approach is to provide a fixed set of control flow constructs. Typical control flow constructs are *sequence, parallel branching* and *conditional branching* as well as *join* to join parallel execution paths. Furthermore, constructs like *while, repeat until* and *for until* loops might be added. A combination of control flow constructs allows to express more sophisticated control flow.

The control flow constructs mentioned so far are well known from programming languages and their semantics correspond to the constructs found there. However, our experience from the deployment of workflow management systems in customer projects shows that constructs as introduced above are not sufficient to model specific application scenarios and their use is often very cumbersome.

For instance, the example of the travel agency requires to model that the booking of rental cars, hotels and flights which might happen in any order. This results in six different sequences: FHC, FCH, HCF, HFC, CFH and CHF:[1]

However, this is not exactly what the application scenario expresses. After having finished the first booking (C, H or F), the travel agency clerk has the choice to continue with either of the remaining two steps (HF or FH, CF or FC, CH or HC). Thus, these conditional branches have to be specified additionally. The interested user is asked to write down the control flow expression that results from this refinement.

A more ergonomic control flow construct to model the above scenario would be

- choice(F, H, C).

The semantics of the "choice" control flow construct can be derived easily.

At first glance, the use of the parallel branching control flow construct could be a solution for the above mentioned problem. However, by using it, all three booking steps would have to be performed; it would not be allowed to skip one, two or all of the steps.

The travel agency example can be extended. Instead of booking just one flight, one hotel and one rental car, multiple flights, hotels and rental cars might be needed.

- choice*(F, H, C)

could be a control flow construct that implements these semantics.

The above discussion reveals that powerful control flow constructs are needed for workflow modeling. However, not all control flow constructs can be anticipated – special application areas need special control flow constructs. Thus, a workflow management system should offer a standard set of control flow constructs which can be used to define more powerful, application-oriented control flow constructs. Building new control flow constructs requires that the syntactical representation is defined as well as its execution semantics. Appendix A shows how the formal syntax is defined. At this point we want to give an over-view only.

Basically every control flow construct has a name and parameters. The name should be chosen according to the meaning of the construct, e.g. *sequence*. A control flow construct might have several parameters which can be of type *workflow*. For instance,

- sequence (workflow: A, B)

needs two workflows as parameters meaning that workflow A is executed before workflow B. Parameters can also be of type *condition*, e.g. in the conditional branching control flow construct:

- conditional_branching(condition: cond; workflow: A, B)

The condition "cond" needs to be evaluated in order to decide whether workflow A or B must be performed. Although parameters mostly are of type workflow or condition, arbitrary other parameter types are allowed. For example, in a loop control flow construct, an integer parameter might delimit the number of loops.

To build a complex control flow specification, control flow constructs can be composed. For instance,

- sequence(A, parallel(B, C))

expresses that after workflow A is finished the workflows B and C must perform in parallel. Control flow constructs can replace parameters of type "workflow" since a control flow construct is of type "workflow".

Semantics Specification of Control Flow Constructs

In our approach the semantics of a control flow construct is defined by a Petri net (Jensen and Rozenberg, 1991). A Petri net is a formal representation which can be used to define dynamics. In Figure 6.10 an example Petri net illustrates how the semantics of the control flow construct "sequence" is to be defined. Circles are called *places* and lines are called *transitions*. The difference between a single-line transition and a double-line transition is explained later.

Petri nets follow the idea of producing and consuming tokens. Instead of formally defining how this is accomplished we explain this behavior with the example of Figure 6.10. Figure 6.11 depicts the execution steps of the Petri net in Figure 6.10. At first, a token is generated and is put into the first place (1). Then, the first line of the double-line transition following the place consumes the token resulting in the execution of A (2). As soon as A has finished the second line of the double-line transition produces a token which is put into the subsequent place (3). After that, the first line of the second double-line transition consumes the token resulting in the execution of B (4). After B has terminated, the second line of the double-line transition produces a token which is put into the third place (5). Finally this token is consumed by the last single-line transition. Workflows A and B have been performed sequentially.

A Petri net used to describe the semantics of a control flow construct starts and ends with a single-line transition. In between, a Petri net is constructed according to the usual rules:

- A (double-line) transition is followed by one or more places.
- Each place is followed by one or more transitions.
- One or more places can lead to a transition.

Further rules of how to construct a Petri net for our purposes are discussed later.

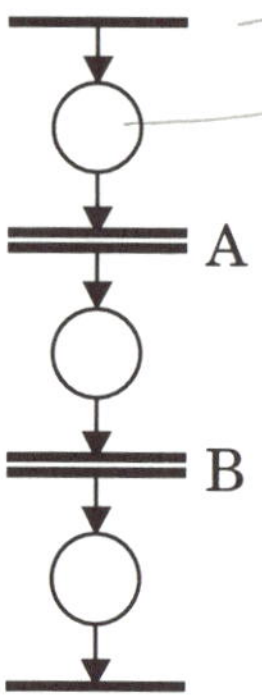

Figure 6.10: Semantics of sequence(workflow: A, B)

Double-line transitions represent place holders and have a name attached. This is the name of a formal parameter of the corresponding control flow construct (workflows A and B in the example of Figure 6.11). At runtime double-line transitions (Figure 6.12(a)) are treated according to the following rules:

- If the actual parameter of a control flow construct is an elementary workflow (e.g. workflow A) the double-line transition is replaced by a single place Petri net representing the elementary workflow (Figure 6.12(b)).
- If the actual parameter of a control flow construct is a composite workflow (e.g. sequence(workflow: A, B)) the double-line transition is replaced by the Petri net representing the control flow of the composite workflow[2] (Figure 6.12(c)).

The functionality of Petri nets described so far is not yet sufficient for serious modeling of control flow construct semantics. In the following we model examples of control flow constructs and thereby introduce additional features which are needed for modeling with Petri nets.

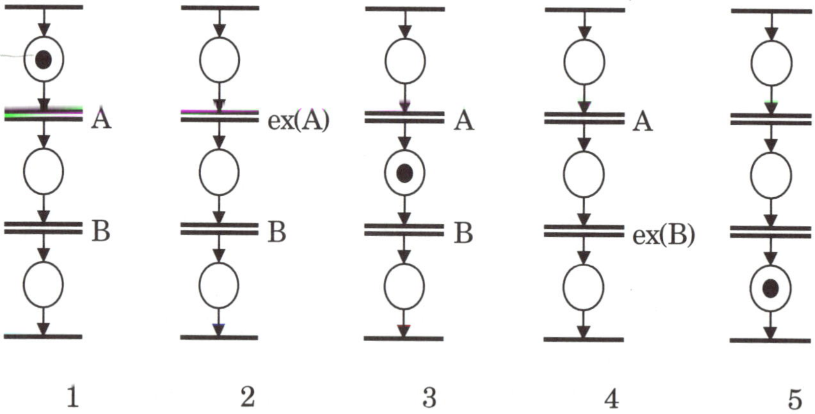

Figure 6.11: Execution of sequence(workflow: A, B)

A control flow construct for *conditional branching* references a condition (here: cond) which decides how to branch execution. The syntactical representation might be

- cond_branch(condition: cond; workflow: A, B)

meaning that if cond evaluates to true A is executed, otherwise B is performed. The symbol "¬" is used to represent the negation of a Boolean value. A Petri net specification of the execution semantics for the cond_branch() construct is shown in Figure 6.13. Conditions are attached to arcs between places and transitions. A token can flow from a place to a transition only if the condition attached is fulfilled.

Another example of a control flow construct that requires a condition is an iteration:

- loop_until_false(condition: cond; workflow: A).

Figure 6.14 shows the semantics of the iteration control flow construct. Workflow A executes as long as condition cond is true.

A control flow construct allowing to execute *n* workflows out of a set of *m* workflows requires as input an integer and a set of workflows:

- n_out_of_m(integer: n; set_of(workflow): m).

To illustrate the behavior of such a control flow construct, Figure 6.15 depicts a simpler version of the general control flow construct where

- *m := 3 (n_out_of_3 (integer: n; workflow: A, B, C)).*

An integer attached to an arc that points to a place indicates the number of tokens that are produced along this arc. For n := 2 two tokens are available which can be

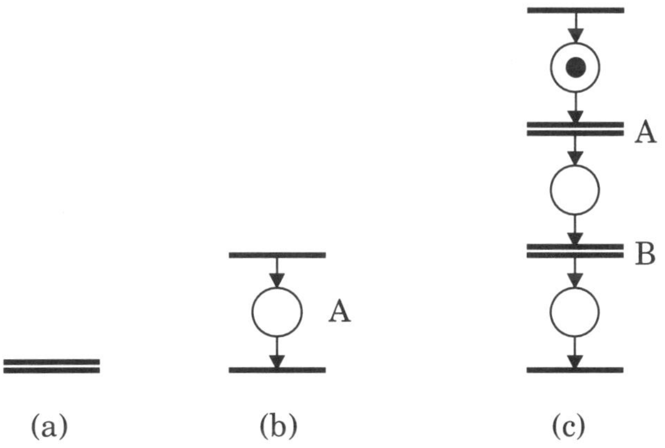

Figure 6.12: Representation of an Elementary Workflow A

consumed resulting in the execution of two subsequent workflows. In order to make sure that n workflows are executed, n tokens are collected after the workflows are executed. Only when n tokens are collected can processing continue (Figure 6.15).

The semantics of the more general construct *n_out_of_m*() is shown in Figure 6.16(a). "n" identifies the number of tokens to be produced and consumed, i.e. the number of workflows to be executed. "m" attached to a double-line transition indicates that *m* workflows have to be inserted in the set. Without specifying further semantics, the workflows are executed independently, i.e. in parallel. If they have to be executed sequentially an additional place has to be added as shown in Figure 6.16(b). When execution starts, this place contains one token and it is empty if a workflow is under execution. If the workflow is finished the place receives another token which allows to perform the next workflow.

Having the *n_out_of_m*() control flow construct in place, *parallel execution* of a set of workflows can be specified easily. Setting *m* to *n* results in the parallel execution of *m* (or *n*) workflows.

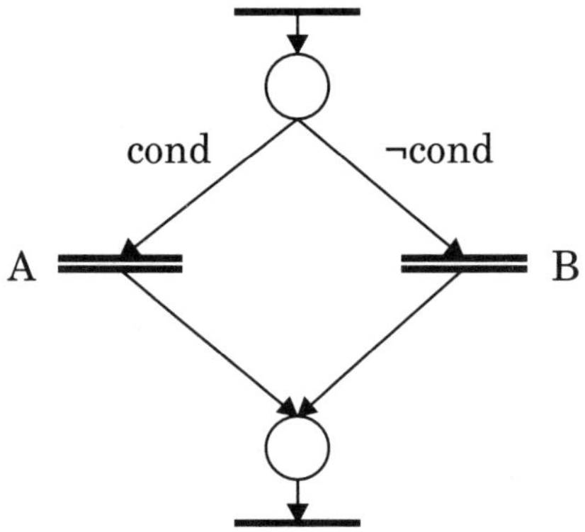

Figure 6.13: Semantics of cond_branch(condition: cond; workflow: A, B)

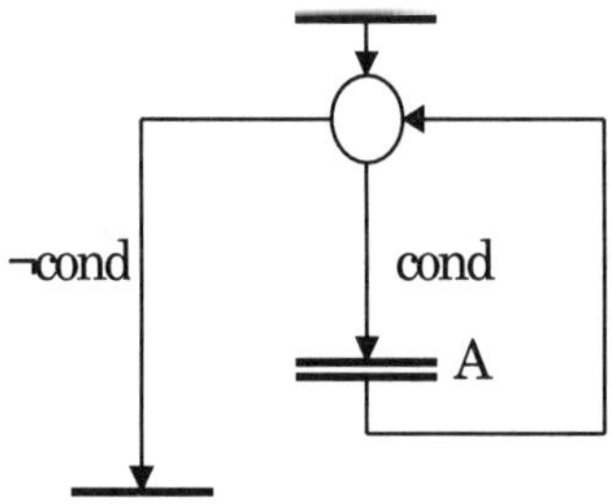

Figure 6.14: Semantics of loop_until_false (condition: cond; workflow: A)

The next example is a *deadline* control flow construct:

- deadline(workflow: W, D)

where D represents the restricting workflow, i.e. the deadline, and W the restricted workflow. Workflow *W* can be executed as long as workflow *D* has not started (Jablonski, 1994). The deadline construct does not prescribe that either workflow *W* or workflow *D* must be performed. Both workflows might be skipped. An example for the application of this construct is the travel agency example discussed before. As long as the invoice is not printed, flights, rental cars and hotels might be booked. However, if the invoice writing activity has started, further bookings are prohibited.

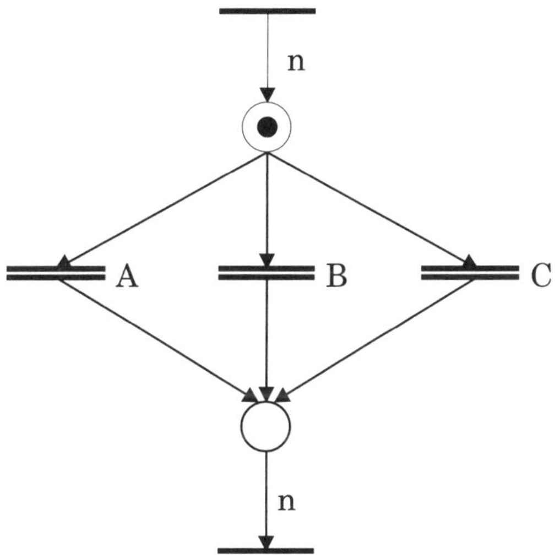

Figure 6.15: Semantics of n_out_of_3(integer: n; workflow: A, B, C)

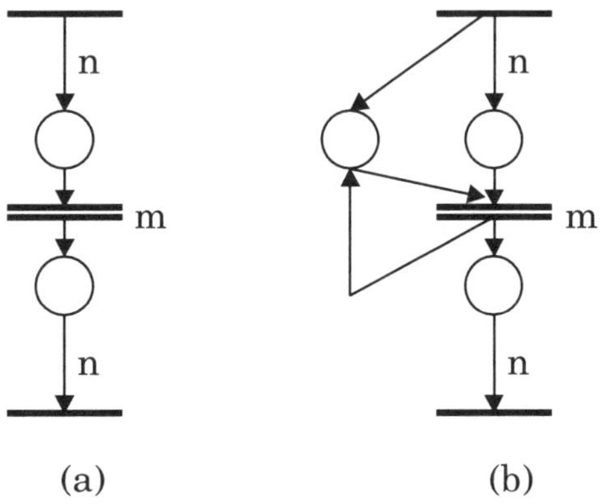

Figure 6.16: Semantics of n_out_of_m(integer: n; set_of(workflow): m)

Figure 6.17 shows the semantics of the deadline construct. At the beginning three tokens are available. In order to express that either workflow *W* or workflow *D* might be skipped a new notation is introduced. A transition labelled "¬A" represents the explicit disabling of the workflow corresponding to parameter A.

The last control flow construct to be introduced is called *repetition*. Repetition means that a workflow type is instantiated several times. The number of repetitions is specified or can be determined by the user. A good application scenario for the repetition control flow construct is damage claim processing. Within such a workflow witnesses of an accident have to be interrogated. For each witness an elementary workflow is started which collects a witness's evidence. Since the number of witnesses is not known a priori, the control flow construct must allow to instantiate as many workflows as needed.

- repetition(workflow_type: A; integer: n)

is a syntactical representation of the repetition control flow construct. Figure 6.18 shows the semantics of repetition.

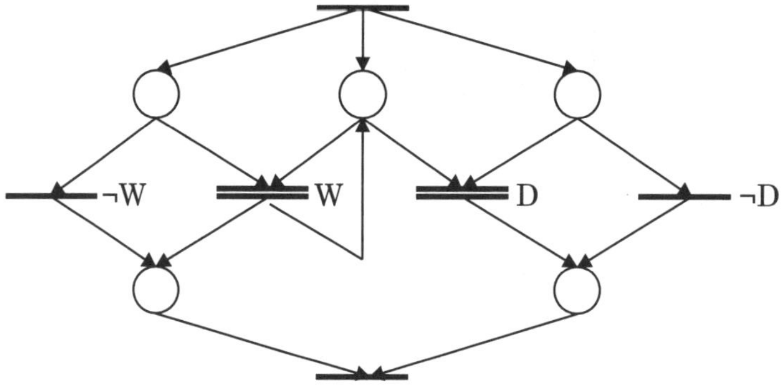

Figure 6.17: Semantics of deadline (workflow: W, D)

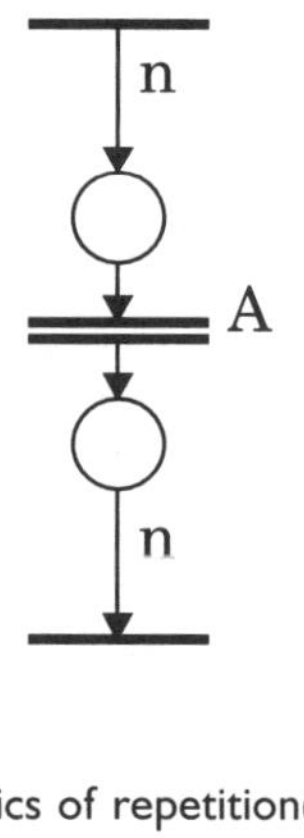

Figure 6.18: Semantics of repetition(workflow_type: A; integer: n):

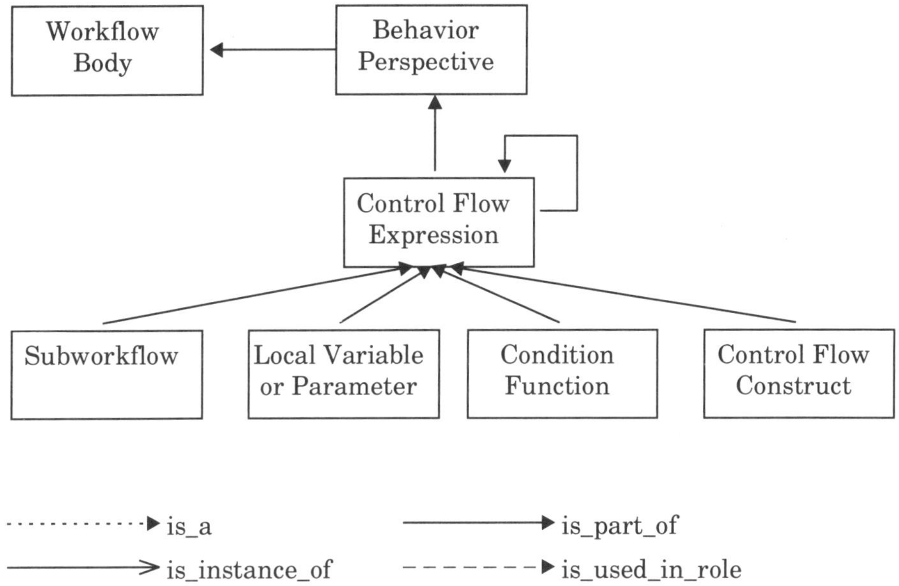

Figure 6.19: Behavior Perspective

It is important to note that Petri nets are only one possible approach to defining the semantics of control flow constructs. Therefore, we do not intend to emphasize the Petri net approach. We rather want to express that a formal way to specify the semantics of control flow constructs must be in place. This is especially important since usually new control flow constructs have to be introduced according to the requirements of the area of deployment.

Behavior Perspective

The behavior perspective defines the execution order of the subworkflows of a workflow. The behavior perspective is constituted by a control flow expression. A control flow expression is either the name of a subworkflow or a control flow construct with its formal parameters replaced by actual ones. Actual parameters are subworkflows, local workflow data, condition functions and constants (Figure 6.19). As already stated, a formal parameter of type workflow can be replaced by a control flow expression as actual parameter. For instance, *sequence(cond_branch (x<0, A, B), C)* defines that after workflow *A* or workflow *B* is executed depending on the evaluation of the condition "x<0", workflow *C* must be performed sequentially.

6.3.2 Example

The travel expense reimbursement example is extended by the specification of control flow.

```
WORKFLOW_TYPE travel-expense-reimbursement (...)
  ...
  SUBWORKFLOWS
    Fill: fill      RUNTIME_CONSTRAINT
                        within_days(2)
                    END_CONSTRAINTS;
    Sign: sign_1    RUNTIME_CONSTRAINT
                        within_week(1)
                    EXIT_CONSTRAINT
                        signed() OR refused()
                    END_CONSTRAINTS,
          sign_2    RUNTIME_CONSTRAINT
                        within_week(1)
                    EXIT_CONSTRAINT
                        signed() OR refused()
                    END_CONSTRAINTS;
    Reimburse: reimburse;
    Archive: archive;
    Information: inform
  END_SUBWORKFLOWS

  WORKFLOW_DATA
    decimal:  amount
              CONSTRAINTS amount > 0
              INITIALIZATION amount := -1;
    boolean:  signed_1, signed_2
              INITIALIZATION signed_1 := false,
                    signed_2 := false
  END_WORKFLOW_DATA

  DATA_FLOW
    travel-expense-reimbursement.trip_id
      →approved.trip_id;
    amount→ sign_1.amount;
    amount→ sign_2.amount;
    sign_1.result→ signed_1;
```

```
    sign_2.result→ signed_2;
    ...
  END_DATA_FLOW

  CONTROL_FLOW
    sequence(
    loop_until_true(
      signed(signed_1AND signed_2),
      sequence(fill, parallel (if_then(NOT
                                 signed_1,sign_1),
                                 if_then(NOT
                                 signed_2,sign_2)))),
    reimburse,
    archive)
  END_CONTROL_FLOW
  ...
END_WORKFLOW_TYPE
```

Until the claim is signed, the filling and signing takes place repeatedly. A sign workflow is only started if there is no signature yet. Thereafter reimbursement and archiving takes place. The subworkflow "inform" is not contained in the control flow specification at all, since this subworkflow runs independently from all other subworkflows. There is only a partial order between subworkflows.

To model the control flow of the travel claim reimbursement example, several control flow constructs have to be modeled:

```
CONTROL_FLOW_CONSTRUCT
  sequence (WORKFLOW: A, B, C)
    (* Petri net specification *)
END_CONTROL_FLOW_CONSTRUCT
CONTROL_FLOW_CONSTRUCT
  loop_until_true (FUNCTION: C,WORKFLOW: A)
    (* Petri net specification *)
END_CONTROL_FLOW

CONTROL_FLOW_CONSTRUCT
  if_then (FUNCTION: C,WORKFLOW: A)
    (* Petri net specification *)
END_CONTROL_FLOW
```

6.3.3 Example Implementation

WorkParty provides a fixed set of control flow constructs. This list cannot be extended.

- *Loop*. Two forms of loop are available: repeat-until and while-for.
- *Choice*. A choice references several workflows which all have to be executed.
- *Parallelism*. Workflows connected by this construct are executed in parallel.
- *Conditional Branching*. A conditional branching construct references several workflows. Each workflow has a condition attached. At run time exactly one workflow is executed. A condition function determines the workflow to be performed. If no condition evaluates to true, a special workflow, the "else" workflow, is executed.
- *Dead End*. Dead ends are used to terminate workflow execution abnormally.
- *Sequence*. A sequence can reference two of the following: an elementary workflow, a composite workflow or an arbitrary control flow construct. The sequence construct is used to model the complete control flow specification of a workflow type.

In contrast to WorkParty, FlowMark does not provide a set of control flow constructs. Instead, it provides a basic mechanism to specify arbitrary control flow. Through transition conditions, enter conditions and exit conditions many kinds of control flow can be defined. However, it is hard to prove whether the specification is semantically correct or is contradictory.

6.3.4 Further Issues

Expressiveness of Modeling Approaches

We have omitted the discussion about the expressiveness of approaches to formulate control flow semantics. Petri nets are one feasible approach. However, it has to be investigated whether other approaches are even more expressive or more user-friendly. When examining this issue, it is most significant that the specific application domain, i.e. workflow management, has to be taken into account.

Compatibility of Approaches

Another important issue is the compatibility of modeling approaches. Since different modelers prefer different modeling approaches (e.g. Petri nets, automata), user-friendliness would be enhanced if each modeler could choose his favorite model.

6.4 Workflow Application

As noted earlier, workflow operations are implemented by application programs. Application programs can be very different in nature (e.g. an executable image to be called by RPC). From a workflow management point of view the technical details of application programs should be made transparent. This section discusses *workflow applications* which provide such an abstraction. Relying on workflow applications a workflow modeler can concentrate on modeling the right functionality instead of having to deal with technical details about application program integration.

Although the focus of this chapter is workflow modeling which should happen without looking into technical details, we have to consider implementation techniques in this section. Otherwise, workflow applications could not be discussed.

6.4.1 Model Elements

In the following a model of workflow applications and their use for workflow operation implementation is introduced. After this a classification of application programs is provided to clarify their different characteristics. Finally, a wrapping mechanism is discussed which provides abstraction from implementation details.

The operation perspective defines the application programs to be used in workflow operations. However, within a workflow operation specification application programs are not referenced directly. An abstraction is used to model application invocations. It is called workflow application. A workflow application specifies the interface to an application program and hides implementation details.

Workflow Applications

Workflow applications follow the idea of separating an interface specification of a function from its implementation. A workflow application has a unique name and parameters. Also constraints might be attached to workflow applications. Their semantics is equal to the semantics of constraints for workflow types (cf. Section 6.1).

Workflow applications bear specific properties which are important for a workflow modeler. A sample property is *reliable*. If a workflow application is reliable, a system failure does not impact its execution consistence. This property should not be mixed with *transactional*. If a workflow application is transactional, its execution effects can be set back to a previous consistent state until execution is committed. Other properties are *interactive* and *batch*.

There is a 1:n relationship between workflow applications and their implementations. Each implementation is characterized by a specific set of properties. The modeler can choose whether a workflow application, i.e. a workflow operation, must show particular properties.

Figure 6.20 shows the components of a workflow application. Missing so far are the application programs implementing a workflow application. They are added later in this chapter since for the moment they are not essential.

Workflow Operations

In general, one or more workflow applications implement a workflow operation. The choice of a workflow application can be influenced by specifying properties that must be fulfilled by the workflow application.

Multiple workflow operations can be specified for a workflow type. The following example stems from the realm of travel expense reimbursement. Reimbursement might take place either by issuing a check or by transferring money. A first workflow operation *reimburse_by_check* is implemented by two workflow applications: *book_amount* and *print_check*. Another workflow operation *reimburse_by_transfer* is implemented by the workflow applications *book_amount* and *transfer_amount*. The workflow application *book_amount* is reused in both operations. The example also reveals that workflow applications within a workflow operation have to obey an execution order.

Between workflow operations and workflow application data flow takes place via their parameters. Furthermore, workflow operations maintain local variables to store intermediate results. They can also be used to implement data flow between workflow applications. As for subworkflows, conversion functions might be necessary before or after workflow applications are executed.

An example for data flow between workflow applications stems from the area of file editing. A non-transactional editor has to be made transactional. In order to accomplish this, the original file to be edited is copied to another place before editing begins ("before image"). The editor is then started. When editing is finished the original file can be overwritten with the new content or the backup copy can be restored. We assume that copying a file, removing and editing it are separate workflow applications. The locations of the files to be handled have to be supplied to the diverse workflow applications. Local variables of workflow operations are used for this purpose.

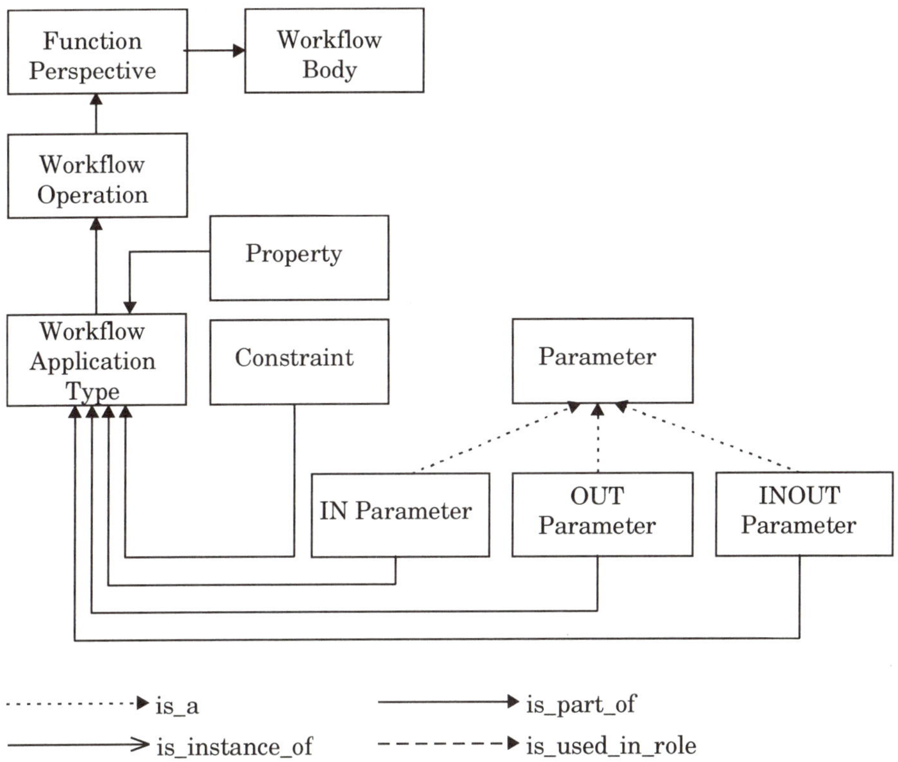

Figure 6.20: Workflow Applications and the Operation Perspective

Classification of Application Programs

Application programs comprise a wide variety of implementation techniques. Executable images, functions from a class library and operating system scripts are different implementation forms which are subsumed under the notion "application program". In general, every piece of code which is used by a workflow operation is an application program.

In order to classify application programs it is helpful to provide a catalog of criteria. They alleviate the design of useful application program wrappers. Requirements posted towards application programs can also be formulated more appropriately when a classification scheme is in place. The following criteria are fundamental:

- *Degree of Modification.* In most cases application programs are already implemented and have to be integrated into workflow management systems a posteriori – the use of application programs to implement workflow operations is not anticipated. Adjustments are often necessary to smoothly integrate application programs into workflows. Not all application programs can be adjusted easily. So-called *legacy application programs* cannot be adapted at all. *Adjustable application programs* can be tailored to the use in workflow operations. A special subclass of adjustable application programs are *workflow aware application programs*. These programs are designed with the goal to integrate them into workflow management systems. In Section 6.4.4 a discussion about the "ideal" application program takes place.

- *System Support*. There is no guarantee that all workflow operations can be supported by application programs. Sometimes, *manual tasks* are needed to implement workflow applications. Although manual tasks are performed outside a computer system, the workflow management system user has to get information about the task to execute. Also, results have to be transferred back to the workflow management system. Forms are used for this necessary interaction with the user. Data to describe the task and data that can be filled with results are provided. To manage the forms, generic application programs are required. They are called *free application programs*.
- *Granularity*. Another criteria to distinguish application programs is granularity. The smallest granularity is an elementary object or an elementary function. To perform it input and output parameters for methods and functions have to be provided. The greatest granularity is an executable image. It probably consists of several hundred functions or manages thousands of objects. In this case parameters might be provided at the invocation time of the image. However, an image might not only depend on invocation parameters but also get data from files or databases. Additionally, an image might produce side effects on files or databases. From the workflow management system point of view, it is important to know what function was executed. In the case of an elementary function this is easy to determine. However, in the case of an executable image it is difficult. In such a case, the user has to be asked to start exactly the particular function that is described in the workflow.
- *Scope*. The scope of an application program defines the set of data which it manipulates (including the data of subsequently called application programs). Two kinds of data can be distinguished: workflow management system internal data and external data. The latter belong to the application area (e.g. flight reservation data). Workflow management system internal data are data stored somewhere in the repositories of the workflow management system. Since all functions implemented by a workflow management system are regarded as application programs themselves, manipulating internal data allows to add new workflow types, to stop workflow instance executions, etc.

- *Coupling.* There are different degrees of how tight application programs are coupled to a workflow management system. At one end of the spectrum, an application program runs in its own sphere of control. If it fails the workflow management system is not impacted. A typical example of this coupling mode is an editor call. The editor runs within its own operating system process. If the editor crashes the workflow management system is not affected. At the other end of the spectrum, application programs run in the same sphere of control as the workflow management system. This means that if the application crashes the calling workflow operation is impacted. The coupling between an application program and a workflow management system is important for failure detection and failure repair. If they run within the same sphere of control failures might be detected and recovered more easily.
- *Invocation Mode.* Application programs can be called synchronously, or asynchronously, involving the usual benefits and drawbacks. When an application program is called synchronously the workflow management system has to wait for the end of the execution. Asynchronous calls allow to perform other requests meanwhile. However, the management of asynchronous calls is more complicated. Either a polling mechanism or a callback function must be provided in order to receive the results of application program execution.
- *Interaction Mode. Interactive application programs* are distinguished from *batch application programs.* The former class of application programs requires user interaction. A further distinction can be made: some application programs only need user input at program start, other application programs require user interaction continuously.

The application program criteria are used to characterize the properties of application program wrappers. Before discussing wrappers some further issues are discussed which are relevant in the context of application programs, namely actions, parameters, execution location and settings.

Sometimes it is important that a user can interrupt the execution of an application program; later on it might be resumed. If the user recognizes that the application program does not deliver expected results, it may even be aborted. These and similar operations on running application programs are called *actions.* An action is an operation that influences the execution of an application program. If actions are not provided by the application programs, the workflow management system should implement them. Actions greatly enhance the usability of application programs.

Parameters consumed and produced by application programs have to be exchanged with the calling workflow operation. In the best case, application programs can handle parameters as in function calls. For other application programs, e.g. legacy application programs, parameters have to be provided manually by the users. Another kind of application program expects parameters to be in a certain location. For instance, parameters are read from and written to a file.

When a user invokes an application program, the computer node the user is residing on must provide the infrastructure required by the application program. If an application program cannot be started at the user's node either the user cannot perform the task or some proxy mechanism makes the application program available at a remote site. This in turn might have severe consequences. If an interactive application program is run remotely the user interface output has to be redirected to the user's desktop.

When an application program is run, the environment variables on that computer node must be set correctly. This can happen shortly before the application is invoked. At the same time the system management effort is kept low. An example environment is the variable that specifies the user's input and output file. This variable is especially used by interactive application programs.

The above discussion reveals the complexity of application program integration. The applicability and usefulness of a workflow management system depends heavily on its ability to integrate application programs. So an expressive mechanism is required to integrate applications with different criteria.

In the following we discuss application wrapping techniques which can be the interface between a workflow management system and an application program.

Application Program Wrapping Techniques

An application program wrapper is a piece of code integrating an application program into a workflow operation. Since a wrapper is the glue between an application program and workflow operations, it exhibits two interfaces. One interface allows the integration of application programs. All communication with application programs is implemented here. This interface is different for every type of application invocation method like RPC, CORBA, operating system call, etc.

The second interface provided by the wrapper connects an application program and workflow operations, i.e. it builds the interface to a workflow management system. This interface is equal for all wrappers since they abstract from the specific implementation details of application programs.

In the following we concentrate on two wrappers which we introduce in detail in order to convey the complexity of application program wrappers. The first wrapper implements the invocation of application programs on a UNIX operating system level. The second implements the invocation of CORBA based application programs. We have chosen these wrappers since they allow to integrate a broad spectrum of application programs into a workflow management system.

In the following we assume the following characteristics of application programs which are wrapped by the so-called *operating system call wrapper*. The application programs to be called are autonomous images and run in their own operating system process in case they are started at a remote site. They are based on X-Windows. Parameters are supplied directly at the time of invocation. Results are expected in a file whose location is determined by an input parameter.

The basic idea is to start a (remote) shell which executes the application program. When the shell is started a string is passed that contains all commands to be executed. The environment variable "DISPLAY" is set by the string, indicating the node where the user works. The application program name is appended to the string specifying the call. Additionally, all parameters as declared in the corresponding workflow application are appended as well as the file name (path) where the result is taken from. In order to extract the result from the specified file another application program call (an application program extracting data from files) which is started after the first application program terminates, is added to the string. Parameters to the second application program specify for which values the application program should look for in the file.

Before *CORBA call wrappers* are presented, a short overview on CORBA must be provided. CORBA follows the idea of client/server computing and the idea of object-oriented programming. CORBA clients have an object-oriented view of the world, distinguishing objects and methods on objects. When a client calls a method on an object it supplies parameters (in CORBA format); CORBA then looks for an appropriate server which can execute the specified method on the specified object.

A CORBA call wrapper has to establish communication with a CORBA server on the local node. Also, it has to transform parameters into the CORBA proprietary format. After an operation is called, the wrapper – acting as a CORBA client – waits for the results. Results have to be transformed back into the representation of the client. Finally, the wrapper has to disconnect from the CORBA server.

CORBA implementations vary with respect to their functionality. Some CORBA implementations allow dynamic binding. This means that if new methods are added to a CORBA server, CORBA clients accessing the server do not have to be recompiled and rebound. CORBA implementations that only support static binding require recompilation whenever a method in the server is modified. From the viewpoint of wrapper design, dynamic binding is more convenient since the same wrapper can be used for a great number of method invocations.

The discussion of the two example wrappers shows that wrapper implementations differ significantly from each other. Being able to abstract from all the internals of a wrapper increases productivity in the context of workflow management systems significantly.

In the following a working subset of the information to be passed to a wrapper is discussed. Not all information is mandatory.

- *Parameters.* The parameters as defined within the workflow application have to be delivered. The designer of the workflow application has to make sure that all required parameters are contained in the workflow application interface.
- *Interaction Mode.* An interaction mode is necessary to indicate that user interaction is needed. Among other things, user interaction requires to set specific environment variables (see above).
- *Coupling.* It has to be specified whether the application program has to execute within the sphere of control of the workflow management system.
- *Invocation Mode.* For the end user there is no difference if the application is called synchronously or asynchronously. However, the workflow management system needs this information in order to work efficiently.
- *Settings.* When settings are different for each application program invocation they have to be specified as parameters. Some settings can only be determined at runtime (e.g. the node name where a user is logged in). If settings are static for an application program, i.e. they have to be set whenever it is invoked, they might be specified in a wrapper instead of passing them as parameters.

Information also flows back from the wrapper to the workflow management system. Some information is provided at the workflow management system user interface:

- *Actions.* As soon as it is clear which coupling mode is chosen and which application program runs the set of actions is returned. This can be made available to a user to influence program execution.
- *Interaction Mode, Coupling, Invocation Mode, Execution Location.* This information is given back as status information. It is relevant to the workflow management system for status reporting.
- *Error Code.* An error code indicates the status of execution. Before execution starts, the error code shows if the parameters are set correctly. As soon as the application program is finished the error code indicates success or failure.

Further application program invocation mechanisms which are not discussed in more detail are shown in Figure 6.21. The figure is by no means complete and only shows some selected invocation mechanisms as well as systems that implement them.

Operation Perspective

A workflow application is implemented by a set of application programs. In order to specify which application program implements which workflow application a relationship between them has to be defined.

Application program instances and application program types have to be distinguished. An application program instance is an occurrence of an application program type on a certain computer node or within a certain server. For instance, the *emacs* editor (application program type) is installed at different nodes (application program instances). An application program type is bound to a certain application invocation mechanism like CORBA or RPC.

Application program types have properties. Each application program instance has also to show these properties. All application program types which implement the same functionality are grouped together as workflow applications. A workflow application therefore represents a functionality independent of its implementation. For instance, besides the *emacs* editor there might be another editor *vi*. Both implement the functionality "editor" and belong therefore to a workflow application *editing*.

The properties of application program types are forwarded to a workflow application. If all application program types support a property the workflow

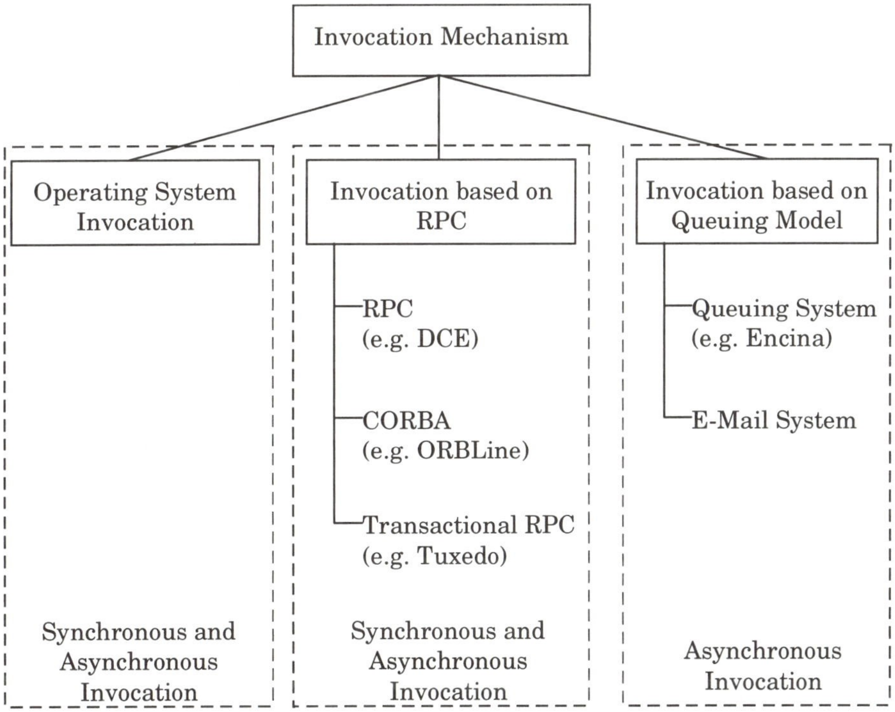

Figure 6.21: Application Program Invocation Mechanisms

application gets it attached also. If only some application program types support a certain property this gets attached to the workflow application with the additional predicate *possibly*. This information is valuable for a workflow modeler to select adequate application programs to implement workflow operations.

Workflow applications often belong to some application area (e.g. accounting, manufacturing). Therefore workflow application groups are introduced to structure workflow applications.

Figure 6.22 must be regarded as an extension of Figure 6.20. It additionally includes application program types and instances as well as workflow application groups.

When a workflow application has to be executed, adequate and appropriate application programs have to be selected. The selection proceeds through several steps:

- All program types implementing the workflow application are examined with respect to their properties. If an application program type does not have the properties specified in the workflow operation, it is dropped. All remaining application program types are candidates for further selection. If no application program types can be found, an error code is returned.
- For the further selection, the location where the application program should be executed is determined. Also, the node where the user interface has to be provided is resolved. All application program instances are then selected which can run on the suggested nodes. If no application program instances can be found, an error code is returned.
- All qualifying application program instances are potential candidates. Based on selection criteria (e.g. workload) an appropriate application program instance is chosen.

The above selection process might be fully automated. Then the user does not have any choice to influence it. Alternatively, all choices must be made by the users. However, a solution which lies between these two extreme alternatives should be most adequate.

6.4.2 Example

The "book_amount" example illustrates how parameters of a workflow application are specified.

```
WORKFLOW_APPLICATION_TYPE book_amount
  (IN decimal: amount;
```

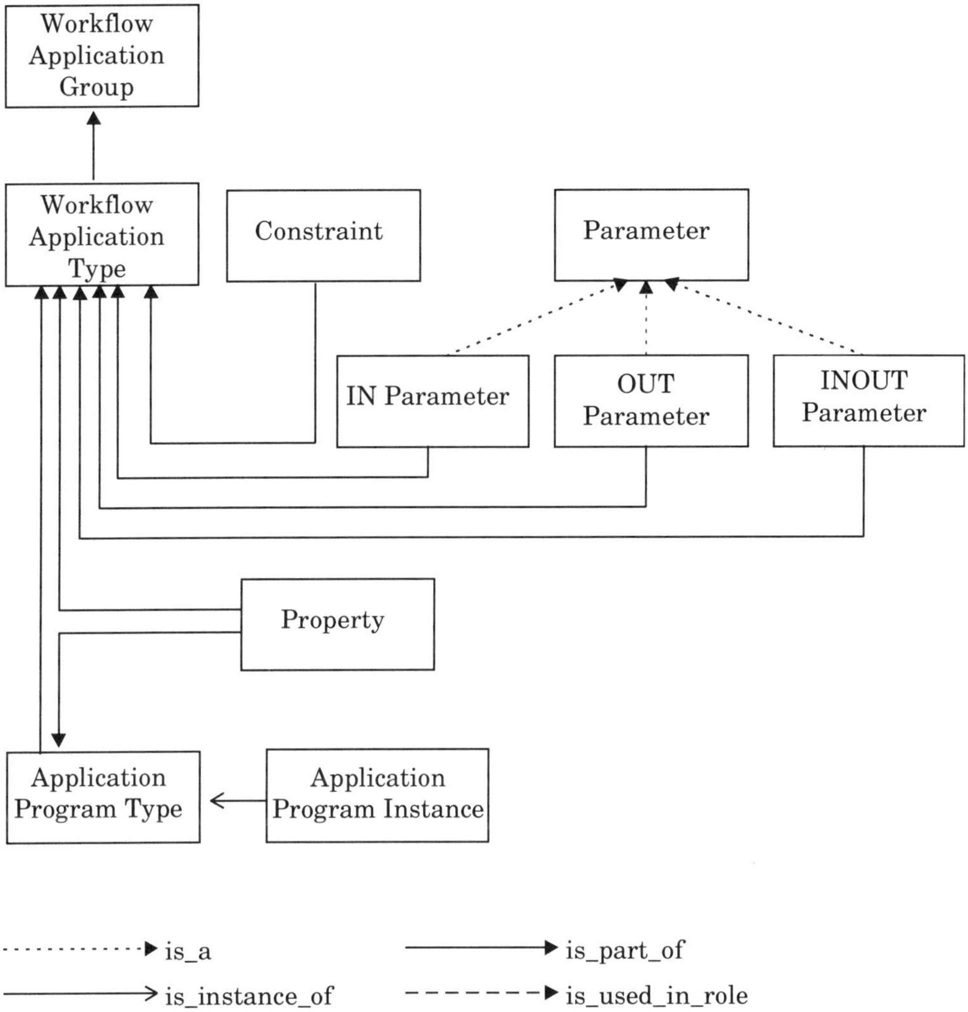

Figure 6.22: Complete Definition of Workflow Application

```
    INinteger:from_account_number,
              to_account_number)
   PROPERTIES
     POSSIBLY XOPEN_compliant, reliable,
     transactional, batch
   END_PROPERTIES
 END_WORKFLOW_APPLICATION_TYPE
```

As an example, the "reimburse_amount" workflow operation is specified next. Two workflow applications *book_amount* and *transfer_amount* are needed.

```
WORKFLOW_APPLICATION_TYPEtransfer_amount
  (IN decimal: amount;
   INinteger: from_banking_account_number,
              to_banking_account_number;
  IN string: from_bank, to_bank)
  PROPERTIES
        reliable, transactional, batch
  END_PROPERTIES
END_WORKFLOW_APPLICATION_TYPE

I_OPERATIONreimburse_amount
  (INdecimal: amount;
   IN integer: from_booking_account_number,
        to_booking_account_number,
        from_banking_account,
        to_banking_account;
   IN string: companys_bank, employees_bank)

  book_amount(amount,
        from_booking_account_number,
        to_booking_account_number);
  transfer_amount(amount,
        from_banking_account_number,
        to_banking_account_number,
        companys_bank,
        employees_bank);
END_OPERATION
```

6.4.3 Example Implementation

The workflow management system COSA (cf. Chapter 2) provides only operating system based invocation. This means that an RPC is not supported at all. However, there is a way to implement an RPC indirectly. Instead of calling a function directly by RPC a program can be started which does the calling instead. Using this kind of indirection every invocation mechanism can be used which is supported on the node the COSA system runs.

COSA asks the workflow modeler to specify where application programs are executed. Application programs can either execute on the node the COSA server runs or on the node where the invoking user works.

FlowMark (cf. Chapter 2) supports three execution environments for application programs: OS/2, AIX and Windows. For each of these environments not only the application program name is specified but also environment specific settings. The specification of application program invocations is done using the workflow modeling script language of FlowMark. FlowMark does not support a direct CORBA or RPC call.

6.4.4 Further Issues

Ideal Application Program

Having mentioned the problems of integrating application programs into workflow applications, the question arises, what an "ideal" application program should look like. Such an application program is so flexible that it can be adjusted to all possible uses. The most important feature of an ideal application program is that its properties can be switched on or off. In this case a workflow management system can configure the application program according to its needs.

Groupware Applications

Workflow management systems intend to support asynchronous cooperation, whereby groupware systems (e.g. conferencing systems) support synchronous cooperation among a group of people (Ellis *et al.* (1991); Greif (1988)). We want to distinguish between these two kinds of applications and disapprove attempts to mix them together such that a workflow management system should implement them both. A workflow management system is not a panacea for every type of communication problem.

Groupware applications and workflow management can be integrated nicely. A groupware application is a special workflow application that is called by the workflow management system. Parameters needed to conduct a groupware conference can ideally be provided by the workflow management system. For example, people who should participate are delivered by the organization perspective of workflow management, documents that should be shared are delivered by the information perspective, etc.

6.5 Organization

The four perspectives of the workflow model introduced so far are concerned with the description of the work itself. They are used to model *what* has to be done (function perspective), *when* workflows have to be executed (behavior perspective), *which data* are processed (information perspective) and *how* tasks are accomplished (operation perspective).

However, so far it is not possible to model *who* is responsible for carrying out tasks modeled by a workflow.[3] The organization perspective discussed in this section provides modeling elements which allow to specify which user (in general: *agent*, since users might also be of non-human nature like machines or software services) is responsible for carrying out tasks (defined by workflow operations).

Most workflow management systems in Chapter 2 provide modeling elements to describe an organization as well as assignment strategies to specify which user is responsible for executing which workflow. However, all these workflow management systems prescribe a fixed set of modeling elements for organization definition. This approach is sufficient as long as the provided modeling elements resemble the semantics required in an area of deployment. However, as soon as the semantics have to be changed or new modeling elements have to be added these systems will fail.

We criticize the inflexibility of the workflow management systems in this respect and present an example which motivates a more flexible approach to model organizations. One of the workflow management systems provides a modeling element "group". A group has members and a manager. The manager of the group is a user who might belong to the group. Members of a group are users. Furthermore, groups can be members of other groups (sub-groups). For example, the shipment group consists of human members and a sub-group for air-freight shipment. If a workflow is assigned to a group the workflow management system assigns the workflow automatically to the members of the group. Also the workflow is assigned to the members of its sub-groups. However, to specify that a workflow is to be assigned to members of a group without assigning it automatically to its sub-groups is impossible.

The above example reveals one scenario where predefined semantics causes problems. Because of this in our approach neither predefined modeling elements nor predefined assignment rules of tasks to agents are provided. In contrast, a set of modeling elements is provided which allow to configure the organization structure, i.e. to define which modeling elements like role, group, user, etc. should be available. Assignment strategies are also not fixed. A modeler can specify assignment strategies arbitrarily as needed. This enables a workflow modeler to specify the organization structure as well as the assignment strategies according to the requirements of the specific deployment area.

6.5.1 Model Elements

Basic Constructs

An organization model in the context of workflow management consists of an organization structure and an organization population. The organization structure defines organizational objects like "user", "role" and "group" as well as organizational relationships like "supervises" and "is a member of". Neither organizational objects nor organizational relationships are predefined, both can be specified as required. The organization population instantiates the organization structure by specifying, for example, users as well as the roles they play and the groups they belong to.

Workflows ready to be processed are assigned to users by notification. Notification makes sure that a user is aware of tasks assigned to him. If several notification techniques like e-mail or worklists are available it can be specified which one is to be used.

Normally, more than one user is eligible to execute a task. However, often only one of the eligible users should actually carry it out. If one user starts to perform a task the other users have to be prevented from doing it also. The requirement that only one out of probably many users may perform a task is specified by a synchronization rule (here: the "1-out-of-many" rule). A "*-out-of-many" rule says that every eligible user can carry out the task. Although in all workflow management systems discussed in Chapter 2 only the 1-out-of-many rule can be found this is not sufficient to model comprehensive application scenarios.

Since not everybody is eligible to execute all workflows, rules have to be in place defining which users are eligible to execute a specific type of workflow. These rules are called task assignment strategies or organizational policies. For example, an organizational policy says that a travel claim has to be signed by a user playing the role "manager".

Components

Organization

The description of an organization in the context of workflow management consists of two parts: an *organization structure* and an *organization population*. The organization structure defines all object types necessary to describe the various elements of an organization. The population of an organization structure defines the individual entities of an organization. It comprises users (described by their names and attributes), roles (like manager and clerk), groups, departments, etc.

Organization Structure

Basically an organization structure is built from *organizational objects* and *organizational relationships*. Organizational objects are entities like role, user, group, department and task force. Organizational objects can be further divided into *agents* and *non-agents*. Agents are objects which can perform tasks. Humans are agents since they perform tasks at their workstations. Machines are agents which use tools to perform a task like drilling a hole. Software services are agents since they perform computations or data operations like computing an interest rate.

Automatic task execution is important. Sometimes tasks can be performed fully automatically. No human intervention is needed at all, neither to start the application nor to finish the task after the application finishes. Often this is subsumed under the operation perspective in the way that a workflow management systems starts an application program itself without assigning it to some agent. In contrast, we do not want to treat the automatic execution as an exceptional case but we want to use the provided modeling objects. For automatic execution *automatic agents* are introduced. From a workflow management system point of view automatic agents behave like other agents: they get tasks assigned which have to be executed. An example of an automatic agent is a software service which runs as a server. Servers query a list of assigned tasks from time to time. As soon as a task is assigned it is executed. The workflow management system itself is not involved in the execution at all.

Non-agents are objects which cannot perform a task by themselves. They structure agents or other non-agents according to some property. An example of a non-agent is a role type. A role groups agents like humans according to their ability to fulfill an organizational function (e.g. clerk, manager). A group is also a non-agent which groups agents like humans according to a membership. For example, all users belonging to a shipment group are members of that group. A group might have another group as a member (sub-group). This is an example that non-agents might group other non-agents. Grouping is based on organizational relationships which are discussed next.

Organizational relationships relate organizational objects. Relations might exist between agents like a supervision relationship, between non-agents like a subordination relationship (a group being a sub-group of another) and between non-agents and agents like a membership relationship. Another important relationship is a substitution relationship between users. This defines which user substitutes for another one if the former is not available (e.g. because he is on a business trip).

Both, organizational objects as well as organizational relationships might have attributes. For example, a human user might be further characterized by his name, telephone number, salary and level of signature. A group might have attributes containing its name, the number of members and its area of expertise. A membership relation might have an attribute associated which contains the start date of the membership.

Organization Population

Before tasks can be assigned to agents the society of agents in which workflows are processed has to be specified. The society of agents, also called the organization population, contains all agents which can have tasks assigned for execution. Furthermore, it describes the relationships between individual agents (e.g. which human user belongs to which group, which machine belongs to which cell, which software service is concerned about flight reservation processing).

All individual entities of an organization population are of a type defined in the organization structure. So "Jim Button" might be of type user and "manager" might be of type role.

Figure 6.23 shows all components discussed so far. Furthermore, an example is added. An agent "Human User" is modeled together with an instance "Jim Button". A non-agent "Group" with an instance "Sales" is shown and an organizational relationship "Belongs to" together with an instance "belongs to". All the instances are part of the organization population.

Notification

As soon as a workflow is ready to be executed and as soon as the agents who are selected to execute the workflow are determined they are notified about the work to do. There are several ways to notify agents about assigned workflows. E-mail is one feasible approach. All information necessary to carry out a task is included in an e-mail message. As soon as an agent selects the task and has carried it out the result is sent back to the workflow management system in another e-mail. Another way to implement notification is to use a customized tool which is provided by a workflow management system. In most cases, this tool is called a worklist. Each agent has a personal worklist which contains all tasks which are assigned to him (see Chapter 13). An agent selects workflow operations belonging to a task in order to execute the workflow. Results are automatically delivered to the workflow management system.

Synchronization

If exactly one agent is assigned to execute a task no problems can arise with concurrency. Often, more than one user is eligible to execute a task. All users are notified about the task, i.e. all have the task available within their worklists. For example, if a purchase order comes in one sales clerk has to take care of it. However, all sales clerks are notified about the task in order to guarantee that it is worked on as fast as possible. As soon as one clerk starts to work on the task the others clerks should not be able to work on it any more. Such a behavior is specified by *synchronization rules*. A typical synchronisation rule is a 1-out-of-many rule.

In principle, a synchronization rule specifies a subset of all assigned users who might execute a workflow. At run time this rule implicitly determines the availability of workflows to users.

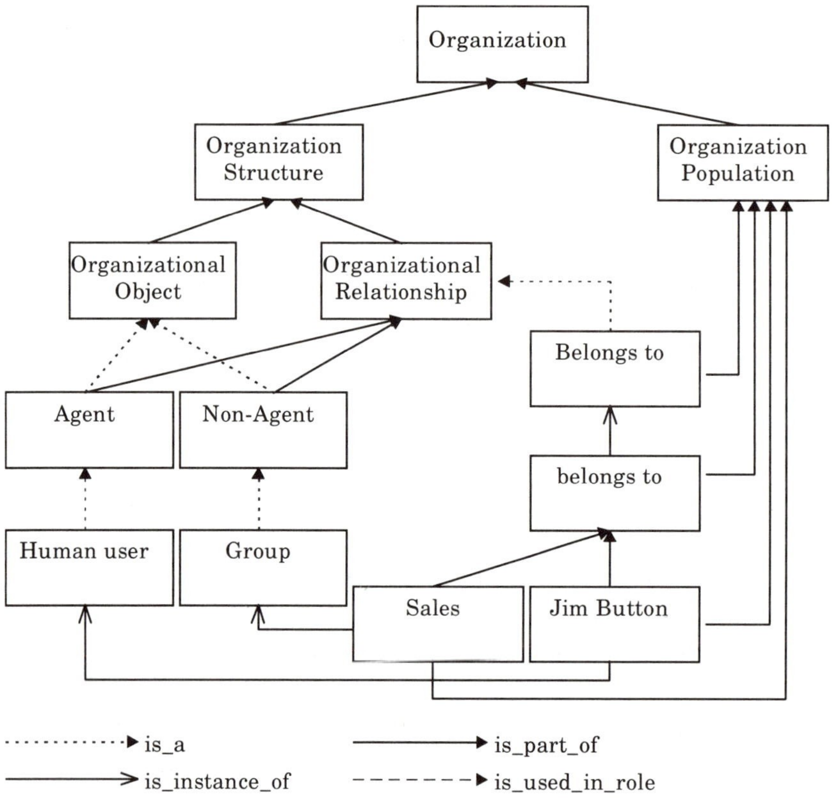

Figure 6.23: Components of an Organization Structure

Organizational Policies

As discussed in Chapter 6.1 a workflow offers multiple workflow operations. A user can execute a subset of the operations of a workflow (sometimes a user can even execute all supported workflow operations). In the following an example is discussed which shows that different users might be able to execute different workflow operations of the same workflow.

An applicant submitting a travel expense reimbursement workflow would like to know about the execution status of his submission, i.e. about the progress of the travel expense reimbursement workflow. The easiest way for him is to call a "inform" workflow operation. However, he is not allowed to invoke the workflow operation "sign" which is also available. At the same time his manager is allowed to invoke the "sign" workflow operation (as well as the "inform" workflow operation).

The example shows that the unit of assignment to users is not a workflow as a whole but workflow operations. In general, different workflow operations of the same workflow instance have to be assigned to different users.

Consequently each workflow operation is synchronized by an individual synchronization rule. The above example illustrates this feature. Not only an applicant can inform himself about the status of the reimbursement process but also other users (e.g. his manager) can. So the "inform" workflow operation is synchronized by a *-out-of-many synchronization rule. In contrast, the "sign" operation is synchronized by a "1-out-of-many" synchronization rule since only one responsible manager must sign (in case there is more than one manager available).

In principle the notification of users about workflow operations to execute can be implemented differently for different operations. The "inform" workflow operation might be sent around by e-mail whereas the "sign" workflow operation is assigned by worklist notification.

There is still one component missing before organizational policy can be defined. *Agent selection predicates* select agents from the organization population based on selection criteria. For example, an agent selection collects all users able to play a specific role. Another agent selection determines all members of a group except its manager.

Agent selection predicates might depend on workflow data. For example, a manager can only sign a travel expense reimbursement workflow if the amount is less than $5000. If the amount is greater a vice-president has to sign it. Workflow data are passed to agent selection predicates through parameters.

Agent selection predicates can be very complex (see Bussler and Jablonski (1995)). For example, if a manager is on vacation, a substituting agent has to sign all travel reimbursement claims of people working in the manager's group. However, if the substituting agent would have to sign his own travel reimbursement claim a second substitute must be found.

The right selection of agents might also depend on the history of workflow execution. An example sheds some light into this problem. To approve a travel reimbursement claim, an arbitrary manager cannot sign but the manager of the employee who was traveling has to sign. The name of the applicant who has posted the travel reimbursement claim can be selected from the workflow history.

Another example where history data are needed in agent selection predicates is the "separation of duty" principle. According to this principle, specific tasks have to be accomplished by different users. When users are selected for such a workflow, the users who have performed the other tasks must explicitly be excluded. The names of these users can be found in the workflow history.

Figure 6.24 shows all components constituting an organizational policy. Organizational policies are the major component of the organization perspective of a workflow type. Basically for each workflow operation of a workflow an organizational policy is defined specifying eligible agents.

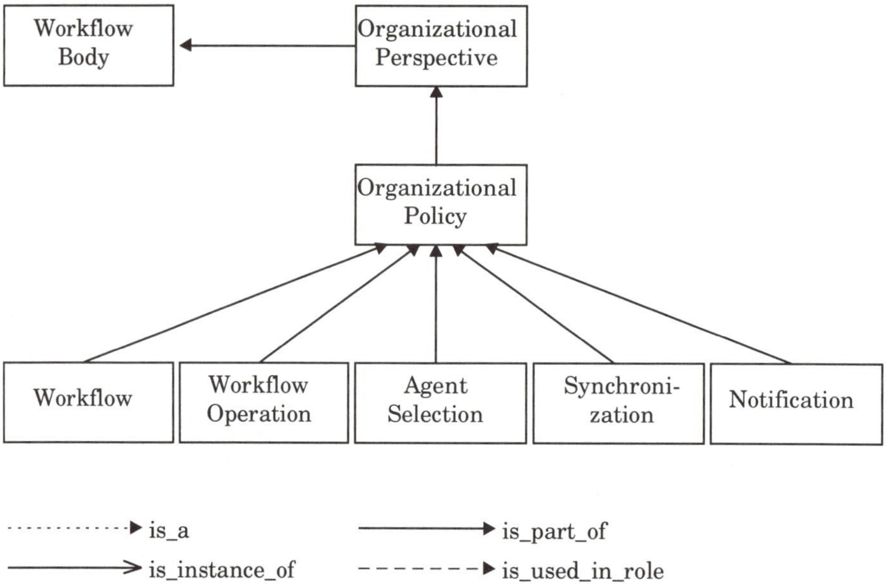

Figure 6.24: The Organization Perspective of a Workflow Type

6.5.2 Example

An example organization type is a hierarchical organization. Basically users belong to a department and play certain roles. A supervision relationship relates users to each other forming a hierarchy.

```
ORGANIZATION_TYPE hierarchical_organization

  ORGANIZATIONAL_OBJECT_TYPES
    AGENTS
      user   ATTRIBUTES string: last_name,
             first_name, tel_#; decimal: room_#
             END_ATTRIBUTES;
    NON-AGENTS
      departmentATTRIBUTES string: name;
                     duties: duties;
                     integer: #_members
                   END_ATTRIBUTES;
      role   ATTRIBUTES string: name;
                     duties: duties;
                     integer: acutal_#_role_players
             END_ATTRIBUTES
  END_ORGANIZATIONAL_OBJECT_TYPES
```

```
    ORGANIZATIONAL_RELATIONSHIP_TYPES
        belongs_toATTRIBUTES string: last_name,
                      first_name, department_name
                  END_ATTRIBUTES
        plays_roleATTRIBUTES string: last_name,
                      first_name, role_name
                  END_ATTRIBUTES
        supervisesATTRIBUTES string:
                      supervisor_last_name,
                      supervisor_first_name,
                      last_name, first_name
                  END_ATTRIBUTES
        manager_ofATTRIBUTES string:
                      manager_last_name,
                      manager_first_name,
                      department_name
                  END_ATTRIBUTES
    END_ORGANIZATIONAL_RELATIONSHIP_TYPES

  END_ORGANIZATION_TYPE
```

A sample organization instance is the Weber company. It is a hierarchically structured company with employees, departments and managers of departments:

```
  ORGANIZATION hierarchical_organization:
  weber_company;
    ORGANIZATIONAL_OBJECTS
      user: "Button", "Jim", "+49 9131 857884",8.153;
      user: "Sera", "Al", "+1 510 791 3381", 127;
      role: "manager", {"supervision", "sign
                        authority"}, 5;
      department: "sales", {"general_sales"}, 3
    ORGANIZATIONAL_RELATIONSHIPS
      belongs_to: "Button", "Jim", "sales";
      belongs_to: "Sera", "Al", "sales";
      plays_role: "Sera", "Al", "manager";
      supervises: "Sera", "Al", "Button", "Jim"
  END_ORGANIZATION
```

In the following we model an organizational policy for the sign subworkflow of the travel expense reimbursement workflow: if the amount to sign is less than 5000 the manager of the applicant signs, otherwise the manager of the department has to sign. The history access is implemented by a function which takes as input a workflow and a workflow operation and returns who executed the operation. Data access is implemented by a function which takes a workflow and the name of the local variable.

```
FUNCTION history (IN WORKFLOW: a_workflow;
                  IN operation: an_operation)
  ...
  returns (string, string) (*last_name, first_name*);

FUNCTION data (IN WORKFLOW: a_workflow;
               IN string: variable_name)
  ...
  returns object (* value *);

AGENT_SELECTION signing_manager (IN integer:amount;
                                 IN string: last_name,
first_name)
  if amount < 5000
  then  select  supervises.supervisor_last_name,
                supervises.supervisor_first_name
        from    user, plays_role, supervises
        where   supervises.last_name = last_name
                and supervises.first_name = first_name
                and supervises.supervisor_last_name =
                                plays_role.last_name
                and supervises.supervisor_first_name =
                                plays_role.first_name
                and plays_role.name = "manager"
  else  select  manager_of.manager_last_name,
                manager_of.manager_first_name
        from    manager_of, belongs_to
        where   manager_of.department_name =
                              belongs_to.department_name
                and belongs_to.last_name = last_name
                and belongs_to.first_name = first_name
END_AGENT_SELECTION

ORGANIZATIONAL_POLICY
  WORKFLOW_TYPE travel_expense_reimbursement
  WORKFLOW_I_OPERATION sign
```

```
    AGENT_SELECTION signing_manager(
            data(travel_expense_reimbursement, "amount"),
            history(fill, fill))
    SYNCHRONIZATION 1
    NOTIFICATION worklist
  END_ORGANIZATIONAL_POLICY
```

Last but not least, organizational policies must be declared. An extended version of the travel expense reimbursement example is presented below.

```
WORKFLOW_TYPE travel-expense-reimbursement (...)
  ...
SUBWORKFLOWS
  Fill: fill   RUNTIME_CONSTRAINT
               within_days(2)
               END_CONSTRAINTS;
  Sign: sign_1  RUNTIME_CONSTRAINT
                  within_week(1)
                EXIT_CONSTRAINT
                  signed() OR refused()
                END_CONSTRAINTS
                ORGANIZATIONAL_POLICIES
                  ORGANIZATIONAL_POLICY
                    WORKFLOW_TYPE Sign
                    WORKFLOW_I_OPERATION sign
                    AGENT_SELECTION
                    direct_manager(
                      history(fill, fill))
                    SYNCHRONIZATION 1
                    NOTIFICATION worklist
                  END_ORGANIZATIONAL_POLICY
                END_ORGANIZATIONAL_POLICIES
                ,
        sign_2  RUNTIME_CONSTRAINT
                  within_week(1)
                EXIT_CONSTRAINT
                  signed() OR refused()
                END_CONSTRAINTS
                ORGANIZATIONAL_POLICIES
                  ORGANIZATIONAL_POLICY
                    WORKFLOW_TYPE Sign
```

```
                    WORKFLOW_I_OPERATION sign
                    AGENT_SELECTION
                    department_manager(
                      history(fill, fill))
                    SYNCHRONIZATION 1
                    NOTIFICATION worklist
                  END_ORGANIZATIONAL_POLICY
                END_ORGANIZATIONAL_POLICIES
                ;
  Reimburse: reimburse;
  Archive: archive;
  Information: inform
END_SUBWORKFLOWS
...
ORGANIZATIONAL_POLICIES
  ORGANIZATIONAL_POLICY
    WORKFLOW_TYPE travel_expense_reimbursement4
    WORKFLOW_I_OPERATION start
    AGENT_SELECTION everybody()
    SYNCHRONIZATION 1
    NOTIFICATION worklist
  END_ORGANIZATIONAL_POLICY
  ORGANIZATIONAL_POLICY
    WORKFLOW_TYPE travel_expense_reimbursement
    WORKFLOW_I_OPERATION stop
    AGENT_SELECTIONdepartment_manager(
                        history(fill,fill))
    SYNCHRONIZATION 1
    NOTIFICATION worklist
  END_ORGANIZATIONAL_POLICY
END_ORGANIZATIONAL_POLICIES

END_WORKFLOW_TYPE
```

Several policies for the travel expense reimbursement workflow are modeled. One for the "sign" operation of the subworkflow "sign_1" and another one for the subworkflow "sign_2". The other subworkflows use the organizational policies as specified in their respective types. No adjustments are made.

A third organizational policy is modeled for the "start" operation of the travel expense reimbursement workflow itself and a fourth one for the "stop" operation. Required agent selections are:

```
AGENT_SELECTION direct_manager (IN string:
                                  last_name, first_name)
  select  supervises.supervisor_last_name,
          supervises.supervisor_first_name
  from    user, plays_role, supervises
  where   supervises.last_name = last_name
          and supervises.first_name = first_name
          and supervises.supervisor_last_name =
               plays_role.last_name
          and supervises.supervisor_first_name =
               plays_role.first_name
          and plays_role.name = "manager"
END_AGENT_SELECTION

AGENT_SELECTION department_manager (IN string:
                                  last_name, first_name)
  select  manager_of.manager_last_name,
          manager_of.manager_first_name
  from    manager_of, belongs_to
  where   manager_of.department_name =
            belongs_to.department_name
          and belongs_to.last_name = last_name
          and belongs_to.first_name = first_name
END_AGENT_SELECTION

AGENT_SELECTION everybody()
  select  user. last_name, user.first_name
  from    user
END_AGENT_SELECTION
```

6.5.3 Example Implementation

The workflow management systems presented in Chapter 2 are almost all characterized by supporting a fixed organization structure and a predefined set of organizational object and relationship types. Also, all these systems offer a standard set of organizational policies. Only three workflow management systems (COSA, Domino and WorkParty) provide more functionality in this respect.

COSA provides a basic set of functions to select users from its organizational database. In addition, the functions can be composed to more complex functions.

For example, one function selects members of a group, another one selects the supervisors of a list of users. Each user might have one or more supervisors. Both functions can be combined to a more complex one which selects the list of supervisors of the members of a group.

In principle, the Domino workflow management system follows the same approach as COSA. A predefined set of functions is supported that can be composed to more comprehensive functions.

A specialized component of the WorkParty workflow management system manages the organization structure. Even though the organizational types and relationships are predefined it is possible to extend them with additional attributes. This allows to implement further attributes if required.

6.5.4 Further Issues

Synchronization

A "*-out-of-many" synchronization rule can be applied to workflow operations which write data, e.g. update local variables of a workflow. In this case many writers for the same data exist. In order not to produce inconsistent data by interleaving write access they have to be synchronized, e.g. by semaphores.

Evaluation of Organizational Policies

For one workflow operation several policies can be specified. For example, workflow types of subworkflow have their own policies specified in addition to those from a superworkflow. In this case an evaluation strategy has to be in place which decides on the overall result. Without going into details here possible strategies are analogous to those of constraints (see Section 6.1.4).

6.6 Further Perspectives

The perspectives described in the previous sections are regarded as being basic. They have to be applied in almost every scenario and are therefore the most important ones. However, they are not sufficient in all cases. Further perspectives can be identified for more advanced scenarios which are discussed in the following. These are *security, causality, history, integrity and failure recovery, quality* and *autonomy*.

6.6.1 Security Perspective

Security is concerned with the question of *who is allowed* to access an object. Access to an object might be denied because of confidentiality (mandatory access control) or because the owner does not allow access (discretionary access control) (Denning, 1983).

The security perspective looks very similar to the organization perspective which defines who can access workflow operations. However, the selection of who *can* access a workflow operation is based on *responsibility* from an organizational point of view. Workflow operations can only be accessed by an actor who is responsible to execute it. This is significantly different to mandatory and discretionary access control.

On the one hand access is restricted because of security reasons and on the other hand organizational policies restrict access because of organizational issues. This does not cause any problems as long as both agree on who can/is allowed to execute a workflow operation. If both grant access or both deny access everything is fine. However, if security rules and organizational policies come to a different conclusion, a conflict occurs. It has to be decided whether access to the corresponding workflow operation should be granted or not. Access to the workflow operation would violate one of the decisions. A common strategy is to combine both decisions such that access is only granted when organizational issues and security issues are both properly satisfied.

An example shows how conflicts as described above can occur. Organizational policies are attached to a workflow type. This defines responsibility for the workflow operations of all instances of this workflow type. Access control specifications are defined on object instances like a file. For instance, a first agent is allowed to access a file whereas another agent is not allowed to access it. When a workflow operation that accesses the file is assigned to the first agent, everything runs without problems. However, if the second agent has to perform the workflow operation a conflict occurs.

6.6.2 Causality Perspective

The causality perspective describes why a workflow type is specified in the way it is and why a workflow instance is executed. Therefore, the causality perspective comprises business policies, enterprise strategies, legal business rules, etc. that regulate the definition of workflow types. For instance, customer orders of more than \$1 000 000 must be approved by at least two vice-presidents. Such a regulation influences the organization perspective. A respective organizational policy must defined. If this business rule changes, the associated organizational policy must also be updated. The causality perspective stores the interrelationship between this business rule and the organizational policy.

Another example describes the dependency of a workflow instance execution on the existence of a project. For this project, new employees should be hired.

Since hiring takes some time, the corresponding workflow instances run for a couple of weeks. The workflow instances only run because of the project that looks for two new members. Before the new employees are actually hired (which is implemented by steps of these workflows), it has to be checked that the project is still ongoing and is running well. Otherwise, the reason to hire new people vanishes and the corresponding workflow instances must be aborted.

In these two examples, the business rule and the project represent so-called causalities of the workflow types and workflow instances, respectively. The existence of a causality justifies the specification of a workflow type or the execution of a workflow instance.

Through causalities workflow types and instances can also be linked together although formerly they were totally independent from each other. An example sheds some light into this concept. A customer inquires for a product which still is not offered by a company. In order to produce this new product the company itself has to look for new suppliers. An employee is therefore asked to visit potential suppliers. The customer inquiry and the employee's trips are modeled as workflows. Hence, the trip workflow is only justified as long as the customer's inquiry holds. If the customer withdraws the inquiry, the trip approvals also must be withdrawn. In this example, the inquiry workflow represents the causality for the trip workflow.

It is up to the workflow management system to maintain dependencies between workflows and their causalities. A simple implementation rule for causalities says that they are checked before a composite or an elementary workflow is executed. So, the integrity of workflow execution can be sufficiently assured.

6.6.3 History Perspective

The history perspective builds up an audit trail for each workflow instance. The audit trail contains information about what happened while a workflow was under execution. An audit trail is used in different contexts: in a system context which deals with computation and recovery and in an application area context which deals with workflow analysis and revision.

The Use of Audit Trail in a System Context

The following two scenarios show where an audit trail is used in a system context.

- *History Access.* As discussed in Section 6.5.2, sometimes it is necessary to find out which agent has executed a workflow operation of a certain workflow instance. This is done by a function querying the history of a workflow.

- *Failure Recovery.* Workflow management system components might fail for various reasons (e.g. a program error or a node crash). A system failure might terminate the execution of workflow instances. As soon as a system is up and running again all interrupted workflow instances have to be set back to a consistent state from which they can continue. To recover from a failure and to find out the last consistent state for a workflow instance, the audit trail of a workflow instance must be inspected.

In both cases the required information has to be recorded in the audit trail. The history perspective must provide a means which allows to specify exactly which information must be recorded depending on how the audit trails of workflow instances are used.

The Use of Audit Trail in an Application Context

Several scenarios can be thought of in the context of an application area.

- *Revision.* A revision of already executed workflow instances has to reveal whether all actions were performed according to established rules.
- *Analysis.* Audit trails can be used to run statistics on executed workflow instances.
- *Reengineering.* Audit trails allow to detect semantic failures and bottlenecks. This kind of analysis might be used to reengineer a workflow so that it runs more smoothly in the future.

Each of the three scenarios requires different information from the audit trail. This observation emphasizes the need for a means that allows to specify individually which history data have to be recorded.

6.6.4 Integrity and Failure Recovery Perspective

In workflow management systems two kinds of failures are distinguished: semantic failures and system failures. Semantic failures are application area dependent. For example, a semantic failure occurs when an applicant fills a form in an incorrect way. As a reaction to this failure the signature is denied and the applicant has to correct the form.

A system failure occurs because of technical problems. A system failure affects the execution of workflow instances so that they cannot be processed further without running a recovery mechanism. A system failure might be caused by erroneous program code, a power failure, a hardware failure, a base service software failure or a network failure.

Semantic Failures

Semantic failures are "normal" in the sense that they are expected to happen. It is not intended but expected that users fill forms wrongly or that users do not obey deadlines. Semantic failures have to be detected and when they are detected they have to be corrected. Failure detection can be implemented in various ways. One way is to declare constraints. Another way is to explicitly test return values.

Constraints

Three types of constraints are introduced in Chapter 6.1.1: enter constraints, exit constraints and run time constraints. If a constraint fails the following recovery actions can be taken:

- *Termination of execution.* This is the simplest form of reaction to a semantic error. An appropriate exit code should be delivered in order to identify the failure.
- *Wait for constraint fulfillment.* If the executing workflow should not be aborted, the workflow management system could wait until the constraint is no longer violated. This requires "continuous" evaluation of the constraint. On the one hand this approach is very appealing. On the other hand it might fail if the constraint never evaluates to true. In this case a fallback strategy is necessary.
- *Start of a repairing workflow.* This approach tries to repair the semantic failure by starting another workflow. The result of the repairing workflow is used to decide if the constraint is finally fulfilled or not. For instance, if there is no approval for a trip even though it is required for reimbursement a repairing workflow could be started asking for a late approval. If this is given, the reimbursement workflow can continue, otherwise it has to terminate.
- *Semantic rollback.* If a constraint is not fulfilled the failing workflow instance has to be rolled back semantically. For example, if travel expense reimbursement is processed but there is not sufficient travel budget (exit constraint), the reimbursement is undone by not releasing the reimbursement check. If an enter constraint is not fulfilled the workflow just terminates with an appropriate error probably causing its superworkflow to roll back (if it was not a top-level workflow itself).

Test on Return Values

Test on return values in the context of workflow management corresponds to the test on return values in normal program design. So it is not necessary to dwell on this kind of failure detection and failure correction. After a subworkflow is finished (or some workflow application or workflow operation) the outcome is tested. If the test is positive the workflow continues normally. If the test is negative the workflow modeler has to deviate from the normal execution path.

Exceptions

Constraints and return value tests deal with unintended but expected failures. However, another class of failures exists: failures which are unintended and unexpected. For instance, a division by zero happens. The result might be a core dump. So the failure correction action produces the dump of the data structure of the program.

In the context of workflow management a core dump is not acceptable at all since a workflow must continue even in the case of unintended and unexpected failure. A workflow instance has to be kept alive even if an unexpected failure occurs. A standard way would be to stop the affected workflow instance and assign it to some agent which is responsible for correcting the failure. This kind of standard mechanism can be used for all kinds of unexpected failures.

System Failures

System failures are different to semantic failures from a modeling point of view. System failures are transparent to a workflow type. A workflow type might model expected semantic failures and how to react to them. However, it does not contain modeling information about how to react to system failures.

As mentioned earlier, a system failure happens because components of a workflow management system or components of underlying base services fail. In principle each component is responsible for recovering from a failure and putting itself back into a consistent state. However, since components communicate with each other, they are not really independent from each other. If one component fails it might affect another one. The other component has to react to the failure as well. For example, if a client calls a server by RPC it is connected to the server. If the server crashes the call will never be returned successfully to the client. The client has to know about the failure in order to issue the call again after the crashed server has recovered.

The situation gets worse if a server called by RPC changes persistent data. In this case it might be the case that the data is changed consistently under transactional control. However, before the success message is sent back to the client the server fails. In this case the client only knows that the server crashed but not that the transaction was executed successfully. If the client calls the server again the server code has to find out whether the call is obsolete because it has already been executed.

Distributed transactions are an appropriate means to deal with this kind of recovery which is very complex. The basic principle is to execute every function in a workflow management system under transactional control. Even client/

server communications follow this principle. If something fails during a call the client as well as the server can be sure that no inconsistent state is left. Basically transactional RPCs or transactional queues (which can be deployed in an X/OPEN protocol to integrate several transactional components) are an appropriate means.

Independence of Semantic and System Failures

From a theoretical point of view effects of system failures should not cause semantic failures and vice versa. If a system failure happens processing of workflow instances should continue normally after the system has recovered. A semantic failure should not crash the system.

However, the independence of semantic and system failures cannot be achieved in reality. For example, if a computer system does not run for half a day semantic failures might be the consequence. But also semantic failures can cause system failures. When a user fills a form with a wrong data value the system might crash (e.g. division by zero).

6.6.5 Quality Perspective

For the sake of this discussion, it is sufficient to associate the quality perspective with time and cost only. There are many more aspects of quality, hence the principal concept of the quality perspective can already be recognized when time and cost are discussed as examples.

Due to the restriction of the quality perspective to time and cost, a high quality workflow instance execution is characterized by not consuming too much time and system resources. In order to measure time and cost, workflows must be prepared. For instance, start and end times of workflow instance execution must be written into a log (preferably the history, cf. Section 6.6.3). The use of resources for workflow instance processing must also be traced. It is possible to analyze this information in order to find execution bottlenecks, resource intensive workflow steps, long-running workflows, etc.

Along with the quality perspective, data needed to assess the quality of a workflow type specification of a workflow instance execution are produced. This means that appropriate log functions have to be incorporated into workflows to be analyzed.

6.6.6 Autonomy Perspective

We regard autonomy as a global concept. Therefore, the autonomy perspective is composed of three aspects: mobility, distribution and execution threads.

Although these aspects seems to be rather different in nature, they can all be traced back to the aim of providing autonomous units of workflow execution.

Mobility

Modern working styles require to use laptops in an off-line fashion (mobile computing). This applies also to workflow management. Work is downloaded on a mobile computer and executed some time later on. As soon as the user reconnects to the network the executed work is transferred back to the workflow management system.

However, some provisions are necessary to guarantee consistent processing:

- *Data and Data Flow.* In the normal case (no mobile computing), data required to execute a task are accessed as soon as its execution starts and are released when its execution ends. Return values are provided at this time also. However, in the disconnected case data have to be accessed before the mobile computer disconnects. Data are released and result values are written after the mobile computer is re-connected to the network.
- *Synchronization.* As detailed in Section 6.5.1 users have to be synchronized. As soon as a user starts working on a task it is synchronized with others who potentially also work on the task. In the disconnected case, synchronization has to take place when the mobile computer disconnects. Instead of actually starting task execution the user merely declares that he intends to work on the task. However, when he re-connects and has not performed the task, synchronization has to be "inverted". Users that were formerly excluded from executing the task get another chance to perform it. Synchronization has to consider the situation of disconnected task execution and has to provide special attributes to indicate it.
- *Deadline.* What happens when a workflow instance executed on a disconnected laptop hits a deadline? In a non-disconnected environment a reaction to a deadline violation could be to notify a responsible agent. However, this is not possible in the case of mobile computing. To avoid such situations, deadline management must be provided on either the mobile computer and the workflow management system.
- *Availability of Workflow Application.* Workflow applications are necessary to execute workflow operations. In principle, all workflow applications needed to perform workflow operations have to be downloaded on the mobile computer.

A more detailed discussion of workflow management and mobile computing can be found in (Bussler, 1995a). However, even though the support requires additional functionality from a workflow management system "mobile workflows" become more and more important. This is also emphasized by the COSA workflow management system which already has the basic functionality in place to support "mobile workflows".

Distribution

Distribution has to be discussed in the context of workflow types as well as in the context of workflow instance execution. However, before this discussion can take place the meaning of "distribution" has to be clarified. An autonomous area of workflow management is called a *logical domain*. Within a logical domain workflow types and other model elements are defined on its own discretion. If several logical domains exist, they act autonomously and their workflow types as well as other workflow related objects evolve differently. For instance, two branches of an enterprise form two autonomous logical domains. Workflow types are modeled independently in each branch. However, some workflows span branch boundaries and therefore cooperation is required. One aspect of cooperation is to build workflow types which reference model elements that belong to different branches.

We differentiate logical from *physical domains*. A workflow management system together with its databases containing workflow types and workflow instances constitutes a physical domain. If one workflow management system is sufficient to manage all workflow types and instances of a logical domain, both logical and physical domains are the same. However, if two or more workflow management systems are required to manage the workflow types and instances of a logical domain (e.g. because of performance reasons) two or more physical domains constitute one logical domain.

Distributed Workflow Types

A workflow type consists of modeling elements of various perspectives. For instance, references to subworkflow are part of a workflow type as well as references to data types, constraints and organizational policies. A distributed workflow type references object types (e.g. subworkflow, data) from another logical domain. A structured way to exchange model objects between logical domains must be found. The definition part of an abstract data type seems to be an adequate and appropriate particle that could made visible to external logical domains. Since in our workflow model, most model elements are described as abstract data types, workflow type distribution is supported appropriately.

Distributed Workflow Execution

A workflow instance can be executed completely within one logical domain if all object types required are available in the logical domain. However, if object types of another logical domain are referenced execution is more complicated. It is possible to execute that part of a workflow which references remote model elements in a remote logical domain. This requires to send a request to the remote domain and to wait for the results. The remote logical domain is fully responsible for the remote execution. Another solution would be to copy remote object types to the local logical domain. However, this is difficult to handle. In most cases, logical domains do not disclose their model elements. They are interested in cooperating with other logical domains but do not want to disclose their assets.

There are several problems that are involved with distributed workflow execution. Status monitoring of a workflow instance which is executed partly at remote sites is one of them. A remote logical domain might be willing to execute a workflow but is not willing to disclose any information about how this is done. This might affect the audit trail. The audit trail of the remote execution cannot be built. This means that status monitoring is principally not possible. Nevertheless, people responsible to execute the remote operations could be asked to do status monitoring on behalf of the workflow management system.

To make distributed workflow execution failure resistant, distributed transactions could be used. Such a distributed transaction would spawn at least two logical domains. The initiator of the transaction therefore can control system resources of the remote logical domain. This might not be acceptable. Therefore it might be necessary to break transactional control between logical domains.

Execution Threads

Workflow instances run independently of other workflow instances as long as they are top level workflow instances. Subworkflow instances run within the scope of their superworkflows. So whenever a workflow starts a subworkflow this is automatically executed within the scope of its superworkflow. This means that a superworkflow waits until its subworkflows are finished.

It might be necessary to start a workflow from within another workflow which executes as an independent top-level workflow itself. This means that the workflow which starts the independent top-level workflow does not wait for the results synchronously. This is modeled by specifying a workflow operation which starts a top-level workflow instance.

---

[1] F stands for booking a flight, C for booking a car and H for booking a hotel. FC denotes a sequence of first F and then C.

[2] Since our Petri nets always start with a transition and end with a transition the replacement of double line transitions with other Petri nets results in a correct Petri net.

[3] In principle, a distinction must be made between a task and a workflow. A workflow is a data structure represented in a workflow management system. Attached to it are data, workflow operations, application programs, etc. A workflow assigned to a user means to carry out a task for him. He uses workflow operations to perform the task. However, to make matters simple, we use task and workflow interchangeably.

[4] The workflow type is specified here even though the organizational policy is defined within the context of the workflow itself. This is because policies can be specified independently from the workflow in which they are used. As a shortcut the workflow type name could be left out if the policy is specified within the scope of a workflow tpye.

7 Workflow Execution Model

The previous chapter discussed a comprehensive workflow model in detail. The main constituents of the workflow model were introduced as well as how they are used to model workflow types. In addition to a structural model it is important to establish an execution model in order to understand the runtime behavior of workflows, i.e. to define their execution semantics. In Section 7.1 a basic workflow execution model based on states and state transitions is introduced. Only some states and state transitions are introduced omitting complexity as much as possible in order to focus on the principle idea. Section 7.2 details some aspects of the execution model. Section 7.3 discusses how model extensions impact the workflow execution model and how dynamic extensions are supported.

7.1 Basic Skeleton

State transition diagrams are an appropriate means to define a workflow execution model. Basically, the execution semantics of workflows is defined like the execution semantics of operating system processes (Tanenbaum, 1987). A state transition diagram defines the states a workflow can be in. Additionally it shows the state transitions which bring a workflow from one state to another one.

A path through a state transition diagram defines the execution semantics of a workflow. There is an initial state as well as a final state. When a workflow is in the initial state its execution starts and when a workflow is in its final state the execution of the workflow is finished. In all states a certain functionality is available. For example, when a workflow is in a state *paused* it can be resumed. If a workflow is in a state *executing* all its workflow operations are available.

Since the workflow model introduced in Chapter 6 consists of two different types of workflows (elementary and composite workflows) two different state transition diagrams are established. In contrast to elementary workflows composite workflows coordinate subworkflows. This requires additional states and state transitions.

When discussing the semantics of elementary and composite workflows we restrict the discussion to the function and behavior perspective. Both perspectives are sufficient to get a good understanding of the basic execution semantics while the state transition diagrams remain simple. Adding further perspectives from the beginning would make the descriptions unnecessarily complicated. Nevertheless, Section 7.2 discusses further issues relevant to the execution semantics and gives an impression about the complexity of workflow execution.

The semantics introduced in the following is one possible semantics which we have found to be applicable in many deployment areas. However, this is not the only semantics conceivable. Looking closer at particular states (e.g. pause) reveals that multiple forms of implementation are feasible: it is possible to wait until all workflow operations of all subworkflows are finished. This would make sure that no workflow application is interrupted, probably causing inconsistent data. A second implementation immediately pauses all subworkflows together with their workflow operations. This would stop the workflow application with the risk of inconsistencies. In the following we show one semantics and make sure that it can be adjusted to different requirements.

7.1.1 Elementary Workflow

The basic state transition diagram defining the execution model for an elementary workflow consists of five states: *not existent, ready, paused, executing* and *done*. *Not existent* is the initial state and also the final state. Figure 7.1 shows the complete diagram together with possible state transitions. The following comments are relevant:

- *Not existent.* A workflow resides in this state before it is instantiated. This state however is very useful to explain the instantiation as well as the deletion of workflow instances.
- *Ready.* A workflow in the *ready* state is fully instantiated and ready to process. However, agents are not notified about the workflow and its operations yet.
- *Paused.* The only workflow operation possible in the *paused* state is the *resume* workflow operation. This workflow operation brings the workflow back to the state *executing*. The workflow is temporarily inaccessible.

- *Executing*. Agents operate on workflow operations in the *executing* state. Previously, they were notified about workflows to be executed. Workflow operation execution orders and synchronization have to be considered in this state also.
- *Done*. A workflow in this state is still accessible. However, workflow operations must not change the workflow internal data structure any more (e.g. workflow local variables). This state is used to give agents an opportunity to query about already executed workflows.

We want to emphasize here that the state transition diagram applies to a workflow instance, not to data objects processed by it. So a workflow instance might be done and finally does not exist any more, although the data objects processed by it might still be alive.

The state transitions are introduced in the following.

1 *Not existent* → *Ready*. The transition from *not existent* to *ready* is caused (besides other things) by instantiating a workflow. A workflow instance is either created because it is next to be executed due to control flow specifications or because a user requests a workflow instance running as a top-level workflow (*start_workflow*). The creation of a workflow instance also involves the flow of data, i.e. the workflow parameters are provided and the local workflow variables are initialized. The agents eligible for the workflow operations are determined. After that the workflow enters the state *ready*.

2 *Ready* → *Executing*. The state *ready* denotes that a workflow is ready to be worked on. Only the notification of the involved agents is left to be done. As soon as the notification took place the workflow is set to the

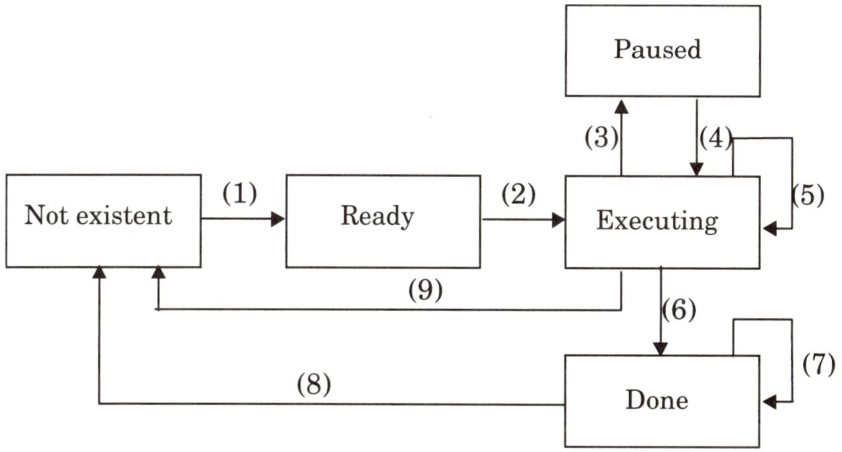

Figure 7.1: Execution Model for an Elementary Workflow

state *executing*. This transition takes place without involving a workflow operation. It is performed by the workflow management system.

3 *Executing → Paused*. When a workflow should cease execution it has to be paused. An agent or the workflow management system can invoke a *pause* operation which implements this transition and puts the workflow into the state *paused*. In this state nothing can be done with a workflow except to resume it and bring it back to the state *executing* again by a workflow operation *resume*. Pause operations are discussed further in Section 7.1.3.

4 *Paused → Executing*. This state transition is caused by the *resume* workflow operation as explained before.

5 *Executing → Executing*. Most workflow operations are executed while a workflow is in the state *executing*. The workflow instance remains in this state after workflow operations are performed. However, by applying the workflow operations *pause* or *finish* the *executing* state is left.

6 *Executing → Done*. Eventually a workflow has to be declared to have finished. The task which is implemented by it is regarded as being fulfilled. After a workflow is finished no changes to its workflow variables and output parameters are possible any more. A workflow is either declared as finished by an agent explicitly invoking an appropriate workflow operation (e.g. *finish*) or implicitly if *finish* is called by another workflow operation. The *finish* operation puts a workflow into the state *done*.

7 *Done → Done*. If a workflow is done it is not deleted yet. It is available to agents, but workflow operations which change workflow local variables or output parameters are not allowed any more. Workflow operations which merely query their contents can be executed. They do not change the internal state of the workflow instance.

8 *Done → Not existent*. A workflow is deleted only if the corresponding workflow operation is called. Then the workflow is unavailable to agents and its system internal representation is deleted. The workflow is put into the state *non existent*.

9 *Executing → Not existent*. This state transition takes place if a workflow is deleted while it is executing.

7.1.2 Composite Workflow

Since the main difference between composite workflows and elementary workflows is the coordination of subworkflows the state transition diagram of elementary workflows has to be slightly extended. Most of the semantics discussed in Section 7.1.1 remains significant so that only the differences are described.

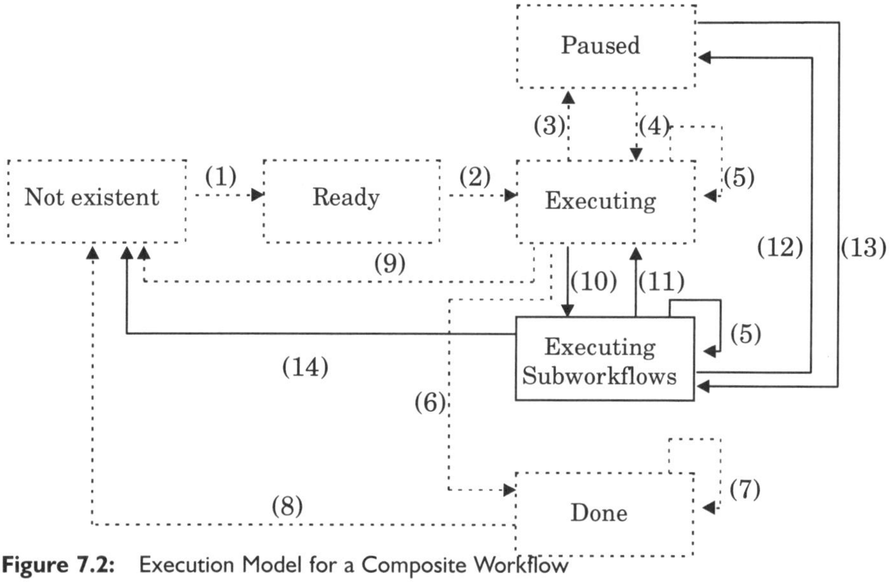

Figure 7.2: Execution Model for a Composite Workflow

Figure 7.2 shows the extended state transition diagram for composite workflows. All components of the previous diagram (see Figure 7.1) are depicted as dashed lines whereas the new parts are depicted as solid lines.

In addition to the already introduced states a new state is added:

- *Executing subworkflows.* The execution of subworkflows takes place while a composite workflow resides in this state. The behavior perspective of the composite workflow is evaluated as long as subworkflows can be started. As soon as all eligible subworkflows are performed the composite workflow leaves this state. Workflow operations can be executed in this state also. For example, it is possible to pause a composite workflow while its subworkflows are executing. The change from state *executing* to state *executing subworkflows* does not influence the execution of workflow operations.

Several new state transitions have to be added:

10 *Executing → Executing subworkflows.* As soon as workflow operations are available to agents, an agent can start subworkflow processing by calling the appropriate workflow operation. This workflow operation is called automatically by an automated agent or explicitly by an agent. Often this workflow operation is related to the idea of taking responsibility for the subworkflow execution by an agent. While subworkflows are executed workflow operations of the superworkflow can still be executed. An example is a query operation that retrieves the status of subworkflow processing or intermediate results.

11 *Executing subworkflows* → *Executing*. When no subworkflow can be executed any more the state *executing subworkflows* is left and the state *executing* is entered.

12 *Executing subworkflows* → *Paused*. Subworkflow execution can be paused and resumed later on. An appropriate workflow operation causes this transition. Usually, if a composite workflow is paused all its subworkflows are also paused. If subworkflows are composite themselves their subworkflows are paused as well. If a workflow is paused by the transition (12) it can be resumed only by transition (13), not by transition (4).

13 *Paused* → *Executing subworkflows*. This transition transitively resumes all paused subworkflows.

14 *Executing subworkflows* → *Not existent*. Like transition (9) this transition will take place when a composite workflow currently executing its subworkflows is deleted.

7.1.3 Interplay between Workflows and Subworkflows

A composite workflow and its subworkflows do not run independently from each other. The behavior of a superworkflow might influence its subworkflows and vice versa. For example, pausing a composite workflow might result in pausing its subworkflows. What happens when a composite workflow should be paused and workflow operations are under execution? There are at least two reactions possible:

- The *pause* operation waits until the executing workflow operations are finished. Any request to start another workflow operation is denied.
- The *pause* operation interrupts the execution of the workflow operations. In this case the executing operations should be transactional in order to not leave inconsistent states.

Instead of offering one *pause* operation it is valuable to have two pause operations available: *deferred_pause* which waits until all workflow operations are finished and *immediate_pause* which interrupts workflow operation execution instantaneously.

When a composite workflow enters the state *executing subworkflows* it results eventually in the instantiation of subworkflows. For a subworkflow to be executed an instance is created and executed according to the state transition diagrams shown in Figure 7.1 and Figure 7.2. When the subworkflow has finished the superworkflow takes over again. It determines whether new subworkflows have to be started. Should the situation arise new subworkflows are instantiated. Otherwise the superworkflow can finish subworkflow execution and switches to state *executing*.

The principal structure of an algorithm for subworkflow execution is given next. This algorithm is evaluated for each composite workflow which is in the state *executing subworkflows*.

```
execute_subworkflows:
  swf :=  evaluate behavior perspective for
          subworkflows to be executed first;
  for each s in swf do
    start s;
  end_for;
  label continue:
  wait for finished subworkflows;
  swf_next := evaluate behavior aspect for further
              subworkflows to be executed;
  if swf_next <> empty
  then  for each s in swf_next do
              start s;
        end_for;
        goto continue;
  else  if there exist running subworkflows
        then goto continue;
        else done;
        end_if;
  end_if;
```

7.2 Integration of Further Perspectives

So far a basic execution semantics is defined for elementary and composite workflows based on the function and behavior perspectives only. In the following further perspectives are incorporated which handle the aspects constraints, application execution and synchronization.

7.2.1 Constraint Evaluation

As introduced in Chapter 6, constraints are used at several places within a workflow type to ensure that consistency criteria are fulfilled. Constraints have to be checked once or several times depending on whether they are enter, exit or runtime constraints. The following describes where constraints are checked:

- *Enter constraint.* Enter constraints are checked at transition (2) when the workflow goes into production.

- *Exit constraint.* Exit constraints are normally checked at transition (6) since they are used to determine whether a workflow completes normally. If execution has to be terminated exceptionally, exit constraints should also be checked at transition (9). However, it is questionable whether a constraint is fulfilled when execution stops exceptionally.
- *Runtime constraint.* Runtime constraints have to be checked continuously. There are several approaches to implement "continuously":
  - A very simple solution is to check runtime constraints of composite workflows before and after every subworkflow execution. Checking at these points does not prevent the constraint being false during workflow operation execution.
  - Another possibility is to check a runtime constraint before and after every workflow operation execution as well as before and after every subworkflow execution. This improves the situation only slightly since during workflow application execution a runtime constraint can be falsified.
  - Another, more rigid possibility would be to check runtime constraints whenever an operation, a subworkflow, a workflow application or an application program is started or finished as well as before and after workflow local variables or parameters are changed. This approach assures high consistency although it produces much additional effort.
  - Runtime constraints can be checked whenever data change that are referenced by them. In this case the check of a runtime constraint is independent of the execution of a workflow.

A trade-off has to be made to select an appropriate evaluation strategy. High consistency normally has to be bought with much additional effort.

7.2.2 Workflow Operation Execution

As for the execution of workflows, an execution model for workflow operations has to be defined. Again this is modeled as a state transition diagram (see Figure 7.3). We explain the diagram from the viewpoint of one workflow operation. As soon as a workflow instance is created workflow operations can be called in principle. This is expressed by the state *not assigned*. However, agents cannot see the workflow operations yet in their worklists. As soon as the organization perspective is evaluated workflow operations are assigned to agents (transition (1)); they enter the state *assigned*. When an agent selects the workflow operation the state *executing* is entered (transition (2)). In this state the workflow applications are executed which implement the workflow operation (transition (5)). During workflow application execution the workflow operation remains in the state *executing*. When all eligible workflow applications are executed the workflow operation is finished and is put into the state *assigned* (transition (6)). Then this operation can be started again. A workflow operation can be paused in the state *executing* (transitions (3) and (4)).

7.2.3 Synchronization

Whenever a user wants to start a workflow operation an appropriate synchronization rule has to be evaluated which either allows a user to continue or denies the execution of the workflow operation. The evaluation has to be done when transition (2) takes place (cf. Figure 7.3).

7.3 Modifications of the Workflow Execution Model

The extensibility of a workflow model was postulated several times. At the model level new modeling constructs have to be added which must fit together nicely with the existing perspectives of the model. At the execution level an extension is more difficult since the state transition diagrams defining the execution semantics of the workflows have to be extended according to the model extension.

A second kind of change on the execution level might not be caused by workflow model extensions but by changes of the execution semantics of the workflow model. As mentioned throughout this chapter, the proposed semantics suggested is only one feasible example. If another semantics is required, the state transition diagrams have to be re-configured to reflect the different semantics. Figure 7.4 gives an overview of possible changes.

As the term "re-configuration" indicates a change in the execution semantics does not necessarily lead to re-programming the system. If the state transition

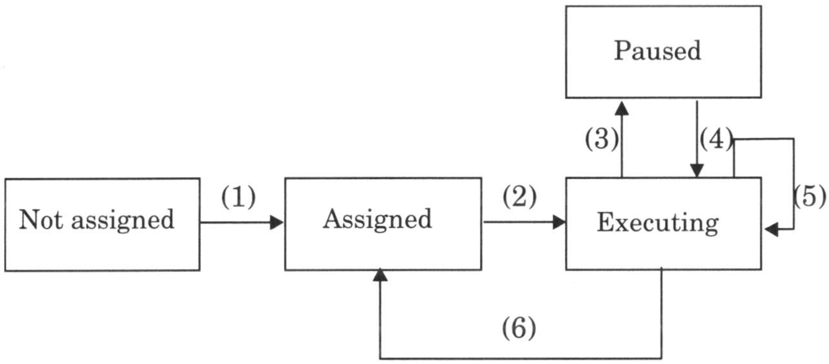

Figure 7.3: State Transition Diagram for Workflow Operation Execution

diagrams shown in the previous chapters are not hard coded in some server code but are interpreted re-programming can be avoided.

However, some problems arise when state transition diagrams are re-configured. First, already running workflow instances have to be considered. They might fail if the execution semantics is changed while they are under execution. Second, already defined workflow types (according to the former version of the workflow model) cannot execute according to the new semantics definition.

A strategy has to be in place when an execution model changes while workflow instances are under execution. It has to be defined how running instances are treated. To wait for the workflow instances to be finished before the execution model is changed is not appropriate in general. Workflow instances might run for a long time (up to several months or even years).

Another approach would be to change the execution model and adjust running workflow instances to the new execution model. However, this might lead to execution inconsistencies.

A better strategy is to maintain different versions of execution semantics (i.e. state transition diagrams). In this case all running workflow instances follow the semantics versions they are designed for.

When new modeling constructs are added to a workflow model, a strategy must be established how to deal with workflow types which are defined according to the former workflow model. There are two basic approaches:

- *Workflow type specifications are not changed.* In this case workflow type specifications of two different versions of a workflow model exist.
- *Workflow specifications are adjusted.* In this case all workflow type specifications following the former workflow model are adjusted.

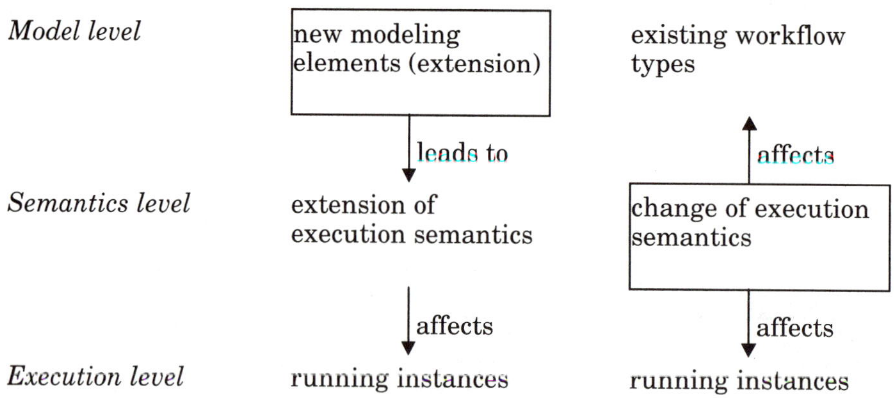

Figure 7.4: Overview over Changes

A change in the workflow model leads to a change in the execution semantics, since the new perspectives or changes of existing perspectives need to be reflected. If after a change all already existing workflow types are adjusted to the new workflow model, the new execution model applies to all workflow instances which will be created.

If two versions of a workflow model coexist it is recommended to maintain two versions of an execution model also. Hence, this requires to implement state transition diagrams in such a way that multiple state transition diagrams also can coexist. The interpretation approach described above is one feasible solution for this issue.

8 Build Time Tools

The introduction of the main constituents of workflow management in Chapter 4 distinguishes between the build time phase and the run time phase. Each phase is further decomposed into the aspects conception, enactment and handling. The first two aspects, conception and enactment, are broadly elaborated in Chapter 6 and in Chapter 7. This chapter presents tools that facilitate the *definition, analysis* and *administration* of workflow types. These issues are elaborated in Section 8.1, Section 8.2 and Section 8.3, respectively.

In order to enhance the usability of tools, they should be graphical. Nevertheless, it is not in the scope of this chapter to show detailed designs of the graphical interfaces of the tools. Following the general approach pursued in this book, we intend to elaborate what basic functionality must be provided by a tool in principle.

Figure 8.1 depicts the three major phases of workflow modeling. Certainly, editing is the first step that has to be performed in order to obtain a workflow description (Definition). The workflow type specification then has to be checked for integrity and consistency (Analysis). Releasing workflow types for production, managing versions of workflow type specifications and withdrawing formerly released workflow types are major tasks of "Administration".

Figure 8.1 also demonstrates that most tasks in the build time phase of workflow management are working against the Build Time Repository which stores unreleased workflow type specifications. The goal of all activities during build time is to release a new version of a workflow type, i.e. to transmit it into the Run Time Repository. Being there, it is available to be used in production.

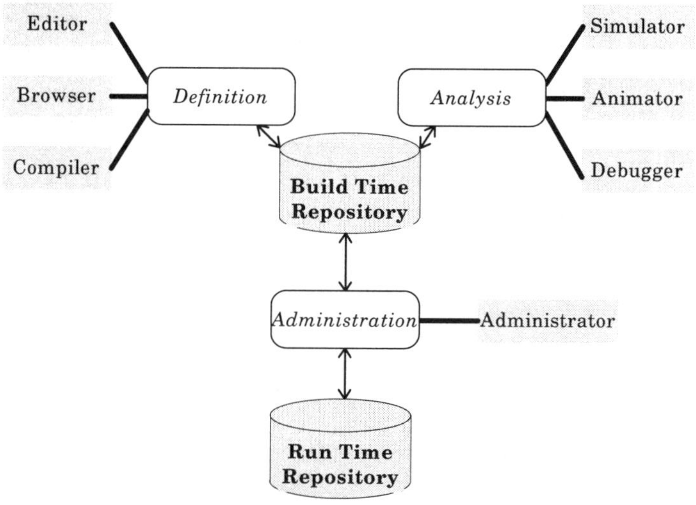

Figure 8.1: Build Time Tools

8.1 Definition of Workflow Schemes

For the implementation of an application system, adequate workflow types have to be specified. The set of all workflow types implementing a specific application system constitutes a so-called *workflow scheme.*[1]

Certainly, the construction of a workflow scheme is the first step to be accomplished during build time. According to the classification of a comprehensive workflow model in independent perspectives, the definition tool, which we call the *Editor*, consists of a couple of independent tools which facilitate the definition of the perspectives of the workflow model (cf. Figure 8.2). To define a workflow, the artifacts specified in the different definition tools are integrated to form a complete workflow description.

The definition of workflows happens in the context of an existing enterprise information processing infrastructure. Therefore, many artifacts which have to be referenced in a workflow specification might already exist. It is of fundamental importance that such artifacts are reused in workflow specifications. If they were newly created without taking into account the existing enterprise information processing infrastructure inconsistencies might develop since logically equal artifacts are developed multiple times. Consistency between these newly generated artifacts and existing artifacts in the repositories of the enterprise information processing infrastructure is difficult to maintain. For example, data describing customers are already stored in an enterprise repository. During the development of workflows such a data structure is defined again without considering the enterprise repository. It is most probable that both definitions are different; this mismatch is a potential source of inconsistencies.

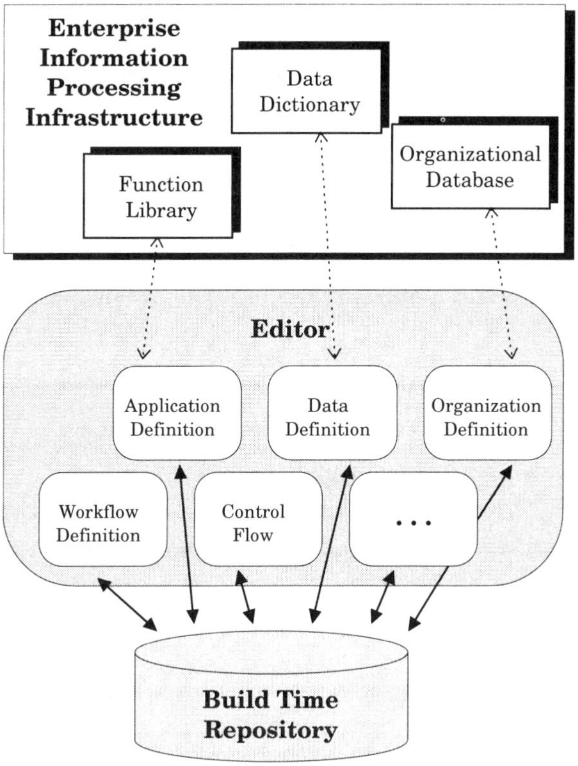

Figure 8.2: Conception of an Editor

Contemplating the above scenario, only one consequence is logical. The definition of workflows must be totally integrated into the existing infrastructure of an enterprise. For instance, data needed in workflow descriptions have to be exported from the global enterprise data dictionary (if this dictionary exists).

Figure 8.2 depicts how the components of the Editor are linked to relevant enterprise repositories. A Data Dictionary, a Function Library and an Organizational Database are presented as example components of an enterprise repository. The figure also shows that all workflow specific specifications are stored in a workflow management system repository called the *Build Time Repository*.

In Part 1 we often remarked that reusability is an essential requirement for modern software development. For the specification of workflows reusability is an important requirement as well. Reusability has to be supported technically. How can a modeler reuse an earlier developed artifact if he does not know that this artifact exists at all? In order to alleviate the reuse of artifacts, a decent workflow management system must offer a *Browser*. Such a tool allows to browse the Build Time and the Run Time Repository for already existing artifacts. A *compiler* translates a workflow specification in an internal format, that is stored in the build time repository.

8.2 Analyzing Workflow Specifications

After having specified workflow types including all their perspectives, a modeler needs to find out whether the specifications are correct. Two kinds of problems are typically encountered:

- the specification is incorrect with respect to syntax and/or semantics
- the specification does not fulfill the requirements posted by the application system to be implemented (pragmatics).

In order to know about the adequacy and correctness of workflow type specifications, they have to be analyzed. There are several forms of analysis, e.g. verification and validation (Deiters and Gruhn, 1994). Verification means to prove that a workflow type has certain properties. For instance, a workflow type should be free of deadlocks and of useless subworkflows. In a deadlock situation, processing of a workflow does not come to an end because two or more consumers are in conflict with respect to the use of the same resources. Useless subworkflows can never be executed because control flow never reaches them.

A workflow modeler verifies a workflow type, looks for undesired properties and modifies a workflow type specification such that these properties are eliminated.

In contrast to verification of workflow types, validation deals with workflow instances. Verification is based on simulation. To simulate a workflow execution means to instantiate a workflow type and to perform the workflow instance. Usually, the effects of workflow application executions are imitated in order to make simulation feasible. There are two ways to exploit simulation. If simulation is animated, i.e. the workflow instance execution is illustrated on a terminal, the workflow modeler can prove whether the workflow behaves as he expected. Also, simulation can produce an execution trace which can be analyzed subsequently. For example, critical paths can be computed. The workflow modeler can exploit such information in order to optimize the workflow type specification.

The above investigation reveals that at least two tools are essential to prove the correctness of a workflow specification, namely a *Simulator* and an *Animator*. Nevertheless, we also see the necessity for another tool. It is called *Debugger*. Let us assume that the workflow modeler recognizes that the workflow does not behave as desired. Just by studying the animation or the simulation traced, the errors cannot be identified. As we know from program debugging, a workflow debugger allows to stepwise inspect the execution of workflows. Thus, error sources are easier to find.

8.3 Administrating Workflow Specifications

Administration during build time means to administrate workflow specifications. The specification of workflow types usually is not accomplished in a single step. Parts of workflow types are already completed while other parts are still to be done. Partial results of workflow specifications must be administered. It must become clear that workflow type specifications are not complete yet but that the design process is still ongoing. If such control were not in place, partially developed workflow types might be referenced in error.

After a workflow type has been designed completely, it still is not available for general use. Each workflow type must explicitly be released by an administrator. Physically this means to move a workflow type from the Build Time Repository to the Run Time Repository. Designs which are stored in the Build Time Repository are regarded as uncompleted and therefore they are not released for use; designs which already reside in the Run Time Repository are regarded as correct and can be used. Often formerly released workflow types must be redesigned, i.e. they must be eliminated from the Run Time Repository and must be stored back into the Build Time Repository.

Over time new versions (and variants) of workflow types will be generated. To produce a new version of a workflow type does not necessarily mean to discard former versions of the workflow type. Workflow type versions must be managed.

All tasks described in this section are accomplished by a tool named *Administrator*. In summary, its main job is to control workflow types during and after editing.

---

[1]The term "workflow scheme" follows the notation "database scheme" from the database area. There, a set of relations constitutes the so-called database scheme which represents the data needed to implement an application system.

Part 3: Run Time

The main goal of Part 3 is to illustrate how a workflow management system could be implemented. The concept described in the next chapters represents one suitable implementation strategy for a workflow management system. Nevertheless, alternative ways for implementation are also conceivable and feasible.

The implementation strategy presented in this book reflects the essential requirements of a workflow management system. A comprehensive set of implementation requirements is discussed in Chapter 9. We use a layered approach to introduce the main features of the architecture. Chapter 10 presents a global view of the implementation, i.e. the implementation model is depicted. Only module interfaces (APIs) and relationships between modules are shown in order to illustrate the inherent structure of the architecture. The platform independent implementation of the modules and their relationships is then detailed in Chapter 11. Chapter 12 superficially presents one platform dependent implementation of the concepts discussed so far. This implementation is a prototype developed at the University of Erlangen according to the concepts developed in this book. Finally, tools necessary to support the run time phase of a workflow management system are identified in Chapter 13.

Part 3 cannot deliver a complete implementation guide for a workflow management system. This guide would fill a book by itself. Nevertheless, the concepts discussed here are proved in a feasibility study, namely for the implementation of the *MOBILE* workflow management system at the University of Erlangen. Developers and project managers who have to conceive an implementation concept for workflow management should be able to obtain important hints when studying Part 3.

Reader's Guide

The following table guides readers with special interests.

Reader's Interest	*Chapters to read*
conceptual architecture	Chapter 9 and Chapter 10
data model, operating system process structure	Chapter 11
implementation issues	Chapter 12
runtime tools	Chapter 13

9 Preliminaries to a Workflow Management System Architecture

This chapter introduces the run time part of the book. First, design principles are introduced that reveal the rationales that form the basis for the development of a workflow management system (Section 9.1). Requirements for the implementation of a workflow management system are discussed in Section 9.2. The meaning of the powerful principle of modularization which is the essential basis for the workflow management system architecture is elaborated in Section 9.3. We dispense with a general comparison of workflow management system architectures in this chapter. Instead, we will discuss related work with respect to an implementation model and an implementation architecture in the following chapters.

9.1 Design Principles

The development of the general workflow management system architecture introduced in the following chapters is based on some design principles. Stating these design rationales explicitly is necessary in order to comprehend the description of the workflow management system architecture.

9.1.1 Design Phases

It is widely accepted that large application systems cannot be designed in a single step. System design phases intend to discover the inherent structure of a problem and describe the solution in a compatible way. On this level of detail, an application system comprises a large collection of modules that are interconnected according to use relationships. Eventually, the results of the system design phase are communicated to the programming teams who are responsible to enact the system design, i.e. to implement the system. DeRemer and Kron distinguished these principle phases of system development and characterized them as programming-in-the-large and programming-in-the-small (DeRemer and Kron, 1976).

Since the design of a large application system is very comprehensive it is recommended to apply abstraction mechanisms to provide design phases. A design phase can be regarded as the refinement of the preceeding phase. Since we humans do not deal effectively with several phases simultaneously, it is also recommended to introduce a system design stepwise, phase by phase. This is what follows in the subsequent three chapters. Hence, we reside on the level of programming-in-the-large since this level better illustrates the principle structure of the approach.

Each design phase is characterized by a set of requirements. Higher levels of design must be illustrative in order to communicate the inherent structure of a problem solution. Lower levels of design must meticulously specify each little artifact that finally constitutes an application system.

The general architecture of a workflow management system is described by three phases (see Figure 9.1):

- *Implementation model.* The major concern of this phase is to construct the basic modules that constitute the overall architecture. Also, the basic interconnections between modules must be specified. The implementation model basically establishes the system structure. However, implementation details are not of interest at all.
- *Implementation architecture.* The implementation architecture considers specific implementation concepts. For instance, it details the interconnection between modules and lays down a client/server relationship. Another detail that is added by the implementation architecture is the use of a database management system to provide persistence for a module. Algorithms that concrete implementation decisions are also part of an implementation architecture. Finally, abstract communication concepts are introduced.
- *Implementation.* The implementation of the workflow management system architecture concretely fixes implementation mechanisms. For

Development of the *Implementation Model*

↓

Development of the *Implementation Architecture*

↓

Implementation of a Workflow Management System

Figure 9.1: Implementation Phases

instance, DCE (distributed computing environment) is selected as basic communication mechanism, INFORMIX is the database management system that has to be deployed and C++ is the overall implementation language.

Because the general mission of this book is to introduce overall concepts rather than to demonstrate concrete implementation details, the implementation model (Chapter 10) and the implementation architecture (Chapter 11) are emphasized in the following. A concrete implementation of the concepts, the *MOBILE* workflow management system, is merely superficially introduced in Chapter 12.

The idea of distinguishing three design layers, implementation model, implementation architecture and implementation, is also influenced by the field of database management systems (Elmasri and Navathe, 1989). For database management systems a three-schema architecture is established that distinguishes external, conceptual and internal levels. Between the levels data independence is sustained which can be described as the capacity to change a schema at one level without having to change the schema at the next higher level. This feature is important for our architectural approach since it is then stable to changes on lower levels. For instance, if another implementation technique is selected, the implementation architecture and the implementation model are not affected.

9.1.2 Modularization

In Chapter 5, modularization was named as the main requirement of workflow modeling. Modularization also is a major prerequisite for a workflow management system architecture. Therefore, the modules of the implementation model are designed as abstract data types. The importance of modularization for the design of large application systems is stated by DeRemer and Kron:

> Modularization helps in finding reliable solutions for complex problems by applying the traditional way of "divide and conquer". (DeRemer and Kron, 1976)

The starting point for modularization of the workflow management system architecture is the division of the workflow model into perspectives. In principle, each perspective is enacted by a dedicated set of modules that are interrelated.

Tightly connected to modularization is the distinction between the presentation of a module and its implementation. The former is established by a set of operations establishing its interface; the latter is the code that actually implements the functionality of the module.

9.1.3 Layered Design

The implementation of a module has two layers. The bottom layer is constituted by so-called base services. A base service is independent of the functionality of a workflow management system. For example, DCE threads can be considered as base services. The top layer represents the individual functionality of the module. This distinction is made in order to better identify a set of base services that are available to implement a workflow management system. When a module calls another module it might not access base services directly but indirectly by calling this other module.

9.2 Requirements

In Chapter 5 requirements for workflow modeling are described. The application-oriented requirements gathered there are relevant for the implementation of a workflow management system. Hence, we take them over and also apply them here. Nevertheless, the so-called model-oriented requirements that merely hold for modeling tasks have to be replaced with requirements that are specific to implementation efforts. Also, requirements must be discussed individually for an implementation model, an implementation architecture and an implementation. Thus, in this section only issues global to these three parts are discussed; specific issues are treated in Chapters 10, 11 and 12.

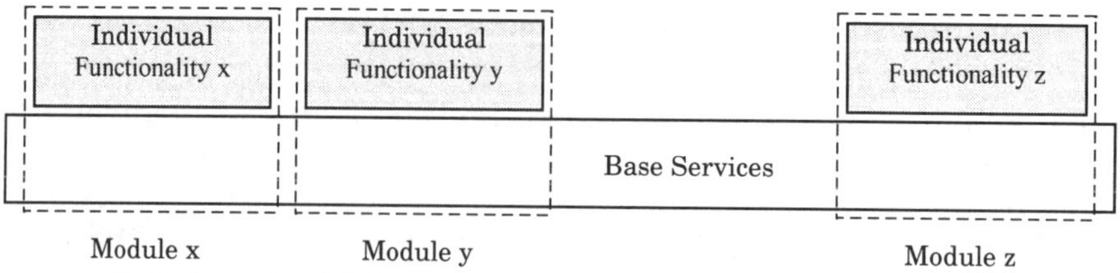

Figure 9.2: Layering within a Module

9.2.1 Application-oriented Requirements

We repeat the application-oriented demands here and discuss their consequences for an architecture of a workflow management system. Details about the application-oriented demands can be found in Chapter 5.

Many Different Forms of Workflows

The fact that not all future application scenarios of workflow management can be anticipated is the reason why a workflow model must be extensible. However, there would be no advantage in extending a workflow model unless the new model elements can also be enacted in the workflow management system. Consequently,

- extensibility

is also a major requirement for the architecture of a workflow management system.

Dynamically Changing Business Requirements

A change management process, a versioning concept and configuration management have to be in place on the workflow modeling level. Consequently, these issues must also be provided on the enactment level.

- dynamic customizability
- adaptability, and
- support of the life cycle of a workflow management system

are prerequisites for effective workflow management. For instance, it must be possible to replace a module that implements one of the perspectives of the workflow model with a new version if new modeling elements have to be offered. This change should not disturb the overall functionality and availability of the workflow management system.

Continuously Growing Application Area

On the enactment level of workflow management, a continuously growing application area makes requirements of

- scalability.

The efficiency of workflow processing should be sustained when many workflow instances are to be executed. The workflow management system must provide means to scale up if a high number of workflows must be processed.

Distributed Heterogeneous Computing Infrastructure

Heterogeneous, autonomous and distributed legacy and new application systems must be integrated into workflow processing (Rusinkiewicz and Sheth, 1995). Therefore, the

- openness

of a workflow management system towards application integration is required (Nutt, 1992; Umar, 1993). APIs for the integration of external application systems and FAP for the communication between external application systems and the workflow management system are of major importance.

9.2.2 Implementation-oriented Requirements

The implementation-oriented requirements discussed in the following are applicable to most system implementations. However, we want to adapt the general discussion to the realm of workflow management. As already mentioned in Chapter 5, the following requirements are tightly connected with the notion of software quality (Hindel, 1993; McCall *et al.*, 1977). In contrast to Chapter 5 where a workflow model is the software product under consideration, in this section the implementation modules of a workflow management system are to be investigated.

- Efficiency

is certainly the first quality that comes to mind in the context of software implementation. Criteria to measure efficiency for workflow management systems are response time and throughput which are slightly interdependent. The criteria "throughput" can easily be discussed. According to general estimations, more than a thousand workflow instances are likely to execute simultaneously. If the workflow management system does not provide high throughput, the overall performance is not acceptable. However, not all components must show the same high degree of efficiency (although this would be ideal). In order to discuss this surprising statement the criteria "response time" needs to be investigated.

There are two groups of services that together make up a workflow management system. The first one is directly involved with processing user requests. An example of such a service is the worklist. When a user wants to obtain some details about a task he is supposed to perform, this request must be handled efficiently by the worklist manager. The second group of components does not directly response to user requests. For example, a module that resolves policies works independent from user requests. Having characterized these different groups of services, the issue "response time" can be revisited.

Services that directly work on user requests must be efficient in order to satisfy user requests as fast as possible. If the response time for user requests is too high, the workflow management system users would refuse to work with the system. In contrast, services that do not directly work on satisfying user requests can tolerate temporary inefficiency better.

As an example, the policy resolution service will be studied. This service must be executed before a workflow can be assigned to worklists in order to be performed by the users. Thus, nobody recognizes whether this service works (temporarily) inefficiently. The only effect for the users is that they are notified a little bit late about new work to do. However, since they usually do not know when the preceding task was completed, the bad performance of the policy service is not recognized.

The above discussion does not intend to spread the idea that efficiency is not a major issue of workflow management. We rather want to demonstrate that efficiency is a debatable feature that even allows some degrees of freedom. To have and to know about this flexibility is very important. An example sheds light onto this observation. Reliability is another feature that must be provided by the implementation of a workflow management system. Nevertheless, implementing reliability (e.g. by using a database management system) reduces performance. Therefore, it is very helpful to know that for some components of a workflow management system the trade-off between efficiency and reliability can be decided in favor of reliability.

The second important feature of a workflow management system has already been mentioned:

- reliability.

The probability of failures during the execution of workflows increases with its lifetime. Loosing the results of a workflow execution just because a failure occurred during processing one of the last workflow steps is not acceptable. Thus, each processing step during workflow execution must be implemented to be reliable such that failure recovery only has to discard some small, still incomplete effects instead of having to eliminate all effects processed so far, i.e. discard the complete workflow.

Without any doubt,

- correctness

is essential for any implementation, therefore also for the implementation of a workflow management system. Consistency, completeness, testability, preciseness and verifiability come along with this feature. See Deiters and Gruhn (1994) for a profound discussion of this issue.

A topic that is often neglected for new software approaches is

- maintainability.

When workflow management is characterized by a continuously growing application area, this issue becomes even more relevant. But also for managing scalability, which normally results in adding further system components, maintainability is a major prerequisite.

The last issue that should be discussed generally in this section is

- portability.

The need for portability can also be derived from the observation that workflow management systems will be deployed in distributed heterogeneous computing infrastructures.

We want to close the discussion of requirements for the implementation of a workflow management system by mentioning once more the major prerequisites that supports their enactment:

- modularity, and
- orthogonality.

From this observation (Hindel, 1993; McCall *et al.*, 1977) the design principle "modularization" is derived (cf. Section 9.1.2).

9.3 Modularization

Modularization is a general concept. Its development started in the early 1970s with the formulation of the principles information hiding (Parnas, 1972) and virtual machines (Dijkstra, 1972). The result of modularization is modules which altogether implement the functionality of an application system.

According to the phases introduced in Section 9.1.1, modularization is a key concept for the implementation model. Nevertheless, since the implementation model is the basis for both the implementation architecture and the implementation itself, modularization is essential for all three phases of the design of a workflow management system. Therefore, it is discussed generally in this introductionary section.

Modularity is also a key requirement mentioned in Section 9.2. It is the prerequisite for the enactment of a well-formed workflow management system.

We begin the discussion of modularization with clarifying its meaning and working out criteria for modularization (Section 9.3.1). Finally, the use of modules in the context of a workflow management system is discussed (Section 9.3.2).

9.3.1 Criteria and Principles

Modularization is the structuring of an application system into parts, i.e. into modules (Denert, 1991). Also, the interrelationship between modules, i.e. the communication protocols (FAP) between them, and the interfaces of modules (API) must be outlined. A module can be described as an abstract data type. If modules are complex they can be decomposed into sub-modules. Sub-modules that compose a module work on the same data.

In general, modularization serves two purposes: understanding and system management. By decomposing a complex application system into comprehensible modules, the overall structure of the complex application system becomes clear. Modules are much easier to administrate compared with monolithically developed application systems because they work only on a part of the complete application.

There are several criteria that help to evaluate a design method with respect to modularity (Meyer, 1988):

- *Modular Decomposability*: decomposing a problem into several sub-problems, whose solution may then be pursued separately.
- *Modular Composability*: modules can be combined freely to produce new composite modules.
- *Modular Understandability*: modules can be separately understood.
- *Modular Continuity*: small changes in a problem specification result in a change of one or just a few modules without affecting the overall system architecture.
- *Modular Protection*: abnormal processing occurring in one module will remain confined to this module.

Based on these criteria a number of design principles for modules can be derived (Denert, 1991; Meyer, 1988):

- *Internal Cohesion* (*Module Strength*, (Myers, 1976)): Cohesion within a module is strong, i.e. functions of a module normally execute without referring to module-external data or functions. A consequence of internal cohesion is that a module must implement a certain issue completely to be independent from other modules.
- *Weak Coupling* (*Module Coupling*, (Myers, 1976)): If modules have to communicate at all, they should exchange as little information as possible.
- *Explicit Interfaces*: All interfaces of a module must be specified uniquely. Whenever two modules communicate, they must not make assumptions about the internal structure of the behavior of the other module.
- *Linguistic Modular Units*: Modules must correspond to syntactic units in the language used.

- *Information Hiding*: For each module interface specification and implementation are separated. Only the interfaces are public and are specifically declared so.
- *Independence*: Changing the internal structure of one module must not affect other modules. Only a change of the interface is recognized by external modules.
- *Testability*: Each module can be tested just by using its interfaces.
- *Integrateable to Larger Units*: Modules must be integrateable to larger software units, here to a comprehensive workflow management system.

Based on these criteria and principles of modularization some guidelines can be derived that support the practical enactment of modularization in application system development. These guidelines are discussed in the following section.

9.3.2 Abstract Data Types

By applying abstraction principles modules can be represented as abstract data types (ADT). Since a module (an ADT) can be very complex, it might be decomposed in further sub-modules (which are themselves ADTs).

Formally a module is described as an ADT with name, external operations, local variables and logical data view. Modules communicate with another by exchanging data. This defines another relationship between modules called the use relationship.

A simple user request can be fulfilled solely by one module. Whenever a complex user request has to be processed, several modules can be involved. They have to be performed in a certain call sequence. Protocols define the sequence of how modules call each other.

A module maintains a logical database. These data are private to the module and can only be accessed by the operations of the module. Since modules are regarded as ADTs, the logical database constitutes external data that are available for the ADTs implementing a module.

10 Implementation Model

In Chapter 9 the goals of an implementation model are named. The basic modules that constitute the architecture of a workflow management system have to be specified. Also, interrelationships and interdependencies between modules must be identified. Implementation details, i.e. the internal structure of modules, are not of interest. Therefore, an implementation model abstracts from implementation details.

In Section 10.1 some specific requirements for an implementation model are discussed. A modularization strategy which is favorable for workflow management system is explained in Section 10.2. Alternative implementation strategies which differ with respect to the modularization strategy are discussed in Section 10.3. Then, the main modules of a workflow management system architecture are introduced (Section 10.4). How the perspectives of the comprehensive workflow model are implemented is shown in Section 10.5. Protocols that define communication between these modules are discussed in Section 10.6. Section 10.7 depicts the implementation of examples of workflow operations. Finally, the flexibility of the chosen implementation model with respect to changes is demonstrated in Section 10.8.

10.1 Specific Requirements

Requirements which apply to the architecture of workflow management systems in general are discussed in Section 9.2. In this section we study some more specific issues towards an implementation model.

An implementation model must be

- complete.

Only if a particular functionality is represented (by one or more modules) in the implementation model, will it be supported by the implementation of a workflow management system. To make the approach practical, it is allowed to omit auxiliary functions of minor importance. For instance, almost all modules need operations like *get_local_variable()* or *put_local_variable()*. However, whether such an elementary function is needed for a specific module cannot be decided before a concrete implementation strategy is chosen (cf. Chapter 11).

An implementation model must also be

- technology independent.

Technology independence means that implementation techniques like relational database management systems, transaction processing monitors or remote procedure calls do not show up. As a consequence, system-related issues like throughput, reliability and even scalability are still not of interest. They do not come into the picture before an implementation architecture is chosen.

10.2 Modularization Design Strategy

Although in Section 9.3 the main issues in the realm of modularization are clearly characterized, there are still degrees of freedom in the way modularization is pursued. In Section 10.3 some alternative approaches to modularization are discussed.

In this section, an approach is selected which is mainly influenced by the structure of the workflow model presented in Chapter 6. This strategy implies the main advantage that workflow model and workflow management system architecture correspond to a maximum degree which significantly supports maintainability: whenever some elements of the workflow model must be changed, the corresponding modules of the workflow management system implementation can be determined easily. The main design rationale for our implementation model is

- to reflect each perspective of the workflow model by a corresponding set of implementation modules.

If new perspectives are added to the workflow model, a new set of implementation modules can be added to the workflow management system. Whenever a perspective is changed, the places where these changes have to be reflected are easy to find, namely the modules implementing the corresponding perspective.

Besides the perspective-oriented definition of modules, there is a higher level classification of modules in the implementation model.

- Modules are classified as to whether they belong to the Kernel, the Shell or the Workspace.

The Kernel is regarded as the central component of a workflow management system. It is responsible to coordinate the execution of workflows. The modules of the Shell support the Kernel and are called whenever a workflow has to be executed. The Workspace represents the interface to the workflow management system user. Normally, the user's worklists are implemented as a module of the Workspace. Kernel, Shell and Workspace modules together contain all the modules that implement the perspectives of the workflow model.

The interested reader will have realized that we put great stress on modularization. We regard modularization as fundamental due to the manifold requirements of a workflow management system. Also, we could learn some interesting but depressing lessons from existing workflow management products which have neglected to stress the modularization issue. Both the products we will now discuss are well known in the market.

The vendor of the first product realized that the organizational perspective had to be made more sophisticated. However, the architect of the workflow management system found out quickly that the change of the organizational perspective would have a dramatic impact on all other perspectives of the workflow management system. So, the vendor decided to freeze the current implementation stream and initiated a complete redesign of the workflow management system.

The second workflow management product was very weak on the functional perspective. Nesting of workflows was not possible. Nevertheless, an important key customer required this feature. It took more than six months to bring out a new release that allows workflow nesting although this issue was handled with highest priority.

It is not very difficult to see that for the two case studies presented above proper modularization would have made it much easier to add new functionality. What that means with respect to satisfying customers and to gaining market share can easily be deduced.

10.3 Alternative Modularization Approaches

Before we describe the modules of the implementation architecture, some selected alternative modularization approaches will be discussed.

Pure Object-Orientation

A first approach to modularization is called *pure object-oriented*. In this case all relevant objects of a workflow model, e.g. workflow, data, control flow construct, organizational policy, would be implemented as an object class. Objects would be data carriers with methods working on their data. The main disadvantage of this approach is that the workflow processing algorithm is somehow spread throughout the various operations of the diverse object classes since all have to contribute to workflow execution.

The main advantage of the pure object-oriented approach is information hiding (Meyer, 1988). However, there are also some serious disadvantages. They mostly are connected with the implementation of algorithms. An algorithm as such does not exist for the pure object-oriented approach. It is implemented by the methods which are associated with the diverse object classes. When many objects are involved in processing an algorithm, the latter is spread across the methods of these objects. Therefore, it is very difficult to realize the complete algorithm as a whole. Whenever some parts of the algorithm have to be changed due to new or changed requirements, it becomes very cumbersome to find out the methods in question.

Pure Functional Programming

Somehow the contrary to a pure object-oriented approach is *pure functional* programming. In this case, all elements of the workflow model would be stored in a global database. A global algorithm would work on these data in order to process a workflow.

The main advantage of the pure functional approach is the ease of finding the algorithm that is responsible to process workflows. However, due to the comprehensiveness of the algorithms, information hiding is not achieved at all. Thus, a change in the underlying database might affect the whole algorithm instead of a small part of it. Besides, failure limitation is hard since the parts of the algorithm are not protected from each other.

Combined Approach

Our approach combines the advantages of both the pure object-oriented and the pure functional approach. Pragmatically, we define object groups which are responsible to implement a certain piece of functionality. Within these object groups, information hiding is guaranteed. However, we do not enforce that all parts of the workflow management system are implement in a pure object-oriented fashion. Parts which naturally involve several objects are extracted and built as independent algorithms. So, it is easy to find the overall algorithms which control workflow processing.

An example sheds some more light into our approach. Let's assume that the workflow operation "start_workflow" has to be implemented. This action involves all perspectives of a workflow and therefore involves the objects which implement them. Pure object-oriented modeling would distribute the algorithm across all the objects being involved. In contrast, we define an extra module called "workflow_execution" which contains the algorithm as a method. Whenever the algorithm has to be changed, it is easy to find. Whenever the implementation of the perspectives has to be modified, the corresponding methods can easily be found with the objects implementing them.

Last but not least we have to explain how we define object groups. Object groups are established according to the perspectives of the workflow model. All objects which implement a perspective or a part of it belong to the same object group. This kind of structuring ensures modularization since the objects implementing a perspective naturally belong together.

10.4 Presentation of the Modules

The modules of the implementation model are presented as abstract data types. In the following, the most important modules of a workflow management system architecture are described. However, the list of modules is not complete but represents a working set. The main modules of a general architecture for workflow management systems are explicitly shown; the description of auxiliary modules is omitted when their functionality is obvious and not very specific for workflow management.

The representation of the modules happens according to the following scheme:

- *Module name.* Each module is identified by a unique name.
- *Internal operations.* Internal operations are solely used by the module itself. They are not available externally.
- *Export operations.* Export operations are accessible for other modules.
- *Import operations.* Import operations are operations of other modules that are used inside a module.
- *Logical data view.* The logical data view defines necessary instance data for a module. Type information is discussed in Chapter 11.
- *Import Modules.* Import modules are used to reuse its functionality.
- *Sub-modules.* Sub-modules are used for internal modularization.

Modules are described according to the following syntax:

```
module ::=
   MODULE module-name
   [internal-operations]
   [export-operations]
   [import-operations]
   [data-views]
   [import-modules]
   [sub-modules]
internal-operations ::=
   {INTERNAL_OPERATION operation-name(parameters)
      (returns data-type);}
export-operations ::=
   {EXPORT_OPERATION operation-name(parameters)
      (returns data-type);}
import-operations ::=
   {IMPORT_OPERATION
      module-name.operation-name();}
data-views ::=
   {DATA_VIEW data-definition;}
import-modules ::=
   {IMPORT_MODULE module-name;}
sub-modules ::=
   {SUB_MODULE module-name;}
data-type ::=
   module-name
   | (* data types as in Chapter 6 *)
```

Figure 10.1 provides an overview on the modules of the implementation model.

The requirements "extensible" and "exchangeable" (Chapter 9) mean that new modules have to be added or existing modules have to be changed or removed. Whether such a modification is easy to perform depends on the communication structure between the modules. If modules communicate only with dedicated ones, the exchange of a module becomes easy. If a module has to be added, only this one has to be altered.

The workflow_execution module is the only module that always has to exist since it forms the backbone of workflow processing (functional perspective). Due to this demand, the workflow_execution module must not make any assumptions about modules outside the Kernel. On the other hand, these modules can assume that the workflow_execution module will always be in place.

"Workflow_operation_execution" is the only module within the Kernel that knows about other modules in the Shell and in the Workspace. This module implements the communication between the Kernel external modules. Therefore,

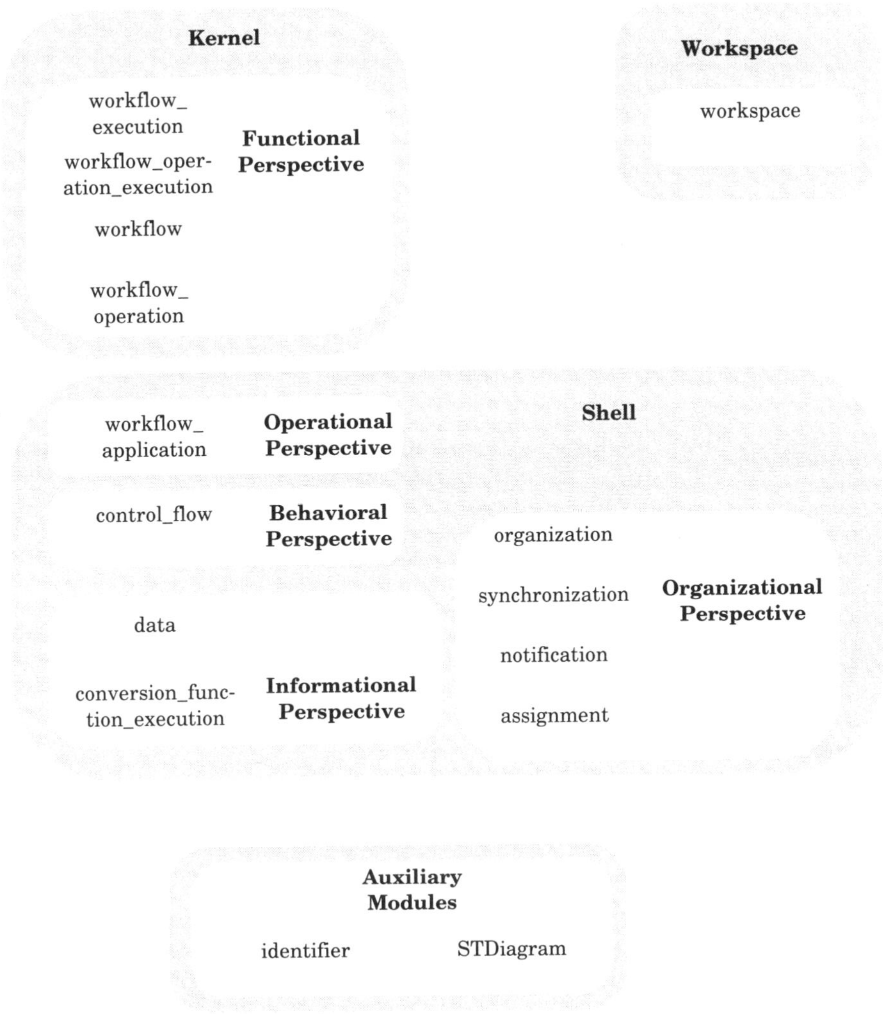

Figure 10.1: Modules of the Implementation Model

it is possible that modules communicate with each other without knowing about each other. At this point the benefit of having a mixed approach between pure object-oriented and pure functional becomes clear. The workflow_operation_execution module implements module operations which do not belong to the other modules but which connect them in order to implement the execution of workflows. Figure 10.2 depicts the structure of the implementation model pursued in this book. Although it is not relevant in the context of an implementation model, the client/server structure of the approach can already be recognized in this figure. The auxiliary modules are omitted.

As can be seen from the representation above the Workspace is different from the other modules. The Workspace is not considered as a perspective, but is an

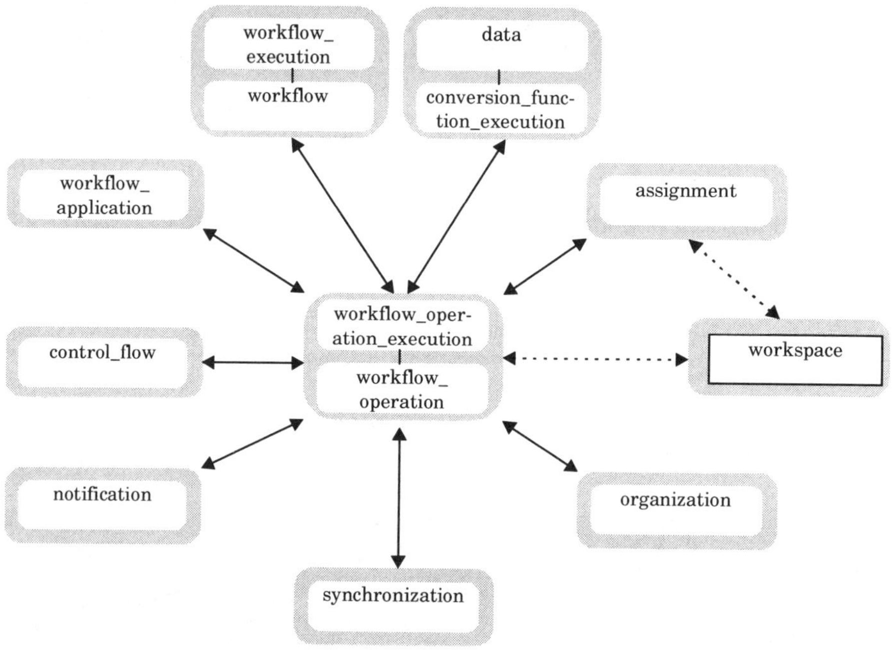

Figure 10.2: Structure of the Implementation Model

interface for the user. Because of this it not only communicates with the workflow_operation_execution module but also with the assignment module to find out assigned workflows for an agent.

As Figure 10.2 shows, all modules are connected by the workflow_operation_execution module. This module implements the communication between the other modules. The question arises why modules do not talk to each other directly. The reason is the requirement of extensibility. Extensibility has two dimensions: adding new modules and removing existing ones. If a module talks only to the workflow_operation_execution module adding a new module requires changes in this place only. The same applies for removing a module.

In contrast, if a module which is removed were called directly by others they would have to be changed in addition to the workflow operation execution module in order to avoid that module operation calls fail.

In the implementation model we therefore stick to this very clear structure. Of course, this structure potentially leads to inefficiency if it were implemented exactly this way. Since the performance requirement cannot be neglected we discuss in Chapter 11 how we modify the structure to obey the performance requirement.

In the following the interfaces of the modules as depicted in Figure 10.1 are specified. Section 10.5 gives an overview of which operations of the modules implement a perspective.

10.4.1 Auxiliary Modules

Besides Kernel, Shell and Workspace modules there are several, so-called auxiliary modules (identifier, STDiagram) which are necessary to implement a workflow management system. They are specified in this section.

MODULE `identifier`

Description. This module provides other modules with unique identifiers.

EXPORT_OPERATION `get_identifier()`
returns `identifier;`
Description. Returns an instance of an unique identifier.

MODULE `STDiagram`

Description. This module implements a state transition diagram (as described in Chapter 7) which consists of states and transitions. Attached to each transition is a set of module operation invocation commands. They have to be invoked before the diagram is put into the next state. For instance, before an elementary workflow is put into state "ready", several module operations have to be invoked (e.g. to determine eligible agents).

EXPORT_OPERATION `create`
`(`**IN** `identifier: diagram_type)`
returns `STDiagram;`

Description. This operation creates an instance of a state transition diagram of type *diagram_type*. The created state transition diagram is in its initial state.

EXPORT_OPERATION `invocations_for_next_state`
`(`**IN** `state: next_state)`
returns `set_of(module_operation_invocation);`

Description. This operation returns a set of module operation invocations which have to be performed before the diagram is set into the next state. The set of modules operations is returned only if the indicated state can be reached from the current state.

EXPORT_OPERATION `set_to_next_state`
`(`**IN** `state: next_state);`

Description. This operation puts the diagram into the state *next_state* (only if this can be reached from the current state).

EXPORT_OPERATION `get_state()`
returns `state;`

Description. This operation returns the current state of a module.

EXPORT_OPERATION `set_STD_context_variable`
`(`**IN** `string: name;`
IN `data_type_constant: value);`

Description. Stores intermediate results between state transitions.

EXPORT_OPERATION `get_STD_context_variable`
`(`**IN** `string: name)`
returns `data_type_constant;`

Description. Retrieves intermediate result.

```
DATA_VIEW state: actual_state;
```
Description. This data value stores the actual state of a state transition diagram.

```
DATA_VIEW identifier: diagram_type;
```
Description. The type of the state transition diagram is stored here.

```
DATA_VIEW identifier: id;
```
Description. The id of the state/transition diagram is stored here.

```
DATA_VIEW
  set_of(string, data_type_constant):
      STD_context_variable;
```
Description. All internal results are stored here.

10.4.2 Kernel Modules

The Kernel is the backbone of workflow processing. Two roles are associated with it. First, it implements the functional perspective. Therefore, it registers whether a workflow is a top-level workflow, a subworkflow or a superworkflow.

Second, as the central component of a workflow management system, the Kernel integrates all perspectives of a workflow. The Kernel processes workflow instances according to the state transition diagrams discussed in Chapter 7. When moving from one state to another, modules that implement the perspectives of a workflow description are called (cf. Section 10.5).

In the following, the two central modules of the Kernel, "workflow_ execution" and "workflow_operation_execution", are described together with modules supporting them (workflow, workflow_operation). The module workflow_execution implements the functional perspective. It knows about all running workflow instances as well as which workflow is a superworkflow of which other workflow. The module workflow_execution implements the execution of workflow operations. Section 10.6.3 shows the protocol for the execution of workflow operations.

```
MODULE workflow_execution
```
Description. The workflow_execution module processes workflow instances. It contains all data required for the processing.

```
EXPORT_OPERATION create_workflow
  (IN identifier: workflow_type)
  returns identifier;
```
Description. This operation creates a workflow instance of type *workflow_type*. The workflow instance is added to the set of actual workflow instances and its identifier is returned.

```
EXPORT_OPERATION set_to_next_state_workflow
  (IN identifier: workflow id;
  IN state: next_state);
```
Description. This operation puts a workflow instance into a subsequent state.

```
EXPORT_OPERATION get_state_workflow
  (IN identifier: workflow_id)
  returns state;
```
Description. This operation returns the actual state of a workflow instance.

```
EXPORT_OPERATION rejected_workflow
  (IN identifier: workflow_id);
```
Description. This operation tells the workflow execution module that a workflow instance is rejected, i.e. it will not be executed any more.

```
EXPORT_OPERATION delete_workflow
  (IN identifier: workflow_id);
```
Description. This operation deletes a workflow instance.

```
EXPORT_OPERATION disable_workflows
  (IN set_of(identifier): disabled_workflows);
```
Description. This operation is called when subworkflows of a workflow are not allowed to execute any more (cf. Chapter 6).

```
EXPORT_OPERATION set_subworkflow
  (IN identifier: workflow_id;
  IN identifier: sub_workflow_id);
```
Description. This operation is used to declare which workflow is a subworkflow of another one.

```
EXPORT_OPERATION next_subworkflows
  (IN identifier: super_workflow_id;
  IN set_of(workflow_type, subworkflow_name):
    next_subworkflows);
```
Description. This operation notifies the workflow execution module about subworkflows that can be executed due to control flow specification.

```
EXPORT_OPERATION get_subworkflows()
  returns set_of(workflow_type, string);
```
Description. This operation returns a list of all possible subworkflows according to the type definition of the workflow type.

```
EXPORT_OPERATION finish_executing_subworkflows
  (IN identifier: workflow_id);
```
Description. This operation notifies the workflow execution module that all eligible subworkflows are executed.

```
EXPORT_OPERATION no_more_subworkflows
  (IN identifier: super_workflow_id);
```
Description. This operation tells the workflow execution module that no further subworkflows are to be executed within the superworkflow.

```
EXPORT_OPERATION exists_executing_subworkflows
  (IN identifier: workflow_id)
  returns Boolean;
```
Description. This operation checks if a subworkflow of a workflow instance is under execution.

```
EXPORT_OPERATION is_top_level_workflow
   (IN identifier: workflow_id)
   returns Boolean;
```
Description. This operation tells if the workflow is a top level workflow.

```
EXPORT_OPERATION is_subworkflow
   (IN identifier: workflow_id)
   returns Boolean;
```
Description. This operation tells if the workflow is a subworkflow.

```
EXPORT_OPERATION get_instance_operations
   (IN identifier: workflow)
   returns set_of(operation);
```
Description. This operation returns a list of all possible workflow instance operations.

```
EXPORT_OPERATION execute_workflow_instance_operation
   (IN identifier: workflow_id;
   IN operation: workflow_operation;
   IN set_of(data_type_constant): parameters);
```
Description. This operation executes a workflow operation. It in turn calls the same operation of the module workflow_operation_execution.

```
EXPORT_OPERATION execute_workflow_type_operation
   (IN identifier: workflow_type;
   IN operation: workflow_operation;
   IN set_of(data_type_constant): parameters);
```
Description. This operation executes a workflow type operation. It in turn calls the same operation of the module workflow_operation_execution.

```
EXPORT_OPERATION exists_executing_workflow_ operations
   (IN identifier: workflow_id)
   returns Boolean;
```
Description. This operation checks if workflow operations of a workflow instance are under execution.

```
EXPORT_OPERATION exists_executing_workflow_operation
   (IN identifier: workflow_id;
   IN operation: workflow_operation)
   returns Boolean;
```
Description. This operation checks if the given workflow operation of a workflow instance is under execution.

```
IMPORT_MODULE workflow;
IMPORT_MODULE workflow_operation_execution;
DATA_VIEW set_of(identifier): actual_workflow_instances;
```
Description. This data value contains all workflow instances which are within the system.

```
DATA_VIEW set_of(identifier,identifier): subworkflows;
```
Description. This data value contains all workflow instances which are within the system.

```
MODULE workflow
```
Description. This module implements a workflow instance.

EXPORT_OPERATION create
(**IN** identifier: workflow_type)
returns identifier;

Description. This operation creates a workflow instance and sets all workflow internal data structures to the default values. In addition it assigns the workflow a unique identifier. Furthermore, a state transition diagram is created and initialized.

EXPORT_OPERATION delete();

Description. This operation deletes a workflow instance.

EXPORT_OPERATION set_to_next_state
(**IN** state: next_state);

Description. This operation puts a workflow instance into the next state.

EXPORT_OPERATION invocations_for_next_state
(**IN** state: next_state)
returns set_of(module_operation_invocation);

Description. This operation returns a set of module operation invocations necessary to put a workflow into the given state.

EXPORT_OPERATION get_state()
returns state;

Description. This operation returns the current state of a workflow instance.

IMPORT_MODULE identifier;

IMPORT_MODULE STDiagram;

DATA_VIEW identifier: id;

Description. This data value implements the identifier of a workflow instance.

DATA_VIEW STDiagram: diagram;

Description. The workflow instance is processed according to the state transition diagram stored in this data view. Every workflow instance possesses its own state transition diagram. This allows that each workflow instance can follow a different state transition diagram type which might implement a different execution semantics.

MODULE workflow_operation_execution

Description. This module takes care of workflow operation execution; it coordinates the execution of all other workflow perspectives.

INTERNAL_OPERATION execute_operation_body
(**IN** identifier: workflow_id;
IN operation: workflow_operation);

Description. This operation executes the body of a workflow operation.

EXPORT_OPERATION execute_workflow_instance_operation
(**IN** identifier: workflow_id;
IN operation: workflow_operation;
IN set_of(data_type_constant): parameters)
returns set_of(data_type_constant): return_values;

Description. This operation is called to execute workflow instance operations. It executes the workflow operation body as specified.

```
EXPORT_OPERATION execute_workflow_type_operation
   (IN identifier: workflow_type;
   IN operation: workflow_operation;
   IN set_of(data_type_constant): parameters)
   returns set_of(data_type_constant): return_values;
```
Description. This operation is called to execute workflow type operations. It executes the workflow operation body as specified.

```
EXPORT_OPERATION exists_executing_command
   (IN identifier: workflow_id;
   IN operation: workflow_operation)
   returns Boolean;
```
Description. This operation checks if workflow operations for a workflow instance are under execution.

```
EXPORT_OPERATION set_to_next_state
   (IN identifier: workflow_id;
   IN operation: workflow_operation;
   IN state: next_state);
```
Description. This operation puts a workflow operation into a subsequent state.

```
IMPORT_MODULE STDiagram;
IMPORT_MODULE workflow_operation;
IMPORT_MODULE notification;
IMPORT_MODULE synchronization;
IMPORT_MODULE workflow_application;
IMPORT_MODULE control_flow;
IMPORT_MODULE data;
IMPORT_MODULE organization;
IMPORT_MODULE assignment;
IMPORT_MODULE workflow_execution;
DATA_VIEW
   set_of(identifier,operation):
        executing_workflow_operations;
```
Description. This data view contains all running workflow operations for a workflow instance. This is used to remember that workflow operations are executing.

```
MODULE workflow_operation
```
Description. This module implements a workflow operation.

```
EXPORT_OPERATION set_to_next_state
   (IN state: next_state);
```
Description. This operation puts a workflow operation into the next execution state.

```
IMPORT_MODULE STDiagram;
DATA_VIEW STDiagram: diagram;
```
Description. The workflow operation is processed according to the state transition diagram *diagram*.

```
DATA_VIEW identifier: id;
```
Description. This data structure contains the identifier of a workflow operation.

10.4.3 Shell Modules

The Shell contains modules that implement all perspectives except the functional one. We pack these modules together to the so-called Shell to illustrate that these modules are grouped around the Kernel which is the central part of workflow processing. We present the modules "control_flow", "data", "organization", "synchronization", "assignment", "notification" and "workflow_application".

MODULE control_flow

Description. This module implements the behavioral aspect. It accesses control flow constructs and instantiates them. In this module a complex data type called *delta_set* is used which we define upfront. A delta set contains the changes in subworkflow execution if another subworkflow is either rejected, finished or used. For example, if a subworkflow is finished, another one might be available because of this. This new subworkflow is then within the delta set. If a subworkflow is rejected another one might be rejected also. This information is contained in the delta set. The structure is:

```
record delta_set is
  set_of(identifier): workflows_to_be_withdrawn;
  set_of(workflow_type, string):
    new_subworkflows_to_be_started;
  Boolean: no_more_subworkflows;
end record
```

```
EXPORT_OPERATION new_workflow
  (IN identifier: workflow_type,
    workflow_id,
    superworkflow_id);
```

Description. This operation tells the control flow module that a new workflow is instantiated. If a subworkflow is instantiated the identifier of the superworkflow is provided also. So, the control flow server knows about functional dependencies between workflows. This operation updates its data views by adding a workflow identifier and instantiating the workflow specified control flow construct.

```
EXPORT_OPERATION derive_subworkflows
  (IN identifier: workflow_id)
  returns set_of(workflow_type, string);
```

Description. This operation asks the control flow module about subworkflows for a workflow. It returns a set of subworkflow types and subworkflow instance names.

```
EXPORT_OPERATION rejected_workflow
  (IN identifier: workflow_id)
  returns delta_set;
```

Description. This operation tells the control flow module that a workflow will not be executed at all.

```
EXPORT_OPERATION finished_workflow
  (IN identifier: workflow_id)
  returns delta_set;
```

Description. This operation tells the control flow module that a workflow is finished.

In turn, the control flow module determines another workflow has to be started or an already started workflow has to be disabled.

```
EXPORT_OPERATION used_workflow
   (IN identifier: workflow_id)
   returns delta_set;
```

Description. This operation notifies the module that a workflow operation was already executed for the workflow. This means that a disable of the workflow is not possible any more.

```
DATA_VIEW set_of(identifier, identifier):
      running_workflow_instances;
```

Description. This data view contains all running workflow instances and the super-/subworkflow relationships.

```
DATA_VIEW set_of(identifier, control_flow_state):
      state_of_behavior;
```

Description. For a composite workflow, this data view contains the state of its control flow.

```
MODULE data
```

Description. This module manages the data flow between subworkflows or workflow operations. It also controls local variables and parameters of workflows and workflow operations.

```
EXPORT_OPERATION set_workflow_parameter
   (IN identifier: workflow_id;
   IN string: parameter_name;
   IN data_type_constant: parameter_value);
```

Description. Sets the value of a workflow parameter.

```
EXPORT_OPERATION set_workflow_parameters
   (IN identifier: workflow_id;
   IN set_of(string,data_type_constant): parameters);
```

Description. Sets the values of all workflow parameters.

```
EXPORT_OPERATION get_workflow_parameter
   (IN identifier: workflow_id;
   IN string: parameter_name)
   returns data_type_constant;
```

Description. This operation retrieves the value of a workflow parameter.

```
EXPORT_OPERATION set_operation_parameter
   (IN identifier: workflow_id;
   IN operation: workflow_operation;
   IN set_of(string, data_type_constant): parameter);
```

Description: Sets the value of a workflow operation parameter.

```
EXPORT_OPERATION get_operation_parameter
   (IN identifier: workflow_id;
   IN operation: workflow_operation;
   IN string: parameter_name)
```

```
    returns data_type_constant;
```
Description: Retrieves the value of a workflow operation parameter.

```
EXPORT_OPERATION set_workflow_local_variable
    (IN identifier: workflow_id;
    IN string: variable_name;
    IN data_type_constant: variable_value);
```
Description: Sets the value of a local workflow variable.

```
EXPORT_OPERATION get_workflow_local_variable
    (IN identifier: workflow_id;
    IN string: variable_name)
    returns data_type_constant;
```
Description: Retrieves the value of a local variable of a workflow.

```
EXPORT_OPERATION set_workflow_context_variable
    (IN identifier: workflow_id;
    IN string: variable_name;
    IN data_type_constant: variable_value);
```
Description: Sets the value of a workflow context variable.

```
EXPORT_OPERATION get_workflow_context_variable
    (IN identifier: workflow_id;
    IN string: variable_name)
    returns data_type_constant;
```
Description: Retrieves the value of a local variable of a workflow context.

```
EXPORT_OPERATION set_operation_local_variable
    (IN identifier: workflow_id;
    IN operation: workflow_operation;
    IN string: variable_name;
    IN data_type_constant: variable_value);
```
Description: Sets the value of a local variable of a workflow operation.

```
EXPORT_OPERATION get_operation_local_variable
    (IN identifier: workflow_id;
    IN operation: workflow_operation;
    IN string: variable_name)
    returns data_type_constant;
```
Description: Retrieves the value of a local variable of a workflow operation.

```
EXPORT_OPERATION new_subworkflow
    (IN identifier: workflow_id,
        superworkflow_id;
    IN identifier: workflow_type);
```
Description. This operation informs the data flow module about a new subworkflow that has started. It checks that required data are already available. This operation returns as soon as the data are available.

```
EXPORT_OPERATION finished_workflow
    (IN identifier: workflow_id);
```

Description. This operation notifies the data module about a finished workflow. This might be a top-level workflow or a subworkflow. In the latter case the data module can go ahead and continue to process the data flow within the superworkflow.

```
EXPORT_OPERATION rejected_workflow
   (IN identifier: workflow_id);
```
Description. This operation notifies the data module about a rejected workflow.

```
EXPORT_OPERATION started_operation
   (IN operation: workflow_operation;
   IN identifier: workflow_id);
```
Description. Notifies the data module about a started workflow operation. It checks that required data are available. This operation returns as soon as the data are available.

```
EXPORT_OPERATION finished_operation
   (IN operation: workflow_operation;
   IN identifier: workflow_id);
```
Description. Notifies the data module about a finished workflow operation.

```
EXPORT_OPERATION delete_workflow
   (IN identifier: workflow_id);
```
Description. This operation notifies the data module about a deleted workflow.

```
DATA_VIEW
   set_of(identifier,set_of(string, data_type_constant)):
     workflow_parameters;
```
Description. Contains all parameters of all workflow instances.

```
DATA_VIEW
   set_of(identifier, operation, set_of(string,
        data_type_constant)):
     workflow_operation_parameters;
```
Description. Contains all parameters of all workflow operations.

```
DATA_VIEW
   set_of(identifier, set_of(string, data_type_constant)):
     workflow_local_variables;
```
Description. Contains all local variables of all workflow instances.

```
DATA_VIEW
   set_of(identifier, set_of(data_type_constant)):
     workflow_context_variables;
```
Description. Contains all context variables of all workflow instances.

```
DATA_VIEW
   set_of(identifier, operation,
        set_of(data_type_constant)):
     operation_local_variables;
```
Description. Contains all local variables of all workflow operations.

```
DATA_VIEW
   set_of(identifier, data_flow_state): data_flow_status;
```
Description. This data view contains the state of the data flow within the composite

workflow for each composite workflow. The state is determined by the progress made when executing data flow rules.

SUB_MODULE `conversion_function_execution;`

Description. (This module is not detailed further.) As discussed in Chapter 6, conversion functions might be used to adjust data formats or data interpretations within the data flow. Due to the halting problem (Hopcroft and Ullman, 1969) the execution of these conversion functions is separated into a module. From an implementation model point of view this is not necessary. However, later on an implementation must be able to deal with the case that a conversion function runs indefinitely. Despite this, the module must work correctly. Having a separated module allows to put it into another process. Thus, the independence of the data module and the conversion function execution module is guaranteed.

MODULE `organization`

Description. This module enacts the organizational perspective.

```
EXPORT_OPERATION resolve_agents
   (IN identifier: workflow_type,
     workflow_id)
   returns set_of(identifier, set_of(operation),
     set_of(identifier));
```

Description. This operation determines a set of agents for a workflow operation based on the evaluation of organizational policies.

MODULE `notification`

Description. This module takes care of notifying agents about workflow operations. It is also required to de-notify agents. This makes already available workflow operations unavailable.

```
EXPORT_OPERATION notify_agents
   (IN identifier: workflow_id);
```

Description. This operation notifies agents about workflow operations they can execute. The agents do not have to be provided as parameters. Neither do the workflow operations. The information about which agent is eligible for which workflow operation is taken from the module *assignment*.

```
EXPORT_OPERATION notify_agents_except_executing_ones
   (IN identifier: workflow_id;
   IN operation: workflow_operation);
```

Description. This operation notifies agents about a workflow operation except those which are executing it already.

```
EXPORT_OPERATION denotify_agents
   (IN identifier: workflow_id;
   IN operation: workflow_operation);
```

Description. This operation de-notifies all agents so that a workflow operation is not available for them any more.

```
EXPORT_OPERATION denotify_agents_except_executing_ones
   (IN identifier: workflow_id;
   IN operation: workflow_operation;
   IN identifier: agent_id);
```

Description. This operation de-notifies all agents except those which are already executing the workflow operation and the one given as the actual parameter.

```
EXPORT_OPERATION denotify_agents_except_executing_ones
   (IN identifier: workflow_id;
   IN operation: workflow_operation);
```

Description. This operation de-notifies all agents except those which are already executing the workflow operation.

```
EXPORT_OPERATION denotify_agents
   (IN identifier: workflow_id);
```

Description. This operation de-notifies the agents of all workflow operations of the given workflow instance.

```
EXPORT_OPERATION delete_workflow
   (IN identifier: workflow_id);
```

Description. This operation tells that a workflow is deleted. It can in turn adjust its data views.

```
DATA_VIEW
   set_of(identifier, operation, notification_state):
      not_states;
```

Description. This data view contains the notification state for each workflow operation.

```
IMPORT_MODULE assignment;
```

Description. This module is used to ask whether a workflow operation that has to be synchronized is still available.

```
MODULE assignment
```

Description. This module stores the actual assignments of workflow operations to agents.

```
EXPORT_OPERATION set_assignment
   (IN identifier: workflow_id;
   IN set_of(operation): workflow_operations;
   IN set_of(identifier): agents);
```

Description. Relates agents with workflow operations. The set as input parameter is used in case an agent can execute more than one workflow operation.

```
EXPORT_OPERATION get_assignment
   (IN identifier: agent_id)
   returns set_of(identifier, operation);
```

Description. Provides assignment information. It returns all workflow operations which are assigned to one agent.

```
EXPORT_OPERATION get_assignment
   (IN identifier: workflow_id;
   IN operation: workflow_operation)
   returns set_of(identifier);
```

Description. This operation provides assignment information. It returns all agents which are assigned to one workflow operation.

```
EXPORT_OPERATION delete_workflow
   (IN identifier: workflow_id);
```

Description. This operation notifies the assignment module that a workflow is deleted.

```
DATA_VIEW
   set_of(identifier, operation, set_of(identifier,
     Boolean)): assignments;
```

Description. This data view contains the set of eligible agents for each workflow operation. The Boolean flag indicates if an agent is already notified about an workflow operation.

```
MODULE synchronization
```

Description. This module takes care of synchronizing agents.

```
EXPORT_OPERATION synchronize
   (IN identifier: workflow_id;
   IN operation: workflow_operation)
   returns {true, false, last_possible_agent};
```

Description. Checks whether a requested workflow operation can execute according to the synchronization rule which is specified. It returns true if the workflow operation can be executed and false if it cannot be executed. It returns last_possible_agent if the requesting agent is the last one. For example, if two agents can execute a workflow operation the first call returns true and the second one returns last_possible_agent. A third call would return false.

```
EXPORT_OPERATION done
   (IN identifier: workflow_id;
   IN operation: workflow_operation)
   returns {true, false}
```

Description. This operation notifies the synchronization module that a workflow operation is finished. In turn the module returns true if the workflow operation can be executed again, otherwise it returns false.

```
EXPORT_OPERATION delete_workflow
   (IN identifier: workflow_id);
```

Description. This operation tells the synchronization module that a workflow does not exist any more. The module can therefore adjust its data views accordingly.

```
DATA_VIEW
   set_of(identifier, operation, synchronization_state):
     sync_states;
```

Description. This data view contains the synchronization state for each workflow operation. For example, if a workflow operation is to be synchronized with a 1-out-of-many rule and has started already other execution attempts are rejected.

```
MODULE workflow_application
```

Description. This module manages and executes workflow applications.

```
EXPORT_OPERATION execute
   (IN identifier: workflow_application,
   IN set_of(data_type_constant): parameter)
   returns set_of(data_type_constant);
```

Description. This operation executes a workflow application. As in the case of workflow operations, parameters and return values are passed to the invocation directly by the caller instead of having to involve the data module.

10.4.4 Workspace Modules

The Workspace is the agents' interface to the workflow management system. All interactions are executed against the Workspace. It is implemented by the module "workspace".

```
MODULE workspace
```
Description. This module lists all workflows assigned to an agent together with the workflow operations an agent is eligible for. Furthermore, workflow operation execution can be initiated here.

```
EXPORT_OPERATION get_workflows
   (IN identifier: agent_id)
   returns set_of(identifier);
```
Description. This operation lists the identifier of all workflow instances which have at least one workflow operation the requesting agent is eligible to execute.

```
EXPORT_OPERATION get_operations
   (IN identifier: workflow_id;
   IN identifier: agent_id)
   returns set_of(operation);
```
Description. This operation lists all workflow operations of a workflow an agent is eligible to perform.

```
EXPORT_OPERATION execute_workflow_operation
   (IN identifier: workflow_id;
   IN operation: workflow_operation;
   INOUT set_of(data_type_constant): actual_parameter;
   IN identifier: agent_id);
```
Description. This operation executes the requested workflow operation.

```
IMPORT_MODULE workflow_operation_execution;
IMPORT_MODULE assignment;
```

Without any doubt, many more workspace module operations can be envisioned, such as *update_workflows* which returns workflow assigned since the last update, *show_executing_operations* which returns all workflow operations currently under execution. These operations would provide a more comfortable interface. However, we only aim to show a basic working set of workflow operations here.

10.5 Overview of the Implementation of the Perspectives

This section demonstrates where the perspectives of the comprehensive workflow model (Chapter 6) are implemented. In principle, the perspectives are implemented by module operations which are called by workflow operations.

In the following we summarize the implementation of perspectives based on the modules described in Section 10.4. We explain how the module operations are used to perform the tasks of the perspective. However, not all operations will be discussed since some are only auxiliary operations.

Section 10.6 shows the protocols which call module operations. These protocols (when executed) do the workflow processing. They show how the different perspectives work together in order to fulfill the tasks of a workflow management system.

10.5.1 Functional Perspective

The functional perspective is implemented by several modules. These are workflow_execution and workflow_operation_execution with the help of the module workflow and workflow_operation.

Whenever a workflow instance is to be created the operation create_workflow of the module workflow_execution is called. A workflow is deleted by delete_workflow. A user rejection of a workflow causes the operation reject_workflow to be called. If an already assigned workflow is not valid any more (e.g. because of control flow reasons), the operation disable_workflow is called. A rejected or a disabled workflow is not available for workflow execution any more.

The execution of subworkflows requires several module operation invocations. In the following we want to summarize what has to happen. When a composite workflow is running its subworkflows are not started automatically. Subworkflows only run when an agent initiates subworkflow execution. When a set of subworkflows is derived the operation next_subworkflows is called which in turn creates these subworkflows by calling a workflow operation start_subworkflow (see Section 10.7). This operation might be called several times depending on the workflow execution progress. The operation set_subworkflow is used to relate subworkflows to their superworkflows. The operation no_more_subworkflows says that there will be no new subworkflows to be executed any more. The operation finish_executing_subworkflows says that all subworkflows which were under execution are finished. In turn a workflow operation finish_subworkflow_execution is called which processes the module operations of transition (11) (cf. Section 10.6.2). Then subworkflow processing of a workflow is completed.

When an agent starts a workflow operation the module operation execute_workflow_instance_operation or execute_workflow_type_ operation of the module workflow_operation_execution is called to actually do it. How a workflow operation body is executed is explained in Section 10.6.3.

10.5.2 Behavioral Perspective

The behavioral perspective is implemented by the module control_flow. As soon as a new workflow (either elementary or composite) is started the operation new_workflow is called. As soon as subworkflow processing is started by an agent the operation derive_subworkflows is executed returning the first set of executable subworkflows according to control flow specifications (the result is then passed to the next_subworkflows operation of the workflow_execution module). If a workflow is finished the operation finished_workflow is called. As a result two sets and a flag are returned. The first set contains new subworkflows to be started because one was finished. This is determined by evaluating the control flow constructs. The second set contains subworkflows which cannot be executed any more even though they might be assigned to agents already (but not started by them). The flag indicates if all subworkflows are processed.

If an agent starts executing workflow operations the control flow module is informed by the operation used_workflow. If an agent denies executing workflow operations the control flow module operation rejected_workflow is called.

10.5.3 Informational Perspective

The informational perspective is implemented by the module data. The perspective distinguishes workflow parameters from operation parameters as well as workflow variables from operation variables. Furthermore, workflow context variables are stored. For each of these classes of data operations for definition and retrieval of the values are available, e.g. set_workflow_parameter and get_workflow_context_variable.

Besides the management of data the module has to implement the data flow. Several operations are available to indicate when data flow has to be evaluated. As soon as a new subworkflow is started the operation new_subworkflow is called. This enables the data module to provide actual parameter values. If a workflow is finished the operation finished_ workflow is called. This triggers the data module to evaluate the data flow (e.g. for the next subworkflows). The operation rejected_workflow indicates that a workflow does not produce an output parameter. The data module can act accordingly. If a workflow is deleted the data module gets a message by calling deleted_workflow. It can in turn update internal data structures. Whenever a workflow operation is started or finished the module operation started_operation or finished_operation is called to allow the data module to evaluate the data flow rules.

10.5.4 Organizational Perspective

The organizational perspective is implemented by the module organization and the module synchronization with the help of the modules assignment and notification. There is only one operation within the module organization. This operation is called when the agents for a workflow and its operations have to be determined.

Workflow operations have to be synchronized. Whenever an agent tries to start a workflow operation it has to be checked if the agent can be synchronized. The operation synchronize is used for this. If the agent can be synchronized it can execute the workflow operation. As soon as a workflow operation is finished the done operation is called indicating the end of the workflow operation execution. As soon as a workflow is deleted the operation delete_workflow is called which allows the synchronization module to update its internal data structures.

The module assignment stores which agent is assigned which workflow operation. Assignments can be set and retrieved through various operations like set_assignment and get_assignment. As in other modules the deletion of a workflow is indicated by the operation delete_workflow.

The assignment is made known to the agent by the module notification. The operations notify_agents and denotify_agents (and their various variants) are used to indicate if an assigned operation can be seen by an agent. This is used to make a workflow operation temporarily invisible for an agent, e.g. because another agent executes the operation.

10.5.5 Operational Perspective

The operational perspective is implemented by the module workflow_application. It consists of one operation execute, which is called whenever a workflow application has to be started.

10.6 Protocols

This section depicts how the various modules described in Section 10.4.1 through 10.4.4 cooperate in order to execute a workflow instance. This is done by demonstrating how the execution protocols introduced in Chapter 7 are associated with module operations.

A protocol describes a complete path through all relationships of modules. In the following we demonstrate how the protocols of Chapter 7 are enacted by module operations, whereby alternative execution paths and a comprehensive discussion of failures will be omitted. The state transition diagrams shown were introduced in Chapter 7. To better illustrate the execution of protocols we show them here again. Module operations are added to the transitions of the diagrams. The set of module operations attached to a transition has to be executed before the transition is completed, i.e. before the state at the end of the transition is reached.

Workflow operations (e.g. start, pause, resume, finish) trigger a workflow to move between states. Workflow operations are performed by the module workflow_operation_execution. It interprets the workflow operation body and triggers appropriate module operations as specified within the workflow operation body. Thus, the workflow_operation_execution module does call those module operations which are specified by state transitions. Figure 10.3 gives a coarse grain overview workflow operation execution.

10.6.1 Executing Elementary Workflows

In this section the execution of elementary workflows is shown. Figure 10.4 depicts the state transition diagram for the execution of elementary workflows. In the following, each transition shown in Figure 10.4 is associated with a set of module operation invocations. The parameters required for these invocations are available in the workflow operation execution context. Whenever a workflow operation is executed it belongs to a specific workflow instance. The workflow instance identifier is then available within the workflow operation (*$workflow_id*) and its type is stored in *$workflow_type*. The parameters of the module operation invocation are available in *$parameter*. The agent performing an operation can be accessed with *$agent_id*.

- Through transition (1) a workflow instance is created (cf. Section 10.7).

```
workflow_execution.create_workflow($workflow_type)
data.set_workflow_parameters($workflow_id, $parameter)
data.set_workflow_context_variable($workflow_id,
  "workflow_id", $workflow_id)
data.set_workflow_context_variable($workflow_id,
  "workflow_type", $workflow_type)
data.set_workflow_context_variable($workflow_id,
  "initiator", $agent_id)
res := <$workflow_id,
  workflow_execution.get_instance_operations(
  $workflow_id), {"default"}>1
res := organization.resolve_agents($workflow_type,
  $workflow_id)
assignment.set_assignment(res)
control_flow.new_workflow($workflow_type, $workflow_id,
  $superworkflow_id)
```

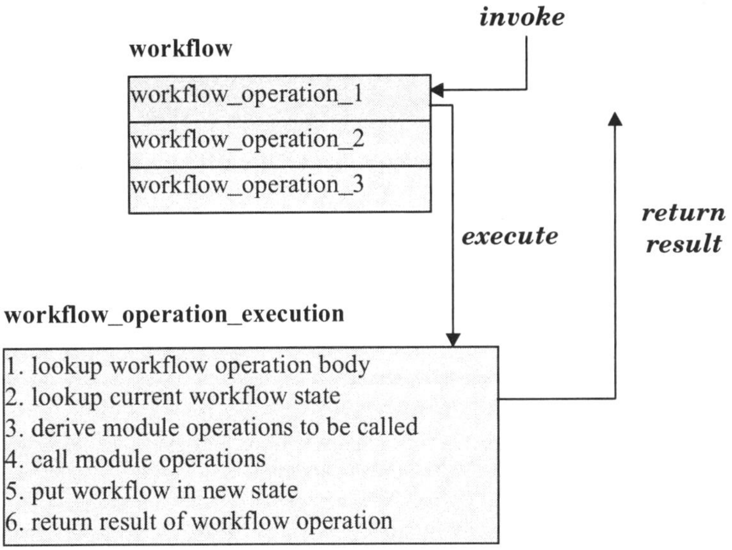

Figure 10.3: Overview on Workflow Operation Execution

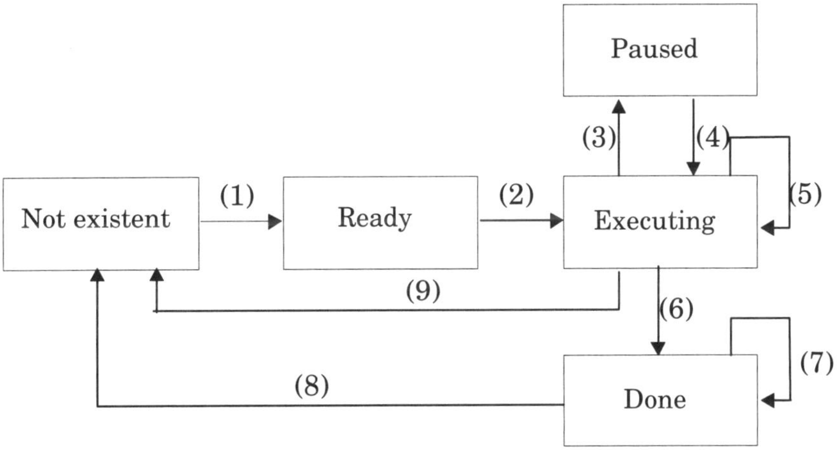

Figure 10.4: Execution Model for an Elementary Workflow

```
workflow_execution.set_to_next_state_workflow(
  $workflow_id, "ready")
```

- Agents are notified by transition (2) about workflows and workflow operations ready for execution.

```
notification.notify_agents($workflow_id)
workflow_execution.set_to_next_state_workflow(
  $workflow_id,"executing")
```

- Transition (3) pauses the execution of a workflow instance.

```
ifworkflow_execution.exists_executing_workflow_operations(
  $workflow_id) = true
```

```
then return with failure
end_if
workflow_execution.set_to_next_state_workflow($workflow_id,
  "paused")
```

- A workflow instance is resumed by transition (4).

```
workflow_execution.set_to_next_state_workflow($workflow_id,
  "executing")
```

- Transition (5) represents workflow operation execution. When a workflow operation is executed the workflow instance remains in the state "executing". Section 10.6.3 details workflow operation execution.
- By transition (6) a workflow operation execution is finished and is put in the state "done". This is only possible if no other workflow operations are executing.

```
if workflow_execution.exists_executing_workflow_operations(
  $workflow_id) = true
then return with failure
end_if
if workflow_execution.is_subworkflow($workflow_id)
then begin
     d := control_flow.finished_workflow($workflow_id)
   if d.new_subworkflows_to_be_startednot empty
   then workflow_execution.next_subworkflows(
     $superworkflow_id,
     d.new_subworkflows_to_be_started)
   end_if
   if d.workflows_to_be_withdrawnnot empty
   then workflow_execution.disable_workflows(
     d.workflows_to_be_withdrawn)
   end_if
   if d.no_more_subworkflows = true
   then workflow_execution.no_more_subworkflows(
     $superworkflow_id)
   end_if
end_if
data.finished_workflow($workflow_id)
workflow_execution.set_to_next_state_workflow($workflow_id,
  "done")
```

- Transition (7) also represents workflow operation execution.
- A workflow instance is deleted in transition (8).

```
data.delete_workflow($workflow_id)
notification.denotify_agents($workflow_id)
notification.delete_workflow($workflow_id)
```

```
synchronization.delete_workflow($workflow_id)
assignment.delete_workflow($workflow_id)
workflow_execution.delete_workflow($workflow_id)
```

- Transition (9) represents the rejection of workflows.

```
if workflow_execution.is_subworkflow($workflow_id)
then begin
  d := control_flow.rejected_workflow($workflow_id)
  if d.new_subworkflows_to_be_startednot empty
  then workflow_execution.next_workflows(
    $superworkflow_id,
    d.new_subworkflows_to_be_started)
  end_if
  if d.workflows_to_be_withdrawnnot empty
  then workflow_execution.disable_workflows(
    d.workflows_to_be_withdrawn)
  end_if
  if d.no_more_subworkflows = true
  then workflow_execution.no_more_subworkflows(
    $superworkflow_id)
  end_if
end_if
notification.denotify_agents($workflow_id)
notification.delete_workflow($workflow_id)
synchronization.delete_workflow($workflow_id)
assignment.delete_workflow($workflow_id)
data.rejected_workflow($workflow_id)
workflow_execution.rejected_workflow($workflow_id)
workflow_execution.set_to_next_state_workflow_instance(
  $workflow_id, "not existent")
```

10.6.2 Executing Composite Workflows

Figure 10.5 depicts the state transition diagram for the execution of composite workflows. This section shows which module operations have to be invoked at the state transitions of Figure 10.5.

State transitions (1) to (9) are explained in Section 10.6.1. Transition (6) has to be modified (see *below). Therefore, only state transitions (10) to (14) are detailed subsequently.

- By transition (6) a workflow operation execution is finished and is put in state "done". This is only possible if other workflow operations or subworkflows are not executing any more.

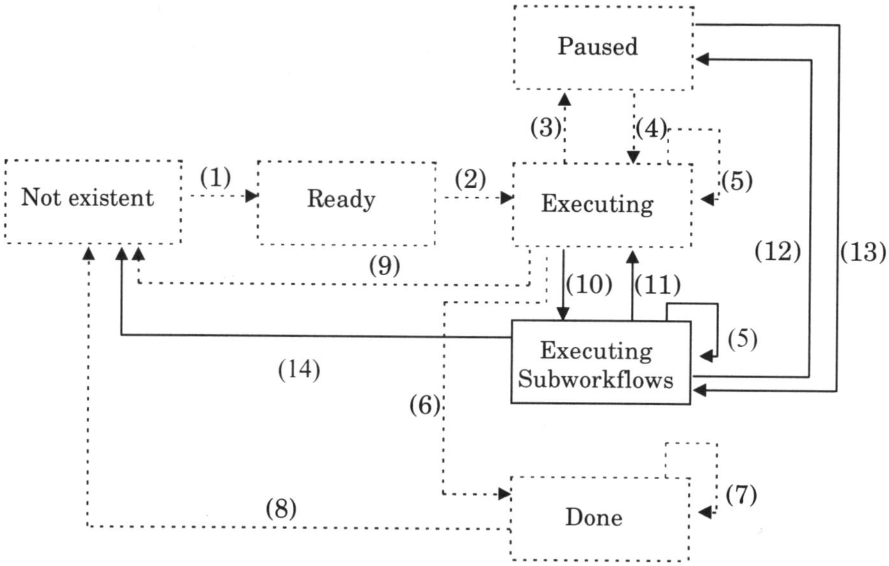

Figure 10.5: Execution Model for a Composite Workflow

```
if workflow_execution.exists_executing_workflow_operations(
  $workflow_id) = true
then return with failure
end_if
* if workflow_execution.exists_executing_subworkflows(
*  $workflow_id)
* then return with failure
* end_if
if workflow_execution.is_subworkflow($workflow_id)
then begin
  d := control_flow.finished_workflow($workflow_id)
  if d.new_subworkflows_to_be_started not empty
  then workflow_execution.next_subworkflows(
    $superworkflow_id,
      d.new_subworkflows_to_be_started)
  end_if
  if d.workflows_to_be_withdrawn not empty
  then workflow_execution.disable_workflows(
    d.workflows_to_be_withdrawn)
  end_if
  if d.no_more_subworkflows = true
  then workflow_execution.no_more_subworkflows(
    $superworkflow_id)
  end_if
end_if
```

```
data.finished_workflow($workflow_id)
workflow_execution.set_to_next_state_workflow($workflow_id,
"done")
```

- Transition (10) starts the execution of subworkflows.

```
sw := workflow_execution.get_subworkflows($workflow_id)²
sw := control_flow.derive_subworkflows($workflow_id)
foreach sub_wf in sw do
  s := workflow_execution.
    execute_workflow_type_operation(
    sub_wf.workflow_type, "start_subworkflow",
    {sub_wf.workflow_type, $workflow_id}, sub_wf.name)
  workflow_execution.set_subworkflow($workflow_id, s)
end_foreach
workflow_execution.set_to_next_state_workflow($workflow_id,
"executing subworkflows")
```

- In transition (11) subworkflow execution is finished.

```
if workflow_execution.exist_executing_subworkflows(
  $workflow_id) = true
then return with failure
end_if
workflow_execution.set_to_next_state_workflow ($workflow_id,
"executing")
```

- Transition (12) behaves as transition (3).
- Transition (13) is analogous to transition (4)
- Transition (14) is similar to transition (9). However, to reject a workflow instance, its subworkflows have to be in a state where rejection is possible.

10.6.3 Executing Workflow Operations

Figure 10.6 shows the state transition diagram for the executing of workflow operations. In the following we complete it by module operations and derive the workflow operation execution protocol from it.

The following module operation invocations are attached to the transitions in the state transition diagram of Figure 10.6. *$operation* contains the operation name of the workflow operation under execution.

- Transition (1) assigns a workflow operation to eligible agents.

```
workflow_operation_execution.set_to_next_state (
  $workflow_id, $operation, "assigned")
notification.notify_agents($workflow_id)
```

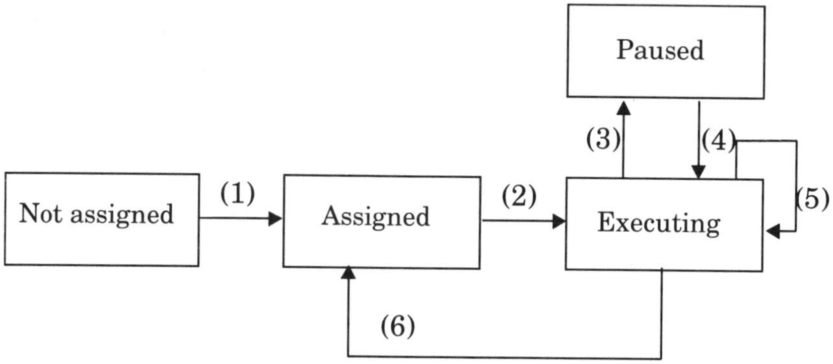

Figure 10.6: State Transition Diagram for Workflow Operation Execution

- By transition (2) agents who are not eligible any more are synchronized and de-notified.

```
x := workflow_execution.exists_executing_workflow_operation(
  $workflow_id, $operation)³
if synchronization.synchronize($workflow_id, $operation) =
  true
then x = false
end_if
if synchronization.synchronize($workflow_id, $operation) =
  false
then x = true
end_if
if last_possible_agent = synchronization.synchronize(
  $workflow_id, $operation)
then x = false
end_if
if x
then return with failure
end_if
if workflow_execution.is_subworkflow($workflow_id)
then begin
  d := control_flow.used_workflow($workflow_id)
  if d.new_subworkflows_to_be_started not empty
  then workflow_execution.next_subworkflows(
    $superworkflow_id,
    d.new_subworkflows_to_be_started)
  end_if
  if d.workflows_to_be_withdrawn not empty
  then workflow_execution.disable_workflows(
    d.workflows_to_be_withdrawn)
  end_if
```

```
    if d.no_more_subworkflows = true
    then workflow_execution.no_more_subworkflows(
      $superworkflow_id)
    end_if
  end_if
  if x = last_possible_agent
  then notification.denotify_agents_except_executing_ones(
    $workflow_id, $operation, $agent_id)
  end_if
  data.set_operation_parameter($workflow_id, $operation,
    $parameter)
  data.started_operation($operation, $workflow_id)
  workflow_operation_execution.set_to_next_state (
    $workflow_id,$operation, "executing")
```

- Transition (3) pauses the execution of a workflow operation.

```
if workflow_operation_execution.
  exists_executing_command($workflow_id, $operation)
  = true
then return with failure
end_if
workflow_operation_execution.set_to_next_state (
  $workflow_id,$operation, "paused")
```

- A paused workflow operation is resumed by transition (4).

```
workflow_operation_execution.set_to_next_state (
  $workflow_id,$operation, "executing")
```

- Executing a workflow operation body does not change the state of a workflow operation. Therefore transition (5) remains in the state "executing".
- After a workflow operation is finished transition (6) puts it into the state "assigned" in case an agent can execute the workflow operation again. If he can actually execute it again is determined by synchronization in conjunction with notification.

```
data.set_operation_parameter($workflow_id, $operation,
  $parameter)
data.finished_operation($operation, $workflow_id)
s := synchronization.done($workflow_id, $operation)
workflow_operation_execution.set_to_next_state (
  $workflow_id,$operation, "assigned")
if s
then notification.notify_agents_except_executing_ones(
  $workflow_id, $operation)
else notification.denotify_agents_except_executing_ones(
  $workflow_id, $operation)
end_if
```

The protocol which executes a workflow operation is shown next. A workflow operation which is about to be called is already in the state "assigned" (cf. Figure 10.6). This transition is triggered by the module operation *notification. notify_ agents()* in the state transition diagram of elementary and composite workflows (transition (2) in Figure 10.4).

The protocol for workflow operation execution starts in state "assigned". The protocol is shown next. It can be derived by walking through the state transition diagram. However, the "pause" state and commands that set new states are omitted.

The protocol is the same for workflow instance operations and workflow type operations.

```
workflow_operation_execution.execute_workflow_instance_operation()
(1) → workflow_execution.exists_executing_workflow_operation()
(2) → synchronization.synchronize()
(3) → workflow_execution.is_subworkflow()
(4) → control_flow.used_workflow()
(5) → workflow_execution.next_subworkflows()
(6) → workflow_execution.disable_subworkflows()
(7) → workflow_execution.no_more_subworkflows()
(8) → notification.denotify_agents_except_executing_ones()
(9) → data.set_operation_parameter()
(10)→ data.started_operation()
(11)→ workflow_operation_execution.execute_operation_body()
(12)→ data.set_operation_parameter()
(13)→ data.finished_operation()
(14)→ synchronization.done()
(15)→ notification.notify_agents_except_executing_ones()
(16)→ notification.denotify_agents_except_executing_ones()
```

Figure 10.7 shows a graphical representation of the workflow operation execution protocol. The module operation execute_workflow_instance is called by the worklist (bold arrow). The order of the module calls within this module operation is indicated by the numbers attached to the normal arrows. (The module operation call number 11 is not detailed since it itself calls module operations.)

The protocol of Figure 10.7 is used for the execution of a workflow operation. Executing a workflow operation is therefore invariant to the specific implementation of a workflow operation.

In the following the execution of the body of a workflow operation is described in more detail. Figure 10.8 shows the corresponding state transition diagram. Data mentioned in this figure might be parameters of a workflow operation, local variables of a workflow operation or context variables of the workflow instance the operation is executed for. Whenever the execution semantics has to be changed, only the corresponding parts of the state transition diagrams must

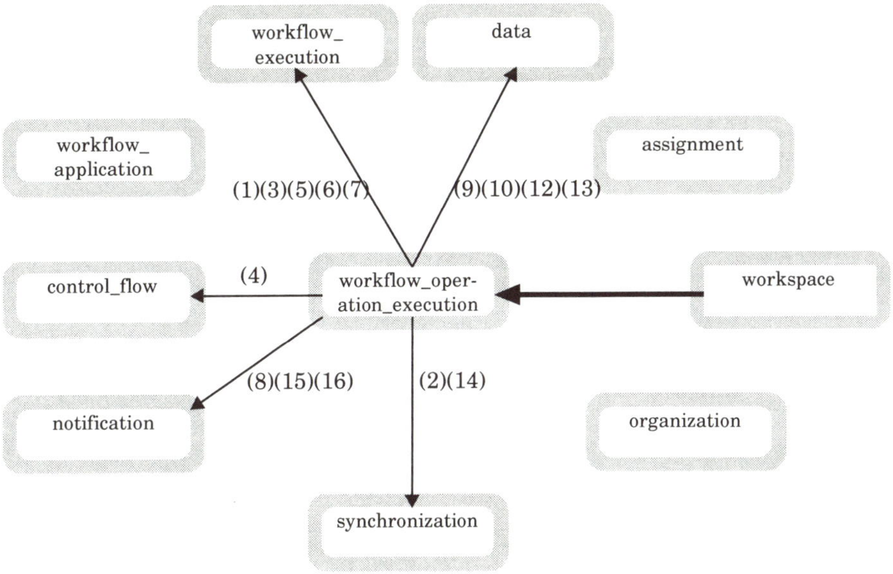

Figure 10.7: Workflow Operation Execution Protocol

be updated, the workflow_execution module does not have to be modified at all. Neither does the module workflow_operation_execution need to be changed. The execution of a workflow operation itself happens according a state transition diagram (Section 10.6.3).

To enhance or change the functionality of workflows only new workflow operations must be defined or existing workflow operations must be updated. It is therefore not necessary to change any other module.

The state transition diagrams of Figure 10.4, Figure 10.5, Figure 10.6 and Figure 10.8 have to be changed if elementary and composite workflows, workflow operations or workflow operation bodies do not meet the requirements any more. This should only happen very rarely. In order to be able to perform such a change, the state transition diagrams are not "hard wired" but can be constructed themselves (see module STDiagram).

To execute an elementary or a composite workflow, the state diagrams of Figure 10.4 or Figure 10.5 have to be performed. Transitions in state transition diagrams are caused by the execution of workflow operations. Figure 10.6 shows that a workflow operation must be assigned to one or more agents to be executable. In case it is executed, state transition (2) of Figure 10.6 is performed. The execution of the workflow operations happens according the state transition diagram of Figure 10.8. The commands mentioned in this figure correspond to the module operations that are attached to the transition of the state transition diagram of the workflow under execution (cf. Figure 10.4 or Figure 10.5). For example, the workflow operation "start" (for an elementary workflow) causes the execution

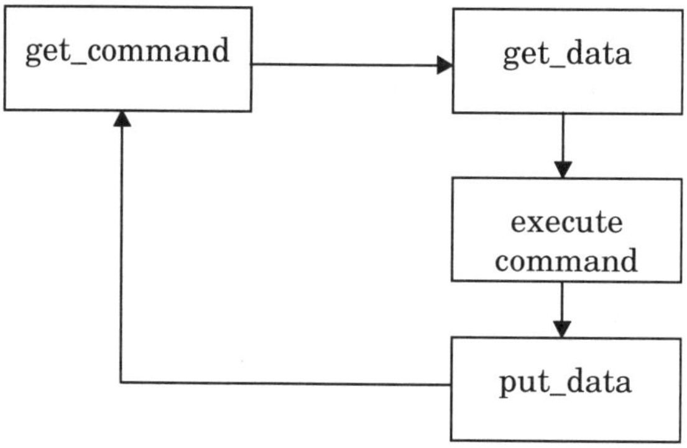

Figure 10.8: State Transition Diagram for the Execution of a Workflow Operation Body

of the module operations attached to transitions (1) and (2) in Figure 10.4. After the module operations are completed, the actions associated with state transition (6) in Figure 10.6 are performed. After that, the workflow operation is done.

10.7 Execution of Example Workflow Operations

In the first part of this section some example workflow operations are specified. The workflow operations shown here form a common working set, i.e. they form a basic set of workflow operations that is needed to perform workflows. The workflow operations start, finish, start_ subworkflow_execution, reject and start_ subworkflow are discussed. A workflow operation sign is added also to show what a workflow operation specific to a workflow type could look like, e.g. travel expense reimbusement.

The second part of the section discusses origins of workflow operation calls. In principle, calls can originate from the workspace of a user or from modules.

10.7.1 Definition of Example Workflow Operations

The workflow operation "start" starts a new top-level workflow. This workflow operation is available for each workflow type, i.e. it works against a workflow type. The specification of the "start" workflow operation follows:

```
T_OPERATION start
   (IN set_of(data_type_constants): workflow_parameters)
      (* these workflow parameters have to be provided
      when the operation is called *)
   commands := $workflow_id.invocations_for_next_state("ready")
                  (* this invocation retrieves the
                  commands from the STDiagram of the
```

```
                    workflow instance which have to be
                    executed before it can be put to the state
                    "ready". These are the module operations
                    from transition (1) *)
  foreach c in commands do
                    (* according to Figure 10.4 this list
                    contains ten module operation
                    invocations *)
      call c;       (* this command is executed *)
  end_foreach;
                    (* now the state "ready" is reached *
  commands := $workflow_id.invocations_for_next_state(
              "executing")
                    (* this invocation retrieves the
                    commands from the STDiagram of the
                    workflow instance which have to be
                    executed before it can be put to the state
                    "executing" *)
  foreach c in commands do
                    (* according to Figure 10.4 this list
                    contains two module operation
                    invocations *)
      call c;       (* this command is executed *)
  end_foreach;
                    (*now the state "executing" is reached
                    and notified agents can start to work *)
END_OPERATION
```

The workflow operation "finish" terminates the execution of a workflow instance. The workflow instance is not deleted, but is still available. The "finish" workflow operation puts a workflow into the state "done".

```
I_OPERATION finish()


commands := $workflow_id.invocations_for_next_state("done")
                        (* this invocation retrieves the
                        commands from the STDiagram of the
                        workflow instance which have to be
                        executed before it can be put to the state
                        "done" (transition(6)) *)
  foreach c in commands do
      result := call c;  (* this command is executed *)
      if result <> ok
      then break;       (* if the command execution leads to an
                        error, the execution of the overall
                        operation is finished. In this case
```

```
                                there might be other workflow
                                operations under execution.
                                So the caller of the finish
                                operation has to call again. *)
      end_if
   end_foreach;
                                (*now the state "done" is reached *)
END_OPERATION
```

The workflow operation "start_subworkflow_execution" is used to start the execution of subworkflows for a workflow instance. It is called by an agent who wants to begin the execution of subworkflows.

```
I_OPERATION start_subworkflow_execution()
   commands := $workflow_id.
     invocations_for_next_state("executing_subworkflows")
                                (* this invocation retrieves the
                                commands from the STDiagram of the
                                workflow instance which have to be
                                executed before it can be put in the
                                state "executing subworkflows"
                                (transition(10)) *)
   foreach c in commands do
      result := call c;   (* this command is executed *)
      if result <> ok
      then break;         (* if the command execution leads to an
                                error, the execution of the overall
                                operation is finished. *)
      end_if
   end_foreach;
                                (* now the state "executing
                                subworkflows" is reached *)
END_OPERATION
```

The workflow operation "reject" prohibits a workflow instance from being started. This workflow instance has not executed yet.

```
I_OPERATION reject()
   commands := $workflow_id.
     invocations_for_next_state("non_existent")
                                (* this invocation retrieves the
                                commands from the STDiagram of the
                                workflow instance which have to be
                                executed before it can be put to the
                                state "executing subworkflows"
                                (transition(9)) *)
```

```
  foreach c in commands do
      result := call c;   (* this command is executed *)
      if result <> ok
      then break;          (* if the command execution leads to an
                         error, the execution of the overall
                         operation is finished. *)
      end_if
  end_foreach;
                         (* now the state "non_existent"
                         is reached *)
END_OPERATION
```

The next workflow operation to be presented is "sign". This operation demonstrates how an editor is invoked. This workflow operation is used to edit a document. It does not affect the state of the corresponding workflow instance. The commands "cp", "edit", "prompt_user" and "rm" are workflow applications invoking appropriate application programs. This workflow operation is specific to a particular workflow type since it implements certain application semantics.

```
I_OPERATION sign(IN string: filename)
  if workflow_execution.get_state_workflow($workflow_id)
    ≠ "executing"
  then return with failure;
                    (* this avoids this operation being called
                    in a state other than execution. *)
  end_if
  workflow_application.execute(cp, {filename,filename
    ∘"bck"});
                    (* making a backup by copying the file
                    into one with the same name and an
                    appendix "bck" *)
  workflow_application.execute(edit, {filename})
                    (* an editor is called *)
  res := workflow_application.execute(prompt_user,
    {"undo changes?"})
                    (* the user is asked if he wants to
                    undo the changes *)
  if res
  then   workflow_application.execute(cp,
           {filename∘"bck", filename});
         workflow_application.execute(rm, {filename∘"bck"});
  else   workflow_application.execute(rm, {filename∘"bck"});
  end_if
END_OPERATION
```

The last workflow operation to be detailed is called "start_ subworkflow". It is used by the workflow_execution module only. Agents are not allowed to trigger it. The workflow operation causes the initiation of a subworkflow of a composite workflow. In contrast, the workflow operation "start" initiates processing of a top-level workflow. This operation is called by workflow_execution whenever a new subworkflow is determined by the module operation next_subworkflows.

```
I_OPERATION start_subworkflow(IN identifier: workflow_type,
  superworkflow_id; IN string: name) returns identifier;
  $workflow_id := workflow_execution.create_workflow(
    workflow_type)
  data.new_subworkflow($workflow_id, superworkflow_id,
    workflow_type)
  data.set_workflow_context_variable
    ($workflow_id, "workflow_id", $workflow_id)
  data.set_workflow_context_variable
    ($workflow_id, "workflow_type", workflow_type)
  data.set_workflow_context_variable
    ($workflow_id, "superworkflow_id", superworkflow_id)
  res := <$workflow_id, workflow_execution.
    get_instance_operations($workflow_id), {"default"}>4
  res := organization.resolve_agents($workflow_type,
    $workflow_id)
  assignment.set_assignment(res)
  control_flow.new_workflow
    (workflow_type, $workflow_id, superworkflow_id)
  workflow_execution.set_to_next_state_workflow(
    $workflow_id,"ready")
  commands := $workflow_id.invocations_for_next_state(
    "executing")
                 (* this invocation retrieves the
                 commands from the STDiagram of the
                 workflow instance which have to be
                 executed before it can be put to the state
                 "executing" *)
  foreach c in commands do
       call c;   (* this command is executed *)
  end_foreach;
                 (*now the state "executing" is reached
                 and notified agents can start to work *)
  return $workflow_id
END_OPERATION
```

10.7.2 Origins of Workflow Operation Calls

The workspace is the main interface to users of a workflow management system. A user can view assigned workflow instances together with the possible workflow operations in the workspace. Most appropriately the workspace is implemented as a graphical user interface.

If a user wants to execute a workflow operation she indirectly calls the module operation execute_workflow_operation (e.g. by pressing a button or by selecting a menu item). In addition, workflow operations can be called by a module. This was discussed in the context of the operation start_subworkflow which is called by the workflow_execution module to start subworkflows. Whenever a new subworkflow is ready to be started (indicated by next_subworkflow) the workflow_execution module calls the workflow operation start_subworkflow.

In the following scenario the execution of workflow operations also originates in a module. The scenario describes how composite workflows are automically terminated. So far, a workflow instance is finished as soon as the workflow operation finish succeeds (see Section 10.7.1). However, this requires that an agent calls this workflow operation. If it fails (because some subworkflow still runs), the agent has to call it again. This behavior is certainly not acceptable in general. Often composite workflow instances should finish automatically. This can be achieved in the following way. Whenever a module recognizes that a composite workflow can be finished it calls the finish operation. For example, if data flow is complete, the data module calls the finish operation. If there are still subworkflows running, the operation execution will fail. If all subworkflows are finished the control flow module itself calls the workflow operation finish. If all conditions are fulfilled under which "finish" can succeed the workflow instance is finally terminated. This protocol can run automatically without agent interaction.

10.8 Sample Change of Execution Model

In this section we discuss how the semantics of the execution model can be changed. Before the discussion of how to add a new perspective in Section 10.8.2 (history perspective) and how to drop an existing perspective in Section 10.8.3 (information perspective) we discuss the scope of changes in Section 10.8.1. The scope of a change defines whether all workflow types and workflow instances are affected by the change or only a certain subset.

10.8.1 Scope of Changes

Changes to the execution model can be threefold: first, adding a new perspective, second, removing an existing perspective, or third, changing an existing perspective. The third case is not further discussed here since changes within an existing perspective take place in the modules implementing this perspective. These changes are not visible within the execution model except if the interfaces of modules are changed. In that case the change can be seen as removing the perspective and adding it after the change.

Adding a perspective means to add one or more new modules to the execution model. As in the case of other perspectives, module operations have to be inserted into the state transition diagrams or the workflow operations.

The state transition diagrams discussed in Section 10.6 are used for the execution of all workflows. If a state transition diagram is changed all workflows are affected from then on. Changes in those diagrams are therefore global to all workflows.

The scope of changes in workflow operations is different. If a workflow operation is local to a specific workflow type only instances of this workflow type are affected in the case of a change. However, if a workflow operation is global to all workflow types all workflow instances are affected in the case of a change.

Removing a perspective means to remove module operation calls from either the state transition diagrams or the workflow operations or both. As in the case of adding module operations, removing them affects all workflow instances or only instances of one workflow type.

10.8.2 Adding History Perspective

Extending the execution model with a history perspective requires to add the operation invocations of a history module to the state transition diagrams where recordings should be made. In the following such a history module is shown. It has two operations, one for storing history relevant events (enter_event) and one for retrieving them (retrieve_event).

```
MODULE history
```
Description. This module records events.

```
EXPORT_OPERATION enter_event
   (IN identifier: workflow_id;
   IN string: event_class;
   IN set_of(string): event_keys;
   IN set_of(data_type_constant): event_data);
```
Description. This operation records an event which belongs to a workflow instance. Besides the data to be recorded (*event_data*) an event class for classifying events is stored. Keys are added also to improve searching.

```
EXPORT_OPERATION retrieve_event
  (IN identifier: workflow_id;
  IN string: event_class;
  IN set_of(string): seach_keys)
  returns set_of(data_type_constant);
```
Description. This operation is used to retrieve history data for a specific workflow. Besides an event class, specific keys can be provided.

```
DATA_VIEW
  table(identifier,
    string,
    set_of(string),
    set_of(data_type_constant)): history;
```
Description. This data view contains all history information.

The workflow operation execution module must know about the history module (this might be done by registering its interfaces there). Additionally, the module operations have to be added to the state transition diagrams or workflow operations. In the following some sample changes are discussed.

As an example we require that starting and finishing of a workflow instance has to be recorded. It has to be recorded who does it and when. Whenever the workflow operation sign is called we would like to know if the changes are undone or accepted by the agent.

Transition (1) of Figure 10.4 is altered in the following way:

```
workflow_execution.create_workflow($workflow_type)
history.enter_event($workflow_id, "workflow_execution",
  {$workflow_id}, {$agent_id, date, "created"})
data.set_workflow_parameters($workflow_id, $parameter)
...
```

In addition the workflow operation start_subworkflow has to be changed to be able to record the creating of subworkflows:

```
I_OPERATION start_subworkflow(IN identifier: workflow_type,
  superworkflow_id; IN string: name) returns identifier;
  $workflow_id := workflow_execution.create_workflow(
    workflow_type)
  history.enter_event($workflow_id, "workflow_execution",
    {$workflow_id}, {$agent_id, date, "created"})
  data.new_subworkflow($workflow_id, superworkflow_id,
    workflow_type)
  ...
  return $workflow_id
END_OPERATION
```

So far the requirement to record the start of a workflow instance is fulfilled. Finishing of a workflow has to be recorded also according to the requirements list. So transition (6) of Figure 10.4 and transition (8) of Figure 10.5 have to be altered. We show transition (6) of Figure 10.4 here:

```
...
data.finished_workflow($workflow_id)
history.enter_event($workflow_id, "workflow_execution",
  {$workflow_id}, {$agent_id, date, "finished"})
workflow_execution.set_to_next_state_workflow($workflow_id,
"done")
```

As soon as a workflow instance is started using the new state transition diagram recording takes place.

What is left is to change the workflow operation sign to record if changes made to a file are accepted or undone:

```
I_OPERATION sign(IN string: filename)
  if workflow_execution.get_state_workflow($workflow_id)
    ≠ "executing"
  then return with failure;
                    (* this avoids this operation being called
                    in a state other than execution. *)
  end_if
  workflow_application.execute(cp,
{filename, filename∘"bck"});
                    (* making a backup by copying the file
                    into one with the same name and an
                    appendix "bck" *)
  workflow_application.execute(edit, {filename})
                    (* an editor is called *)
  res := workflow_application.execute(prompt_user,
    {"undo changes?"})
                    (* the user is asked if he wants to
                    undo the changes *)
  if res
  then   workflow_application.execute(cp,
            {filename∘"bck", filename});
         workflow_application.execute(rm, {filename∘"bck"});
         history.enter_event($workflow_id,
            "operation_execution",
            {$workflow_id, $operation},
            {$agent_id, date, "undone"})
  else   workflow_application.execute(rm, {filename∘"bck"});
         history.enter_event($workflow_id,
```

```
            "operation_execution",
            {$workflow_id, $operation},
            {$agent_id, date, "not undone"})
    end_if
END_OPERATION
```

10.8.3 Removing Information Perspective

As another example to study the flexibility of the introduced implementation model we drop the information perspective. This results in a workflow model without any data flow.

Figure 10.4 shows the state transition diagram for elementary workflows. If all module operation invocations of the data module are removed from the state transition diagram these operation are not invoked any more at runtime. If all operation calls to the data module within all state transition diagrams as well as within all workflow operations are dropped the information perspective is completely eliminated. This is all that has to be done in order to drop the information perspective. It is to be emphasized that no change in the programmed code of a system has to take place if state transition diagrams or workflow operations are stored as data.

---

[1]This specifies a default assignment of all workflow instance operations to a default user called "default". If there is no organization module integrated this default assignment is taken. However, if an organization module is available, it overwrites the default assignment.

[2]This is a way to determine the default set of subworkflows in case no control flow module is available. In case it is, the default set is overwritten.

[3]This defines the default synchronization rule: one out of all possible agents are allowed to execute a workflow operation. If a synchronization module exists the value can be overwritten by it.

[4]This specifies a default assignment of all workflow instance operations to a default user called "default". If there is no organization module integrated this default assignment is taken. However, if an organization module is available, it overwrites the default assignment.

11 Implementation Architecture

This chapter constitutes the second phase of the implementation of a workflow management system. The implementation architecture of a workflow management system is detailed here, i.e. implementation concepts are analyzed and synthesized to a comprehensive architecture of a workflow management system. Processes, databases and communication have to be specified. Finally, the modules of the implementation model have to be mapped to the components of the implementation architecture. The implementation architecture therefore enacts the contents of the implementation model.

Section 11.1 summarizes requirements that are specific for an implementation architecture. The three major components of an implementation architecture, processes, databases and communication are discussed in Section 11.2, Section 11.3 and Section 11.4 present a general implementation architecture. Section 11.5 evaluates the presented implementation architecture.

11.1 Specific Requirements

The implementation architecture of a workflow management system has two major requirements. The first requirement is general in nature and aims at the

- completeness

of its description. Not only the main functions of a workflow management system must be specified (as needed for the implementation model), but also the so-called auxiliary functions (e.g. *shutdown_process()*) for the administration of the system need to be defined.

Since processes, databases and communication are constituting components of an implementation architecture, it is characterized by

- technology dependence.

Technology dependence implies that implementation decisions like using processes or threads, taking a relational or an object-oriented database management system and applying message passing or procedure calls must be made. Nevertheless, the description of an implementation architecture should not name actual products that have to be used. For instance, it is therefore not relevant to select one specific database management system vendor.

By having selected specific implementation means, the resulting workflow management system obtains properties that are inherited from the properties of the underlying implementation components. For example, if the implementation is based on a database management system, reliability is a property of the overall workflow management system.

There are a lot of system properties that are essential for the implementation architecture of a workflow management system:

- response time
- throughput
- reliability (and failure tolerance)
- scalability
- extensibility, and
- portability

are fundamental for each implementation (cf. Chapter 9). The implementation architecture decides whether these requirements are fulfilled and how they are implemented. Replication and partitioning of databases might be one means to achieve reliability and failure tolerance. However, we see replication as part of the implementation (see Chapter 12).

11.2 Components

This section introduces the components that an implementation architecture is constituted of. While an implementation model must only consider application-related issues, an implementation architecture must also take process structures, database concepts and communication techniques into account.

There are some basic assumptions about the computer system a workflow management system resides on. These assumptions influence the implementation architecture and have to be stated explicitely.

- *Distributed Computer Network*. We assume a network of nodes; each node runs an operating system which supports processes. We do not assume that process threads are also available. A database is installed at each computer node.
- *Distributed Processing*. Since nodes are atonomous and independent we will focus on distributed processing. Servers as well as clients are distributed over the network. We do not discuss the case of a (monolithic) mainframe architecture. Such an infrastructure would require different design with respect to process structure, databases and communication. For example, communication between processes would mainly be based on shared memory data what is not adequate for communication in a distributed environment.
- *Distributed Agents*. Each agent involved into workflow processing is associated with a certain workstation (i.e. node in the network). Either (s)he can directly work at this workstation or (s)he can log in remotely.

In the next three sections, the three main components of an implementation architecture, processes, databases and communication, are investigated with respect to design alternatives for the implementation of a workflow management system.

11.2.1 Process Structure

One major step from an implementation model to an implementation architecture is to associate modules with processes, i.e. it has to be determined which modules (cf. Chapter 10) run within one operating system process.

There are a number of issues that are directly impacted by the design of the process structure for a workflow management system. One issue is parallelism. Under the assumption that threads are not necessarily provided, parallelism for a module can only be guaranteed when the functionality of the module is implemented by several processes running on the same or on different computer nodes. Parallelism enhances throughput and provides fast response time.

Failure resistance also requires support. When processes run on different computer nodes continuous operation and graceful degradation can be sustained (Gray and Reuter, 1993). The first phenomena means that operation provision continues when single computer nodes fail since the service is still supported on other computer nodes. However, the overall performance will slightly be decreased (graceful degradation).

When considering the number of processes that run on behalf of a workflow management system the administration issue must be tackled. Exchange of modules by new versions, system startup and shutdown must be easy to handle. A complex process structure limits ease of use.

Besides the process structure the processing model has to be determined. Synchronous and asynchronous processing modes (function calls) have to be deployed such that the overall performance of the workflow management system will be optimized. The processing model also influences the implementation of the algorithms. When requests are processed synchronously, the calling process has to wait passively for the response. Asynchronous function calling allows to work on further requests meanwhile. However, request/response management gets more difficult in the asynchronous case.

Considering the issues mentioned so far, several design alternatives have to be discussed. They are distinguished by the way they provide for modularization (recall that modularization is one of the key requirements; cf. Chapter 9 and Chapter 10). In the context of an implementation architecture modularization refers to the association of modules to processes.

A first design approach would support n:m mapping between operating system processes and workflows (types and/or instances). There are some mapping alternatives:

(1) Each workflow instance corresponds to one operating system process. An operation system process must be created for each top level workflow and for each subworkflow.
(2) Each top level workflow corresponds to one operating system process. All subworkflows of the top level workflow run within one operating system process.
(3) All workflow instance of one workflow type run in one operating system process. The top level workflow and all its subworkflows are associated with the type-specific operating system processes.
(4) All workflow instances of all workflow types run in one operating system process.

Due to the proportional relationship between workflow instances and operating system processes, scalability cannot be reached in cases (1) and (2). The number of operating system processes increases proportionally with the number of workflows instantiated. The more different workflows are served by an operating system process, the less failure isolation can be provided (especially in cases (3) and (4)).

All four alternatives lack failure isolation. Extensibility is not easy to implement since whole operating system processes are impacted by such a modification which means that many workflows which are not directly concerned by an extension are also affected.

Due to the deficiencies of the mapping between operating system processes and workflows (types and instances) we prefer to map perspectives to operating system processes. One or more operating system processes act as a server class which implements a specific perspective, i.e. contains the modules implementing a perspective. If the workflow model (and the architecture) has to be extended, a new server class can easily be integrated without impacting the already existing modules. As a consequence of this mapping strategy workflows are represented as data (not as operating system processes) residing in the underlying databases. Thus, scalability is easy to accomplish. This issue only tackles the implementation of the various perspectives and is not related to the number of workflows. If the implementation of one perspective does not perform adequately, new servers implementing this perspective (i.e. new operating system processes) can be started to overcome the bottleneck. Section 11.3 provides a broad discussion of this implementation strategy.

11.2.2 Databases

The topic "databases" summarizes all tasks that are connected with the design of data repositories. When using relational database management systems, this means to define attributes, attribute domains, relations and consistency criteria.

Due to the distributed implementation of a workflow management system, database design also is concerned with distributing – and if necessary replicating – data. Hereby, a trade-off between performance and reliability must be decided. Replication can result in better performance since read requests can be handled locally. Nevertheless, the coherence between data replicas must be maintained by expensive protocols (e.g. a distributed two-phase commit protocol (Gray and Reuter, 1993)) in case data are changed.

Database design in the context of workflow management must comprise at least the logical data views introduced in Chapter 10. Hence, further issues arise. For instance, the workflow management system itself must be administered in databases. Besides other things, dedicated relations reflect the current configuration of the workflow management system.

Due to the operating system process mapping strategy introduced in Section 11.2.1, each server class (which implements a certain perspective of the workflow model) is associated with a database. There will also be a centralized data repository, storing among other things workflow type information. Due to the independence of the server classes, the databases associated with them can be heterogeneous in nature. Data are exchanged via messages between servers. The distributed servers normally do not need to talk to each other directly.

11.2.3 Communication

In a workflow management system different communication mechanisms have to be applied. When user requests have to be answered synchronously, performance is the main demand. When the user does not directly wait for a response to the request (e.g. an e-mail is sent) then reliability might be more important than performance. Altogether, different forms of user request processing require different types of communication mechanisms.

The modules of a workflow management system are spread across a computer network. Therefore, continuous communication is required and communication failures are rather probable. Communication mechanisms that provide failure transparency drastically reduce recovery work. For instance, when a server breaks locally during processing a client's request, the client should not be aware of this (temporary) failure. Thus, the client does not have to perform any recovery activities.

Communication takes place within physical domains. However, communication also has to cross physical domains in order to implement enterprise-wide workflows. The situation even becomes more difficult if enterprise boundaries have to be crossed during processing of inter-enterprise workflows. Since different physical domains, different divisions of an enterprise and different enterprises might deploy manifold communication mechanisms, gateways must be provided to bridge the gaps between them.

Communication mechanisms differ with respect to their ability to support synchronous invocation (e.g. RPC), asynchronous invocation (e.g. message passing) or both (e.g. CORBA (OMG, 1992)). Reliability is another issue that characterizes communication mechanisms (see above). Being able to buffer requests is another feature of communication mechanisms. Gray and Reuter (1993) give an introduction into the area of communication.

For the purpose of the following discussion, one feature of a communication mechanism must be discussed in more detail. We call it the dependency between a caller and a callee. If failures of a server directly affect the client, the underlying communication mechanism is called *tight* since it couples caller and callee tightly. Otherwise, it is called *loose* because caller and callee are only coupled loosely. For instance, communication via (persistent) queues (Gray and Reuter, 1993) provides loose coupling since caller and callee are independent with respect to failures.

Loose coupling is advantageous, especially in the context of workflow management systems where communication continuously takes place. For instance, when deploying persistent queues errors do not spread across the whole workflow management system but are limited by queues. Therefore, we prefer loose communication via persistent queues for workflow management systems (cf. Section 11.4).

11.2.4 System Failure, Backup, Administration and Configuration

Process structure, database design and communication mechanisms are not the only issues that are relevant for an implementation architecture. Nevertheless, they constitute a working set that conveys a deep insight into the implementation of the main functionality of a workflow management system.

System failure recovery, backup strategies, administration and configuration management are not worked on in this book even though they are extremely important in the area of workflow management system. We think that there are no different requirements in the realm of workflow management systems than in other systems. Therefore, experience and techniques developed in similar application systems might be deployed in the workflow management area.

11.3 Processes and Databases

Section 11.2 presents general concepts for an implementation architecture. Since modules have to be associated with processes and data views have to be defined for modules, it is practical to discuss processes and databases together. In Section 11.4, the communication design of the general implementation architecture is presented. Databases and processes can be seen as the basic building blocks which are composed into a comprehensive and complete system by a communication infrastructure.

Figure 11.1 gives an overview of the general implementation architecture. The association of modules to server classes, the definition of logical databases and the design of the communication system is depicted. Note that each server class might consist of several operating system processes of the same type (servers), e.g. one worklist for each user within the system. Each logical database might be partitioned into several "smaller" ones which are used by single operating system processes implementing a module. In addition Section 11.3.5 discusses alternatives to the process structure of Figure 11.1.

Subsequently, the implementation of the Kernel, the Shell and a Workspace is demonstrated. The descriptions will be as complete as necessary to convey a general understanding of the implementation architecture. Unessential details that are not specific for the chosen design are omitted.

11.3.1 Auxiliary Modules

Module Identifier

Identifiers are used by every module to attribute its managed objects like workflows or control flow states. This way each object becomes distinguishable

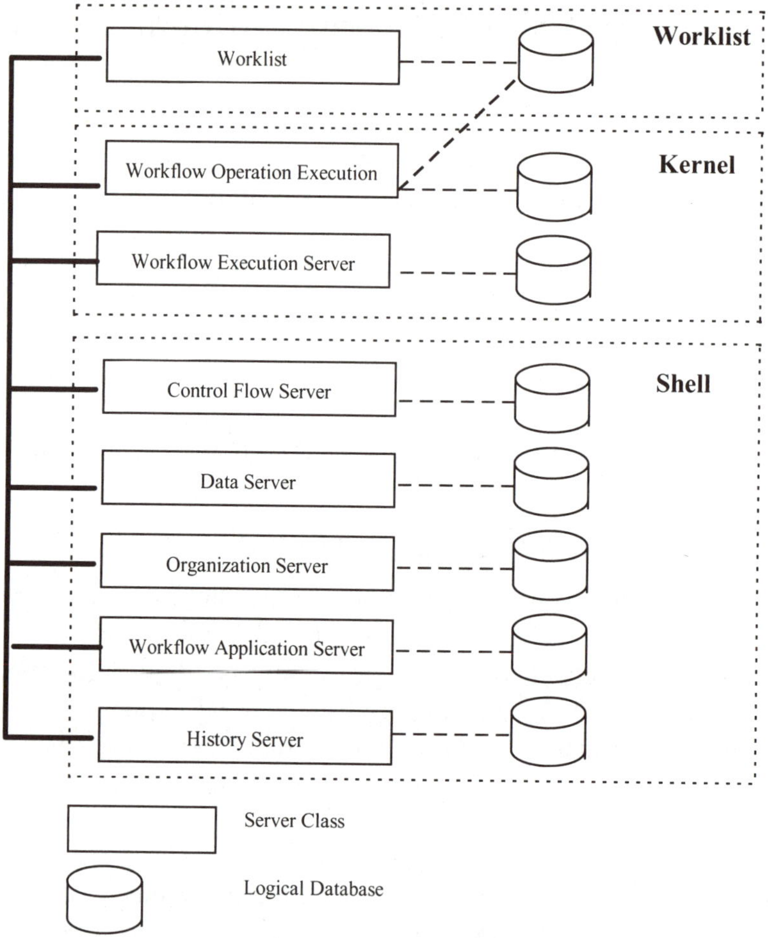

Figure 11.1: Implementation Architecture

from other objects since identifiers are unique. A table is defined storing the last identifier used. To keep things simple we do not reuse identifiers in case objects are destroyed.

```
Identifier (current_id)¹

  integer  current_id
```

Module STDiagram

In Chapter 7 and Chapter 10 the use of state transition diagrams is discussed. Chapter 10 discusses four different types of state transition diagrams. These different types of diagrams are stored in one database table STDiagram_Type.

```
STDiagram_Type (std_type_name,
  {context_variable_name, context_variable_type},
  initial_state, final_state,
  {from_state, to_state, command}) (* transitions *)

  string std_type_name
  set_of (string, string)
        {context_variable_name, context_variable_type}
  string initial_state
  string final_state
  set_of (string, string, string)
        {from_state, to_state, command}
```

Each workflow and each operation instance is processed according to a state transition diagram of a certain type. For each instance the current state has to be recorded as well as the type of diagram it is using.

```
STDiagram_Instance (std_instance_id, std_type_name,
  {context_variable_name, context_variable_value},
  actual_state)

  integer  std_instance_id
  string   std_type_name
  set_of (string, string)
           {context_variable_name, context_variable_value}
  string   actual_state
```

11.3.2 Kernel

The Kernel is constituted by two major modules, workflow_execution and workflow_operation_execution. The workflow_execution and the workflow_operation_execution modules are associated with private databases. In the database of the workflow_execution module, workflow type definitions and workflow instance states are stored. The workflow_operation_execution module controls a database that stores the states of workflow operation execution.

Each module is implemented by a dedicated operating system process since both modules should execute independently. The workflow execution process is concerned with managing workflows. The execution of workflow operations is done by the workflow operation execution process.

Module Workflow Execution

The functional perspective defines the type of a workflow as well as its subworkflows. The following tables contain the type information describing the functional perspective.

```
WF_Type (wf_type_name)

   string wf_type_name

Subworkflows (subworkflow_name, superworkflow_type_name,
   subworkflow_type_name)

   string subworkflow_name
   string superworkflow_type_name
   string subworkflow_type_name
```

Each workflow possesses a state of execution. This has to be stored in the workflow instance table which is shown below.

```
WF_Instance (wf_instance_id, std_instance_id,
   {subworkflow_instance_id})

   integer  wf_instance_id
   integer  std_instance_id
   set_of(integer)
            {subworkflow_instance_id}
```

Module Workflow Operation Execution

The workflow_operation_execution module executes workflow operations. The table WF_Operation stores the definition of workflow operations.

```
WF_Operation (wf_type_name, wf_operation_name, kind,
   wf_operation_body, std_diagram_name)

   string wf_type_name
   string wf_operation_name
   {T, I} kind (* workflow type or instance operation *)
   string wf_operation_body
   string std_diagram_name
```

The table WF_Operation_Instance stores the execution state of a workflow operation which is an instance of a state transition diagram.

```
WF_Operation_Instance (wf_operation_id, wf_instance_id,
   std_instance_id)
   integer  wf_operation_id
   integer  wf_instance_id
   integer  std_instance_id
```

The state transition diagrams for workflow operation processing are also kept in the workflow_operation_execution database. The existence of several versions of the state transition diagrams is motivated in Chapter 7.

11.3.3 Shell

Module Control Flow

Control flow constructs like sequence and loops have to be stored as well as the control flow expressions which define the execution behavior of the subworkflows of a workflow.

```
Control_Flow_Construct (control_flow_construct_name,
  {control_flow_construct_parameter_name,
    control_flow_construct_parameter_type},
  control_flow_construct_semantics)

  string control_flow_construct_name
  set_of(string, string)
        {control_flow_construct_parameter_name,
        control_flow_construct_parameter_type}
  string control_flow_construct_semantics (* i.e. Petri-Net *)

Control_Flow_Expression (wf_type_name, control_flow_expression)

  string wf_type_name
  string control_flow_expression
```

At all times the control flow server has to know how far a workflow is executed in terms of control flow. This state is stored in a separate table Control_Flow_State.

```
Control_Flow_State (wf_instance_id, control_flow_state,
  {subworkflow})

  integer  wf_instance_id
  string   control_flow_state
  set_of(identifier)
           subworkflow
```

Module Data

Data, such as parameters and local variables as well as data flow, have to be specified. This is done within the following tables.

```
WF_Parameter_Definition (wf_type_name, parameter_name,
  parameter_type, direction, kind)

  string wf_type_name
  string parameter_name
  string parameter_type
  {in, out, inout}
        direction
```

```
   {mandatory, optional}
          kind

WF_Operation_Parameter_Definition (wf_type_name,
   wf_operation_name, parameter_name, parameter_type,
   direction, kind)

   string wf_type_name
   string wf_operation_name
   string parameter_name
   string parameter_type
   {in, out, inout}
          direction
   {mandatory, optional}
          kind

WF_Local_Variable_Definition (wf_type_name, variable_name,
   variable_type)

   string wf_type_name
   string variable_name
   string variable_type

WF_Operation_Local_Variable_Definition (wf_type_name,
   wf_operation_name, variable_name, variable_type)

   string wf_type_name
   string wf_operation_name
   string variable_name
   string variable_type

WF_Context_Variable_Definition (wf_type_name, variable_name,
   variable_type)
   string wf_type_name
   string variable_name
   string variable_type

Data_Flow (wf_type_name, source, sink, via_variable)

   string wf_type_name
   string source
   string sink
   string via_variable

Conversion_Function (conv_function_name, {parameter_name,
   parameter_type}, conv_function_body)
```

```
string conv_function_name
set_of(string, string)
      {parameter_name, parameter_type}
string conv_function_body
```

Actual values of parameters and local variables as well as the state of the data flow within workflow instances is stored in the tables shown next.

```
WF_Parameter (wf_instance_id, parameter_name, parameter_value)

  integer  wf_instance_id
  string   parameter_name
  string   parameter_value

WF_Operation_Parameter (wf_instance_id, wf_operation_id,
  parameter_name, parameter_value)

  integer  wf_instance_id
  integer  wf_operation_id
  string   parameter_name
  string   parameter_value

WF_Local_Variable (wf_instance_id, variable_name,
  variable_value)

  identifier
        wf_instance_id
  string variable_name
  string variable_value

WF_Operation_Local_Variable (wf_instance_id, wf_operation_id,
  variable_name, variable_value)

  integer  wf_instance_id
  integer  wf_operation_id
  string   variable_name
  string   variable_value

WF_Context_Variable (wf_instance_id, variable_name,
  variable_value)

  integer  wf_instance_id
  string   variable_name
  string   variable_value

Data_Flow_State (wf_instance_id, state)
```

```
integer  wf_instance_id
string   state
```

Module Organization

The organization schema, agent selections and organizational policies are stored within the following tables.

```
Organization_Type (org_type_name, {org_object_types},
  {org_relationship_types}))

  string org_type_name
  set_of(string)
        {org_object_types}
  set_of(string)
        {org_relationship_types}

Organizational_Objects (org_object_name, {attribute_name,
  attribute_type}, is_agent)

  string   org_object_name
  set_of(string, string)
          {attribute_name, attribute_type}
  boolean  is_agent

Organizational_Relationships (org_relationship_name,
  {attribute_name, attribute_type})

  string org_relationship_name
  set_of (string, string)
        {attribute_name, attribute_type}

Agent_Selection (agent_selection_name, {parameter_name,
  parameter_type}, agent_selection_body)
  string agent_selection_name
  set_of (string, string)
        {parameter_name, parameter_type}
  string agent_selection_body

Organizational_Policies (org_policy_name, wf_type_name,
  wf_operation_name, agent_selection_name,
  synchronization_rule_name, notification_rule_name)

  string org_policy_name
  string wf_type_name
  string wf_operation_name
```

```
string agent_selection_name
string synchronization_rule_name
string notification_rule_name
```

The instance of an organization is stored in the Organization_Instance table.

```
Organization_Instance (org_instance_name, org_type_name,
  {org_object, {attribute_name, attribute_value}},
  {org_relationship,{attribute_name, attribute_value}})

  string org_instance_name
  string org_type_name
  set_of(identifier, set_of(string, string))
    {org_object, {attribute_name, attribute_value}}
  set_of(identifier, set_of(string, string))
    {org_relationship, {attribute_name, attribute_value}}
```

Module Notification

Notification rules are stored in the database table Notification_Rule. They are used by organizational policies to define which workflow operation is associated with which notification rule.

```
Notification_Rule (notification_rule_name,
  notification_rule_body)

  string notification_rule_name
  string notification_rule_body
```

As soon as a workflow operation is attached to agents an entry can be found in the Notification_State table. This table stores the notification state of each workflow operation.

```
Notification_State (wf_instance_id, wf_operation_id,
  notification_state)
  integer  wf_instance_id
  integer  wf_operation_id
  string   notification_state
```

Module Assignment

The assignment table stores the assigned agents for each workflow instance and for each workflow operation instance. Furthermore it is stored whether the agent is already notified.

```
Assignment (wf_instance_id, wf_operation_id,
  {agent, notification_state})
```

```
integer  wf_instance_id
integer  wf_operation_id
set_of(identifier, boolean)
         {agent, notification_state}
```

Module Synchronization

As in the case of notification synchronization rules have to be specified. These are used within organizational policies.

```
Synchronization_Rule (synchronization rule name,
  synchronization_rule_body)

  string synchronization_rule_name
  string synchronization_rule_body
```

The actual synchronization state of a particular workflow operation of a workflow instance is stored in table Synchronization_State.

```
Synchronization_State (wf instance id, wf operation id,
  synchronization_state)

  integer  wf_instance_id
  integer  wf_operation_id
  string   synchronization_state
```

Module Workflow Application

Workflow applications specifications are defined in table Workflow_Application.

```
Workflow_Application (wf app name, {parameter_name,
  parameter_type}, {property}, wf_app_body)

  string wf_app_name
  set_of(string, string)
         {parameter_name, parameter_type}
  set_of(string)
         {property}
  string wf_app_body
```

Module History

History information is kept in table History.

```
History(wf instance id, event_class, {event_key}, {event_data})

  integer  wf_instance_id
  string   event_class
  set_of(string)
```

```
            {event_key}
    set_of(string)
            {event_data}
```

11.3.4 Workspaces

A Workspace represent the user working area. The main component of a Workspace is the user's interface to the run time system of the workflow management system (see Chapter 13). Each user can establish his own Workspace. Usually, it runs in an operating system process on the user's workstation or Personal Computer.

A Workspace of a user displays a list of tasks (i.e. workflows) the user is responsible for. In order to retrieve all tasks assigned to a user the user's Worklist accesses the assignment module database. When a user wants to see whether a new task has arrived the Worklist accesses the assignment database again fetching the newly assigned tasks. Since the assignment database represents the actual state of task assignment a Worklist does not maintain its own database.

11.3.5 Overview of Processes and Libraries

A short discussion follows about the implementation of modules as servers or as libraries. In general both alternatives are possible for each module depending on some properties of the module which are discussed subsequently.

When instances of a module do not hold the states of module operation executions in local variables but store intermediate results in a database, other instantiations of the same module can have the same view on the data. In this case they can coordinate themselves based solely on the database entries. Therefore it is possible that instances of modules become either independent processes (except identifier and STDiagram) or are bound to existing processes as libraries. This is possible since every module instance shares its state with every other module instance through database entries. An extreme case is that every user has a process running his worklist and all the other modules are bound to that process. This means that every user running a worklist runs a full workflow management system. There are no directly cooperating servers but all worklists and their modules cooperate solely using one database containing all data (cf. Figure 11.2).

In contrast, when an instance of a module holds intermediate results in local variables other module operation calls have to go to the same instance of the module. Otherwise the result of a module operation will be incorrect. In this case only one module instance can exist within the workflow management system. This module instance runs as a process to be available for others. In

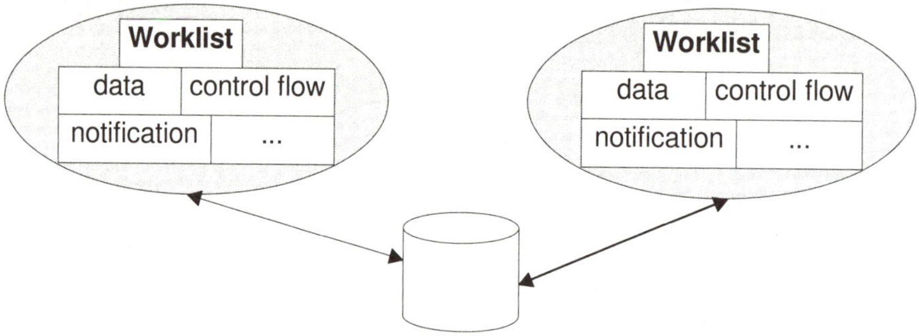

Figure 11.2: One Process per User

consequence each module corresponds to one process and all processes have to cooperate (cf. Figure 11.3).

In general a particular design lies somewhere in between. Some modules run within processes whereas others are bound as libraries. For example, the workflow_operation_execution module might be bound to the worklist module. This means that every user has an own workflow_operation_ execution module. In consequence, all these module instances run in parallel so that performance might be improved (cf. Figure 11.4).

Table 11.1 gives an overview of which modules can be implemented as processes and which can be offered via libraries. As indicated, most modules can be used in both ways.

11.4 Communication

For the implementation of communication we do not favor a certain technology. In principle, every communication technology can be used. However, properties like reliability, throughput or response time require certain technologies.

11.4.1 General Philosophy

According to Figure 11.1 every server is connected with every other server through a communication infrastructure. Network nodes were intentionally left out of the figure to avoid prescribing an allocation of servers to nodes. In principle, each server can reside on a separate node. It is also possible that all servers run on one node. For instance, if a user has access to a workstation his Worklist process runs most likely at this node. In the case of several users this means that as many Worklist processes are distributed over the network as users work.

However, servers cannot be placed arbitrarily within a network of nodes when certain requirements have to be fulfilled like performance or throughput. In the following section we discuss some criteria for how servers can be distributed over a network.

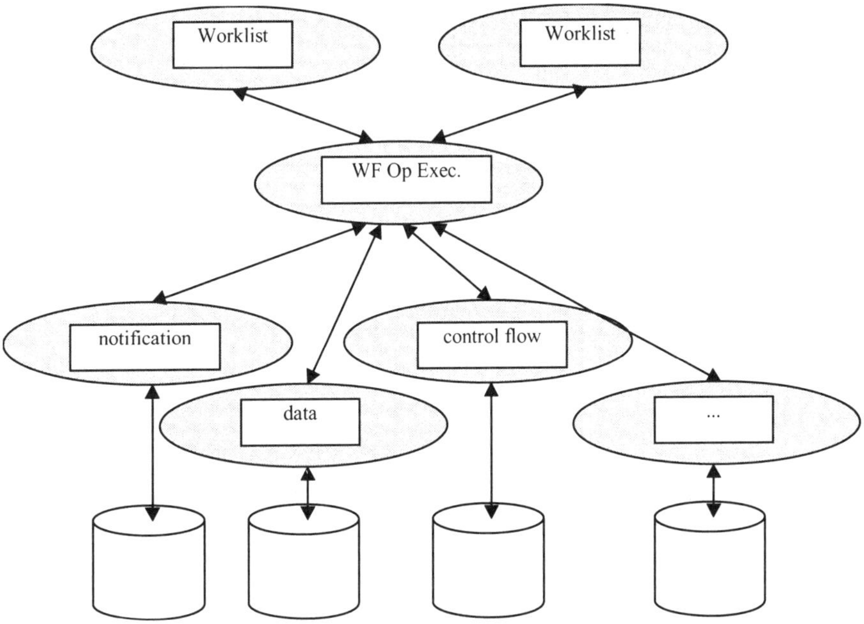

Figure 11.3: Each Module Corresponds to one Operating System Process

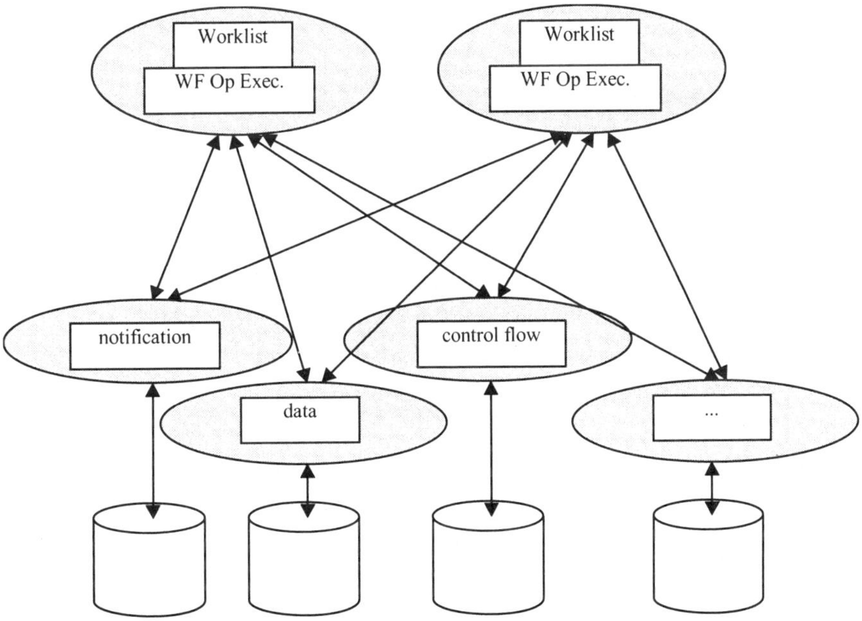

Figure 11.4: Grouping of Modules into Operating System Processes

Table 11.1: Overview of Processes and Libraries

	Process	*Library*
Worklist	√	
Workflow_execution	√	√
Workflow_operation_execution	√	√
Control Flow	√	√
Data Flow	√	√
Organization	√	√
Workflow_application	√	√
History	√	√
Synchronization	√	√
Notification	√	√
Identifier		√
STDiagram		√
Assignment	√	√

11.4.2 Topology Considerations

Without going into too much detail the placement of servers within a network of nodes is discussed. Placement is usually not done arbitrarily but is controlled by specific requirements.

One important requirement is performance. User requests should be executed fast so that a user does not have to wait for a response. A good design would place the servers involved in request processing near to the user, i.e. on the same node where the Worklist of the user runs. This design is fine in the case of one user. However, if there are several users, servers have to be placed such that the response time is equally good for all of them. In this case servers are placed "in the middle" of all users. In general, this means that servers run on nodes different from the nodes where the Worklists reside. As soon as a request is executed by servers on a different node from the node where the Worklist runs the communication between the nodes plays an important role for the overall performance. If a node cannot be reached through a reliable and fast connection it is probably not good for executing user requests.

Even though it sounds trivial and obvious, sometimes there is no choice and low bandwidth connections have to be used. In this case the correct server placement becomes even more important. To illustrate a good and a bad placement in the presence of a low bandwidth connection to user nodes we give an example. Assume that all user nodes are connected with a low bandwidth connection to a fast node. A decision is made that at each user node a Worklist and a workflow_operation_execution process is installed and all the other servers are placed on the fast node. As can be seen from the code of workflow operations (see Chapter 10) in most cases a lot of different servers are involved (control

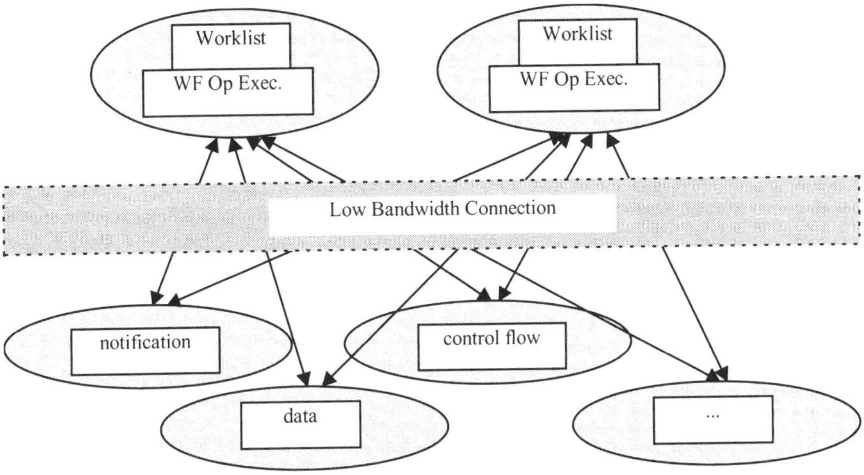

Figure 11.5: High Traffic over Low Bandwidth Connection

flow server, data server, etc.). Each call to such a server requires communication over the network. In our scenario this communication would take place over a low bandwidth connection. Needless to say, the execution of workflow operations will be slow (cf. Figure 11.5).

A better choice would be to place the workflow_operation_execution process on the fast node instead on the user nodes. In this case a user request to execute a workflow operation would be transmitted to the fast node within one message. Requests from the workflow_operation_ execution process to other servers are in this case local to the fast node and therefore performance is much better than in the alternative case (cf. Figure 11.6).

Other criteria to place servers are their interaction frequency. If they do not interact at all, their nodes might be not connected at all. If they interact very often a high speed connection might be the best choice.

Another alternative would be to place servers with a high interaction frequency on the same node. In this case the interaction pattern is important. If servers cooperate synchronously both can sit on the same node. In this case only one server executes at a time. However, if both can work in parallel even though they call each other it might be more appropriate to place them on different nodes to enable real parallel processing.

There are many more requirements which influence server placement within a network. Besides performance requirements reliability and failure tolerance might be important. Chapter 12 discusses some of them in more detail.

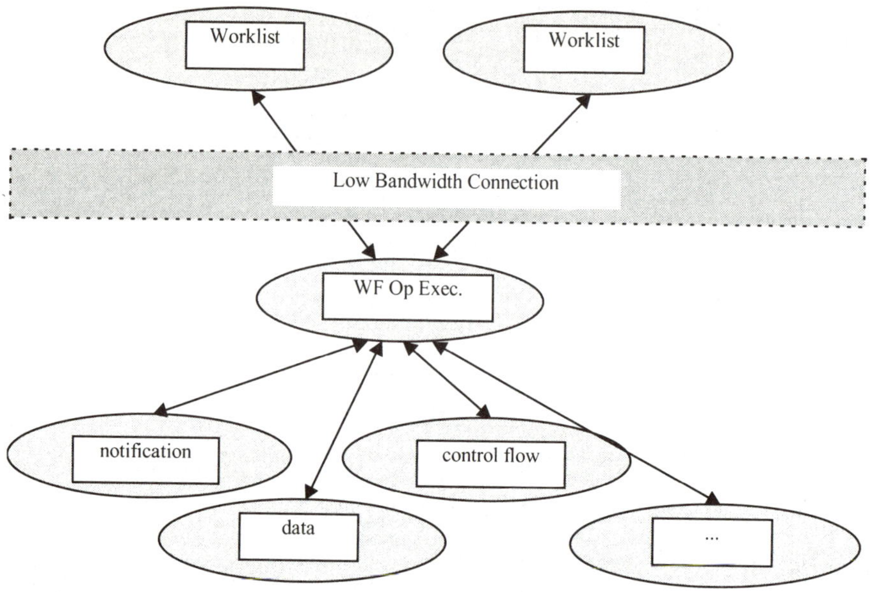

Figure 11.6: Low Traffic over Low Bandwidth Connection

11.5 Evaluation of Design Criteria

The implementation architecture discussed so far is complete and fully operational. We will call it the "basic architecture". In the following its properties are discussed as well as where and how improvements are possible. One important indicator of implementation architectures of workflow management systems is the number of processes involved in executing workflows. In our basic architecture one server is responsible for each perspective. This server processes only one perspective, but for all workflow instances in the system. If we assume a fixed number of users, the number of processes to execute their workflows is fixed because for each perspective there is one server and for each user there is one Worklist process. This number increases only if new users enter the system. The number of processes is independent of the number of workflow instances processed. This is important since the number of operating system processes on one machine is limited.

The basic architecture is failure tolerant. As discussed, workflow operations call module operations of different modules implementing the perspectives. Module operation calls result in server calls. If a workflow operation does not require a certain server for its execution it can be processed even if the server is not available. Therefore if a server fails it is still possible to continue workflow operation execution and therefore workflow processing.

The requirement of extensibility is also fulfilled by the basic architecture. Since every server implementing a perspective is only called by the workflow_operation_execution module they do not depend on each other. A new perspective must be reflected by the workflow operations and the state transition diagrams only (as discussed in Section 10.8).

Other requirements listed in Section 11.1 like response time, throughput, reliability, scalability and portability depend much more on the specific implementation than on the implementation architecture. However, since the implementation is not independent from the architecture the architecture must also support these requirements. At least, the architecture must not make it impossible to fulfill them.

Chapter 12 discusses implementation decisions complementing the basic architecture. Trade-offs are discussed of how to fulfill certain requirements which are not or cannot be addressed by the basic architecture.

---

[1]Database tables are specified by a table name followed by a list of attributes in brackets. Attributes in "{}" denote a set. Identifying primary attributes are underlined. The data types of attributes are specified after the table definition. The specified tables are not normalized.

12 Implementation

This chapter discusses a possible implementation. However, we do not show pieces of code. This would be too difficult to discuss because too many details would have to be introduced. First, we describe our computing system environment in which the development takes place (Section 12.1). Section 12.2 evaluates the basic architecture and highlights areas where implementation decisions are to be made. In Section 12.3 we describe such implementation decisions made to make our system operational. These decisions will be discussed in the framework of the implementation architecture.

12.1 Implementation Environment

This section describes our installed computing environment. Hardware as well as software is listed to give an impression of the size and installed computing power.

12.1.1 Network

Basically four types of machine are available within the local network within our department. The nodes comprise 2 AXP 3000/800 machines, 9 AXP 3000/300 machines and 10 VAXstation 3100 machines from Digital Equipment, 5 SPARCstation 20 from Sun Microsystems and 2 Pentium PCs.

The AXP machines run the operating system OSF/1, the VAXstations run VMS, the SPARCstations run SOLARIS and OS/2 is installed on the PCs.

The network protocols used are TCP/IP and DECnet.

12.1.2 Programming Language

For coding the execution logic the programming language C++ is used. Compilers for the compilation of the script language discussed in Chapter 6 are implemented with the UNIX tools lex and yacc in combination with C++ and a database. Graphical user interfaces are implemented with Tcl and Tk (Ousterhout, 1994; Welch, 1995) together with C++.

12.1.3 Database

As a database system we use Informix. In addition the Informix XA package is installed in order to link several separate databases to the TP monitor Encina. This configuration provides distributed transaction management over multiple resource managers.

12.1.4 Communication Mechanisms

The workflow management system internal communication is done with transactional RPCs and transactional persistent queues which are provided by Encina (Transarc, 1994).

Workflow applications are called based on several different communication tools like CORBA implementations (ObjectBroker from Digital Equipment, ORBline from PostModern Computing Technologies), RPC provided by DCE, Tuxedo and transactional RPC as well as transactional persistent queues from Encina.

12.2 Evaluation of the Implementation Architecture

The basic implementation architecture leaves many areas open for implementation decisions. This is intended because depending on the requirements of a real implementation decisions have to be made which cannot be done within the architecture. An implementation architecture supports some basic requirements but cannot solve all requirements at the same time. This is especially true if conflicting requirements have to be dealt with. Because of this an implementation architecture has to be flexible and open enough to provide freedom for implementation alternatives.

The basic architecture results in a high communication effort. One reason for this is the design of minimal module operation interfaces. If a server is asked to perform some operation based on a workflow instance it is sometimes necessary to know the workflow type the instance belongs to (e.g. if type information has to be read). If this information is not passed in the first place, the server has to ask another server to provide the workflow type name for a workflow instance. Subsequently this results in communication effort. Section 12.3.1 discusses this issue in more detail.

Another reason for a high communication effort is that the implementation architecture does not support inter-server communication. This was done intentionally to foster extensibility. However, if extensibility is not a requirement, inter-server communication might be appropriate to save communication effort and speed up workflow operation processing. Section 12.3.2 discusses inter-server communication in more detail. Another approach for speeding up workflow operation processing is server internal multiplexing. Server internal multiplexing makes use of waiting times by executing several requests at the same time. Each request is cut into pieces which execution interleaves. Section 12.3.4 discusses this approach in more detail.

The basic architecture was not designed for a specific type of communication mechanism. The mechanism used depends on several things. First, from a pragmatics point of view it might be necessary to use the already installed communication mechanism. In this case there is no choice. Second, requirements like performance or throughput might be important. Section 12.3.3 discusses how different communication mechanisms might be deployed.

Failure tolerance is supported to a certain extent within the basic architecture. So far a clear separation of concepts is reflected in a clear modularization. This modularization leads to a perspective-oriented server structure which gives failure tolerance upfront since the failure of one server does not stop the whole system. Additional failure tolerance can be achieved by enhancing the communication mechanism and deploying transactional services (see Section 12.3.5) as well as partitioning the underlying databases (see Section 12.3.6).

12.3 Implementation Decisions

This section is devoted to the discussion of implementation decisions and choices. We will show where decisions can be made which lead to more flexibility and better support requirements as discussed in Section 10.1.

12.3.1 Extended Interfaces

As can be seen from the module operations of Chapter 10, the key of a workflow instance is a workflow instance identifier. During workflow processing it is sometimes necessary to consult workflow type data in order to process a workflow instance. For example, if a workflow instance is created the data server is called providing the actual parameter values of the workflow instance. This is done by a module operation "set_ workflow_parameter" (see Section 10.4.3). In order to check if the actual value fits the specified data type the data module must access workflow type information. In order to do so it has to find out the workflow type of the created workflow instance. This knowledge is stored within the workflow_execution server. In the distributed case this is a server call just for finding out which workflow type the workflow instance belongs to.

This is not acceptable from the viewpoint of communication cost. A much better approach would be to provide, in addition to the workflow instance identifier, the workflow type it belongs to. So, communication effort can be saved. This improvement is in principle valid for all module operations. In the example the data server would know the workflow type immediately and would be able to check the actual parameter values against the specified data type without further server communication.

A similar argument applies for a different area. As discussed in Chapter 6 control flow constructs might depend on workflow local data like parameters and variables. Whenever a control flow construct is evaluated and data are necessary for evaluation the data has to be accessed. This results in one data server call for each accessed data value. If we stick to the basic architecture this call could not be done directly from the control flow server but via the workflow operation execution process. As in the discussion above this is not acceptable since the communication effort is high. A much better solution would be to provide the data of a workflow instance each time the control flow server is called because of this workflow instance. This would save a lot of communication between servers. In contrast to the above case, here a lot of data would be moved (because a workflow might have lots of parameter values and local variables). However, this could be optimized so that only those data of a workflow instance which are accessed by control flow expressions are provided to the control flow server. This can be derived from the workflow type information where the control flow expressions are defined for a workflow type.

12.3.2 Inter-Server Communication

The communication effort in the basic architecture is high. One way to save communication was discussed in Section 12.3.1 where interfaces of module operations were extended. This enables to reduce communication effort.

Another way to reduce communication cost is to implement direct server-to-server communication without involving the workflow_ operation_execution module. This change violates the requirement for independence of servers. If a server assumes the existence of another one dependencies are introduced which have to be obeyed later on. If one server is dropped the other one is affected because its calls are not returned correctly. If interfaces are changed at one server others have to change their invocations accordingly.

However, sometimes there is no choice and performance is more important than the effort to implement changes. As an example, one area is discussed where direct server communication is possible instead of communication via the workflow_operation_execution module. Transition (2) in Section 10.6.3 calls a module operation "control_flow.used_ workflows()". This module operation returns a data structure ("delta_set") which is analyzed and results in several module operations of the workflow_execution module. All these module operations are initiated by the workflow_operation_execution module. As an optimization the following scenario might be envisioned. The delta_set is not returned to the workflow_operation_execution module but analyzed in the control_flow module itself and this module might issue the resulting workflow_execution module operations itself. If the communication cost between the control_flow module and the workflow_execution module is less than between the workflow_operation_execution module and the workflow_execution module an improvement is gained.

Communication costs can also be saved by introducing active servers. An active server can notify another server about changes. This avoids polling for changes. An example is the interplay between a Worklist and the assignment module. The assignment module stores all tasks assigned to a user. The assignment module updates its database if new tasks arrive for a user or if already assigned ones are removed. If a user wants to know about changes in task assignment his Worklist accesses the assignment module and fetches the changes. Depending on the frequency with which the user updates the Worklist, a lot of communication takes place often without resulting in an update at all. To avoid this the assignment module should be active (as a process). In this case the assignment server could notify the Worklists of all users affected by changes in the assignment database. In this case communication takes place only when updates are made. However, since not all assigned workflow operations will be executed by an agent but by other eligible agents this might still cause a lot of unnecessary calls to the workspace.

12.3.3 Communication Types

The requirements of throughput, scalability and response time are dependent on types of communication in conjunction with the way servers are implemented. To start the discussion two extreme scenarios are given. The first one assumes that only a synchronous communication mechanism is available and the second one assumes only an asynchronous and buffered communication mechanism. If there is only a synchronous communication mechanism available only one user request can be processed at a time. This is because a user request resulting in a server call blocks the server until the call is done. If the call in turn calls another server this is blocked also. In the basic architecture every user call is processed by the workflow operation execution module. If there is only one process executing workflow operations only one workflow operation can be processed at a time. Replicating the workflow operation execution process does not help much since every other server can handle only one call at a time. However, because of this structure the system is very performant and response time is the best possible since no effort has to be made to coordinate different user requests executing at the same time.[1]

If asynchronous and buffered communication is available each user request is represented as a message submitted to the workflow operation execution process. This process takes a request message at a time to find out what to process. If processing involves another server, the workflow operation execution process sends another message to that server and remembers that a request was sent. In the meantime the workflow operation execution module can take another request message and process it. If the server (which runs in parallel) is finished it sends back the result to the workflow operation execution process. As soon as the workflow operation execution process has time it takes the result and continues processing the corresponding request. This way an interleaved processing of user requests is possible at each server. This way of processing user requests requires more coordination effort in comparison to the first scenario, however, the throughput is much better since there are no waiting states within the servers (except when there is nothing to do). Also scalability is much better since the open requests depend only on the buffer size of the communication mechanism. If the size is big a lot of requests can be handled simultaneously.

As the discussion revealed, synchronous communication mechanisms are good for performance whereas asynchronous and buffered communication is good for throughput and scalability (Gray and Reuter, 1993). In principle, good response time, throughput and scalability are important within workflow management. If differentiated carefully one can find out the following: when a user wants to execute a workflow operation in which he expects an application program to start, good response time is important. If the application program is not started almost immediately the user is not satisfied and he cannot work efficiently. When a user calls a workflow operation in which no application program is called (i.e. where he does not observe a side effect) response time is no issue at all. Workflow operations showing this characteristic are finish operations and workflow steps performing automatically.

From the discussion so far it becomes clear that some workflow operations should be executed based on synchronous communication because of performance issues, whereas other workflow operations can be executed based on asynchronous and buffered communication to support throughput and scalability. Therefore both types of communication should be supported in a workflow management system.

If reliability is an important requirement not only the servers have to be reliable to keep state information but also communication has to be reliable to preserve an exactly once semantics. Both types of communication which are discussed above are available as reliable services. As synchronous communication mechanism transactional remote procedure calls can be used (TRPC, (Transarc, 1994b)). An asynchronous and buffered communication mechanism is implemented as a transactional queue (TQ, (Transarc, 1994a)).

12.3.4 Server Internal Request Multiplexing

If implemented in a straightforward approach a server can execute one request at a time. Parallel execution is possible only if at least two servers are installed. However, this approach probably leads to a high number of servers (operating system processes) which in turn might lead to a slow system. If servers are created dynamically the number of servers corresponds to the number of current requests. If this cannot be controlled (e.g. by an upper limit) a node might fail because too many operating system processes are created at the same time.

If a server has waiting states while executing requests (e.g. if a server waits for an answer from another server) the question arises if these waiting states can be used processing some other request meanwhile. The answer is yes if the requests can be broken down into smaller parts which can be executed separately.

Basically each request arriving is broken down into smaller parts. The algorithm within the server executes a request part by part. If the execution of a part cannot be done by the server itself it asks a foreign server to execute the part and remembers the fact that a part of a request is executed by some foreign server. It then executes a part of a second request. When this part is executed the server finds out if a result arrived from the foreign server. If a result arrived the server continues executing the first request remembering the execution state of the second request. If not the server continues executing parts of the second request.

This way a server multiplexes requests internally within the same operating system process. The number of requests which can be executed this way depends on the possibility to store requests in different execution states. The size of the storage is the critical factor in this case (and not the number of possible operating system processes).

12.3.5 Failure Tolerance

Workflow management systems have to be failure tolerant. This term comprises not only that a workflow management system can continue with workflow processing in the presence of server failures but also that they do not lose state information. Reliability is very important.

Reliability can be achieved by deploying transactional services. As discussed already, states of workflow types and instances are stored within the server databases. If all changes within a workflow management system are done under transactional control reliability is guaranteed. Of course, if a workflow operation involves several servers they have to join the transaction in which the workflow operation is executed. This is possible by deploying databases which support open distributed transactions (e.g. following the X/OPEN protocols (Gray and Reuter, 1993)). Transactional communication mechanisms provide an exactly once semantics which makes failure detection and failure handling much simpler than in the non-transactional case.

Failure tolerance can also be improved by enhanced communication technologies. If we look at asynchronous and buffered communication with transactional queues we can observe that between two servers there is one queue in either direction. These queues are used to send and receive messages in the role of requests and answers to requests. In total four objects have to be distributed over nodes: two servers and two queues. If we have two nodes and place a server on each node the question arises where to put the queues. If we put one queue on each server the following error scenario arises: if a node crashes, one server and one queue cannot be reached any more. The other server is affected by this crash since it cannot fetch or put a message on the queue on the crashed server (Figure 12.1).

A possible improvement is to introduce another two queues and arrange the message flow as shown in Figure 12.2. In the new design two queues are responsible for both directions. A server puts a message in its queue and the queue forwards its contents to another queue from which the receiving server fetches the messages (forward queues). If each of the two queues is placed on a different server a server failure does not affect the other server at all. This is because each of the servers has access to a full set of queues. If one server is down the other can still handle messages.

This queue-based communication hides failures in contrast to threads in conjunction with synchronous communication. All the following error types are hidden: server crash, node crash, queue crash and communication failure between nodes. If any of those error occurs at one node the other does not realize it at all. Of course, this kind of failure tolerant communication is expensive since queueing a message or dequeueing is done within a transaction.

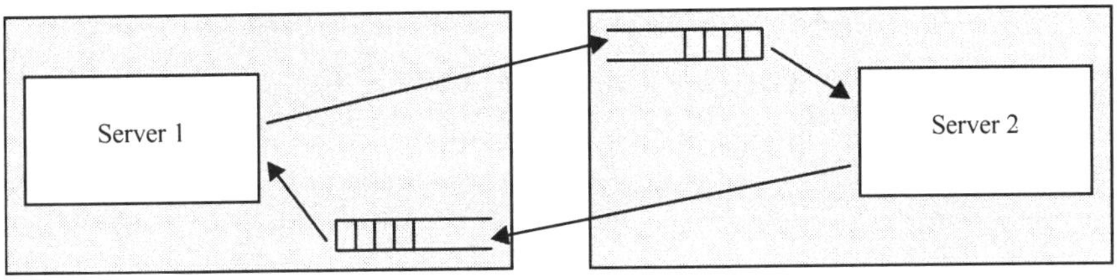

Figure 12.1: Distribution of two Servers and two Queues over two Nodes

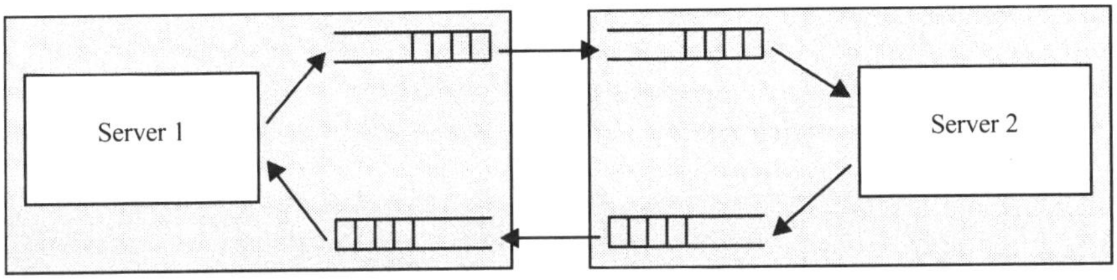

Figure 12.2: Forward Queues

12.3.6 Partitioning and Replication

As indicated partitioning and replication are a means to improve the availability of server functionality as well as to increase failure tolerance. In general data partitioning and replication have to be distinguished from server replication. However, both have to be combined in a good way to gain significant benefit.

Data replication is an area of extensive research. In contrast to the research effort database products provide little functionality. The basic drawback is the effort to update replicas synchronously when they are frequently changed. When data must be updated synchronously replication might require more effort than it saves (Ceri and Pelagatti, 1984). Since in our case a lot of status information is frequently updated we refrain from discussing data replication further.

Data partitioning separates the complete database into several smaller ones. If the smaller portions are stored at different nodes parallel and independent access is possible. This improves not only performance (because of parallel processing) but also failure tolerance and availability (because the databases are independent from each other). In our case data are already partitioned according to the perspectives. It is possible to store the data of each server in a different database running on a separate node. However, further partitioning within a server database is possible because of the following property. The servers work on data belonging to workflow instances. Workflow instances share data only, if they belong (transitively) to the same top-level workflow. Workflow instances belonging to different top-level workflows do not share data at all. Therefore partitioning can take place according to top-level workflows. This is true for every server except the assignment database. This exception is discussed later on.

Partitioning the databases does not help much if they are served by the same server. In this case the server becomes the bottleneck. A better solution is to have a separate server for each partitioned database. In this scenario not only the databases but also the servers run independently from each other. From a parti-tioning point of view this scenario is perfect. However, one problem remains to be solved: if for example two data flow servers are available, each working on a different set of workflow instances a caller of control flow module operations has to know which server to address. Obviously the server to be addressed depends on the workflow instance.

An obvious solution is to extend the workflow instance identifier with server information. This server information would contain a server address for each perspective. This server is the one which possesses the instance information with respect to the perspective the server works on. Whenever a server is contacted by a caller the caller could derive the right server address from the workflow instance. Even if this solution is simple it bears a lot of problems. The most critical issue is the fact that a caller would have to find out a server address. Therefore servers would have to know about partitioning.

A more sophisticated approach is discussed in the following. This approach makes the assumption that no server has to know about partitioning. By extending the communication mechanism with a server addressing scheme based on workflow instance identifiers the server addressing can be hidden from the servers. A server, e.g. the workflow_ operation_execution server, calls the control flow server without knowing that the control flow server is partitioned. The communication layer itself is aware of partitioning however. It takes the request from the workflow_operation_execution server and looks up its internal server addressing schema. When it detects an entry the requested service is partitioned and a selection has to take place. Based on the workflow instance identifier an appropriate server is selected and the server call is executed. Figure 12.3 shows the basic principle and a sample invocation sequence. Server A calls Server B. B is partitioned into B′ and B″. The server address resolution component within the communication layer derives that the workflow instance A deals with belongs to Server B′. The call from A is redirected therefore to B′.

However, partitioning of the assignment data of the assignment module is not that easy. In a first attempt it looks good to partition this database according to users. For example, all users within a certain department belong to each other and their assignments are stored within one database. Therefore as many assignment database partitions as departments exist. This is fine as long as workflow operations of a workflow instance are assigned to users of one partition only. If workflow operations are assigned to users of different partitions a problem arises. Even though Worklists of users must access only one assignment database (their

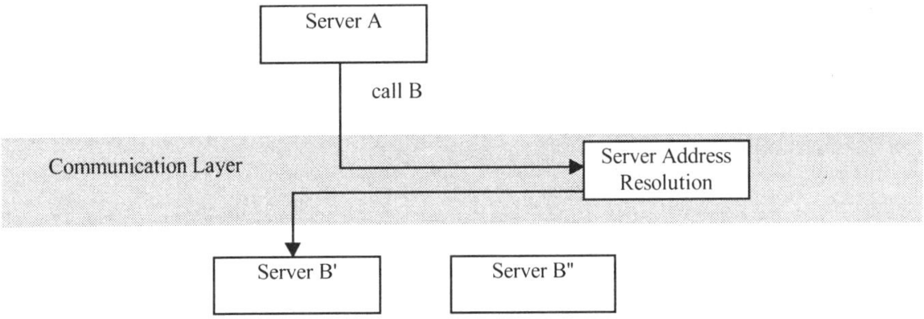

Figure 12.3: Partitioned Server Addressing

partition) other modules must access several assignment databases in this case because the workflow instance is referred to by several of them. If a workflow instance is to be deleted, several assignment databases have to be searched in this case and all assignments referring to the workflow instance have to be deleted.

Basically this means that the server address resolution component in the communication layer has to track that several data partitions are involved. It therefore has the ability to figure out that a server has to access more than one partition or not.

As discussed the workflow_operation_execution module executes workflow operations. Workflow operations are triggered by users pressing buttons on their Worklist. In order to speed up workflow operation processing to each Worklist a workflow operation execution module can be attached. If two users want to execute a workflow operation, both instances of the workflow operation execution module can run in parallel.

---

[1]It could be argued to use threads within a server for multi-threading. If only user-level threads are available the same arguments apply as in the non-threaded case, since there can be only one user-level thread involved in process external communication. This thread would block the whole thread package. This is different in case of kernel-level threads. In this case several kernel level threads can be involved in process external communication. But there is another argument against threads: if a server fails, all user requests executed at this server fail also and all user requests have to be started from the beginning. As we will later see, this can be avoided using other communication mechanisms.

13 Run Time Tools

According to Chapter 4 both the build time and the run time phases of a workflow management system are divided into the three aspects conception, enactment and handling. The conception of a workflow management system is broadly discussed in Chapter 10. The principle functionalities of a workflow management system are defined there and their interrelationships and interdependencies are specified. Chapter 11 and Chapter 12 deal with the enactment part of the run time phase of a workflow management system. Here, the functional components of a workflow management system are mapped to active components of an operating system, data are collected in databases and communication mechanisms are selected to implement the interactions between functional components of the workflow management system. This chapter therefore has to cover the handling aspect of the run time phase, i.e. it introduces the tools necessary to support workflow processing.

Figure 13.1 depicts the main tools deployed for the run time phase of workflow management. Administration mainly has to deal with configuration management. Users, applications and modules have to be managed by system administrators (cf. Section 13.1). Analysis is the second main task to be covered by run time tools; Section 13.2 dwells on this issue. From an end user perspective, worklist management is the most important issue (Section 13.3).

It is remarkable that the tasks "analysis" and "administration" are also relevant in the build time phase (Chapter 8). Nevertheless, the contents of these tasks in the two phases differ slightly. Since their basic meaning and purpose are similar we have chosen equal names.

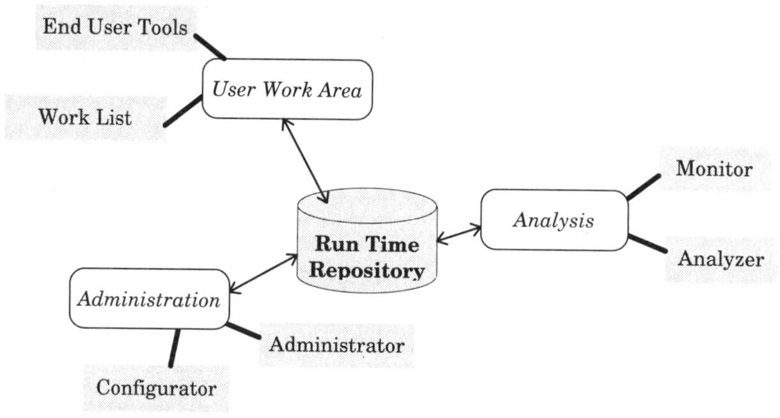

Figure 13.1: Run Time Tools

13.1 Administration

During run time administration comprises two related tasks:

- administration of workflow processing, and
- configuration management.

The first issue deals with all tasks that are necessary to ensure workflow processing (*Administrator*). During the execution of workflows conflicts may occur because application programs are not available, data are not allowed to be accessed, users are not eligible to execute functions, etc. Although these matters should be allowed due to the specification of workflows, problems arise due to wrong handling of these sources. For example, without notifying the workflow management system administrator, access rights to application programs are improperly changed. This can be possible since the workflow management system might not have full control of all components of the underlying computer system. In such a case, workflow processing is blocked and the administrator has to solve the conflict.

Configuration management copes with the configuration of the workflow management system itself (*Configurator*). The allocation of queues that implement communication between modules, the creation of processes that implement a specific server class and the allocation of databases that implement the data view of a server class are typical tasks to accomplish by the workflow management system configuration manager.

In summary, administration comprises all tasks that are necessary to ensure continous workflow processing. The results conducted by analysis (cf. Section 13.2) give valuable hints to the administrator to configure the workflow management system optimally.

13.2 Analysis

Analysis is also a major task in the build time phase (Chapter 8). However, there is a big difference between the implementation of this tasks in the two phases. During build time, analysis can only rely on simulated and animated workflow data; run time provides for real workflow execution data that allows realistic assessments (Deiters and Gruhn, 1994).

To evaluate actual workflow processing is the main issue of the task analysis. Runtime bottlenecks and real semantic errors (e.g. superfluous steps) can be detected and eventually can be resolved. To implement this functionality, a monitoring tool is needed (*Monitor*). This tool has to gather relevant workflow processing information. Thus, it will be working closely with the history module of a workflow management system (if this exists at all).

Not all data collected by the Monitor must be used for analysis. Often it is necessary just to observe workflow processing in order to get hints for further improvements. These improvements might be on a semantic level which can never be dealt with by automatic analysis (*Analyzor*).

One special task of analysis is "on-line assistance" for workflow processing. This issue might be implemented by the Monitor. Due to the enormous complexity of workflow processing, it might sometimes be necessary to actively change the current thread of workflow processing. For instance, due to the occurrence of a deadlock, processing of a workflow must be interrupted. The Monitor must allow such interventions without violating the integrity of workflow processing.

While administration (Section 13.1) is more concerned with system-related issues (e.g. processes, data, communication links), analysis (Section 13.2) deals more with application-related issues (e.g. optimal processing of tasks).

13.3 User Work Area

A user work area constitutes the end users' interface to the workflow management system. A worklist is the most relevant component for an end user since it is the only component of the workflow management system that is dealt with directly. The administrator has to take care that an end user's worklist is configured according to his/her individual requirements. A worklist contains all work to do by an end user. There are many forms of implementation: a worklist might be implemented in an e-mail like fashion: an end user will actively be informed about new work to do. It can also be implemented as a table in a database management system. This implementation is passive and the end user himself is responsible for retrieving new work from the database.

The following figures demonstrate how a worklist might be implemented.

Figure 13.2 shows an empty worklist. Pressing the button OpenWorklist fills the worklist with workflows assigned to the agent who started the worklist program (Figure 13.3). The button RefreshWorklist looks up new assignments for the agent and adds or removes new or finished workflows.

Each entry of a worklist has workflow operations attached which are available to the agent of the worklist. Figure 13.4 shows the operations of a step of the travel expense reimbursement workflow.

Figure 13.5 shows how to log out from a worklist.

The end user needs access to tools (e.g. text editor, calculator, spreadsheet) in order to process work to do. These tools must be integrated into the user work area seamlessly such that they can easily be called when requests have to be processed.

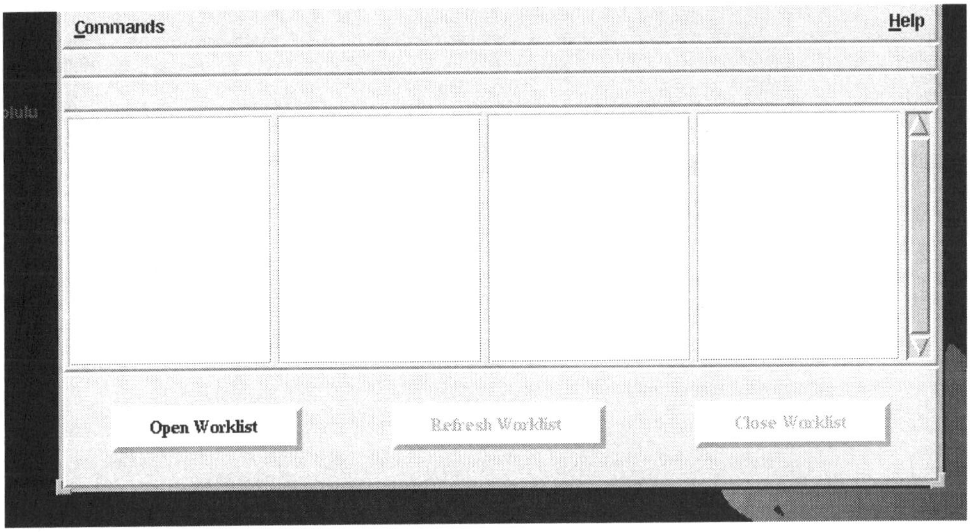

Figure 13.2: Empty Worklist

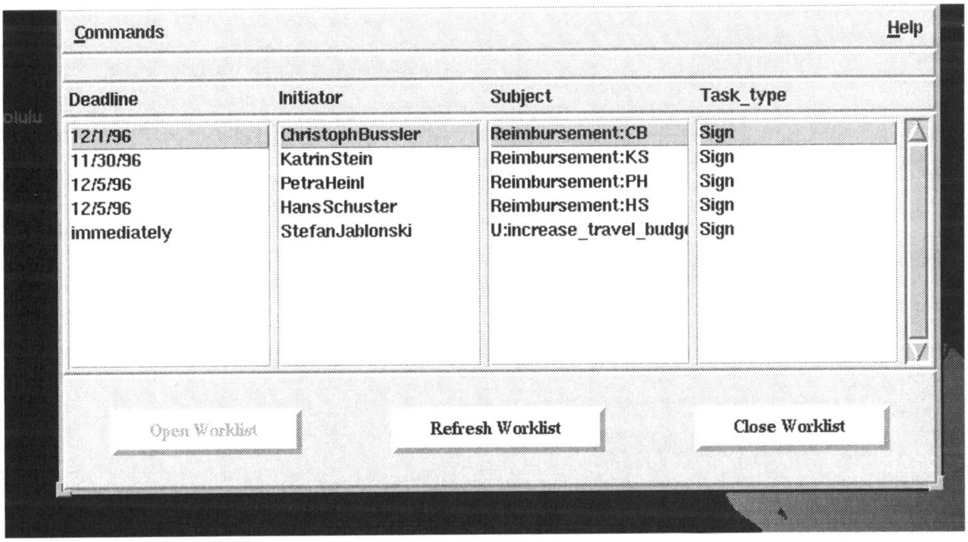

Figure 13.3: Worklist Filled with Assigned Workflows

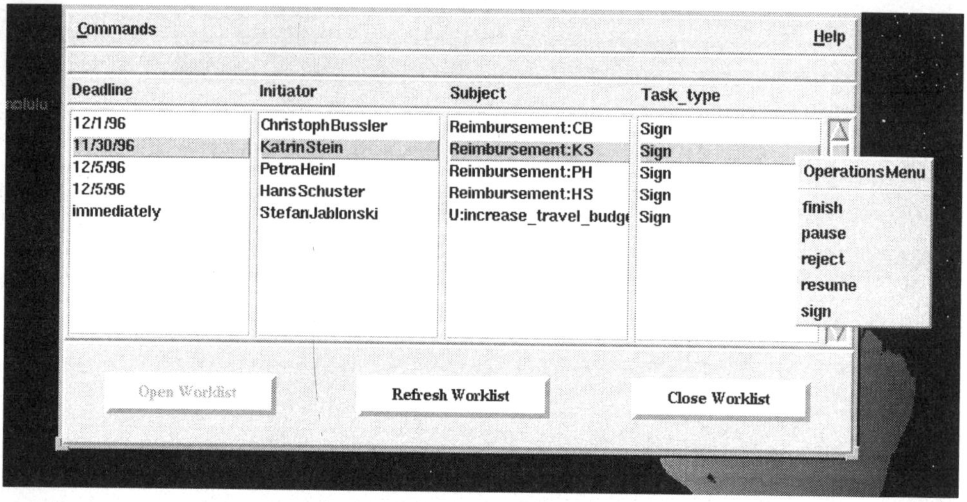

Figure 13.4: Workflow Operations of an Assigned Workflow

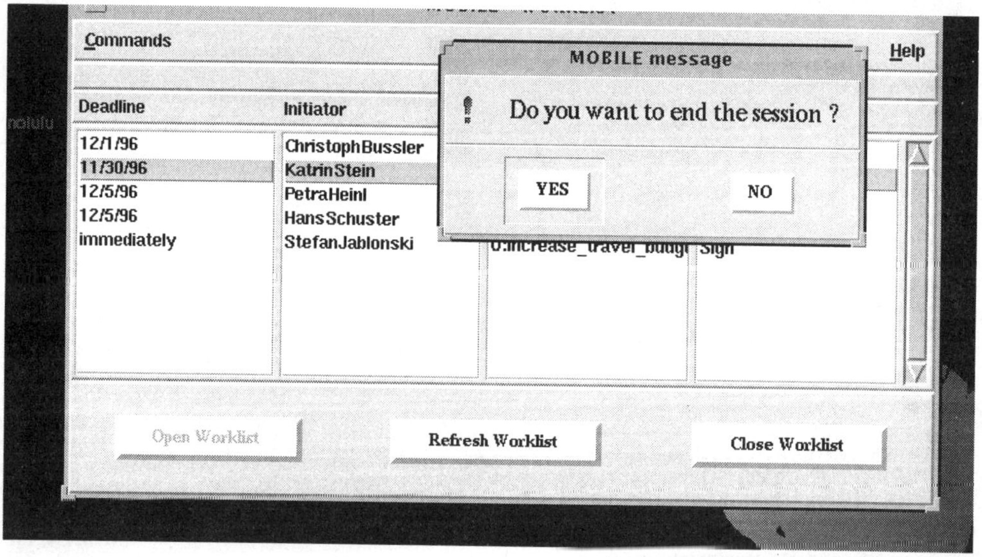

Figure 13.5: Logging out from a Worklist

Part 4: Conclusion

Part 4 concludes the book by summarizing the main concepts presented and by providing an outlook on open research and engineering issues in the area of workflow management.

The introduction of generations of workflow management technology in Chapter 1 reveals that this technology is still in the learning phase. Many improvements are still necessary to deliver matured workflow management systems that can effectively and efficiently support enterprise-wide workflow applications. In this sense, the discussion of related work in Chapter 2 unveils drawbacks and pitfalls of actual workflow management technology. Nevertheless, progress in workflow management research and engineering has definitely been made already and many good examples of workflow management technology promise the advent of a new generation of tools that makes enterprise-wide enactment of business processes possible. Part 2 and 3 present many of these concepts and form a decent basis for future research and engineering efforts in workflow management.

Chapter 14 summarizes the major concepts presented in this book. The main design rationales applied are presented and justified. Chapter 15 contains open issues in the area of workflow management. Their solution requires effort in workflow research and workflow engineering.

14 Summary

This chapter summarizes the main ideas and concepts presented in this book. Its purpose is to recall design rationales that lead to the form of workflow modeling as shown in Part 2 and of workflow management system implementation as depicted by Part 3.

The concepts of Parts 2 and 3 present one eligible alternative to enact the requirements towards workflow modeling and execution as discussed in Chapters 5 and 9, respectively. It is not said that this approach is the only one that fulfills these requirements adequately. Nevertheless, the approach chosen has been checked for practicability, effectiveness and efficiency and therefore is justified to be presented as the example approach throughout the book.

Section 14.1 recalls all issues regarding workflow modeling tackled with in Part 2. Accordingly, Section 14.2 summarizes issues of workflow management system implementation presented in Part 3. Both sections list the main concepts of this book without broad interpretation. They resemble check-lists. Readers should use them to check whether they have grasped the main concepts introduced in the book. Subsequently, Section 14.3 delivers an interpretation of these concepts from the viewpoint of design rationales. The main contributions of this book, that form its distinctive character, are reported there.

14.1 Workflow Modeling

Chapter 5 discusses preliminaries for workflow modeling. As a consolidation of related approaches a workflow model should encompass the following perspectives:

- function perspective
- operation perspective
- behavior perspective
- information perspective
- organization perspective

These five perspectives seem to be fundamental for almost all application fields of workflow management technology. There are a number of further perspectives that are worth mentioning: causality perspective, integrity and failure perspective, quality perspective, history perspective, security perspective and autonomy perspective. This open list comprises perspectives that are essential for specialized application fields.

Because of their importance the design principles of a workflow model must also be repeated. The representation of model elements as abstract data types and the differentiation between definition and use foster the enactment of the requirements extensibility, dynamic customizability, adaptability, reusability, openness, ease of use, readability, abstraction, correctness, integrity, preciseness, testability, verifiability and maintainability. The modularity and orthogonality of a workflow model are the necessary prerequisites to meet all these demands.

Chapter 6 presents a comprehensive workflow model. The main constituents of a workflow model are composite and elementary workflow types. Constraints reduce their use in order to assure consistency. A workflow can be manipulated by execution workflow operations. *Start*, *activate*, *deactivate*, *suspend* and *resume* are often used sample workflow operations.

The information perspective of a workflow is based on data types, parameters and workflow local variables. They are applied to define data flow between workflow instances.

Control flow constructs – which can be defined as application-specific – are required to formulate control flow between workflow instances. They determine when instances of a workflow are ready to be performed.

Workflow applications and workflow operations constitute the operation perspective of a workflow. In general, one or more workflow applications implement a workflow operation.

The organization perspective comprises the organization structure, organizational population, notification, synchronization and organizational policies. Together these concepts specify what agents are eligible to perform a workflow.

The semantics of the workflow model elements is defined in Chapter 7. In order to be able to dynamically change the execution model of workflows, the semantics of elementary and composite workflow execution and workflow operation execution is defined by state transition diagrams. By changing actions that are executed at a state transition the semantics of workflow model elements can be customized to special needs.

Chapter 8 concludes the expositions about workflow modeling by presenting tools required to model workflows. Here, workflow modeling is sub-divided into the three tasks definition, analysis and administration.

Part 2 presents all relevant aspects of workflow modeling. Their implementation might be arguable in detail, but their global meaning and purpose are unassailable.

14.2 Workflow Execution

Preliminaries to a workflow management system architecture are reported in Chapter 9. The most important characteristic of the approach presented in Part 3 is the classification of the architecture of a workflow management system into implementation model, implementation architecture and implementation.

The implementation model re-constructs the basic modules of an overall architecture for workflow management systems. The modules constitute the principle structure of the workflow management system. The implementation architecture maps implementation concepts onto the implementation model. Communication techniques, database support and algorithms are conceived to put the implementation model in concrete form. Finally, an implementation is one specific instantiation of the implementation architecture. It describes an operating workflow management system.

Another design rationale for the architectural part of a workflow management system is the modularization approach that is chosen. The model elements of the workflow model and some so-called base services are strictly modeled as modules. These modules constitute the implementation model of a workflow management system.

As requirements for a workflow management system the following issues are elaborated: extensibility, dynamic customizability, adaptability, scalability, openness, efficiency, reliability, correctness, maintainability and portability. Again, modularity and orthogonality are considered to be mandatory prerequisites when enacting these demands.

The implementation model is designed in such a way that each perspective of the workflow model is implemented by a set of modules. These modules can be classified as belonging to the Kernel, the Shell or the Workspace of a workflow management system. Chapter 10 presents the major modules of a general implementation architecture. Chapter 11 takes the modules and implements them by operating system processes, databases and communication mechanisms. In Chapter 12 one instance of the implementation architecture is presented as a concrete implementation.

Finally, Chapter 13 introduced tools that are obligatory for workflow execution. Three tool suites can be determined: tools for the user work area, for analysis and for administration.

The design of a workflow management system depicted by Part 3 can serve as an implementation template for a workflow management system. Although it is not complete – this would definitely be out of the scope of the book – a system engineer should be able to derive a concrete implementation specification out of the explanations in Part 3.

14.3 Distinctive Features

This section compiles the distinctive features of the approach presented in this book. The workflow model (Part 2) is characterized by the following two features.

The Workflow Model is Open

By definition, the conceptual approach pursued with the workflow model does not assume that all model elements of all potential application areas can be anticipated. Experiences and upcoming needs require to adjust and to extend the workflow model over time. The syntax and the semantics of the workflow model meet this requirement. For instance, the workflow semantics is defined by state transition diagrams that can easily be modified to reflect new application-specific demands.

The Workflow Model is Constructive

Before a model element can be used within the specification of a workflow type, it has to be defined explicitly. This approach even applies to basic control flow constructs like the construct for sequential execution. Although the semantics of this control flow construct is obvious it must be explicitly defined.[1] To enhance the practicability of the approach, it is recommended to ship a handful of basic model elements with a workflow management system.

The distinctive feature of the implementation approach for workflow management systems depicted in Part 3 is the classification of three architectural layers (implementation model, implementation architecture, implementation). Based on this design strategy, data independence can be achieved which results in the following benefits.

Distinction Between Conceptual Model and Implementation Architecture

The implementation model only deals with the logical design of a workflow management system. Modules are used to constitute this conceptual model. This is a general approach that does not imply implementation techniques to be used later in order to implement the workflow management system. Implementation techniques are not described before the implementation architecture comes into the picture. Here, adequate techniques are selected to guarantee an optimal enactment of the logical concepts.

Most other approaches avoid introducing an implementation model explicitly and start the architectural design at the level of an implementation architecture. Consequently, this description of a workflow management system architecture implies a certain implementation technique. For instance, some implementation architectures rely on the trigger approach. Interrelationships and inter-dependencies between elements of the implementation architectures are described by event–condition–action rules. It is natural that later on an implementation technique should be selected that better resembles the trigger approach.

Distinction Between Implementation Architecture and Implementation. Implementation techniques are introduced principally on the level of the implementation architecture. For instance, it is determined that the use of a reliable queue best fulfills the requirements of a specific communication problem.

The implementation techniques are not instantiated before the implementation layer is entered, i.e. concrete systems are selected. For example, Encina's persistent queues are taken to implement transactional asynchronous communication.

[1]Even for this control flow construct there are at least two different interpretations possible. A → B might mean that B can be started after A has terminated, or it might mean that B can be started after A has started execution.

15 Outlook and Future Work

Neither research nor engineering work in the field of workflow management is mature yet. Nevertheless, we are in the middle of the conceptual phase of the development of workflow management technology (cf. Chapter 1) and promising steps towards the development of a powerful technology have successfully been made already. The examples discussed in Chapter 2 confirm this observation in an illustrative way.

In this last chapter we will summarize open issues in the area of workflow management. Throughout the book when discussing concepts for workflow modeling and workflow execution open problems in the various areas of workflow management have been mentioned. Here we only want to mention principal directions where future research is still necessary.

The following discussion first deals with conceptual issues (Section 15.1) and then tackles technical issues (Section 15.2).

15.1 Conceptual Issues

Conceptual issues deal with the question of whether and where to apply workflow management technology.

Delimitation of Workflow Management

Though workflow management has been a hot topic in research and development for the last couple of years, it is still not clear what the concept workflow management comprises. In particular, there is much confusion with the related areas of business process reengineering and workgroup computing (groupware).

Towards the establishment of a consolidated view of the interrelation and interdependency between workflow management, workgroup computing and business process reengineering, we delimit workflow management from workgroup computing in Chapter 1 and from business process reengineering in Chapter 3. Nevertheless, this is merely one single attempt which needs further investigation.

Integration into Systems Engineering Lifecycle

Along with the delimitation of workflow management technology, its embedding and integration into a systems engineering lifecycle must be studied thoroughly (cf. Chapter 3). For the specific concept of workflow management, new and customized techniques in the areas of requirements engineering are needed. Methodologies to build workflow applications are also still missing. In this context, the association to business process engineering approaches must be investigated.

Reference Models for Workflows

To enhance the productivity of workflow application system development, reference models for workflows must be defined. Such reference models show how typical workflow applications (e.g. order entry processing, travel claim reimbursement) can be processed. Reference models for workflows should be delivered with workflow management systems in the form of application area specific class libraries. Hereby, methods like domain analysis should be applied (Arango, 1989; Prieto-Díaz and Arango, 1991).

15.2 Technical Issues

When it is decided to apply workflow management technology, the next question to be answered is how to apply it, i.e. how to conceive a workflow management system that implements the required functionality.

Internal Structure of a Workflow Management System

In the main sections of this book, the complexity of the field of workflow management becomes obvious. Among other things, the perspectives of a work-flow model introduced in Chapter 6 reveal the diversity of workflow management technology. Most probably, every application area of workflow management is characterized by requiring a specific subset of perspectives. Thus, an ideal workflow management system should rather be a toolbox containing specialized modules each implementing a specific function. These modules might even be offered by different vendors. For instance, a database vendor delivers a specialized module that allows to implement the history perspective of workflow management.

In order to be generally applicable, monolithic workflow management systems would have to support all functionality described in Parts 2 and 3. Such approaches bear major drawbacks. They would be very expensive since a maximum amount of functionality has to be bought. Also, they would unnecessarily involve too many system resources. A workflow management toolbox would eliminate these problems. However, a general toolbox approach is not yet in sight.

Distributed Workflow Execution

It is often mentioned that the real benefit of workflow management can be gained when larger parts of an enterprise are supported by workflow management technology. The distributed execution of workflows inherently introduces serious problems. One problem is due to implementation issues. In a highly distributed environment several workflow management systems have to cooperate in order to execute a distributed workflow. Here, the interoperability of workflow management systems is demanded. Although some basic steps towards workflow management system interoperability have already been investigated (e.g. by the WfMC), concepts for complete interoperability between workflow management systems are still not available.

The interoperation of distributed workflow management systems does not only produce problems of technical interoperability. Semantics problems have also to be tackled. This is due to the fact that different workflow management systems interpret similar concepts in a different way. A common and general semantics of workflow management terminology has therefore to be developed first.

Workflow Management and/as Middleware Service(s)

Workflow management is mostly regarded as middleware service (Bernstein, 1996). Middleware services sit between platforms, constituted by a processor architecture and an operating system, and applications. Naturally, higher middleware services (as workflow management services) are based on lower middleware services (e.g. for transaction processing). Middleware services must be distributed, portable and standard. In order to meet these requirements and to achieve synergy, workflow management services are based on lower middleware services that provide distribution and portability. However, so far there are no matured concepts on how to base workflow management systems on services like OSF DCE, OMG's CORBA and X/Open's DTP.

Workflow Management and/as Legacy Application(s)

In Chapter 6 and in Chapter 10 the problem of how to integrate legacy applications into workflows is discussed broadly. Workflow management systems struggle with the integration of legacy applications. Since in the area of workflow management the legacy problem is experienced extensively, precautions should be taken such that workflow applications themselves will not finally become legacy applications. How this can be achieved is not quite clear yet, although valuable ideas can be taken from the concepts of open systems.

Appendix A: Workflow Modeling Language MSL

In the following a structured workflow language is laid out to formally specify a workflow type together with other necessary elements. We call it MSL, *MOBILE* Script Language. The language is introduced according to the perspectives discussed throughout the book.

Section A.1 discusses the function perspective, Section A.2 the information perspective, Section A.3 the control flow perspective, Section A.4 workflow applications and Section A.5 the organization perspective. Section A.6 contains auxiliary definitions which are required to define the other perspectives.

A.1 Function Perspective

A.1.1 Workflow Definition

An elementary or composite workflow type together with its constraints is declared using the following language elements:[1]

```
workflow ::=
  WORKFLOW_TYPE workflow-type-name ([parameters])
    [constraints]
    workflow-body
  END_WORKFLOW_TYPE

workflow-type-name ::=
    identifier

constraints ::=
    [enter-constraint]
    [runtime-constraint]
    [exit-constraint]
  END_CONSTRAINTS

enter-constraint ::=
  ENTER_CONSTRAINT expression

runtime-constraint ::=
  RUNTIME_CONSTRAINT expression

exit-constraint ::=
  EXIT_CONSTRAINT expression
```

A workflow body implements all perspectives of a workflow type and is structured as follows.

```
workflow-body ::=
    subworkflows-specification
    workflow-operations-specification
    data-specification
    data-flow-specification
    control-flow-specification
    policy-specification
    (* further perspectives *)
```

A.1.2 Subworkflow Definition

One major perspective of a workflow body is the function perspective. Because of the use of workflows as subworkflows in a certain context it might be necessary to adjust the organizational policies of a subworkflow as well as its constraints. Therefore the specification of subworkflows has to be extended with policy and constraints specifications.

```
subworkflows-specification ::=
  [SUBWORKFLOWS subworkflow-specification
    {; subworkflow-specification}
  END_SUBWORKFLOWS]

subworkflow-specification ::=
    workflow-type-name: subworkflow-name
    [constraints]
    [policy-specification]
      {, subworkflow-name
      [constraints]
      [policy-specification]}

subworkflow-name ::=
    identifier
```

A.1.3 Workflow Operation Definition

Workflow operations are specified according to the following syntax. Workflow type operations have to be distinguished from workflow instance operations.

```
workflow-operations-specification ::=
  [OPERATIONS [I_|T_]workflow-operation-specification
    {; [I_|T_]workflow-operation-specification}
  END_OPERATIONS]

workflow-operation-specification ::=
  OPERATION workflow-operation-name ([parameters])
    workflow-operation-body
  END_OPERATION

workflow-operation-name ::=
    identifier

workflow-operation-body ::=
    statement-list

statement-list ::=
    statement {; statement}

statement ::=
    (* see Chapter 10 for examples *)
```

Operations are either type operations denoted by "T_" or instance operations denoted by "I_". Parameters are to be specified also, their syntax is shown later on. We do not define the syntax of statements since there is nothing special in comparison to other languages. Chapter 10 contains examples which demonstrate the use of statements.

A.2 Information Perspective

Basic data types have to be defined first. We do not put too much emphasis on this well-understood area. The following constructs represent one feasible way to specify basic data types. A more advanced way would be to deploy object-oriented class specifications here. However, this would make the language very complex.

A.2.1 Data Type Definition

```
data-type ::=
     elementary-type
     | composite-type
     | pointer-type
     | user-defined-type

elementary-type ::=
   BOOLEAN
   | INTEGER
   | DECIMAL
   | REAL
   | STRING
   | (* further elementary types *)

composite-type ::=
     record-type
     | array-type
     | list-type
     | (* further composite types *)

pointer-type ::=
   POINTER TO data-type-ref

data-type-ref ::=
     elementary-type
     | pointer-type
     | data-type-name
     | record-name
     | array-name
     | list-name
```

```
user-defined-type ::=
  DATA_TYPE data-type-name: data-type-ref
    [CONSTRAINTS expression]
    [INITIALIZATION data-assignment]
  END_DATA_TYPE
data-type-name ::=
    identifier

data-assignment ::=
    data-type-constant

data-type-constant ::=
    boolean-constant
    | integer-constant
    | decimal-constant
    | real-constant
    | string-constant
    | pointer-constant
    | user-defined-type-constant
    | record-constant
    | array-constant
    | list-constant

record-type ::=
  RECORD record-name
    BEGIN record-elements
  END_RECORD

record-name ::=
    identifier

record-elements ::=
    record-element {; record-element}

record-element ::=
    data-type-ref: element-name {, element-name}

element-name ::=
    identifier

array-type ::=
  ARRAY array-name [integer-constant..integer-constant]
  OF data-type-ref
```

```
array-name ::=
     identifier

list-type ::=
  LIST list-name OF data-type-ref

list-name ::=
     identifier

data-operator ::=
     boolean-operator
     | =
     | <
     | >
     | (* further data operators *)

boolean-operator ::=
     AND
     | OR
```

A.2.2 Workflow Parameter Definition

The syntax for defining parameters is presented next. We distinguish mandatory from optional parameters and their "direction" like IN, OUT or INOUT.

```
parameters ::=
     parameter-kind parameter-type parameter
       {; parameter-kind parameter-type parameter}

parameter-kind ::=
  | (* empty *)[2]
  | MANDATORY
  | OPTIONAL

parameter-type ::=
  | (* empty *)[3]
  | IN
  | OUT
  | INOUT

parameter ::=
     data-type-ref : parameter-name {, parameter-name}

parameter-name ::=
     identifier
```

A.2.3 Workflow Variable Definition

Workflow local variables are declared as described in the following. In addition constraints can be defined which constrain the values of a variable as well as initial values.

```
data-specification ::=
   [WORKFLOW_DATA
     variable {; variable}
   END_WORKFLOW_DATA]

variable ::=
     data-type-ref: variable-name {, variable-name}
   [CONSTRAINTS expression]
   [INITIALIZATION data-assignments]

data-assignments ::=
     variable-name := expression
     {, variable-name := expression}

variable-name ::=
     identifier
```

A.2.4 Data Flow Definition

Data flow is either direct between parameters or indirect via local variables.

```
data-flow-specification ::=
   [DATA_FLOW
     data-flow-rule {; data-flow-rule}
   END_DATA_FLOW]

data-flow-rule ::=
     source→ sinks[4] {, source→ sinks}

source ::= data-location

sinks ::=sink [VIA variable-name]
     | {, sink [VIA variable-name]}( sink [VIA variable-name])

sink ::= data-location

data-location ::=
     workflow-type-name.parameter-name
     | variable-name
     | function-name.parameter-name
     | workflow-operation-name.parameter-name
     | subworkflow-name.parameter-name
```

A.3 Behavior Perspective

A.3.1 Control Flow Construct Definition

Language constructs to specify control flow constructs are introduced first. A control flow construct consists of its syntax definition and its semantics definition. We omit the exact syntax to define Petri nets here.

```
control-flow-construct ::=
  CONTROL_FLOW_CONSTRUCT
    control-flow-construct-name ([control-flow-parameters])
    control-flow-construct-semantics
  END_CONTROL_FLOW_CONSTRUCT


control-flow-construct-name ::=
    identifier

control-flow-parameters ::=
    control-flow-parameter {; control-flow-parameter}

control-flow-parameter ::=
    control-flow-parameter-type:
      control-flow-parameter-name
      {, control-flow-parameter-name}

control-flow-parameter-type ::=
    data-type-ref
    | WORKFLOW
    | FUNCTION

control-flow-parameter-name ::=
    identifier

control-flow-construct-semantics ::=
    (* Petri-net specification *)
```

A.3.2 Control Flow Definition

The behavior perspective is modeled according to the following syntax.

```
control-flow-specification ::=
  [CONTROL_FLOW
    control-flow-expression
  END_CONTROL_FLOW]
```

```
control-flow-expression ::=
     subworkflow-name
     | {subworkflow-name {, subworkflow-name}}5
     | control-flow-construct-name(
        [control-flow-term {, control-flow-term}])

control-flow-term ::=
     expression
     | control-flow-expression
```

A.4 Workflow Application

The language representation restricts itself to workflow application specification and their use. Wrapping application programs is not supported by a workflow modeling language but is implemented as code. The following language construct allows to define workflow applications.

```
WORKFLOW_APPLICATION_TYPE
   workflow-application-type-name([parameters])
   [constraints]
   [properties]
END_WORKFLOW_APPLICATION_TYPE

workflow-application-type-name ::=
     identifier

properties ::=
   PROPERTIES
     property {, property}
   END_PROPERTIES

property ::=  [POSSIBLY] property-name

property-name ::=
     identifier
```

A.5 Organization Perspective

The organization perspective has to be defined in three steps that logically depend upon each other. First, an organization structure is built up. Based on this, organizational policies are specified. Finally, organizational policies are related to workflow specifications.

An organization, the organization structure and organizational relationships are typed objects.

A.5.1 Organization Type Definition

```
ORGANIZATION_TYPE organization-type-name
  organizational-object-types
  organizational-relationship-types
END_ORGANIZATION_TYPE

organization-type-name ::=
    identifier

organizational-object-types ::=
  ORGANIZATIONAL_OBJECT_TYPES
    [agents]
    [non-agents]
  END_ORGANIZATIONAL_OBJECT_TYPES

agents ::=
  AGENTS
    agent-type {; agent-type}

agent-type ::=
    agent-type-name
    [ATTRIBUTES attributes END_ATTRIBUTES]

agent-type-name ::=
    identifier

attributes ::=
    attribute {; attribute}

attribute ::=
    data-type-ref: attribute-name {, attribute-name}

attribute-name ::=
    identifier

non-agents ::=
  NON_AGENTS
    non-agent-type {; non-agent-type}

non-agent-type ::=
    agent-type

organizational-relationship-types ::=
  ORGANIZATIONAL_RELATIONSHIP_TYPES
```

```
      organizational-relationship-type
        {; organizational-relationship-type}
    END_ORGANIZATIONAL_RELATIONSHIP_TYPES

  organizational-relationship-type ::=
      organizational-relationship-type-name
      [ATTRIBUTES attributes END_ATTRIBUTES]

  organizational-relationship-type-name ::=
      identifier
```

A.5.2 Organization Instance Definition

An organization instance is defined with the following language construct.

```
ORGANIZATION organization-type-name:
    organization-instance-name;
  ORGANIZATIONAL_OBJECTS
    organizational-object-type-name: attribute-values
    {; organizational-object-type-name: attribute-value}
  ORGANIZATIONAL_RELATIONSHIPS
    organizational-relationship-type-name:
      attribute-values
    {; organizational-relationship-type-name:
      attribute-values}
END_ORGANIZATION

organization-instance-name ::=
    identifier

organization-object-type-name ::=
    identifier

attribute-values ::=
    attribute-value {, attribute-value}

attribute-value ::=
    data-type-constant
```

A.5.3 Agent Selection Definition

The specification of organizational policies assumes the existence of agent selection predicates.

```
agent-selection ::=
  AGENT_SELECTION agent-selection-name ([parameters])
    agent-selection-body
  END_AGENT_SELECTION

agent-selection-name ::=
    identifier

agent-selection-body ::=
    (* this can be implemented in many ways. We use some
    kind of SQL dialect for illustration *)
```

A.5.4 Organizational Policy Definition

The organization perspective as well as the organizational policies are specified according to the following syntax.

```
policy-specification ::=
  ORGANIZATIONAL_POLICIES
    organizational-policy {; organizational-policy}
  END_ORGANIZATIONAL_POLICIES

organizational-policy ::=
  ORGANIZATIONAL_POLICY policy-name
    WORKFLOW_TYPE workflow-type-name
    [WORKFLOW_T_OPERATION workflow-operations]
    [WORKFLOW_I_OPERATION workflow-operations]
    AGENT_SELECTION agent-selection-expression
    SYNCHRONIZATION synchronization-number
    NOTIFICATION notification-mechanism
  END_ORGANIZATIONAL_POLICY

policy-name ::=
    identifier

workflow-operations ::=
    workflow-operation-name
    | {workflow-operation-name
     {, workflow-operation-name}}[6]
    | *[7]

agent-selection-expression ::=
    agent-selection-call
    | agent-selection-call set-op-2 agent-selection-call
    | (agent-selection-expression)
```

```
agent-selection-call ::=
     agent-selection-name ([parameter-values])

parameter-values ::=
     parameter-value {, parameter-value}

parameter-value ::=
     expression
     | agent-selection-call
set-op-2 ::=
   AND
   | OR
   | DIFFERENCE

synchronization-number ::=
     integer-constant

notification-mechanism ::=
   e-mail
   | worklist
   | ...
```

A.6 Auxiliary Definitions

In the following some auxiliary definitions are given. The elements defined are used all over MSL so we have separated them from the rest.

```
identifier ::=  [{"a"|"b"|...|"z"}+ | {"A"|"B"|...|"Z"}+]
             {0|1|2|...|9|"a"|"b"|...|"z"|"A"|"B"|...|"Z"}*

function ::= FUNCTION function-name ([parameters])
     BEGIN
        (* implementation of body *)
     END
     returns data-type-ref;


function-name ::=
     identifier


function-call ::=
     function-name ([expression {, expression}])

boolean-expression ::=
     boolean-constant
     | boolean-expression boolean-operator
        boolean-expression
```

```
      | NOT boolean-expression
      | ( boolean-expression)
      | expression data-operator expression

   expression ::=
      data-constant
      | variable-name
      | workflow-type-name.parameter-name
      | subworkflow-instance-name.parameter-name
      | workflow-operation-name.parameter-name
      | function-name.parameter-name
      | function-call
      | ( expression)
      | expression data-operator expression
      | boolean-expression
```

---

[1] We use a BNF-like notation. Terminals are written in bold font, non-terminals in normal font. "[.]" represent that the content (represented by ".") is optional and "{.}" represent that the content can be iterated 0, 1, 2, ... times. A "+" after "{.}" indicates that the content can be iterated 1, 2, 3, ... times. "[. | .]" means that either of the two choices has to be taken.

[2] The default is **MANDATORY**.

[3] The default is **INOUT**.

[4] Data might flow from a source to several sinks.

[5] The brackets {} denote a set of subworkflows. If this set is specified no execution order is definied and each of the subworkflows can be started as chosen by the users at runtime.

[6] The bold "{}" denote a set of elements, in this case a set of workflow operation names.

[7] The "*" denotes all workflow operations of a workflow.

References

Abbott and Sarin, 1994
Abbott, K.R.; Sarin, S.K.: Experiences with Workflow Management: Issues for the Next Generation. *Proceedings ACM 1994 Conference on Computer Supported Cooperative Work*, Chapel Hill, NC, 113–120

Action Workflow, 1992
Workflow Management System, Architecture and Technology. Action Technologies, Inc., Alameda, CA, USA, 1992

Action Workflow, 1993
Action Workflow, White Paper. Action Technologies, Inc., Alameda, CA, USA, 1993

Ahmed *et al.*, 1993
Ahmed, R.; Albert, J.; Du, W.; Kent, W.; Litwin, W.; Shan, M.-C.: An Overview over Pegasus. *Proceedings of the Conference on Research Issues in Data Engineering: Interoperability in Multidatabase Systems (RIDE-IMS '93)*, Vienna, Austria, 1993

Ansari *et al.*, 1992
Ansari, M.; Ness, L.; Rusinkiewicz, M.; Sheth, A.: Using Flexible Transactions to Support Multi-system Telecommunication Applications. *Proceedings of the 18th Conference on Very Large Databases*, Vancouver, Canada, 1992

Arango, 1989
Arango, G.: Domain Analysis – From Art Form to Engineering Discipline. *Proc. 5th International Workshop on Software Specification and Design*, 1989

Attie *et al.*, 1993
Attie, P.; Singh, M.; Sheth, A.; Rusinkiewicz, M.: Specifying and Enforcing Intertask Dependencies. *Proceedings of the 19th Conference on Very Large Databases*, Dublin, Ireland, 1993

Bernstein, 1996
Bernstein, P.A.: Middleware: A Model for Distributed Systems Services. *Communication of the ACM*, Vol. 39 (1996), No. 2, 86–98

Bock, 1993
Bock, G.: Workflow as Groupware: A Case for Group Language? *Proc. GroupWare '93*, San Jose, CA, 168–170

Booch, 1991
Booch, G.: *Object Oriented Design with Applications.* Benjamin/Cummings, Redwood City, CA, 1991
Borghoff and Schlichter, 1995
Borghoff, U.M.; Schlichter, J.H.: *Rechnergestützte Gruppenarbeit: Eine Einführung in verteilte Anwendungen.* (Computer Based Cooperative Work: An Introduction in Distributed Applications) Springer-Verlag, Berlin, 1995
Bracchi and Pernici, 1984
Bracchi, G.; Pernici, B.: The Design Requirements of Office Systems. *ACM Transactions on Office Information Systems*, Vol. 2 (1984), No. 2, 151–170
Breitbart *et al.*, 1993
Breitbart, Y.; Deacon, A.; Schek, H.-J.; Sheth, A.; Weikum, G.: Merging Application-centric and Data-centric Approaches to Support Transaction-oriented Multi-system Workflows. *SIGMOD Record*, Vol. 22, No. 3, 1993
Brodie and Ceri, 1992
Brodie, M.L.; Ceri, S.: On Intelligent and Cooperative Information Systems: A Workshop Summary. *Journal of Intelligent and Cooperative Information Systems*, Vol. 1 (1992), No. 3
Bussler, 1995a
Bussler, C.: User Mobility in Workflow-Management-Systems. *Proceedings of the Telecommunications Information Networking Architecture Conference (TINA '95).* Melbourne, Australia, February 1995
Bussler, 1995b
Bussler, C.: Workflow Management Systems as Enterprise Engineering Tools. *Proc. IFIP Working Conference Models and Methodologies for Enterprise Integration*, Heron Island, Queensland, 1995
Bussler and Jablonski, 1994
Bussler, C.; Jablonski, S.: An Approach to Integrate Workflow Modeling and Organization Modeling in an Enterprise. *Proc. 3rd IEEE Workshop on Enabling Technologies: Infrastructure for Collaborative Enterprises (WET ICE)*, Morgantown, WV, 1994, 81–95
Bussler and Jablonski, 1995
Bussler, C.; Jablonski, S.: Policy Resolution for Workflow Management. *Proceedings of the Hawaii International Conference on System Sciences – 28.* Maui, Hawaii, January 1995
Ceri and Pelagatti, 1984
Ceri, S., Pelagatti, G.: *Distributed Databases: Principles and Systems*. McGraw-Hill, New York, NY, 1984
Chrysanthis and Ramamritham, 1990
Chrysanthis, P.K.; Ramamritham, K.: ACTA: A Framework for Specifying and Reasoning about Transaction Structure and Behavior. *Proc. ACM SIGMOD*, Atlantic City, NJ, USA, May 1990
Cleetus, 1994
Cleetus, K.J.: Working Group Report on Enterprise Modelling and Workflow Management. *Proceedings of the 3rd Workshop on Enabling Technologies: Infrastructure for Collaborative Enterprises*, Morgantown, WV, 1994
COSA, 1994a
COSA Administration Manual, Software-Ley GmbH, Pulheim, Germany, 1994
COSA, 1994b
COSA Programming Manual, Software-Ley GmbH, Pulheim, Germany, 1994
COSA, 1994c
COSA Reference Manual, Software-Ley GmbH, Pulheim, Germany, 1994

Crowston, 1991
Crowston, K.: *Towards a Coordination Cookbook: Recipes for Multi-Agent Action.* Doctoral Dissertation, MIT Sloan School of Management, Cambridge, MA, 1991

Curtis *et al.*, 1992
Curtis, B.; Kellner, M.; Over, J.: Process Management. *Communications of the ACM,* Vol. 35, No. 9, 1992

Dayal *et al.*, 1988
Dayal, U.; Blaustein, B.; Buchmann, A.P.; Carey, M.; Chakravarthy, U.; Hsu, M.; Jauhari, R.; Ladin, R.; Livny, M.; McCarthy, D.; Rosenthal, A.: The HiPAC Project: Combining Active Databases and Timing Constraints. *SIGMOD Record,* Vol. 17 (1988), No. 1, 51–70

Dayal *et al.*, 1995
Dayal, U.; Hanson, E.; Widom, H.: Active Database Systems. In: Kim, W. (Ed.): *Modern Database Systems: The Object Model, Interoperability, and Beyond.* ACM Press, 1995, 434–456

DEC, 1992
TeamRoute Programming Guide. Order Number: AA-PM6FA-TE, Digital Equipment Corporation, Maynard, MA, June 1992

Deiters and Gruhn, 1994
Deiters, W.; Gruhn, V.: The FUNSOFT Net Approach to Software Process Management. *International Journal on Software Engineering and Systems Engineering,* Vol. 4 (1994), No. 2

Deiters *et al.*, 1993
Deiters, W.; Gruhn, V.; Weber, H.: Software Process Evolution in Melmac. In: Cooke, D.E. (Ed.): The Impact of CASE Technology on Software Processes. *Series on Software Engineering and Knowledge Engineering,* Vol. 3, World Scientific Publishers, 1994

Denert, 1991
Denert, E.: *Software Engineering.* Springer-Verlag, Berlin, 1991

Denning, 1983
Denning, D.: *Cryptography and Data Security.* Addison-Wesley, Reading, MA, 1983

DeRemer and Kron, 1976
DeRemer, F.L.; Kron, H.H.: Programming-in-the-Large versus Programming-in-the-Small. *IEEE Transactions on Software Engineering,* Vol. 2 (1976), No. 2, 80–89

Dijkstra, 1972
Dijkstra, E.W.: Notes on Structural Programming. In: Dahl, O.-J.; Dijkstra, E.W.; Hoare, C.A.R. (Eds.): *Structured Programming.* Academic, New York, 1972

Dinkhoff *et al.*, 1994
Dinkhoff, G.; Gruhn, V.; Saalmann, A.; Zielonka, M.: Business Process Modeling in the Workflow Management Environment. In: Loucopoulos, P. (Ed.): *Entity-Relationship Approach - ER '94, Business Modelling and Re-Engineering.* 13th International Conference on the Entity-Relationship Approach, Manchester, UK, December 1994. Appeared as Lecture Notes in Computer Science 881, Springer-Verlag, Berlin, 1994

Ellis, 1983
Ellis, C.: Formal and Informal Models of Office Activity. In: Mason, R. (Ed.): *Information Processing 83,* North-Holland, Amsterdam, 1983

Ellis and Bernal, 1982
Ellis, C.; Bernal, M.: Officetalk-D: An Experimental Office Information System. *1st Proc. SIGOA Conference on Office Automation Systems,* 1982

Ellis and Nutt, 1980
Ellis, C.; Nutt, G.: Office Information Systems and Computer Science. *ACM Computing Surveys,* Vol. 12 (1980), No. 1, 27–60

Ellis and Wainer, 1993
Ellis, C.; Wainer, J.: Goal Based Models of Groupware. *Technical Report CU-CS-668-93,* University of Colorado at Boulder, Department of Computer Science, 1993
Ellis *et al.*, 1991
Ellis, C.A.; Gibbs, S.J.; Rein, G.L.: Groupware Some Issues and Experiences. *Communications of the ACM,* Vol. 43 (1991), No. 1, S. 39–58
Elmagarmid, 1992
Elmagarmid, A. (Ed.): *Database Transaction Models for Advanced Application.* Morgan Kaufmann, San Mateo, CA, 1992
Elmasri and Navathe, 1989
Elmasri, R.; Navathe, S.B.: *Fundamentals of Database Systems.* Benjamin/Cummings, Redwood City, CA, 1989
European Committee for Standardization, 1994
European Committee for Standardization (CEN TC310 WG1): An evaluation of CIM modelling constructs - Evaluation report of constucts for views according to ENV 40 003. *Computers in Industry,* Vol. 24 (1994), No. 2–3, 159–236
Fichman and Kemerer, 1992
Fichman, R.G; Kemerer, C.F.: Object-Oriented and Conventional Analysis and Design Methodologies: Comparison and Critique. *IEEE Computer,* Vol. 25 (1992), No. 10, 22–39
FlowMark, 1994
IBM FlowMark. Workflow Modeling. Release 1.1. International Business Machines Corporation, Vienna, Austria, 1994
FlowMark, 1995
IBM FlowMark. Programming Guide. Version 2.1. International Business Machines Corporation, Vienna, Austria, 1995
Fox and Gruninger, 1994
Fox, M.S.; Gruninger, M.: Ontologies for Enterprise Integration. *Proceedings 2nd Conference on Cooperative Information Systems,* Toronto, Canada, 1994
Fritz, 1994
Fritz, F.: Overhead Projector Slide Set. SAP AG, Waldorf, Germany, 1994
Georgakopoulos et al., 1995
Georgakopoulos, D.; Hornik, M.; Sheth, A.: An Overview of Workflow Management: From Process Modeling to Workflow Automation Infrastructure. *Distributed and Parallel Databases,* No. 3, 1995
Goldberg and Robson, 1989
Goldberg, A.; Robson, D.: *Smalltalk-80, The Language.* Addison-Wesley, Reading, MA, 1989
Gray and Reuter, 1993
Gray, J.; Reuter, A.: *Transaction Processing: Concepts and Techniques.* Morgan Kaufmann, San Mateo, CA, 1993
Greif, 1988
Greif, I. (Ed.): *Computer-Supported Cooperative Work: A Book of Readings.* Morgan Kaufmann, San Mateo, CA, 1988
Gruhn and Jegelka, 1992
Gruhn, V.; Jegelka, R.: An Evaluation of Funsoft Nets. In: Derniame, J.C. (Ed.): *Proceedings of the 2nd European Workshop on Software Process Technology (EWSPT '92),* Trondheim, Norway, 1992. Lecture Notes in Computer Science No. 635, Springer-Verlag, Berlin
Hales and Lavery, 1991
Hales, K.; Lavery, M.: *Workflow Management Software: the Business Opportunity.* Ovum Ltd., London, UK, 1991

Hammer, 1990
Hammer, M.: Reengineering Work: Don't Automate, Obliterate. *Harvard Business Review,* July–August 1990, 104–112
Hammer and Champy, 1993
Hammer, M.; Champy, J.: *Reengineering the Corporation, A Manifesto for Business Revolution.* Nicholas Breadley, London, 1993
Hess *et al.*, 1994
Hess, T.; Brecht, L.; Österle, H.: Metamodell Prozessentwurf. (Meta Model for Process Design) *Bericht Nr. IM HSG/CC PRO/13, Hochschule St. Gallen,* 1994
Hindel, 1993
Hindel, B.: How to ensure Software Quality for Real Time Systems. *Control Engineering Practice,* Vol. 1 (1993), No. 1, 35–41
Hopcroft and Ullman, 1969
Hopcroft, J.; Ullman, J.: *Formal Languages and their Relation to Automata.* Addison-Wesley, Reading, MA, 1969
Humphrey, 1989
Humphrey, W.S.: *Managing the Software Process.* Addison-Wesley, Reading, MA, 1989
Humphrey and Feiler, 1992
Humphrey, W.S.; Feiler, P.H.: Software Process Development and Enactment: Concepts and Definitions. *Technical Report SEI-92-TR-4.* Software Engineering Institute, Carnegie Mellon University, Pittsburgh, PA, 1992
ICEIMT, 1992
Proceedings of International Conference on Enterprise Integration Modeling Techniques (ICEIMT), Proceedings, Hilton Head, SC, 1992
Jablonski, 1994
Jablonski, S.: MOBILE: A Modular Workflow Model and Architecture. *Proc. International Working Conference on Dynamic Modelling and Information Systems,* Noordwijkerhout, Netherlands, 1994, 1–30
Jablonski and Ruf, 1990
Jablonski, S.; Ruf, T.: Data and Process Integration in a Flexible Manufacturing System, *Proceedings CSME Mechanical Engineering Forum,* Toronto, Canada, 1990
Jensen and Rozenberg, 1991
Jensen, K.; Rozenberg, G. (Eds.): *High-level Petri Nets: Theory and Application.* Springer-Verlag, Berlin, 1991
Johansen, 1988
Johansen, R.: *Groupware: Computer Support for Business Teams.* Free Press, New York 1988
Johansen, 1991
Johansen, R.: *Leading Business Teams.* Addison-Wesley, Reading, MA, 1991
Joosten *et al.*, 1994
Joosten, S.; Aussems, G.; Duitshof, M.; Huffmeijer, R.; Mulder, E.: *WA-12 An Empirical Study about the Practice of Workflow Management.* University of Twente Service Centrum, Enschede, 1994
Karbe and Ramsperger, 1989
Karbe, B.; Ramsperger, N.: Electronic Circulation Folders for the Design, Processing, and Migration of Office Processes. *Proc. Online Conference 1989,* Hamburg, Germany, 1989
Karbe and Ramsperger, 1990
Karbe, B.; Ramsperger, N.: Influence of Exception Handling on the Support of Cooperative Office Work. In: Gibbs, S. Verrijn-Stuart, A.A. (Eds.): *Multi-User Interfaces and Applications.* North-Holland, Amsterdam, IFIP, 1990

Karbe and Ramsperger, 1991
Karbe, B.; Ramsperger, N.: Concepts and Implementation of Migrating Office Processes. In: Brauer, W. Hernández, D. (Eds.): *Verteilte Künstliche Intelligenz und kooperatives Arbeiten* (Distributed Artificial Intelligence and Cooperative Work). 4. Internationaler GI-Kongress Wissensbasierte Systeme, Munich, Germany, October, 1991 (Proceedings), Springer-Verlag, Berlin

Karbe et al., 1990
Karbe, B.; Ramsperger, N.; Weiss, P.: Support of cooperative work by electronic circulation folders. *Proceedings Conference on Office Information Systems*, Cambridge, MA, 1990, 109–117

Karbe *et al.*, 1991
Karbe, B., Ramsperger, N., Vogel, P.: Office Work Coordination Using a Distributed Database System. *Proceedings of the 2nd International Symposium on Database Systems for Advanced Applications (DASFAA'91)*, Tokyo, Japan,1991

Katz, 1990
Katz, R.L.: Business/Enterprise modeling. *IBM Systems Journal*, Vol. 29 (1990), No. 4, 509–525

Kellner *et al.*, 1991
Kellner, M.I.; Feiler, P.H.; Finkelstein, A.; Katayama, T.; Osterweil, L.J.; Penedo, M.H.; Rombach, H.D.: ISPW-6 Software Process Example. In: Katayama, T. (Ed.): *Proc. 6th International Software Process Workshop: Support for the Software Process*, Hakodate, Japan, 1990, IEEE Computer Society Press, 1991, 176–186

Khoshafian et al., 1992
Khoshafian, S.; Baker, A.B.; Abnous, R.; Shepherd, K.: *Intelligent Offices: Object-Oriented Multi-Media Information Management in Client/Server Architectures.* Wiley, New York, 1992

Klein, 1991
Klein, J.: Advanced Rule Driven Transaction Management. *Proc. IEEE COMPCON*, San Francisco, CA, 1991

Kosanke, 1992
Kosanke, K.: CIMOSA – A European Development for Enterprise Integration, Part 1: An Overview. *Proc. International Conference on Enterprise Integration Modeling Technology (ICEIMT)*, Hilton Head, SC, 1992, 179–188

Koulopoulos, 1995
Koulopoulos, T.M: *The Workflow Imperative: Building Real World Business Solutions.* Van Nostrand Reinhold, New York, 1995

Kreifelts, 1991
Kreifelts, T.: Coordination of Distributed Work: From Office Procedures to Customizable Activities. In: Brauer, W., Hernández, D. (Eds.): *Verteilte Künstliche Intelligenz und kooperatives Arbeiten* (Distributed Artificial Intelligence and Cooperative Work). 4. Internationaler GI-Kongress Wissensbasierte Systeme, Munich, Germany, October, 1991 (Proceedings), Springer-Verlag, Berlin

Kreifelts *et al.*, 1993a
Kreifelts, T.; Hinrichs, E.; Klein, K.-H.; Seuffert, P.; Woetzel, G.: Experiences with the Domino Office Procedure System. *Proceedings of the 2nd European Conference on Computer-Supported Cooperative Work (ECSCW '91)*, Amsterdam, Netherlands, 1991

Kreifelts *et al.*, 1993b
Kreifelts, T.; Hinrichs, E.; Woetzel, G.: Sharing To-Do Lists with a Distributed Task Manager. *Proceedings of the 3rd European Conference on Computer-Supported Cooperative Work (ECSCW '93)*, Milan, Italy, 1993

Kreifelts and Seuffert, 1988
Kreifelts, T.; Seuffert, P.: Addressing in an Office Procedure System. In: Speth, R. (Ed.): *Message Handling Systems, State of the Art and Future Directions*. Proceedings of the IFIP WG 6.5 Work Conference on Message Handling Systems, Munich, Germany, 1988

Krishnakumar and Sheth, 1995
Krishnakumar, N.; Sheth, A.: Managing Heterogeneous Multi-System Tasks to Support Enterprise-Wide Operations. *Distributed and Parallel Databases*, No. 3, 1995

Leymann and Altenhuber, 1994
Leymann, F.; Altenhuber, W.: Managing business processes as an information resource. *IBM Systems Journal*, Vol. 33 (1994), No. 2, 326–348

Lochovsky, 1983
Lochovsky, F.H.: Improving Office Productivity: A Technology Perspective. In: Tsichritzis, D. (Ed.): Beta Gamma, *Technical Report CSRG-150*, University of Toronto, Toronto, Canada, 1983

Malone and Crowston, 1994
Malone, T.W.; Crowston, K.: The Interdisciplinary Theory of Coordination. *Computing Surveys*, Vol. 26 (1994), No. 1, 87–120

Marca and Bock, 1992
Marca, D.; Bock, G.: *GROUPWARE: Software for Computer-Supported Cooperative Work*. IEEE Computer Society Press, Los Alamitos, 1992

Martin, 1990
Martin, J.: *Information Engineering*. Prentice-Hall, Englewood Cliffs, NJ, 1990

Martin, 1993
Martin, J.: *Principles of Object-Oriented Analysis and Design*. Prentice-Hall, Englewood Cliffs, NJ, 1993

McCall *et al.*, 1977
McCall, J.A.; Richards, P.K.; Walters, G.F.: *Factors in Software Quality*, Vol. I-III. Rome Air Development Center, 1977

McCarthy and Bluestein, 1991
McCarthy, J.C.; Bluestein, W.M.: *The Computing Strategy Report: Workflow's Progress*, Forrester Research Inc., Cambridge, MA, October, 1991

McCarthy and Dayal, 1989
McCarthy, D.R.; Dayal, U.: The Architecture of an Active Database Management System. *Proc. ACM SIGMOD*, Portland, Oregon, 1989

McCarthy and Sarin, 1993
McCarthy, D.; Sarin, S.: Workflow and Transactions in InConcert. *Bulletin of the Technical Committee on Data Engineering*, Vol. 16, No. 2, 1993

Medina-Mora *et al.*, 1992
Medina-Mora, R.; Winograd, T.; Flores, R.; Flores, F.: The Action Workflow Approach to Workflow Management Technology. *Proceedings of the ACM 1992 Conference on Computer-Supported Cooperative Work*, Toronto, Canada, 1992

Medina-Mora et al., 1993
Medina-Mora, R.; Wong, H.; Flores, P.: Action Workflow as the Enterprise Integration Technology. *Bulletin of the Technical Committee on Data Engineering*, Vol. 16, No. 2, 1993

Melling, 1994
Melling, W.P.: Enterprise Information Architectures – They're Finally Changing. *Proc. ACM SIGMOD*, Minneapolis, Minnesota, USA, 1994, 493–504

Mertens, 1985
Mertens, P.: *Industrielle Datenverarbeitung. Band I: Administrations- und Dispositionssysteme* (Data Processing in Industrial Applications. Vol. 1: Administration and Decision Support Systems). Betriebswirtschaftlicher Verlag Dr. Th. Gabler, Wiesbaden, Germany, 1985

Meyer, 1988
Meyer, B.: *Object-oriented Software Construction,* Prentice-Hall, Englewood Cliffs, NJ, 1988
Myers, 1976
Myers, G.J.: *Software Reliability.* Wiley, New York, 1976
Nutt, 1992
Nutt, G.: *Open Systems.* Prentice-Hall, Englewood Cliffs, NJ, 1992
OMG, 1992
The Common Object Request Broker Architecture and Specification (CORBA). OMG, Framingham, MA, 1992
Opper, 1988
Opper, S.: A Groupware Toolbox. *Byte,* December, 1988
ORM, 1994a
ORM, Organization and Resource Management, Version 1.2. Siemens Nixdorf Informationssysteme AG, Paderborn, Germany, 1994
ORM, 1994b
ORM, Basics Manual, Version 1.2. Siemens Nixdorf Informationssysteme AG, Paderborn, Germany, 1994
Ortner, 1994
Ortner, E.: Linguistically Based Information System Development – A Constructive Approach. *Proceedings 4th International Conference Information System Development,* Bled, Slovenia, 1994, 141–152
Ortner, 1995
Ortner, E.: Elemente einer methodenneutralen Konstruktionssprache für Informationssysteme. *Informatik Forschung und Entwicklung* (Elements of a Material Language Approach for the Development of Software), Band 10 (1995), 148–160
Ousterhout, 1994
Tcl and the Tk toolkit. Addison-Wesley, Reading, MA, 1994
Parnas, 1972
Parnas, D.L.: On the Criteria to be used in Decomposing Systems into Modules. *Communication of the ACM,* Vol. 15 (1972), No. 12, 1053–1058
Porter, 1985
Porter, M.E.: *Competitive Advantage.* Free Press, New York, 1985
Prieto-Díaz and Arango, 1991
Prieto-Díaz, R.; Arango, G.: *Domain Analysis and Software Systems Modelling,* Tutorial, IEEE Computer Society, 1991
Reinwald, 1994
Reinwald, B.: Workflow-Management. *Tutorial 13th IFIP World Congress,* Hamburg, Germany, 1994
Rumbaugh *et al.*, 1991
Rumbaugh, J.; Blaha, M.; Premerlani, W.; Eddy, F.; Lorenson, W.: *Object-Oriented Modelling and Design,* Prentice-Hall, Englewood Cliffs, NJ, 1991
Rupietta, 1994
Rupietta, W.: Organization Models for Cooperative Office Applications. In: Karagiannis, D. (Ed.): *Database and Expert Systems Applications.* 5th International Conference, DEXA '94, Athens, Greece, September 1994, Proceedings. Springer-Verlag, Berlin, 1994
Rusinkiewicz and Sheth, 1995
Rusinkiewicz, M.; Sheth, A.: Specification and Execution of Transactional Workflows In: Kim, W. (Ed.): *Modern Database Systems: The Object Model, Interoperability, and Beyond.* ACM Press. 1995, 592–620

SAP, 1995
SAP Business Workflow. Funktionen im Detail. System R/3. SAP AG, February, 1995
Sarin and Greif, 1985
Sarin, S.; Greif, I.: Computer-based Real-time Conferencing Systems. *IEEE Computer,* Vol. 18 (1985), No. 10, 33–45
Sarin *et al.*, 1991
Sarin, S.; Abbot, K.; McCarthy, D.: A Process Model and System for Supporting Collaborative Work. *Proceedings of the ACM SIGOIS Conference on Organizational Computing Systems*, Atlanta, GA, 1991.
Schienmann, 1995
Schienmann, B.: Objektorientierte Spezifikation betrieblicher Informationssysteme. *Tagungsband Wirtschaftsinformatik '95* (Object-oriented Specification of Information Systems), Frankfurt, Germany, 1995
Schwab, 1993
Schwab, K.: *Konzeption, Entwicklung und Implementierung eines computergestützten Bürovorgangssystems zur Modellierung von Vorgangsklassen und Abwicklung und Überwachung von Vorgängen* (Conception, Development and Implementation of a Computer Based Office System for the Modeling of Activity Classes and Execution and Control of Activities). Dissertation, University of Bamberg, Germany, 1993
Shan, 1993
Shan, M.-C.: Pegasus Architecture and Design Principles. *Proceedings of the 1993 ACM SIGMOD International Conference on Management of Data*, Washington, DC, 1993
Singh, 1989
Singh, B.: On Coordination Systems. *Proc. Conference on Organizational Computing,* Austin, TX, 1989
Tanenbaum, 1987
Tanenbaum, A.: *Operating Systems, Design and Implementation.* Prentice-Hall Englewood Cliffs, NJ, 1987
Transarc, 1994a
RQS System Administrator's Guide and Reference. Transarc Corporation, Pittsburgh, PA, USA, 1994
Transarc, 1994b
Executive Programmer's Reference. Transarc Corporation, Pittsburgh, PA, USA, 1994
Umar, 1993
Umar, A.: *Distributed Computing: A Practical Synthesis.* Prentice-Hall, Englewood Cliffs, NJ, 1993
Vernadat, 1992
Vernadat, F.B.: CIMOSA - A European Development for Enterprise Integration. Part 2: Enterprise Modelling. *Proc. International Conference on Enterprise Integration Modeling Techniques (ICEIMT),* Hilton Head, SC, 1992, 189–204
Vernadat, 1996
Vernadat, F.: *Enterprise Modeling and Integration: Principles and Applications.* Chapman & Hall, London, 1996
Vogel and Erfle, 1992
Vogel, P.; Erfle, R.: Backtracking Office Procedures. In: Tjoa, A.M., Ramos, I. (Eds.): *Database and Expert Systems Applications (DEXAA'92)*, Springer-Verlag, Berlin, 1992
Wächter and Reuter, 1991
Wächter, H.; Reuter, A.: The ConTract Model. In: Elmagarmid, A.K. (Ed.): *Transaction Models for Advanced Database Applications.* Morgan Kaufmann, San Mateo, CA, 1991
Welch, B.B., 1995
Practical Programming in Tcl and Tk. Prentice-Hall, Englewood Cliffs, NJ, 1995

WfMC, 1993
The Workflow Reference Model, Version 0.6, Workflow Management Coalition, 1993
WfMC, 1995a
Workflow Process Definition Read/Write Interface, WFMC-WG01-1000. Workflow Management Coalition, 1995
WfMC, 1995b
Workflow Management Coalition Application Programming Interface (WAPI) Specification, WFMC-TC-1009. Workflow Management Coalition, 1995
WfMC, 1995c
http://www.aiai.ed.ac.uk/WfMC/
WfMC, 1995d
http://www.aiai.ed.ac.uk/WfMC/
WfMC, 1995e
http://www.aiai.ed.ac.uk/WfMC/
White and Fischer, 1994
White, T.; Fischer, L.: *New Tools for New Times: The Workflow Paradigm.* Future Strategies Inc., Alameda, CA, USA, 1994
Wilson, 1991
Wilson, P.: *Computer Supported Cooperative Work.* Intellect Books, Oxford, UK, 1991
Wirfs-Brock *et al.*, 1990
Wirfs-Brock, R.; Wilkerson, B.; Wiener, L.: *Designing Object-Oriented Software.* Prentice-Hall, Englewood Cliffs, NJ, 1990
Wirth, 1971
Wirth, N.: The Programming Language Pascal. *Acta Informatica*, Vol. 1, 1971
Woetzel and Kreifelts, 1993
Woetzel, G.; Kreifelts, T.: The Use of Petri Nets for Modeling Workflow in the Domino System. *Workshop on CSCW, Petri Nets and Related Formalisms. International Conference on Application and Theory of Petri Nets*, Chicago, IL, 1993
Wöhe, 1984
Wöhe, G.: *Einführung in die Allgemeine Betriebswirtschaftslehre* (Introduction to Business Management). Verlag Franz Vahlen, Munich, Germany, 1984
WorkParty, 1994a
WorkParty. Organizer Tool, Version 1.1. Siemens Nixdorf Informationssysteme AG, 1994
WorkParty, 1994b
WorkParty. Technical Information. Siemens Nixdorf Informationssysteme AG, 1994
Wortmann, 1994
Wortmann, H. (Ed.): Computers in Industry. *CIM Architectures*, Vol. 24 (1994), No. 2–3

Index

gunzip -c filename | lp -d printer